LAW AND LITERATURE

The Law and Literature series publishes work that connects legal ideas to literary and cultural history, texts, and artefacts. The series encompasses a wide range of historical periods, literary genres, legal fields and theories, and transnational subjects, focusing on interdisciplinary books that engage with legal and literary forms, methods, concepts, dispositions, and media. It seeks innovative studies of every kind, including but not limited to work that examines race, ethnicity, gender, national identity, criminal and civil law, legal institutions and actors, digital media, intellectual property, economic markets, and corporate power, while also foregrounding current interpretive methods in the humanities, using these methods as dynamic tools that are themselves subject to scrutiny.

Judicial Uses of Images

Vision in Decision

PETER GOODRICH

OXFORD
UNIVERSITY PRESS

OXFORD
UNIVERSITY PRESS

Great Clarendon Street, Oxford, OX2 6DP,
United Kingdom

Oxford University Press is a department of the University of Oxford.
It furthers the University's objective of excellence in research, scholarship,
and education by publishing worldwide. Oxford is a registered trade mark of
Oxford University Press in the UK and in certain other countries

Published in the United States of America by Oxford University Press
198 Madison Avenue, New York, NY 10016, United States of America

British Library Cataloguing in Publication Data
Data available

Library of Congress Control Number: 2023908043

ISBN 978–0–19–284877–2

DOI: 10.1093/oso/9780192848772.001.0001

Printed and bound by
CPI Group (UK) Ltd, Croydon, CR0 4YY

Preface

The plethora of pictures in the present work is only in part the expression of an inclination towards the visual. It is much more a matter of principle and a principle of mattering. To take the appearance of images in judicial judgements seriously as a jurisprudential topic, as a matter of normative significance, requires attending to, scrutinizing, allowing the eye to wander and the mind to open to the depiction viewed, as apparition, as visual material and as normative expression. Appearances, to purloin a notion from a recent study, are compelling, and sense and perception are the social form of the mediation of life, the first and primary encounter with law: 'Things show themselves and become perceptible in the public sphere—in other words they become real in the world—through appearance. This is why the form cannot be separated from the content without destroying the phenomenon itself, *along with its specific meaning*'.[1] Skin, colour, tone, sound, smell, masks, and clothes are the immediate theatre of legality because it is inevitably, initially and continuingly a spectacle of things unseen. In such a context the initial protocol of visual jurisprudence, here termed retinal justice, is that of viewing law as a sensible form, a chameleon of appearances, which apparitions include law's texts, its varied writs, typography, and other scriptural injunctions as well as its diversity of plastic and imaginal, cinematic and streamed virtual relays.

The key argument is that images, the figuratively depicted matter of legality, are not reducible to texts, discursive descriptions, typography and tympanum.[2] It is neither, if an early refutation of a legal solecism is permissible, that the picture speaks for itself, nor that it is the equivalent of a thousand words, nor that it is obvious. The principle of the present work is precisely that of debunking such legal fictions, the blinkers of eyes accustomed only to archival gloom, the regimentations of the page, printed columns, monochromacy, and attending to the visual in the juridical, the picturing of the norm in judicial decisions in their optical plenitude. The large number of images—good, bad, and ugly—drawn from precedential determinations across the common law influenced world are there so that they can be viewed and their pictorial identity and scopic distinctiveness from the linear text of the scriptural law can be discerned.[3] The point of departure is thus

[1] Barbara Carnevali, *Social Appearances: A Philosophy of Display* (New York: Columbia University Press, 2020) at 33.

[2] On typography and the semiotics of fonts, see Thomas Giddens, *The Font of Justice: Typography and the Common Law* (Edinburgh: Edinburgh University Press, 2024).

[3] It is noted here that the plenitude of such images has been restricted by the Press which has refused to publish third party images reproduced in judgements where permissions for works clearly in the

the opposite of a search for visual literacy and is resistant for the same reason to any inculcation of a method of reading pictures. To look, to view, to glimpse, gaze, stare, watch or espy is to enter the domain of the image as a corporeal and optical experience, an affective journey, a reaching out and a responding to the picturing as it appears, haptically, visibly in time and space, here and now, returning our gaze as for our part we are recipients who change with the images we view.

Increasingly, in a media driven, imaginally saturated social sphere, we watch the law. It appears, and it is through appearances that we view, react, follow, or infract. There is nothing especially novel in thinking of legality as a spectacular mode of social presence, but the availability and ease of reproduction of pictures now means that judicial decisions and other juridical and jurisliterary promulgations contain an augmenting number of figures. For common lawyers, this means that the legal code must now also be decoded visually. What does it mean for the norm to be relayed as an image? What is the juridical status of a picture? How does it bind? Should it hold sway over future cases? The absence of a method, of established protocols for viewing precedential pictures, and on occasion affect-laden emojis, screenshots, gifs, memes, tokens, nfts, all impel an opening of law, interior and exterior, to the ontography of images and to a study of the critical apparatuses that produce and interpret the pictorial. What lawyers early on dubbed *veritas falsa*, the picture as a depiction that is paradoxically both true and errant, real and illusory, is all that there is, the theatre of law being the scope of its manifestations and then the modes of its disappearances.[4] The process, development, and expansion of visualizations of the norm suggest a loosening of law, a certain escape from the text and the protestant strictures of *sola scriptura*. There is an element of flight from the linear and lectoral mode of inscribed exclusivity, a glimpse into the subtext and the 'hors-texte' as an aesthetics of law is developed to appreciate the performative force of the pictorial and the affective drive of the imaginal. A technically unwritten law returns in the form of imagistic depictions, in dynamograms best looked upon as spectral presences that technology now makes available in the *perpetuum mobile* of diverse on-screen modalities, as well as in the form of pictorial insertions and hyperlinks to imagery and video in the text of judgements.

public domain, or squarely within the doctrine of fair use, cannot be obtained. To coin a phrase, that which one cannot see remains hidden. Such observed and noted, I have included a hyperlink to such images which are also, of course, available, for those with access, in the reported cases: https://larc.cardozo.yu.edu/faculty-online-pubs/61/. The posted figures are listed by page and numbered as eFigures.

[4] This is the theme of Julie Stone Peters, *Law as Performance: Legal Theatricality, Spectatorship, and the Making of Law in Ancient, Medieval, and Early Modern Europe* (Oxford: Oxford University Press, 2022) at 86: 'The advocate's artful reality effect, heightened through *actio*, did not offer a mere illusion of reality (as the actor's did): it made reality appear as real as it really was'. As for disappearance, images still often get excluded from the reports and even the online reports, and where they are reproduced the quality is low and will often preclude close scrutiny and analysis. As for the legal concept of *veritas falsa*, the source is Andreas Alciatus, *Notitia utraque ... Disputatio Adriani aug. et Epicteti philosophi* (Basle: n.p., 1552) 'Quid est pictura? Veritas falsa'. The *Altercatio* is published as an appendix to the 1552 edition. For discussion, see Goodrich, 'The Comediography of Law', forthcoming.

The erudite and ergonomic Emanuele Coccia traces a short history of what he terms the 'iconification' of law in antiquity. To become a form of life, a *modus vivendi*, before *nomos* was even named as such, governance had to be imagined and relayed as image. At its root, this genealogical tracking suggests, it is the ethical and existential lessons, the precepts of iconic lives that act as precedential narratives and hold up to view the proper institution of life. An iconic nature 'is the form that law has to assume to apply to life'.[5] This is especially true of a common law system in which it is the biographical stories told in cases, the casuistry of persons, encounters, and events that is the model and relay of the rules that we live by and the institutions we inhabit. A legal form that is transmitted through stories, through actions upon the case and the peripatetic of casuistry, is necessarily one that relies upon the image of the event, the matter of dispute, to have an effect, to endure, and so to rule on. It is as close to painting as to writing, imagining as narrating, figuring the forms of licit modes of acting, a theatre to view much more than a merely textual, literal, monastic exposition of the doctrinal content of the norm. The reason is not just that sociality requires a prototype, a recognizable pattern of behaviour, icons to aspire to and imitate, but also that law attaches to the subject. The *nomos* of the earth, which common lawyers are most fond of referencing in the form of the *leges terrae*, *justissima tellus*, the alluvion of itinerancy and tradition since time out of mind, are only ostensively tellurian in that it is subjects, persons, *propositi*, the literal bodies of the *corpus iuris* whose paths are being tracked and whose habits and habitations, relations, rambunction, and rumpus that are being viewed. It is the image of the law that escapes both text and territory to become an interior norm, the economy of emotion, the administration of affections. In the terms elaborated by the late Pierre Legendre, the image enlaces the subject in desire and so, as is exponentially visible in contemporary social media, 'politics is the power to signify love of the image'.[6] It is a short step from such an aperçu to recognizing that the enlacing of legal decisions in the relay of imagery is an explicit politicization of law in the form of the exposure of the judicial embrace of desire. The nooks and alcoves, crannies and zawns that hid the rhetorical *inventio* or motive of arbitral decision in the gaps of the precedential text now appear to the eye in pictorial form as the image of decision or *imago decidendi* in the untrustworthy Latin of archaic legal declensions.

[5] Emanuele Coccia, 'Form of Life: How the Law Became an Image', in Christian Delage et al. (eds), *Law and New Media: West of Everything* (Edinburgh: Edinburgh University Press, 2019) at 156. The juridical genealogies of iconic lives are numerous (and mainly Latin). See Barthèlemy Aneau, *Jurisprudentia. A primo & divino sui ortu, ad nobilem* (Lyon, 1554); and Giuseppe Aurelio di Gennaro, *Respublica jurisconsultorum* (1731), available also in a truncated French version, *La République des jurisconsultes* (Paris, 1768). Both provide biographical lists of great (male) legal lives.

[6] Pierre Legendre, *L'inestimable objet de la transmission: Étude sur le principe généalogique en Occident* (Paris: Fayard, 1985) at 55. In translation, there is Pierre Legendre, *God in the Mirror: A Study of the Institution of Images* (London: Routledge, 2019).

To say that the image alights or springs from the text, that the *imago* flaps its imaginal discs and takes flight, is simply to reiterate that the visual acts differently, affectively and effectively, and in doing so it generates both the danger and the opportunity of a law relayed in optical forms. The sense of the dissonance or the rend—the *déchirure* in Didi-Huberman's erudite argot or argute vocabulary—generates an opening, a sense of possibility as well as a path to the other scene of knowledge.[7] The normative image as nascent visual regimen or prescient visiocratic governance is an as yet inchoate space of potential and possibility. It presages law unbound, an angelological and imaginal normativity in the sense of being free of text and territory, constantly mobile and plural because the image as the object of perception exists outside the subject while also enveloping the interior life as response to and desire for that which is imaged. It is multiple, mobile, unbound and changing. The medial, as imaginal, is a phenomenon of the spirit and exists without any specific tellurian ties, in externality to mind and body as exterior and exteriorization: 'Every image is the Being of knowledge that acts outside of the subject, a sort of objective unconscious'.[8] Just as the oneiric image is an alien and escaping interior plurality of forms, the exterior image is the projection of perception, the unconscious appearing outside the body, or as an internal diffraction in the juridical text. It is the latter sense, as the transmission and mattering of apparition in judicial reasoning, the dissonant medium of relay which is to be our focus. The law becoming imaginal is the next stage of jurisprudential development, already foreshadowed in rhetorical figures, in film and law, in legal aesthetics, in the jurist's theatrical accoutrements, and the elaborate staging of juridical spectacles.[9] All trials are show trials, all legal texts are picture books haunted by the images they bear, the imaginal spectres that they invoke, the affects that escape repression in the form of figure, likeness, face.[10] The enlacement of law with desire in the image is thus not a novelty, but it is a sleight of legal transmission that

[7] On the rip, rend, slash, or tear—*déchirure*—of the image, see Georges Didi-Huberman, *Confronting Images* (State College: Pennsylvania State University Press, 2005): one who 'desires *to see*, or rather to look, will lose the unity of an enclosed world to find himself in the uncomfortable opening of a universe henceforth suspended, subject to all the winds of meaning; it is here that synthesis will become fragile to the point of collapse; and that the object of sight, eventually touched by a bit of the real, will dismantle the subject of knowledge, dooming simple reason to something like a rend'. The root of such analysis lies in Aby Warburg's sense of the seismography of the image, the dynamogram of the depiction that surives as the affective force of a form. On which, see Georges Did-Huberman, *The Surviving Image: Phantoms of Time and Time of Phantoms: Aby Warburg's History of Art* (University Park: Pennsylvania State University Press, 2017) at 108–111.

[8] Emanuele Coccia, *Sensible Life: A Micro-ontology of Images* (New York: Fordham University Press, 2014) at 52. Continuing to argue that '[s]ensible life goes beyond the nature and the identity of things because it represents the exodus of forms from their material existence ...'.

[9] For recent and powerful work on legal spectrality in terms of a theory of show trials, see Başak Ertür, *Spectacles and Spectres: A Performative Theory of Political Trials* (Palo Alto: Stanford University Press, 2022).

[10] Goodrich, '*Imago Decidendi*: On the Common Law of Images', 1 *Art and Law* 1 (2017).

awaits its proper syntagms, its albums and galleries, exhibitions and installations.[11] The imaginal extends the text and forces the scripture of law outside of itself and into the intimate public sphere of juridical affect and lawful attachment. It is in sum and substance an impersonal medium because communal in intellection and enterprise. By extension, the images that judges use provide a distinctive and differently shared avenue and manifestation of judicial intent, of the affect and drive that triggers and focuses decision upon the novelty of its expression and the publicity of its relay. The choice to insert is to graft a distinct form into the lineal text and in doing so the judge incorporates the dominion of appearances, figures of the everyday, objective images with histories, archives, critical discourses, visions and decisions of their own and of which the precedential proponent is quite frequently entirely unaware. The copula, *vision in decision*, plays of course also on the element of indecision, the indeterminacy and productivity that the image brings into the text. It is for this reason that the present work strives in part to mirror the method of the courts and of common law by following the judicial gaze, the ambulation of the eye, the lateral reasoning, so far as this can be discerned, into what is not seen, the scotomized, the blind spots, the shadows of juridical vision, the opaque optics of the anecdata or personal choices that subtend the rendering in imaginal form.

The exempla and indeed the precedents that this study uses as its focus are images, the figurative visual manifestations and captured depictions of judgement.[12] These novel yet daily augmenting modes of judicial expression raise significant questions that engage the ocular and the textual, the aesthetic and normative, art and law in ways that have not been studied or systematized. This book aims first to review in critical and analytic fashion the visual materials that are to be found in legal judgements across the common law world. Its second objective is to provide an initial categorization, historical and theoretical, of the contexts and uses that judges make of such imagery, creating the nascent possibility of an atlas or gallery of legally manipulated visual material. Third, no harm in a trinity, even an evaporating one, the new media of law pose stark questions of method and juristic status. The image is not a norm and yet relayed in a legal judgement, a picture takes its place in a normative decision being handed down to regulate subsequent courts and judgements. The image is variously probative, explicatory, affective, evidential, identificatory, comedic, or peripheral, and yet in its very incorporation into a judicial decision must also gain the aura and context if not yet the explicit force of a norm. Increasingly law looks a particular way, not simply as a spectacular presence but as a mode of manifestation in a gaze,

[11] For a recent and admirably produced account of the earlier history of images in juridical texts, see Michael Widener and Mark Weiner, *Law's Picture Books: The Yale Law Library Collection* (Clark, N.J.: Talbot, 2017).

[12] It is time to take the opportunity to note that I retain the middle 'e' of judgement in antipathy to legalistic truncation. See Goodrich, 'Weird Judgement: Agon, Omniscience and the Absence of an "e"', *Ordine internazionale e diritti umani* (2021a), 130–139.

a visual response to and depiction of what judges have seen. Such a dialectic of legal vision deserves critical recognition as well as empirical acknowledgement of a law increasingly disseminated through new media and social platforms that carry their own *dispositif* of theoretical and social connotations, implications, and attributions. Retinal justice as a critical ambition starts with the examination of those platforms, apparatuses, and imputations as they have emerged through precedent.

Frequently drawing its images from social media and then returning those images, in judicial text or fragments of rulings, to the selfsame virtual relays, the line between linear legal rule, black letter gravamen, and the free play, the distinctly unruly dialogue of the web, the comedy of bites, nibbles, clips, grabs, memes, tweets, nimbs, nebula, and Instagrams of internet domiciliaries becomes ever more fluid. The legal subject is constituted as a viewing subject, the persona of the judge is depicted and apprehended *ad apparentiam*, as an aesthetic form and visual figure, joining belatedly the imaginal domain, the videosphere of the contemporary. If images, in sum and pestle, abound and make up the media fare of daily life, of news, of legal bites and nibbles, circulating on multiple mobile devices in a diversity of transitory contexts as evanescent meanings, an account of how law appears in those crypto domains of the imaginal and virtual is overdue. You are welcome. Insofar as it cannot ignore the pixelated realms and circulating imagery of websites, emails, SMS, and all the other platforms of remediation, as the judiciary seeks to communicate virtually as well as *in vivo*, in visual mode as well as textual elaboration, the role played by imagery drawn from social media and other platforms and sites will only increase. The last point to be made in this extended excursion into the judicial imaginary is that retinal justice is a method of training the eye to comprehend the aesthetic and political implications, the implexities of a visual law that rules and is relayed by appearances, and so reasons in significant part, wittingly and unconsciously, *ad apparentiam*, towards apparition, propelled by premonition and becoming.[13]

[13] The term implexity comes from Georges Didi-Huberman, 'Image, Language: *The Other Dialectic*' (2018) 23:4 *Angelaki* 19, at 22, meaning internal complexity, the element of one color in the other, of one aspect implicated in and inseparable from others.

Acknowledgements

I shall begin, because no one else will, by thanking myself. This work would not have been possible without me. In my absence it would have remained incomplete. An extraordinary and commendable if erratic attention to the development of the project lay almost entirely on my finger grapes and the emanations of my proboscations. I hasten to add that this gratulation is neither philodoxy nor ipsative intimacy in that I have, by the same token, only myself to blame. Deep inside the study, however, are innumerable figures, tones, and hues of friends and helpmeets, comrades and correspondents, who have diversely aided and beneficially impeded the work of writing and the travails of picturing. Emergent over the course of a decade, I can but scan the surface and provide the appearance of acknowledging intellectual debts, sartorial choices, oenophile diversions, onomastic inventions, and common bibliophilic excursions. First, the frisson of recognition, which is to say that the work of Julie Stone Peters, Chiara Bottici, Richard Sherwin, Tom Mitchell, Paolo Heritier, Marco Wan, Linda Mulcahy, Bradin Cormack, Subha Mukherji, Gary Watt, and Emanuele Coccia, has been an invaluable source of admiration and of rapidly exorcized feelings of inadequacy. Their variably supportive and reluctant, persisting or abandoned correspondences have left me both intimidated and improved. Neil Duxbury has been an extraordinary and gratuitous reader, a benevolently insightful and beneficially opaque commentator. Then there is London calling, *cosmos polis*, and Nathan Moore, Maria Aristodemou, Adam Gearey, Piyel Haldar, Elena Loizidou, as also Conal Parsley, Jorge Bellido, and Thanos Zartaloudis from the suburbs, who have provided a maelstrom of erudition and on their good days exemplify the proper flirtation with the excitement of ideas. Ultramontane and antipodean, Desmond Manderson has become indispensable as an inspiration and protagonist of optical insight and the aesthetic opificers of a visual jurisprudence. In unparalleled extroversion Daniela Gandorfer, *femina fenestris*, provided constant insufflation of ideas, astronomical materializations of sub-atomic proton alignments, and a reliable matterphorical relay of photographs of evanescent bicycles, and light spangled pigeons in Vienna. The imaginosum of Valérie Hayaert in the realm of esoteric emblems and the espionage of art are daunting and yet worn lightly. Elizabeth Huang emerged virtually, apparently from the isolarion of fogbound Cambridge, to provide sustaining wit and unexpectedly optimistic projects at the eleventh hour. The oneiric moods and nebulous humours of Deepak Unnikrishnan provide a subtly melancholic timbre and a Raya of light for us all. Phillip Mitsis, *nunc demitsis*, towers above the merely tellurian zetetic efforts of an imperite such as I. Barton Beebe kindly stirred himself both from normal occupancy of his day bed and his elevated empirical juristic endeavours to comment upon my analyses of copyright law. And Sabarish Suresh has been tormented by my requests for research and yet retained his equanimity and intellective bonhomie. He provided the bulk of the database of judicial images, corralled permissions, and commented cartographically. Jibraan Mansoor nobly stepped up when Sabarish left for further and higher exploits. The apologetic endeavours and unrestrained goodwill of Simon Stern and Bob Spoo, the editors of this series, are as remarkable and as elongated as is my debt to their energetic ministrations. And, of course, nothing can express my thanks to David Garland.

Then there are the boots and braces, those nearby and in the family. The Olympian Marinos Diamantides affects us all with a sense of erudite humour and aesthetic homelessness. The unrestrainedly effervescent advocate of intellectual accidents, the prize bespattered Swethaa Ballakrishnen keeps me grounded. The meticulously percipient apperceptions of Ronnie Goodrich time and again robustly refocus my viewings of familiar images and forgotten words. The laser vision of Linda Mills, her sense of colour and unparalleled propensity for affective reasoning defy verbal circumscription though I can say that she is the cause of my being here. Which returns me to my topic and subject. But for this fork and thimble, *sine qua non*, the stretch and hide of Petrus Bonus Dives, the chimera of this upright corpse, the alignment of these eyes with those of the many, there would be one book less in the atlas of scribblings.

A special word of thanks, a paragraph on their own, for the two artists, Charis Entwistle and Isobel Williams, who have so dexterously reproduced depictions that the Press lawyers, for reasons exclusively their own, have deemed were without permission. These, together with a number of other images that the Press chose not to reproduce in the book, are posted on the website, the cemetery of censored images, the link to which is provided in the now excitingly multimedia text.

Peter Goodrich

New York
April 1, 2023

Contents

List of Figures xiv

1. Introduction: A Morphology of Judicial Images 1
2. Maps, Diagrams, Schemata 25
3. Surplusage: Out of an Abundance of Words 70
4. Comedy of Eros 97
5. Evidential Expositions 128
6. Extispicious Depictures 164
7. Retinal Justice 196
8. Conclusion: Remediations 239

Table of Cases 257
Bibliography 262
Index 271

List of Figures

1.1 A & B. Insertion of his own photographs by Judge Richard Posner (dissenting) in *Construction & General Laborers' Local Union No. 330 v Town of Grand Chute* (2016). By permission of Richard Posner 2

1.2. Screenshot from *Aileen Brooks v IT Works Marketing* 2022 WL 2079747 (2022) 4

1.3. Insertion of court-generated image by Justice Stevens (dissenting) in *Capitol Square Advisory Board v Pinette* (1995) 10

1.4. Insertion of court-generated image by Justice Souter *Capitol Square Advisory Board v Pinette* (1995) 13

1.5. Insertion by Judge Amir Weizebbluth in *Dahan v. Shacharoff*, 30823-08-16 (Herzliya Small Claims Ct. Feb. 24, 2017) 15

2.1. From Guillaume Rouille, *Alenconiensis causidici in legibus licêtiati* (1570). Rare Book Collection, Lillian Goldman Law Library, Yale Law School 28

2.2 A & B. From John Speed, *Theatrum imperii magnæ Britanniæ* (1611 & 1612 respectively). Reproduced by kind permission of the Syndics of Cambridge University Library 30

2.3. Insertion of Supreme Court in *Siddiq v Mahant Suresh* (2019) 36

2.4. Insertion of Supreme Court in *Siddiq v Mahant Suresh* (2019) 37

2.5. Insertion of Justice Mann in *Nigel Peter Moore v Brent Waterways Board* [2009] 40

2.6. Insertion by Judge Patricia McCullough in *Kruge v Workers' Compensation Appeal Board* (2014) 43

2.7. Insertion by Judge Alex Kozinski in *US v Lizarrago-Tirado* (2015) 44

2.8. Insertion of Judge Christopher Kehoe in *Long v State of Maryland* (2019) 46

2.9. Insertion of Judge Christopher Kehoe in *Long v State of Maryland* (2019) 46

2.10. Insertion of Judge Daniel Friedman (dissenting) in *Long v State of Maryland* (2019) 48

2.11. Insertion of Associate Justice Moore in *New South Wales Aboriginal Land Council v The Minister Administering the Crown Lands Act* (2015) 49

2.12. Insertion of Associate Justice Moore in *New South Wales Aboriginal Land Council v The Minister Administering the Crown Lands Act* (2015) 50

2.13. Insertion of Associate Justice Moore in *New South Wales Aboriginal Land Council v The Minister Administering the Crown Lands Act* (2015) 51

2.14. Insertion by Judge Fred Biery in *HouseCanary, Inc. v Quicken Loans, Inc* (2018) 54

2.15. Insertion by Deputy High Court Judge Kwok in *Chan Chuen v Forestside Limited* (2016) 58

2.16. Insertion by Deputy High Court Judge Kwok in *Chan Chuen v Forestside Limited* (2016) 59

2.17. Insertion by Associate Justice Derham in *Clare and Ors v Eva Bedelis* [2016] 61

2.18. Insertion by Associate Justice Derham in *Clare and Ors v Eva Bedelis* [2016] 62

3.1. Insertion by Chief Judge Charles Marvin in *Jackson v Beasley* (1998) 77

3.2. Frontispiece from Père le Moyne, *De l'art des devises* (1666). Permission by P. Goodrich 78

3.3. Insertion by Judge Fred Biery in *HouseCanary, Inc. v Quicken Loans, Inc* (2018) 82

3.4. Insertion by Judge Fred Biery in *HouseCanary, Inc. v Quicken Loans, Inc* (2018) 83

3.5. Insertion by Judge Michael Walker in *Michael Dick v Pilot Travel Centers, LLC* (2018) 85

3.6. The world upside down, from John Taylor, *Mad Fashions* (1642). Permission by P. Goodrich 89

3.7. Insertion by Judge Richard Posner in *Omar Grayson v Harold Schuler* (2012). Photo © David Corio 91

3.8 A & B. Insertion by Judge Arnold Goldin *Robertson v Clarksville-Montgomery County School System* (2018) 93

3.9. Insertion by Judge Arnold Goldin in *Robertson v Clarksville-Montgomery County School System* (2018) 94

4.1. Insertion by Judge Rares in *Metro Business Centre v Centrefold Entertainment Pty Ltd* [2017] 105

4.2 A & B. Insertion by Lord Justice Jacob in *European Central Bank v Document Security* (2008) 110

4.3 A & B. Insertion by Lord Justice Jacob in *European Central Bank v Document Security* (2008). Photo by Philippe Halsman © Philippe Halsman Estate 111

4.4. Insertion by Justice Birss in *Hearst Holdings v A.V.E.L.A.* [2014] 113

4.5. Insertion by Justice Birss in *Hearst Holdings v A.V.E.L.A.* [2014] 114

5.1. Still from video clip posted by the Supreme Court in *Scott v Harris* (2007) 130

5.2. Insertion by Judge Pierre Bergeron in *Milatz v City of Cincinnati* (2019) 134

5.3. Insertion by District Judge Brantley Starr in *Rincon v Home Depot USA* (2019) 136

5.4. Insertion by Justice Sarah Beth Landau in *Richard Culotta v Doubletree Hotels LLC* (2019) 137

5.5 A & B. Insertion by District Judge Paula Xinis in *Schaefer v United States* (2017) 140

5.6 A & B. Insertion by Judge Ann Walsh Bradley (dissenting) in *Kochanski v Speedway SuperAmerica LLC* 850 N.W.2d 160 (2014) 141

5.7. Insertion by DCJ Cash QC in *Ring v Commissioner for Police* (2019) 144

5.8. Insertion by DCJ Cash QC in *Ring v Commissioner for Police* (2019) 144

5.9. Insertion by CJ Quinlan in *Sanders and Others v City of Perth* [2019] 145

5.10. Insertion by CJ Quinlan in *Sanders and Others v City of Perth* [2019] 146

5.11. Insertion by Judge Katzmann in *Gill and Others v Ethicon Sàrl* (2019) 148

5.12. Insertion by Judge Katzmann in *Gill and Others v Ethicon Sàrl* (2019) 149

5.13. Insertion by Justice M. Wong in *R v Shaun Burgher* [2016] 151

5.14. Insertion by District Judge Jorge Alonso in *Jeans v John Varga Warden* (2019) 153

5.15 A & B. Insertion by Chief Judge Edwards (dissenting) in *Evers Welding Co. v Occupational Health and Safety Review Commission* (1980) 155

5.16. Insertion by Judge Richard Posner in *Sandifer v United States Steel Corporation* (2012). Permission by Timothy Shapiro 158

6.1. Insertion by DCJ Levy in *Lange v Timothy O'Corrigan* [2015] 168

6.2. Insertion by DCJ Levy in *Lange v Timothy O'Corrigan* [2015] 170

6.3. Insertion by Justice Makaula in *State v Redhouse and Another* [2018] 175

6.4. Insertion by Judge Birss QC in *Samsung Electronics (UK) Ltd v Apple Inc* [2012] 177

6.5 A & B. Insertion by Judge Birss QC in *Samsung Electronics (UK) Ltd v Apple Inc* [2012] 179

6.6 A & B. Insertion by Judge Birss QC in *Temple Island Collections v New English Teas Limited* [2012]. By permission of Temple Island Collections 182

6.7 A & B. Insertion by Judge Richard Posner in *Sikhs for Justice v Badal* (2013) 186

6.8. Insertion by District Judge Robert Conrad in *La Michoacana Natural, LLC v. Maestre* 611 F.Supp.3d 87 (2020) 189

6.9 A & B. Insertion by Federal Magistrate McInnis in *Melbourne's Cheapest Cars v Melbourne Street Cars* [2004] 192

7.1. Insertion by U.S. Magistrate Judge Mark Dinsmore in *Randolph v Forever 21 Inc* (2017) 197

7.2. Insertion by U.S. Magistrate Judge Mark Dinsmore in *Randolph v Forever 21 Inc* (2017) 199

7.3. Insertion by the House of Lords in *Designers Guild Ltd v Russell Williams (Textiles)* [2001]. By permission of Parliamentary Archives, Houses of Parliament, Westminster 209

7.4. From *Spicer v Commissioner for Police of the Metropolis* [2019] 217

7.5. Inserted by Judge Gerard Lynch in *Warhol Foundation v Goldsmith* (2021). By permission of Lynn Goldsmith 220

7.6. Insertion by Judge George Draper III in *State v Walter* 479 S.W. 3d 118 (2016) 225

7.7. Insertion by Judge George Draper III in *Ferdman v CBS Interactive* (2018) 228

7.8. Insertion by District Judge Vernon Broderick from *Walsh v Townsquare Media* (2020). Image courtesy of Rebecca Fay Walsh // FAYMOUS 230

7.9. Insertion by District Judge Vernon Broderick from *Walsh v Townsquare Media* (2020) 231

8.1. Naked Rambler seated, by Isobel Williams http://isobelwilliams.org.uk/ 244

8.2. Naked Rambler in the dock http://isobelwilliams.org.uk/ 247

8.3. Insertion by Circuit Judge Damon Keith in *Northeast Coalition for the Homeless v Husted* (2016) 253

1
Introduction
A Morphology of Judicial Images

A judge springs out of his car on the way to court in downtown Chicago and takes photographs of an inflatable rat. A while later he inserts these photographs into a decision involving another balloon rodent. Begin, however, at the beginning. The majority opinion opens: 'Rats. This case is about rats. Giant inflatable rats which unions use to demonstrate their unhappiness with employers ... Cats too—inflatable fat cats wearing business suits and pinkie rings strangling workers'.[1] Judge Easterbrook, feeling perhaps that verbal description is inadequate to the enormity of the spectacle, or that such things should not be left to the imagination, then reproduces passport sized photographs of the rat and the cat in the judgement. The doctrinal issue, for the majority, was whether the inflatables, staked to the ground, were 'structures' that conveyed a message in contravention of a Municipal Code which required a permit for such monumental symbolic effigies. Little is otherwise said about the feline and rodent in the majority judgement, although it is of course legally notable that the decision contains precedential pictures of a swollen rat and an aureate cat, presumably as indicators of structural status and as lending visibility and providing a reality effect for the contested symbols of protest.

The dissenting judge, a top ten public intellectual in the United States according to a survey that he conducted himself, goes rather further.[2] Judge Posner focuses solely on the rat and is of the view that prohibiting the inflatable commensal creature is only lawful if it causes harm 'the prospect or possibility of which justified the town in forbidding' its placement near the road. The town argued aesthetic and safety concerns to which the judge has a surprising response. He argues that for some the rat is rather handsome and bears 'at least a faint resemblance to Tyrannosaurus Rex' and as such there is no substantial aesthetic complaint. As to safety, the judge regales the patient reader with the story that he sometimes drives to downtown from the south side of Chicago along Martin Luther Drive and that he had seen a rat, named Drape, on the east side of the street, during the course of a different dispute. He continues: 'Every time I drove past the rat I glanced at it,

[1] *Construction & General Laborers' Local Union No. 330 v Town of Grand Chute* 834 F.3d 745 (2016). For another example of judicial photographers, see *Clare and Ors v Eva Bedelis* [2016] VSC 381, discussed in detail in Chapter 2.

[2] Richard Posner, *Public Intellectuals: A Study in Decline* (2003) 209–214, ranking is based on scholarly citation.

Judicial Uses of Images. Peter Goodrich, Oxford University Press.
 DOI: 10.1093/oso/9780192848772.003.0001

as it was the only noteworthy sight on my route. This glance never caused me to swerve, crash, crouch in my seat, avert my eyes, hit a pedestrian or cause mayhem'. This was so, even though 'this rat, like its Grand Chute cousin', was close to the street. 'I took a close-up photo of it and another from across the street'.[3] Here, he concludes the anecdote, are the two photos. (Figures 1.1 A & B)

The majority judgement shows the rat so as to see and address the ropes and stakes that potentially turn it into a structure—if the workers had held the ropes, or put weights on the inflatable there would have been no contravention of the Code—while the dissenting judge shows his own photographs of a different rat in a distinct location so as to argue, presumably by analogy—the commensal is commensurate—that this rat is neither aesthetically offensive nor a threat to vehicular or pedestrian safety. In neither instance of judgement is the depictive image directly probative and the dissenting judge even goes so far as to admit that his personal photographs may 'scandalize some readers who think it improper for the judge to stray outside the official record'.[4] While it may be hard to think that it is scandalous in the sense of irreligious or indeed in the old language of common

(a) (b)

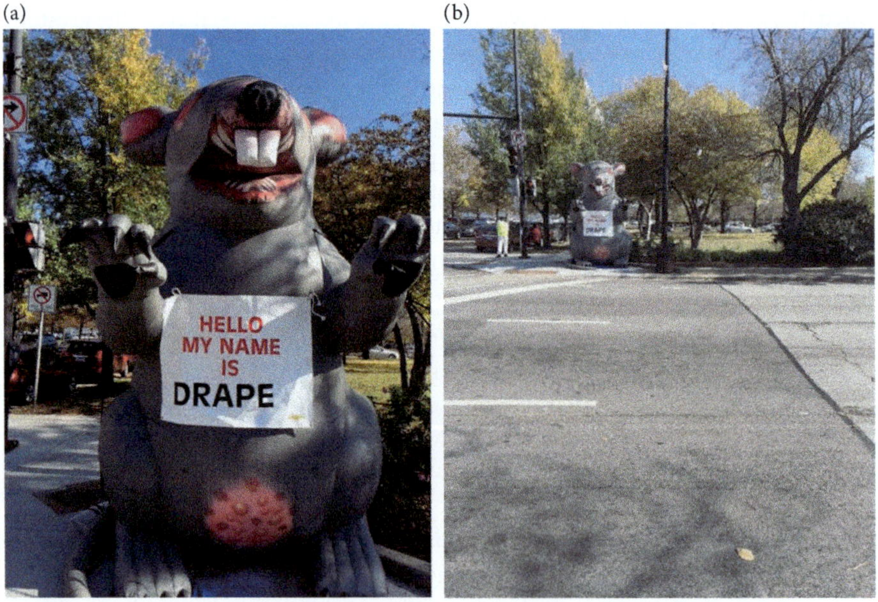

Figures 1.1 A & B Insertion of his own photographs by Judge Richard Posner (dissenting) in *Construction & General Laborers' Local Union No. 330 v Town of Grand Chute* (2016).
By permission of Richard Posner.

[3] *Construction & General*, at 756.
[4] Ibid. at 755.

law, contempt of court, it is a conflation of different media, distinct locations and separate scenes. It also represents a sea change in judgement, an inversion of the constraint of law and the linear discourse of the text in favour of a novel arbitral freedom. The change in medium, the visual ambulation of the optic lens scanning figures in judgement portends decision making that is normatively surprising while also being, mostly unwittingly, both transparent in its motives and visible in its imaginal moments of invention. The image escapes the ruins of the text.

The sea change is aligned with Judge Posner's notion that in posting his own photographs he is doing something that may scandalize. There is in historical terms a certain demitting of the office of the judge and a transgression of the formal separation of subject and *ideona persona* or invested institutional figure. Judicial office is traditionally a dignity, a position of record, a clerical role bounded by rules and strictly confined to the *in vivo* theatre of trial within the court, and doctrinally within the text. There could be no more striking example of the change exemplified by the judicial amateur photographer stepping out of court to provide his own witness statement than the classical decision on 'misnosmer' in *Marriot and Pascalls Case*. The specific issue was an error in naming, the misnomer of a hospital in a lease in which Le Savoy was inscribed rather than de le Savoy. The lease was adjudged utterly void for the conveyance had to be *idem re, idem nomine*, the same in the thing and in the name.[5] What is important is the reasoning. The lease was not *unum in sensu*—'not in your understanding as private persons, but in your judicial knowledge upon the record, *quod coram vobis residet*, as Judges of record'.[6] It was judicial knowledge that governed, not private perception, to which the court adds 'the record is your eye of justice, and you have no other eye to look unto the cause depending upon you, but the record'.[7] To support this a citation to a case of 7 H.4 108 is relayed, where a judge on his way to the assizes had witnessed a murder and later sat on the bench at the trial of another man arraigned and in conclusion convicted of the murder. What the judge had seen was private knowledge and irrelevant to the process and verdict of trial. The only image relevant to law was the image created in the theatre of justice and truth, the trial conducted within the theatrical confines of unity of time, place, and meaning.[8]

Photographs of chthonian creatures taken en route to court on other occasions and in relation to different disputes, without any visible stakes in the ground, used not as evidence but as an aspect of judicial determination, part of the reasoning of the judgement, transgresses the extant legal rule of exclusively literary legal argument while simultaneously opening the judge's interior perception of the case to

[5] *Marriot and Pascalls Case* 1 Leonard 159, at 161: *Qui haeret in litera haeret in Cortice.*
[6] Ibid. at 161 (because our court is resident there).
[7] Ibid. at 161.
[8] See Julie Stone Peters, *Law as Performance* (Oxford: Oxford University Press, 2022) 298 discussing Bacon and Bentham on '*nihil ex scenâ*' and for the latter '*multum ex scenâ*', differentially referencing images internal to the theatre of law.

public scrutiny. With the escalation and acceleration of access to images at every stage of the legal process, their novel status as figures of precedential reasoning, *obiter depicta* or *imago decidendi,* things seen along the path to decision and the image of the ruling, have to be addressed. The jurisprudence of the imaginal is in its infancy. The judicial depictions used in support or legitimation of judgement have no explicit normative status and are frequently omitted from the law report.[9] No explanation is deemed necessary for the omission and where, as is more increasingly the case, images are reproduced, their quality is frequently so low as to make discernment of the judicial optical argument either difficult or impossible. In *Aileen Brooks v IT Works Marketing,* to use a recent example, the plaintiff had purchased products on the defendant's website and the question, a common one in U.S. contract law, was whether the Terms and Conditions of Use, hyperlinked on all the site webpages, were sufficiently prominent to put the plaintiff on notice inquiry, and so bind her to the terms (Figure 1.2).[10] The relevant portion of the judgement, is as follows:

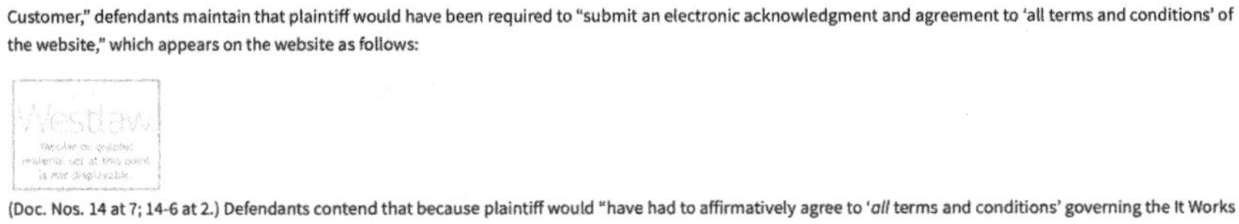
Customer," defendants maintain that plaintiff would have been required to "submit an electronic acknowledgment and agreement to 'all terms and conditions' of the website," which appears on the website as follows:

(Doc. Nos. 14 at 7; 14-6 at 2.) Defendants contend that because plaintiff would "have had to affirmatively agree to '*all* terms and conditions' governing the It Works

Figure 1.2 Screenshot from *Aileen Brooks v IT Works Marketing* 2022 WL 2079747 (2022).

The reproduction, viewing, and interpretation of the image is clearly neither a judicial priority, nor deemed legally significant. The judicial eye is simply to be taken on trust or believed, presumably because there is nothing controversial or disputable in the evidence of the eye. The vision in decision, the optical aspect of the judgement, is paradoxically veiled, a seeming scotomization or blindspot at that very point where the judge has sought to show their reasoning. The old law that restricts what is seen and judged to the interior time and space of the courtroom lingers to the effect of excluding or downgrading the images that actually appear in the record of the trial and as potential visual precedents for future courts. The vestiges of the old law haunt, but novel technologies now overcome such restraint and images proliferate in judgements despite such hesitations. The visual is now a part of legal reasoning and determination. The outside comes inside, and myriad depictions—emojis, photographs, films, screenshots, animatrix, graphics, Instagrams, memes, gifs, nfts—increasingly populate the law reports

[9] Rebecca Tushnet, 'Worth a Thousand Words: The Images of Copyright', 125 *Harvard Law Rev.* 684 (2012) at 720 makes the point that visual material is often not even included in the report online, but rather the viewer encounters: TABULAR OR GRAPHIC MATERIAL SET FORTH AT THIS POINT IS NOT DISPLAYABLE. A decade later, the point has been ameliorated but not essentially changed.

[10] *Aileen Brooks v IT Works Marketing* 2022 WL 2079747.

as visual emblems, inserted depictions of boundary lines, portrayals of subject matter, views of causes of accidents or dispute, and parties or victims are variously depicted as what in the old language would be termed *vividæ rationes*, ambulant—or better 'bimbling'—images motivating judgement and constituting an ocular dimension to the record, even where the optical is haphazardly omitted.[11] There has been significant work already done on the visual turn in law, the plethora of different depicted dimensions of advocacy and argument, film and on-screen appearances in court and in the forums of trial, but little has been written on the judicial use of images as part of judgement.[12] It is the sea change in the medium of judicial determination, the insight into the drive, the synaesthetic and visual propulsion of judging that the rapidly augmenting pictorial scope of determinations now makes available to analysis.[13] These are images in and of judgement, the depiction constituting what I will term the *imago decidendi*, the affective source of judicial decision as well as frequently being the effectively binding facet of the rule upon the eyes of future coordinate and lower courts, lawyers, advocates, and academics. This novelty will be elaborated as retinal justice, meaning the law that strikes the eye and impacts the thalmus prior to thought.[14] The cathartic concussion or affective force of vision needs to play an exponentially augmented role in the critical and cultural analysis of law. As Linda Mulcahy formulates the point, the incursion of the visual into the legal has extensive interpretative implications:

[11] For an extraordinary example from the UK, where the issue for the Supreme Court to determine was precisely that of the visual similarities and differences of two suitcase designs, the official BAILII report omits the images, while the court ready online report on LEXIS reproduces a judgement where colour is a key component of the analysis and determination in monochrome: *PMS International v Magmatic* [2016] UKSC 12.

[12] For an important overview and methodological outline of digital legal design and visual law, see Colette Brunschwig, *Visual Law and Legal Design: Questions and Tentative Answers* (Bern: Weblaw Editions, 2021), and also her earlier account of *Iurisprudentia picturata*, in Brunschwig, *On Visual Law: Visual Legal Communication Practices and their Scholarly Exploration* (Bern: Weblaw, 2014). There is some doctrinal literature addressing image and law, reviewed, for example, in E. Porter and K. Watts, 'Visual Rulemaking', 91 *NYU Law Rev.* 1183 (2016); Sionaidh Douglas Scott *Law After Modernity* (London: Routledge, 2014); Voker Boehme-Neßler, *Pictorial Law: Modern Law and the Power of Pictures* (Springer, 2011), and one important empirical study of judicial perception, D. Kahan et al., 'Whose Eyes Are You Going to Believe? *Scott v Harris* and the Dangers of Cognitive Illiberalism' 122 *Harvard Law Rev.* 837 (2009). On the technology of legal vision, see Neal Feigenson and Christina Speisel, *Law on Display: The Digital Transformation of Legal Persuasion and Judgment* (New York: NYU Press, 2015).

[13] On the theory subtending this pathway, see, for a conspectus of works, Desmond Manderson, *Danse Macabre: Temporalities of Law in the Visual Arts* (Cambridge: Cambridge University Press, 2019); Richard Sherwin, *Visualizing Law in the Age of the Digital Baroque: Arabesques and Entanglements* (London: Routledge, 2012); Desmond Manderson (ed.), *Law and the Visual: Representations, Technologies, and Critique* (Toronto: Toronto University Press, 2018); Elizabeth Porter, 'Taking Images Seriously', 114 *Columbia Law Rev.* 1687 (2014).

[14] This is a complicated point that I take initially from studies of early cinema when viewers would duck, scramble away, dive for cover when danger appeared to be coming at them from the screen. See the discussion of a 'shark aesthetic' in Gabriele Pedullà, *In Broad Daylight: Movies and Spectators after the Cinema* (London: Verso, 2012) 79 et seq.; there is no pure viewing but rather a system of mediating via the thalmus and emotional coding via the amygdala. The meaning of the image is never simple, and it requires complex reconstruction or unpacking of the pathways that the picture has prompted. My thanks to Christina Spiesel for epistolary discussion of this point.

'Unlike the text which must be read in English from the left to the right, line after line, images are more anarchic'.[15] The regimentations of the page are torn apart by the insertion of pictures because the eye acts differently in viewing than in reading. It is that escape from the exclusively linear that unsettles and excites. It is an opening up to vision that potentially both expands and threatens the confinement and the restraint of legal reasoning. The eye wanders when looking and so the image brings the world, interior and exterior, into the courtroom, and to that extent it takes the law out of the textual and out of the constraints of trial and courthouse, no longer *in camera* but now *ex camera*. In another formulation, addressing how filming a tribunal alters the nature of the process: 'the camera intervenes in even the forensic ritual of coding violence and threatens to topple the media conversion of act to language in favor of another: act to image'.[16]

Judicial Uses of Images utilizes a constantly augmenting corpus of over 400 images taken from decisions across the common law influenced world, specifically the United States, the United Kingdom, India, Pakistan, Canada, South Africa, Mauritius, Singapore, Hong Kong, New Zealand, and Australia to inaugurate both an archive of precedential imagery and a critical method for apprehension and reception of such visual dimensions of legal judgement. The focus will be upon how judges use images in their decisions, and specifically the variety in the types of depiction utilized, the range of analyses, implicit and explicit, that are offered in the reasoning of the determinations, and the diversity of interpretations that can be extracted from them. The atlas or album of judicial images has yet to be compiled, there are simply disparate and variable pictorial manifestations in judgements and so the analysis has to begin, as I began, with the somewhat haphazard character of these visual insertions and a sense of their novelty as a dimension of legal reasoning or manifestation of juridical intent.[17] There is an unwitting sense both of lack and excitation. The sensed lacuna is that of sensibility, the absence of animation in the dead letter of the text, the desiccated linearity of scriptural reason.[18] The affect of the image is thus that of the intimation of an epistemic gap that can be filled by a picture, a reality effect that can be inserted to justify and exemplify the judgement.

[15] Linda Mulcahy, 'Eyes of the Law: A Visual Turn in Socio-legal Studies', 44 *J. Law & Soc.* 111 (2017) at 123. For the theoretical roots of such a distinction, see Jean-François Lyotard, *Discourse, Figure* [1975] (Minneapolis: University of Minnesota Press, 2011) and the excellent elaboration in Laurence Moinereau, *Le générique de film: De la lettre à la figure* (Rennes: Presses Universitaires de Rennes, 1995).

[16] Cornelia Vismann, 'Tele-Tribunals: Anatomy of a Medium', 10 *Grey Room* 5 (2003) at 15.

[17] Tushnet, 'Worth a Thousand Words' provides a useful analysis of the legal addiction to the text even in relation to copyright law where it is images that are frequently the source and the subject of dispute. See also Jose Bellido, 'Looking Right: The Art of Visual Literacy in English Copyright Litigation', 10 *Law, Culture, and the Humanities* (2014) at 66. Richard Sherwin and Anne Wagner (eds), *Law, Culture and Visual Studies* (Dordrecht: Springer, 2014) provides an expansive survey of the emergent discipline. Mateusz Stępień, 'Say it with Images: Drawing on Jerome Frank's Ideas on Judicial Decision Making', 32 *Int. J. Semiotics of Law* (2019) at 321 also provides a valuable overview of current work.

[18] A useful counterpoint to this sense and sensibility of texts can be found in Katherine Biber et al. (eds), *Law's Documents: Authority, Materiality, Aesthetics* (Abingdon: Routledge, 2021).

Visualization here generates a false sense of certainty, an unreflective reality effect that Barthes analyses in terms of the referential illusion used as a weapon against the intelligible.[19] The sole function of the reality effect is that of signalling the reality of the description that the judge offers, the verisimilitude of 'what is' or at least has been. The aesthetic is provided with the alibi of referential constraints. It is the affect of seeing, however, the need to view, the desire to raise what were classically the downcast eyes of the judge, that signal the excess of meaning, the aesthetic and ethic of judgement. The reality effect can thus act as the sign of the significance of the insignificant, the advenience or first mark and symptom of transmission of the affective substrate of determination, the drive of deciding.

Common law operates according to a Roman logic of analogy—*procedere ad similia*—rather than one of appearances—*procedere ad apparentiam*—and so the fiction or 'as if' of the insertion of an image is initially that it is similar to writing, an illustration of the textual point, to be read rather than viewed. It is normative by association and is presumably restricted in import to the words that reduce and describe it. As Mnookin correctly observes: 'Most significantly, it may well be that judges were unlikely and sometimes unwilling to innovate, preferring to analogize the photograph to familiar forms. A genuinely new form of evidence could be disruptive and destabilizing; better then for a judge to conceptualize the photograph as another iteration of already established representational forms'.[20] The desire to insert an image—a photograph, a video, an animated clip, a hyperlink to pictures and film—is thus most usually conclusory in that it is predetermined by the prior discourse and assumed self-evidently to show what has been adjudged and decided already. Photograph and film, the screenshot and hyperlinked images, are presented to prove irrefragably what the judge has been elaborating in accepted linear textual form by way of reason for deciding. The varied depictions express a desire for a non-scriptural excess, for affect and world, and yet ironically they are supposed to do no more than demonstrate or show what has been said and concluded in the preceding—precedent—text. The old maxim, both theological and legal, beware of all novelty—*novum omne cave*—dictates a conservative approach, one in which the image is stilled, immobilized, and simply shows what the untutored eye of the judge and absent atlas or gallery of juridical images takes it to represent.[21] It joins the dead letters of the text as one more corpse, and this despite the change in medium, the differences of the eye and of visual apprehension.

[19] Roland Barthes, 'The Reality Effect', in *The Rustle of Language* (New York: FSG, 1986) at 141.

[20] Jennifer Mnookin, 'Photographic Evidence and the Power of Analogy', in Dianne Dufour (ed.), *Images of Conviction: The Construction of Visual Evidence* (Paris: Editions Xavier Barral, 2015) at 13.

[21] On the theological roots of this priority of the past and of print, see the extraordinary treatise of John Favour, Doctor of Lawes, *Antiquitie Triumphing over Noveltie: Whereby it is Proved that Antiquitie is a True and Certaine Note of the Christian Catholicke Church and Verity, against all new and upstart heresies* (1619) London: Field, at 141.

A desire for demonstrative certitude, for the specific particular, the *certum* of the visible, is satisfied at the cost of visual veracity and dismissal of the distinctiveness of figuration. There is little sense of the mobile and open quality of images apprehended as material forms, as encounter and event, extant in their own right.[22] The photograph, or now more often the digital screen capture, CCTV, streamed video, is a theatrical performance interpreted by the eye. Taking up the etymology of performance, as forming (*per-formo*) a being (*entia*), there is both mobility, historicity, and sensibility in any image, be it diagrammatical, schematic, pictorial, or digital. The art historian Didi-Huberman explains that the image should be viewed as a materiality, imbued with a haptic quality which in imaginal terms is its visibility as an apparition and so temporal locus of affect and desire. The *pupa*, in biological argot, is a transitional entity that results in the *imago*, an image, a living and usually winged insect.[23] There is in this optical conception both *eros* and *telos* to the image, which can be apprehended best by thinking of it as mobile and alluring in the manner of the flesh which insufflates and exhales, opens and closes, is alive to desire while also being the tactile bearer of an unseen and inexhaustible interiority. To view is to pierce and to be perceived, the image has to be opened up so as to release its sense to the viewer who in turn is discerned by the depicted, looked back upon by the brittlestar of the imaginal, the sensibility of the community of thought. The image constitutes the viewer, as much as the subject who looks insufflates and composes the picture that is seen. A sense of imaginal history, of the archive of artistic presences, the gallery of judicial pictures, is needed to combat in critical modes the lazy eye of the law. Thus, to take an early example, a formative instance, when Justice Stevens introduces a photograph of a 'Latin cross' outside the statehouse in Columbus Ohio into the reported decision of the US Supreme Court, the image itself receives no analysis but is treated as the self-evidence of the textual point being advocated. The persuasive force, affect, and allure of the image go unsaid and, as it were, below the radar of discursive analysis as a species of sub-intellective relay, as unconscious baggage. A case of Homer, or here Stevens, nodding.

Capitol Square Advisory Board v Pinette involved the Klu Klux Klan's application to place a cross in the Capitol Plaza in Columbus, Ohio, and the refusal by the Board to grant permission.[24] The grounds for denial were that the proximity of the cross to the statehouse and other government symbols would indicate governmental endorsement of the religion in contravention of the Establishment clause which

[22] On the immobilization of images, see Georges Didi-Huberman, *The Eye of History* (Cambridge, Mass.: MIT Press, 2018).

[23] George Didi-Huberman, *L'Image ouverte: motifs de l'incarnation dans les arts visuels* (Paris: Gallimard, 2007) at 230. And specifically on Aby Warburg's Atlas, see Didi-Huberman *The Surviving Image: Phantoms of Time and Time of Phantoms: Aby Warburg's History of Art* (University Park: Pennsylvania State University Press, 2017) at 108–111.

[24] Ohio Rev. Code Ann. § 105.41 (1994) gave the Capitol Square Review and Advisory Board responsibility for regulating public access.

requires religious neutrality. In a dissenting judgement, Justice Stevens argues that the cross in Capitol Square 'quite obviously' has the 'principal or primary effect of advancing or inhibiting religion' and then concludes that 'in this case we are dealing with a *visual display*—a symbol readily associated with a religion, in a venue readily associated with the State. This [is a] clear image of endorsement ... '[25] As to the photograph inserted into the opinion, the justice states laconically: 'the picture appended to this opinion demonstrates ... [that] a reasonable observer would likely infer endorsement from the location of the cross erected by the Klan in this case' (Figure 1.3).[26] The photograph is seemingly self-evident to the eyes of the judge and so nothing is said about the provenance or the composition of the image: and this despite the fact, as one commentator put it, 'the unfamiliar inanimate object, together with an unnaturally low angle, creates the impression of a giant cross—a cross larger than surrounding buildings, capable of crushing an innocent bystander (there is a figure discernible on the edge of the right side of the picture and seemingly only a fraction of the cross's height) should it fall.'[27] The reasonable observer in this particular depiction would be an insect, prone on the ground close to the holy rood, gaze centred on the Capitol building, and looking up directly at it as if desiring to enter with the crucifix or at least with its image close to mind.

There is no viewing, description, or critical analysis proffered in the various judgements, beyond conclusions of various sorts. Justice Souter, in a concurring opinion, appends two pictures, one of which presents a panoramic photograph of the Capitol square in which the cross is invisible due in large part to the poor quality of the grainy black and white reproduction, but nonetheless seems to prompt the remark that 'Given the domination of the square by the government's own displays, one would not be a dimwit as a matter of law to think an unattended religious display here was endorsed by the government' (Figure 1.4).[28] The reasonable dimwit could easily view the cross, 'displayed immediately in front of the Ohio Statehouse, with the government's flags flying nearby, and the government's statues close at hand', without any other displays on the square at the time, as giving the appearance of endorsement of the message.[29] As the panoramic image provides no direct visual confirmation of any point that Justice Souter is embellishing, it must, like the use of Latin, have another function: that of symbolizing an occluded reality which only the judge can truly see and dictate as the normative reason of their discursive, linear, monochrome decision. It is in Vico's terms, *verum* and not *certum*, truth rather than the particular and probable empirical subject of precedential

[25] *Capitol Square Advisory Board v Pinette* 515 U.S. 811, 115 S.Ct. 2440 (1995) at 2471.
[26] Ibid. at 2469.
[27] Hamton Dellinger, 'Words are not Enough: The Troublesome Use of Photographs, Maps and Other Images in Supreme Court Opinions', 110 *Harvard Law Rev.* (1997) 1704, at 1727.
[28] *Capitol Square* at 2458 (Justice Souter).
[29] Ibid. at 2461 (Justice Souter).

Figure 1.3 Insertion of court-generated image by Justice Stevens (dissenting) in *Capitol Square Advisory Board v Pinette* (1995).

matter.[30] Not only are there no flags or statues visible, but the cross is in this image too small to be visible, which perhaps fits with the other justification for the decision, namely that there were no other signs in the square to provide a diversity of viewpoints and so dissipate the sense of dimwitted or, in the case of the judge, rational perceptions of endorsement. A giant menorah had recently been removed and of course its absence is visible only in its non-apparition, but that is hardly the visual analysis that the justice is proffering, accurate though it might be in its failure to show what is being discussed as not there. In sum and pestle, Souter's use of the image is gauged to show nothing because the absence of any visible symbols, statues, or flags, serves to confirm his conclusion which is that the Board should have ordered some sign disavowing any endorsement, so filling in the blank space between the diminutive yet present Latin cross and the serried steps and looming columns of the government building.

The desire for an irrefutable demonstration of the point being made, an affective urge to show in an accessible and material visual form the real – the hermeneutic aesthetic – of the dispute, is seemingly what leads Justice Stevens to insert a photograph with neither code nor scale, nor any delineation of the photographic trompe l'oeil that makes the cross look bigger than the government building. The myriad questions of focus, perspective, aperture, aspect ratio, depth of field, frame, selective chromatic, and similar are ignored in favour of simply confronting the reader of the decision, and future courts, with a strangely accentuated and basillic close up perspective on the cross as the lens through which the government buildings are perceived. It makes an exaggerated and from most perspectives an inaccurate visual point. Despite its insertion in the judgement, its position and status as precedential reasoning, it would be very hard to argue that the photograph is an unbiased or neutral depiction of the scene under judicial consideration or that it has any normative force without further critical analysis. The pictorial incursion simply manifests in material and visible form the desire to win an argument, to advocate, to persuade viscerally and visually, to conclude a line of reasoning with an exhibit, the thing itself, if not *in vivo* at least in photogram, as a species here of legal phantasmography. Where words are failing, as Christian Delage so convincingly argues in relation to the Nuremberg trials, on 29 November 1945, film is introduced, pictures are proffered, and the image is ventured so as to save the indictment of Nazi war criminals from being buried by paper and tedium, the theology of law. The visual medium changes the scene from a room full of five million documents to one that effects an encounter, footage of concentration

[30] See, for a detailed examination of the *certum*, Charles J. McNamara, *Quintilian's Theory of Certainty and its Afterlife in Early Modern Italy* (Columbia PhD, 2016). *Verum*, is *aequitas*: the *in camera* rustle of parchment rules, the archival realm of inscriptions, extant and elaborated in forms and processes unseen by the commons. The *certum*, by contrast, is the decision and application in public, so that law is enacted and emerges as both governed by and informing the *verum* for future cases.

camp victims, to which viewers can attach and respond.[31] 'On that day, for the first time in legal history, the American prosecutors showed a film as incriminating evidence'.[32] When transferred from the evidentiary to the normative in the opinion of the judge, the image brings with it a prior and presumed status as a depiction of the real, as obvious, as plain to the eye, whereas its principal untutored effect is affective, an expansion of the judicial medium of discourse, and a sea change in the relations between judge, audience, and subjects judged. The appearance of the real in perceptible, which is to say familiar and frequently encountered visual forms, shifts the path of determination from the linearity of the text to the scopic and more lateral ambulation of the eye. It is a transfer, a remediation that transitions from the stasis of the legal text to the image as the accessible, mobile and open frame of a momentary depiction. The vision in decision is the optical rhizome, the field of ocular associations that the image inserts and portends.

Time, technology, and new media all propel the jurist to novel visual and viserbal forms.[33] The tralatitious character of common law means that it moves on by dint of the exponential increase in the methods and media of relay since our previous example of black and white photographs of the mid-1990s, reproduced in the poorest quality as merely occasional incidents of judgement. In a more contemporary context, the plethora of images unleashes the scopic drive that underlies the use of figurative forms of judicial argument and expression, and in potential the reasoning of law is liberated and expanded by the altered and plural forms of media that now attract the judicial retina and engage a more visceral response. Dash cams, body cams, CCTV, mobile camera applications on a plethora of hand-held devices mean that law is witnessed and visible in colour and *in actu*, with sound and motion, in nearly all of its encounters. Judges have to view as well as read, look as well listen, so as to render judgement in apposite and ethical form. Retinal justice references this augmentation of the visual from linear to figural as the current cutting edge of legal practice by asking the prior and generally dispositive question of how judges look, what panoptic or panoramic perception is embedded in arbitral noticing, what awareness manifests in the judicial gaze? Retinal justice means taking account and providing an analysis of lines of sight and blindspots. The extant literature suggests, continuously and fairly uniformly, whether deemed for good or ill, that the image is powerful, that it should be taken seriously, that it

[31] Christian Delage, *Caught on Camera: Film in the Courtroom from the Nuremberg Trials to the Trials of the Khmer Rouge* (Philadelphia: Pennsylvania University Press, 2014).

[32] Christian Delage, 'Confronting the Nazis with Images of their Crimes', in Dufour (ed.), *Images of Conviction*, 133.

[33] The inelegant neologism of viserbality aims to stress the visual quality of all text, of words as signs, while also pointing to the augmentation generated by insertion of pictures. For the context and for discussion of the term, see Goodrich, 'Viserbal Laws: On an Arbitral Modality Recently Adopted in Judgments', 9 *African Yearbook of Rhetoric* (2019) 50–60.

Figure 1.4 Insertion of court-generated image by Justice Souter *Capitol Square Advisory Board v Pinette* (1995).

is worth a thousand words, and such emphasis is a starting point.[34] Retinal justice references a pre-reflective visual apprehension that mobilizes a shadow archive of images, a preconscious relay of emblematic affects, archetypes, and adumbrations of persons, things, and actions that structure and constitute both sociality and positive law. The image precedes thought because the imagination triggers discourse—the unconscious, as Freud puts it, thinks in images—and yet jurisprudence has failed to accord a distinct status to the pictures that precede, subtend, and now increasingly manifest in judgements. The starting point for an analysis of retinal justice thus has to be an accounting of a distinct conceptual and analytic space of the image, a heterotopia of the visual, a haptic and hepatoscopic (divinatory) site within the imaginal recognition of law. There is a jurisdiction of the

[34] In addition to the previously cited literature, an excellent and lasting history of the power of images is David Freedberg, *The Power of Images: Studies in the History and Theory of Response* (Chicago: Chicago University Press, 1989). For a psychoanalytic account of the disruptive and motive power of images, see Georges Didi-Huberman, *Confronting Images: Questioning the Ends of a Certain History of Art* (State College: Penn State University Press, 2005). For a political analysis, see Retort, *Afflicted Powers* (London: Verso, 2005). The first jurisprudential work to address these questions was Goodrich, Oedipus Lex: *Psychoanalysis, History, Law* (Berkeley: University of California Press, 1995), and the first collection on this topic was Costas Douzinas and Lynda Nead (eds), *Law and the Image: The Authority of Art and the Aesthetics of Law* (Chicago: Chicago University Press, 1999) and then Richard Sherwin, *When Law Goes Pop: The Vanishing Line between Law and Popular Culture* (Chicago: Chicago University Press, 2002). For a recent and commendably comparative argument in support of addressing the visual in the textual, see Greta Olson, *From Law and Literature to Legality and Affect* (Oxford: Oxford University Press, 2022).

image, an imaginal sensibility, which historically has preceded and overlain the real in the form of the text as the sign of law which now is in the process, by dint of technological transformations and media accessibility, of metamorphosing into pictorial relays and a scopic economy that increasingly structures legality.

The image is more than it seems. It is a multiplicity, a plateau in Deleuze's argot, and it is linked rhizomatically, in subterranean form to other multiplicities, other images, and to the distinctive—frequently anachronic—temporality and distinct relay of visibilities.[35] The other space of the image is frequently threatening, disruptive of law's settlement and its precedential certainties precisely because the heterotopic quality of the pictorial within the legal text is that of an alien form, an unclassified and so at least initially disturbing intrusion upon both convention and classification, the formulae of the juridical structure and order. The image is a ghost, a spectre, and in Hobbes' diction a 'Mask or Visard' of things exterior to both text and law. There is initially a sense of displacement, an anxiety or otherness both by dint of the appearance of images in the record, the scripture—*ratio scripta* in the antique argot—of law, and by virtue of the accession of law, despite its resistant textual form, to the profusion of images circulating in social media, in mobile forms, in email, sms, Instagram, and tweets that surround and impinge upon the clerks, interns, litigants, jurors, judges, and lawyers. The text, which was solid, unfolds into the spectral. The rule book, code or precedent, which was inscribed on skin—wethers—then embossed on vellum, latterly printed in leather bound and then card bound volumes is anxiously dislodged, fragmented, and rendered virtual, no longer controlled and now capable of taking multiple forms whose ontological status is mobile and indeterminate. Law, to borrow from Bottici, is becoming imaginal, increasingly taking place in images, in pictorial representations, and these are more or less real, subjective and objective, with and without ontological status, true and false.[36] In classical terms, the picture is *veritas falsa* as the Renaissance lawyers put it, because it shows something and because it is not what it shows.[37]

Retinal justice references the process of deciding that takes account of the incalculable moment of the image and renders it real by making it appear. The eye is evidently here the medium and scopic drive of deciding. A multi-million-dollar contract can be formed by text messages: 'NO LIMIT', in all caps, followed by 'awesome', constituting *consensus ad idem*.[38] Or take an English child custody case in which the judge inserted an emoji several times in the judgement. The latter

[35] Gilles Deleuze and Félix Guattari, *A Thousand Plateaus* (1988) at 22.

[36] Chiara Bottici, *Imaginal Politics: Images Beyond Imagination and the Imaginary* (New York: Columbia University Press, 2014), and in a similar vein, also engaging the imaginal, see Emanuele Coccia, *Sensible Life: A Micro-ontology of the Image* (New York: Fordham University Press, 2016).

[37] The term emerges from an anonymous Latin text printed in Andreas Alciatus, *Notitia utraque … Disputatio Adriani aug. et Epicteti philosophi* [Basle: n.p., 1552]: Quid est pictura? Veritas falsa. For expansive Occitan commentary contemporary with Alciatus, see Jean de Coras, *Altercacion en forme de dialogue, entre l'Empereur Adrian et philosophe Epictéte* (Toulose: Porterie, 1558).

[38] *CX Digital Media Inc. v Smoking Everywhere* 2011 WL 1102782.

case begins ironically with an order prohibiting the publishing or broadcasting of 'any picture' of the participants, and then proceeds to publish an emoji, a smiley face, which the police claimed was winking on screen and so indicated the opposite of what the accompanying text stated, whereas the judge reproduced the emoji four times and concludes 'I don't agree that the ☺ is winking. It is just a ☺'.[39] The Honorable Mr Justice Peter Jackson reproduces unwinking smiley faces but misses the point that on screen emojis act quite differently to emojis in word documents and that without knowing the algorithmic source of the emoji or the platform and program of its delivery onscreen it is impossible to state with certainty what form, appearance, dance, or sign it will make. The same problem arises in an Israeli case where applicants for the lease of an apartment, after visiting the flat, texted the following message to the landlord: '"Good morning 😊 Interested in the house 💃👯✌️🌠🐿️🍾"' (Figure 1.5).[40]

The judge determined that the message, 'a dancing woman, a dancing couple, a "V-sign with fingers", a shooting star, a squirrel and a bottle of champagne' indicated 'great optimism', and together with repeated use of the 'smiling face' emoji, might fall short of a contract but did give rise to a promissory estoppel, and so the senders were liable for losses incurred by the landlord as a result of removing the apartment from the property listings. In an ironically Christian interpretation of the emojis, viewing them from left to right, from dancer to popping cork, the judge may have inadvertently treated the images as distinct and different in form but nonetheless proffers a thoroughly conservative, swift, and shallow interpretation. The obvious sexual connotations of the SMS that the couple sent are ignored,

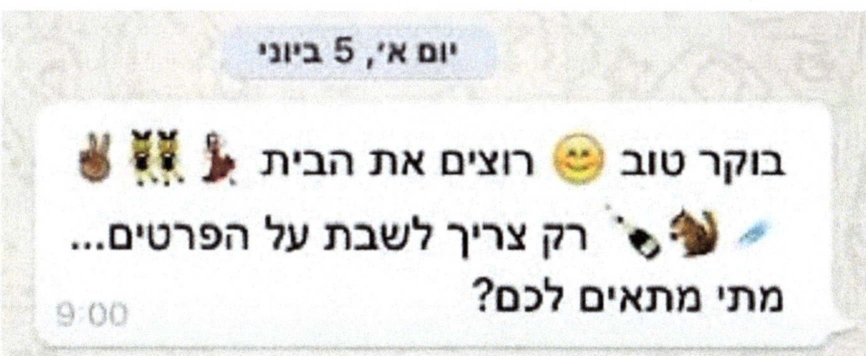

Figure 1.5 Insertion by Judge Amir Weizebbluth in *Dahan v. Shacharoff*, 30823-08-16 (Herzliya Small Claims Ct. Feb. 24, 2017).

[39] *Lancashire County Council v Mr A and Mr B The Children* (By their Children's Guardian) (2016).

[40] *Dahan v. Shacharoff*, 30823-08-16 (Herzliya Small Claims Ct. Feb. 24, 2017). For discussion of the case, see Moshe Berliner, 'When a Picture is not Worth a Thousand Words', 41 *Cardozo Law Rev.* (2020) 2161.

the images themselves are neither scrutinized nor interpreted beyond a generic designation and conclusion. The chipmunk displayed is called a squirrel, what is clearly a lesser mark is labelled champagne, and the propulsive ball or ejaculating projectile is detumescently termed a shooting star without any further deliberation or analysis. The flash of blue that opens the second line is not even noticed, let alone remarked. Colour gains no mention. What is introduced is tucked away.

The legal anxiety towards images is apparent in these cases primarily in the lack of analysis and the desire to distance the pictorial and return to the scriptural. Mr Justice Peter Jackson simply shows the emoji and in effect says 'look', it doesn't move, it is not winking. That, however, as adverted already, is a feature of the program being used, the context of the emoji, the platform and the mobile optimization or other medium of transfer of the text and image. There are also frequently glitches due to updates and changes in program that the attentive user or viewer might want to take into judicial conusance. If the court's programming was not updated, for example, the emoji would appear as a black box. In a similar vein, it is certainly difficult to imagine that a text would receive such brief and bald interpretation as is given by the Herzliya judge to the string of emojis used by the apartment seekers. The smiling face, just for a start, has many different significances in different contexts and different cultures. Like any other sign it can also, according to site of insertion, be ironic, allegorical, moral, or spiritual. As for the string of emojis, the lack of a code or key leaves a bewildering array of possibilities, even if one ignores the fact that there is no squirrel in the string, but rather a lowly chipmunk. The champagne looks suspiciously like prosecco, the dancing couple are decked out as bunnies, the asteroid could as easily be a cricket ball, a football, a baseball, and the V might well be interpreted as an expletive, an Anglican version of *digitum impudicum*, flipping the bird, or giving the finger. And that is only a start because no attempt is yet made to account for the imaginal character of the emojis and the fact that they are viewed differently as images and so not subject to the linear law, the left to right symbolæography of the Christian written page.[41] More than that, seeking the hole in the heart of the law, it does not take Freud to recognize the juxtaposition of feminine and phallic, the V and the shooting star, male and female, emissive and receptor, leading visually to the chipmunk's erect tail and the cork ejaculated from the aroused bottle. The dancing lady, in Christian visual symmetry, is marching towards a climactic copulation. This is likely more significant of the searching couple's relationship to each other, or their future plans, than it is of their rental intentions. The point is that there are multiple possible viewings of the depictions, that the image is always more than it seems and the indeterminacy or *ambulatio* of the eye in the imaginal exercise of looking.

[41] As stated in Bartolus de Saxoferrato, *Tractatus de Insigniis et armis*, edited and translated as O. Cavallar et al., *A Grammar of Signs* (Berkeley: University of California Press, 1994) at 154. Inserted in a Hebrew text, as visible in Figure 1.5, the imagery presumably is to be viewed from right to left.

The string of emojis could be an obscenity, a sexual proposition, an invitation, a rejection, a joke or, in the peculiar language of the law, because nothing should be excluded a priori, a bottle bung, an estoppel, a foreclosure of alternate meanings, legal preclusion from changing the manifest expression of intention upon which the landlord has relied.[42]

Retinal justice thus signals a willingness to account, address, attend, and apprehend the novelty and the heterotopic distinctiveness of the legal imaginal, the profusion of images within judicial texts, the virtual pages, the retrolutionary scroll pages, the digital figurations and animations of the decisions and rules of a supposedly and perhaps increasingly common law. The key signifier of the new methodology is the willingness to look, to acknowledge and analyse the manifestations of the legal gaze in all of their haptic, symptomatic, and hepatoscopic force. To look is to leave the linearity of the text and accept the lateral and fluid ambulation of the eye as it scans and processes the image utilizing that vast storehouse of an essentially visual Mnemosyne, the optical atlas that is both the body and its knowledge. The heterotopia of the imaginal takes us elsewhere and specifically into a regime of images, the order of the visual, the iconocratic or visiocratic hierarchy of the optical with its own laws and anxieties, constraints and potentials. No beginning without looking and acknowledging the eye, the scopic, the relay of sight, sound, smell, movement, and colour. Thus the irony, to take an image of retinal justice as presently practiced, of a case that involves the validity of patents owned by Pfizer, the pertinent one being '411 Patent Method of Treating Eye Infections with Azithromycin'.[43] The anatomy of the eye is indicated with a picture of the manifold mechanisms that the oculus uses to keep fluids and solids out. The defensive structure runs from the penthouse lids, to the tear film, to the cornea and conjunctiva, all of which must allow light in but exclude other objects or fluids from reaching the retina which channels illumination to the optic nerve. The retina, like retinal justice, is heavily defended and in relation to the latter those defences remain largely intact and not least, if the most obvious point is made, by the fact that the image of the eye used to diagram the various elements and functions is itself poorly reproduced and somewhat blurred even in the digital text of the report, the record itself.[44]

What the picture of the eyeball most immediately conveys, precisely in its lack of focus, is the judicial perception of the secondary quality and incidental character of the visual transmission of law. The image is deemed merely rhetorical leaving

[42] The source of the rule, in case common lawyers think that inelegant law French neologisms—*cacozelia*—are original contributions to jurisprudence, is Justinian, *Digest* 50.17.75 (Papinian): *Nemo potest mutare consilium suum in alterius iniuriam*—no one can change their counsel to the harm of another.

[43] Diagram of the eye, from *Insite Vision Inc. v Sandoz Inc.* (2013). An artist's mock-up of the image is also provided courtesy of Charis Entwistle, eFigure 1. https://larc.cardozo.yu.edu/faculty-online-pubs/61/.

[44] *Insite Vision Inc. v Sandoz Inc.* 2013 U.S. Dist. LEXIS 1602.

its impact as pre-reflective. It is an affective as well as cognitive sign, sighted at the body and the impact of showing. That the image is not an argumentative priority but rather a medium of influence is a common feature of many of the judicial depictions, the screenshots, the low resolution web capture and dash cam images, the splash-pages and other digital screen captures or downloads of web sourced portraits, portrayals, and pictures whose origin and composition is seldom acknowledged and whose manner and context of fabrication and insertion is thus generally missing from the normative analysis. There is an element of the overlooked, and in reconstructing the genesis, morphology, and transmission effectuated by legal images this constitutes an important starting point. The written document not only has priority, but also governs the image. Thus, the tendency has been for the picture to be reduced to the text not simply in the sense of being incorporated into the reasons for the decision, the linear script of record, but more dramatically as being subject to print methodology and the hermeneutics of 'being read' as if the image were a text, as if literacy, visual but also of course lectoral and verbal, was what was needed for viewing images. Visual literacy is already a distortion, a desensitization of the gaze, a cabining and cribbing of viewing. It is also an understandable and historically explicable prioritization of writing over image and in juristic terms closure as preferable to the indeterminacy and affect of opening and unfolding. Even when a judge, Posner again, advocates explicitly for the use of images in judgements, the figures inserted into the decision are neither explained nor evaluated by the transmitting author.[45] In the case in question, he is determined to impress upon the attorneys the importance of precedent and so to make litigants pay attention to applicable court decisions and their governing rules, but the images that he inserts to make this point are nowhere referenced to a source, nor are they analysed as figures, let alone as precedential pictures, as ocular norms.

Gonzalez-Servin v. Ford Motor Company involved two consolidated appeals from District Court decisions dismissing class action lawsuits brought by foreign nationals, on the grounds of *forum non conveniens* (wrong forum). The Seventh Circuit Court of Appeals, in a decision authored by Judge Posner, dismisses the complaint fairly summarily. The decision relies upon precedents of the same court, and specifically *Abad v. Bayer Corp.*, decided two years earlier, incidentally by Posner again, that had dismissed appeals in circumstances which the judge defines as 'nearly identical' to those of the present case. In justifying the refusal of the appeals, the judge goes out of his way to censure the appellants' attorneys for failing to address the appropriate, binding authority.[46] 'Where there is apparently dispositive precedent, an appellant may urge its overruling or distinguishing or

[45] The article in which Posner advocates for images in judgements is Richard Posner, 'Judicial Opinions and Appellate Advocacy in Federal Courts—One Judge's Views', 51 *Duquesne L. Rev.* 3 (2013) at 12–13.

[46] *Gonzalez-Servin v. Ford Motor Company* 662 F.3d 931, at 933 (2011).

reserve a challenge to it for certiorari but may not simply ignore it'.[47] Such a lesson is unremarkable in itself, but the judge then proceeds to reproach the appellants' advocacy as 'unacceptable' and depicts it as 'an ostrich-like tactic'. He then inserts two pictures into the judgement.[48] The first, in monochrome in the printed report, in colour in the online version, is of an ostrich with its head in the sand. The second is of a seemingly male figure, a lawyer presumably, in a brown suit, kneeling, with his head in the sand.

As the decision purports to offer a lesson on the importance of precedent and specifically asserts the dispositive quality of prior judgements in similar circumstances, it is unquestionably necessary to address the precedential status and import of the images that form the most striking aspect of the decision handed down. It is necessary to ask whether the pictures are part of the reasoning of the decision, whether they bind future courts, and what precisely is their priority and normative status in relation to apparently similar cases to come, concerned with *forum non conveniens*, with tort actions, with professional conduct, and with legal method. In reading, or better, viewing the decision, it would be a grave error and indeed would exacerbate the poor advocacy denounced by the judge simply to ignore this visual depiction of willful ignorance. Such, however, has generally been the fate of images in judgements for the principal reason that lawyers have neither training nor skill in visual advocacy nor in the history of the art of law. The medium betrays the message and Posner is in effect hoisted with his own petard: he is determined to indicate that precedent should be taken seriously, but then he fails to do so himself. More than that, to extrapolate from Posner's visual agnosia, there is a reason for his limited apprehension of the images, which is not just age, but rather that legal method has no concept of how to incorporate depictions into the prosaic logic of precedent. In what follows I will suggest that the history of the use of images in legal texts can be used to construct a new version and vision of the humanistic *mens emblematica*, a legally devised methodology that apprehends pictures not *ad similia*, as text, by way of analogy, which is generally the lawyer's rule, but *ad apparentiam*, by dint of how they appear and the rhizomatic multiplicity of other images that a depiction will invoke and relay. The anachronic quality of iconic images, the emblematic significations of visual representations, and the history of the *ius imaginum*, which one can imaginatively define as the law of the mask, of faces, figures, and frames of governance, can provide the tools for curating an atlas of pictorial law, of precedent pictures which generate the vision of precedence.

[47] *Gonzalez-Servin*, at 934.

[48] Ostrich and Attorney, from *Gonzalez-Servin v. Ford Motor Company* (2011) https://larc.cardozo.yu.edu/faculty-online-pubs/61/, eFigures 2 and 3. For a recent similar example, in this case a picture, a meme, of two costumed spidermen figures pointing at each other, aimed at quieting the administrative agents' litigation strategy of blaming each other as their defence to a claim that they had delayed access to court filings, see *Courthouse News Service v Brenda Forman* 606 F.Supp.3d 1200 (2022), eFigure 4.

The examples of apparently random, visually dissonant, affectively disorientating insertions of images will be multiplied and analysed in the ensuing chapters. What follows is in large part a classification of types of judicial images and their potential curation as the visual repository, storehouse, atlas, and album of optical equity conceived in terms of retinal justice. What is needed is a mapping of visual insertions and a coda or key to their interpretative uses, a heuristic unpacking of their sources, elements, and affective connotations. It is indeed with maps, graphic linear depictions, that the judicial use and apprehension of the sensible in the textual historically begins. The diagrammatic will thus be the first category of the legal imaginary. The linear graphic representation of occupation of territory is the most frequent early usage of visual materials. The reason for this is that they share a linear quality with the textual and discursive and so appear on first viewing to represent rationally the object mapped or diagrammed. The atlas, as also other schema, diagrams, and charts are pictures but are not thought of as such because of their seemingly merely linear and abstract character. The map lays claim historically to an epistemic purity that is perceived juridically to align it with text as denotative rather than figurative. It is also, however, as will be tracked in Chapter 2, aesthetic and sensible, affective and ontographic, in that it creates its object and further, it will be argued, is performative, an encounter and perspective upon inconstant surfaces that set beings and events in motion. Bluntly, it is in origin a nationalistic aesthetic, and imperial performance of subjecting the territories or properties mapped to the law of the cartograph, the charter of ownership. The opening category of image analysis is simply that of the appearance of the real in the judgement, as part of the record, in a diagrammatical form that aligns with the text and will usually carry a visual coda and a verbal key. It is the reality effect that jurists initially crave in the image as demonstrative proof, the *certum* of the visible particularity.[49] The map, however, is also an imaginal, which is to say, a visually depicted mode of disseminating law and so marks a beginning of retinal justice, of the manifestation of the vision in decision.

The reality effect is potentially highly persuasive but is of variable doctrinal and decisional relevance. At present, in the corpus of cases in which judges insert images, the data that forms the basis of the current study, the image most often falls into the category of surplusage, meaning depictions that are somehow out of place in the decision, spectres that in Derrida's terminology haunt the record and signal sights that are out of joint with the text.[50] Surplusage, however, as will

[49] *Certum* is classically contrasted to *verum* which, as Vico points out, is often a mere synonym for *aequum* or theological truth. The *certum* of visibility is that of particularization, leading Vico to the position that 'In good Latin certum means particularized, or, as the schools say, individuated; so that, in overelegant Latin, certum and commune, the certain and the common, are opposed to each other'. *The New Science* (Ithaca: Cornell University Press, 1984) at 93 (cxi).

[50] Jacques Derrida, *Specters of Marx: The State of the Debt, the Work of Mourning, and the New International* (New York and London: Routledge, 1994) at 10. For recent commentary, see Başak Ertür, *Spectacles and Specters: A Performative Theory of Political Trials* (Palo Alto: Stanford University Press)

be elaborated in Chapter 3, also has a legal meaning in that the presumption of juridical interpretation is against the unnecessary or superabundant. The image produces an effect of affect rather than any more deliberative or directly evidential insertion into the reasoning of judgement. The imaginal depiction will variably give weight, sense, feel, and direction to the decision but this will most often go unsaid, as self-evident demonstration, like an identity-kit picture, like a document, as in documentary or super-doc which in law means a winning piece of advocacy in images. Excess words, and pictures in excess of words, are alike, however, in critical terms to be presumed to be significant. These are images that nonetheless, or more accurately because of their silent apparition, become open, unfold, lead to other images, further rhizomes of the regimen of the scopic and the optical order of visiocracy, the governance of sight. Visual figures inserted into precedents are self-evidently incomplete, and so exponentially expansive in potential and implication, and yet they are installed without analysis or even adumbration of impact and influence, and in that sense are discordant with the linear rationality of decision. Chapter 3 thus reviews images as surplusage, out of joint depictions that are at the same time also indexical and indicative of the motive of decision, of the vision that subtends determination.

The paradox of surplusage, the relevance of the superabundant, leads, in Chapter 4, to the analysis of the most explicit disjunction between text and image, the category of erotic and comedic judicial uses, of which the images of ostrich and lawyer in *Gonzalez-Servin* are one early example of the *comédie humaine* as comedy of law *au jus*. This is to say that images introduce the theatrical into the legal text, the pictures mirroring the drama of trial, while also invoking the sense of *serio-ludere* or comic gravitas that is in essence the judiciary giving expression to parodic, satirical or ironic affects, and at times also striving to add force to reason, as well as aspiring to make their judgements accessible and persuasive to the populace. The humorous images are strikingly emotive insertions while also being the most incongruous and so most revealing of visual depictions. The corporeal and comedic pictures bear a histrionic and frequently explicitly erotic undertone, constituting in manifest though lateral form judicial affects that are glimpsed fleetingly in the exposure of something seen and underpinning judgement, a flash or symptom of invention, the glimpse of unconscious choice. Again, it is not that the images should be discounted as otiose or insignificant, but rather the juristic surplusage of the humorous bears its own meanings and precedential importance. The comico-erotic ranges from the jocular to the satirical, from the parodic to the punitive, and can present images directly or via hyperlink but nonetheless incorporated into judgement as affective performances and hermeneutic excursions,

developing Derrida's 'spectrality effect' in relation to the haunting of trials by images of violence that undo the order of temporality allowing both past and future to render the present indeterminate and the time of violence undifferentiated, as then, now, and in the future.

interfaces via and into the figurations of the visual. These are best interpreted as visceral and invested appearances, the most explicitly emotive depictions of the text and the most directly symptomatic of the motive of judgement. The optical projection, desire for, and laughter at the real in the mode of insertion of a picture is indicative of condensation of affect, the compressed expression of the intersection of several associative chains that require disentanglement and analysis.[51] The *in vivo* character of the theatre of trial or scene of encounters, of persons and propriety that the image relays in displaced form, carries a libidinal force and intensity of energy that proffers an elliptical view of the ground of judgement, of the drive of determination. Here, I will argue, the viewer confronts the eye of the judgement, and despite the resistance of the judiciary to aesthetic and material analyses, the visibilities of transmission are expressions of retinal justice directly manifesting the scopic propulsion of the outcome of the *duello* or agonism of trial.

The libidinal force of the image, in the most part unwittingly introjected into judgement, heralds the persuasive evidential use of pictures that is tracked in Chapter 5. Here the insertion is both for its affective force and its demonstrative sense of the *certum*, as evidence and proof in legitimation of the reasoning of the determination. The picture shows the *ratio* of judgement, the *imago decidendi* as I coin it, rather as the identikit or mugshot will frame a subject. The force of the inserted visuals tends to be promoted by the assertion of their obviousness: the evidential image is indisputable because, to the judge, it manifests and makes real the object of decision and the reason for an outcome. It appears here to have both an empirical and a normative valence in judgement, even if that probative value and precedential status are inexplicit. The assumption is that it is certain because it is visible, it can be photographed, filmed, screen captured, and brought into court and into judgement. Yet the visual is no more unitary than the discursive, indeed probably less so because the multiplicity of optical options and associations are not as familiar to the judiciary, to those trained as lawyers in the linearity of the printed page and taught to judge blindfold or at least with downcast eyes, in the pretence of being impartial lectors, neutral arbiters, unseeing eyes.

Starting from the verbal, trained in linear textuality, scriptural reason, judges are slow to credit the eye with hermeneutic or decisional status. Picking up on pictorial plurality or ocular polysemy, the final category of analysis, excoriated in Chapter 6, is that of extispicious or divinatory uses of images. The concept has its roots in the hepatoscopic methods of medical and shamanistic diagnostics, the reading of entrails and the significance of organs and body parts that becomes in psychoanalytic practice the method of oneiric interpretation, the reviewing of the

[51] It is Vico, *The New Science*, at 390, who most directly addresses the jurisprudence of images, in the context of the poetics and *carmina* or songs of law. The *iura imaginaria* or 'rights invented by imagination' are the extension of the old legal narratives—*antiqui iuris fabulas*—and he further proffers the instructive view that 'Men of limited ideas take for law what the words expressly say'. The idea of Vico's jurisprudence was to predicate the religion of words (*religio verborum*) upon prior imagination.

corporeal symptoms expressed in dream. Extispicious images house the judicial utilization of depictions that signal features of decision and of its motivation that are pictorially available, and striking, without being as easily conveyed or as convincing if merely verbally described. The reference is to the transmission of sights that relay prognostications, viewings of an outside that are deemed probative and give rise to the reason for judgement, and so become part of a binding record, the visual *imago decidendi* that results from the retinal character of decision making. Here the image provides direct insight into judicial affect and advocacy in that the judgement is persuading, reasoning in imagery so as to relay a depth and force—a shark aesthetic—that *ratio scripta*, the written reason of determination, cannot transmit. The extispicious images that judges use exemplify the degree to which focus upon retinal justice can bring to the fore an imaginal iconomy of law that has previously slept between the lines of the text or emerged only partially in inchoate cartographic and schematic forms. Retinal justice, the subject of exposition and viewing in Chapter 7, has extensive forebears in legal humanism, in jurisliterary texts, as also in the *mens emblematica* and the *ars iuris* understood as the aesthetics of law, as visual *elegantia*, is a discipline that is now urgently in need of revival, rejuvenation, and renovation in light of law's remediation.[52] It is necessary to the apprehension and appreciation of the burgeoning visibility of legal judgement, of the normative and governmental, in the visions of decisions. These are exuberant—extra—depictions that diversely indicate legitimatory grounds for the decision while manifesting in sensible visual form the event that triggered the legal reasoning of the case. The imaginal manifestation of judicial visions suggests an additional and oneiric sense, the other scene and semiotic that the image relays, the spectral figure, the *impersona* of the mask, the communal sensibility that pictures signal, as also the further causes and secluded spaces of judgement that retinal justice unveils to analysis.

In Chapter 8 a schema for *ius imaginum*, a law of images redivivus, is sketched. Alongside the obvious but necessary collation and classification of images used in judgements is the elaboration of the distinctiveness or relative autonomy of the pictorial. Using the methodological resources of art history and aesthetics is a necessary precursor to any gallery of law's optical reasonings or album of precedent. The visual epistemology of the juridical has to provide a genealogical accounting of pictures used. This requires not only close scrutiny of the images themselves, of their composition, their editing and selection, perspective and scale, their colour and encoding, but also of sound and motion where it is moving pictures, film, or streamed video that is utilized or more often hyper-linked. Colour, it will be argued, is a major blindspot in both visual and material senses. Judges seem to

[52] On the jurisliterary and *elegantia iuris*, see Anne Teissier-Ensminger, *Fabuleuse juridicité: sur la littérarisation des genres juridiques* (Paris: Classiques Garnier, 2015). For an anglophone account, see Goodrich, *Advanced Introduction to Law and Literature* (Cheltenham: Elgar, 2021).

scotomize the colour of the imagery used and introduce red arrows, coloured codes and keys, yellows, greens, and blues on maps, on video stills, as if these had no influence or persuasive force in their visual impact upon the viewer, the jury of their peers, as a further *arcanum* or mystery of legal forms. Law, in the main, sees and reasons monochromatically, in black and white. This default visual dualism, the counterposition of the extremes of the spectrum, tends to make legal reasoning binary and antinomic, depriving it of nuance, and specifically failing to see the diversity of colours, the individuation of all appearances. Even in copyright decisions, where similarity and difference are the subject of determination, colour generally counts for little or rather tends to be discounted as somehow lacking in originality and merely an incident or accident of the putative reality that is depicted. What Warburg coined as the dynamogram, the aesthetic form and impelling force of the image is precisely aligned with its colour, the stains of appearance, the tinctures of survivance. Throwing caution to the wind, colour could be called the materiality of the image, and is a distinctive feature of the figuration of the depicted and a crucial aspect of its aesthetic and affective relay. The implexity of the visual depiction has to include the symptom of colour and the rhizomatic nexus that it connotes and incorporates in the lateral transfer of imagination.

2
Maps, Diagrams, Schemata

The enthusiastic and public spirited satirist Myles Na Gopaleen picks judiciously on maps and diagrams as curious features of legal judgement. In one fictional case of trespass, the plaintiff sought a plenary injunction 'and a declaration of fief in agro'. Although the case was free of any cartography, His Honour Judge Twinfeet reprimanded the lawyers for the lack of a 'Guard in court to prove certain maps and measurements. That was a serious matter; it showed disrespect to the court'.[1] In future, so His Honour opined, a Guard must always be present because 'one never knew when a map would be produced'. Whereas in later precedent the Cruiskeen Court of Voluntary Jurisdiction lampoons estreats and estoppels, fees, fiefs and entails as terrorizing law French nomenclature, and parodies latin maxims and 'philologico-juridical obscurantism' besmirching Dame Justice, maps which mark a lawscape are bemoaned as markedly missing.[2] *In ludo veritas,* with or without beer, the map has the juristic virtue of being visible and easily admissible. It proffers the comforting appearance of simple reference while at the same time it unsettles the text and, in the figurative depiction of Justice Twinfeet, requires for that reason a Guard so as to keep it pristine and untouched.

The root of jurisdiction, and of all other real property rights, lies historically in mapping, and in being present on the map, taking livery and seisin in the old rite of possession, so as to mark visually a place attested scripturally. The map becomes the territory, the parchment displacing its tellurian referent, the alluvial or aquatic site that is supposedly being defined and appropriated by the diagrammatology or schematics of the cartograph, the charter of ownership. It is precisely the textual warrants, the *carta*, the lines of amity, that define a space of belonging and over time become the 'only real that ends up mattering … [reflecting] the accelerating reality at common law that what matters—what is material at law—is not, say, the land you live on, but the land that gets onto parchment or paper to be imagined, conveyed, inherited, forfeited *there* … '[3] It is in that early modern shift from terror

[1] Myles Na Gopaleen (Flann O'Brien), *The Best of Myles* (New York: Walker, 1968) at 137–138.
[2] Na Gopaleen, *Best of Myles*, at 143.
[3] Bradin Cormack, 'Paper Justice, Parchment Justice: Shakespeare, *Hamlet*, and the Life of Legal Documents', in Donald Bleecher et al. (eds), *Taking Exception to the Law: Materializing Injustice in Early Modern English Literature* (Toronto: Toronto University Press, 2015) 44, at 50. On the etymological and legal historical links between terror, territory, and text, see Pierre Legendre, *L'Empire de la verité: Introduction aux espaces dogmatique industriel* (Paris: Fayard, 2001) at 224: 'remember the jurist's play of words: *territorium* comes from *terreo*, which means to produce terror; it is the liminal space of the frontier where power can legitimately exercise the *ius terrendi* or the right to terrorize, which one can translate as the right to erase from the map'. See *Digest* 50.16.239.8. (submovendi)

Judicial Uses of Images. Peter Goodrich, Oxford University Press.
 DOI: 10.1093/oso/9780192848772.003.0002

to territory to text that the roots of the juridical legitimacy of the maps, atlases, and other topographical depictions that appear in case law originally resides. Their appeal lies in the familiarity and allure of the scriptural, the analogy to linear representation, the homonymy of book and atlas, printed page, and the contours and keys of the cartograph.

The nation, city, town, village, estate, home, dock or mooring exist as diagrammatic representations of a pictorial competence and assert an objective and homogenous collective parchment and latterly digital though printable identity that will also gain expression in flags, statues, emblems, monumental inscriptions, and other figures commonly found in juristic and administrative texts.[4] The drawing of the territory brings with it the legitimation of government, of Leviathan, sovereign, Church, and populace as the elements of the authorized hierarchy, a community over which reigns one who, as Hobbes' frontispiece has it, is without superior on earth—*non est potestas Super Terram quæ comparetur*. The shift from the images of memory to written record, the lines on the page, was a transition to the inscription of ownership of property, the warrant of possession that was best symbolized, because most directly, graphically and visually expressed in the form of a drawing of what was owned.[5] The linear image was deemed closest to the referent, the drawing reproduced in a coded yet recognizable form the property claimed and as such represented, even if in displaced aspect, the *certum* of being visible. Lawyers were the earliest to make comprehensive use of maps, *charta* and *carta* being homonyms in medieval Latin for authentic representations and legitimate records. The charter, as we would term it, was also a leaf, an object, a parchment, which connotation fits well with the Latin for map, *mappa mundi*, as *mappa* according to Isidore of Seville's *Etymologies* means napkin and latterly piece of cloth.[6] The graphic schema inscribes in a material form and produces effects that exceed mere linearity. The reference of *mappa*, like the English colloquial use of map to refer to the face, is to the physical quality, the material and potentially mobile form of the support of the drawing or diagrammatic table. The map, like the flag or the earlier imperial *stellae*, is a physical and aesthetic object, the support of proprietary title, as well as the exemplification of that which it carries, namely the semiotic figure of a fictive commonality, a view of space that early lawyers termed chorography, the description of people and places, because possession was simply the relation between the two.[7]

[4] John Selden, *Titles of Honor* (London: Stansby, 1631 edn) is a good common law example, although its primary source is Guido Pancirolus, *Notitia utraque dignitatum, cum Orientis, tum Occidentis ultra arcadia honorique tempora* (Lyon: Gabiano, 1608).

[5] The key work on the shift from objects and acts to inscriptions is Michael Clanchy, *From Memory to Written Record: England 1066-1307* (Chichester: Wiley-Blackwell, 2013).

[6] S. Barney et al. (eds), *The* Etymologies *of Isidore of Seville* (Cambridge: Cambridge University Press, 2008) at 388.

[7] 'Chorographical description' is the subtitle, and principal import of William Camden, *Britannia: sive Florentissimorum regnorum Angliæ, Scotiæ, Hiberniæ et insularum adiacentium ex intima antiquitate chorographica descriptio* (London: Bishop & Norton, 1600), arguing in his preface to the readers

The juridical significance of the map resides in the coded yet purportedly direct relation between picture and referent. It is a linear image, a measured representation to scale, a drawing that schematizes and portrays in what is taken to be a rational, mathematical, semiotic fashion. The attraction of the map as a diagram of place is thus paradoxically that it is not seen as an image but rather as an encoding, a *tabula* or table that shows in easily decoded and so logical form the territory that it represents. Maps, of course, as is well travelled, distort, and invent. The survey and inscription involve choices and misrepresentations, often of egregious kinds, and glaring omissions. The cartograph is a unifying image of community, they are 'representations that reproduce a reality "out there" and of necessity express the idea of what people think that reality is, what they have chosen as worthy of representation ... Any map is an image, but an image that reflects a choice'.[8] The medieval map, as Bottici continues to elaborate, was made from the qualitative perspective of the human, showing what the traveller needed to know, with multiple and overlapping jurisdictions, whereas the modern map is political and quantitative, measuring space as a uniform and quantifiable reality. The chorographic is replaced by the demographic and statistical that are necessary keys to the actuarial and biopolitical governance of numbers.

That said, the relevance of maps to the advent of the visual in the legal, and specifically in judicial reasoning, lies in their being linear depictions of their object, schematic diagrams, and generally ornamented and editorialized renderings of place, as territories, administrative districts, or of a concept, as in the early legal depiction of justice in the *carte de tendre*, the fortresss Britannia, or earlier in the figure of a tower—*turris iustitie typus* (Figure 2.1). The lawyer Guillaume Rouille maps injustice in the depiction of a twelve legged dragon, which I reproduce here as an expansive version of the conceptual frame of mapping, more obviously a projection and interpretation in the early illustrated representations, the imaginative depiction of concepts as animate and animal, works to establish attributes that matter, lines that etch a point, and figures that will legitimate or delegitimate the territory, office, or here delineate the concept of injustice—*monstrum iniustitie*—that is being charted and whose patterns are being inscribed. The cloven hooves, claws, tail, horns, and gaping cavernous embouchement all signal the graphic choice of sites, atmospheres, and judgements placed on a visual figure of an abstract idea of indisciplines.[9] It is a map of morals, an imaginal depiction of a fictional unity in the form of a horned dragon, with twelve sins defined on its twelve legs. The basic idea is that of representing a perspective, of offering vivid

that the chorographical tables (*tabulas Chorographicas*) throw both aesthetics and light on the literary descriptions—*pictura oculis esse iucundiores*, the picturing of the eyes being pleasing or, perhaps better, comic.

[8] Chiara Bottici, *Imaginal Politics: Images Beyond Imagination and the Imaginary* (New York: Columbia University Press, 2014) at 93. Also noting at 91 that 'a community is not *a* community until it is gathered together and unified in a pictorial (re)presentation'.

[9] Guillaume Rouille, *Alenconiensis causidici in legibus licêtiati. Justicie et iniusticie descriptionû compeniû* (Paris: Chevallus, 1570).

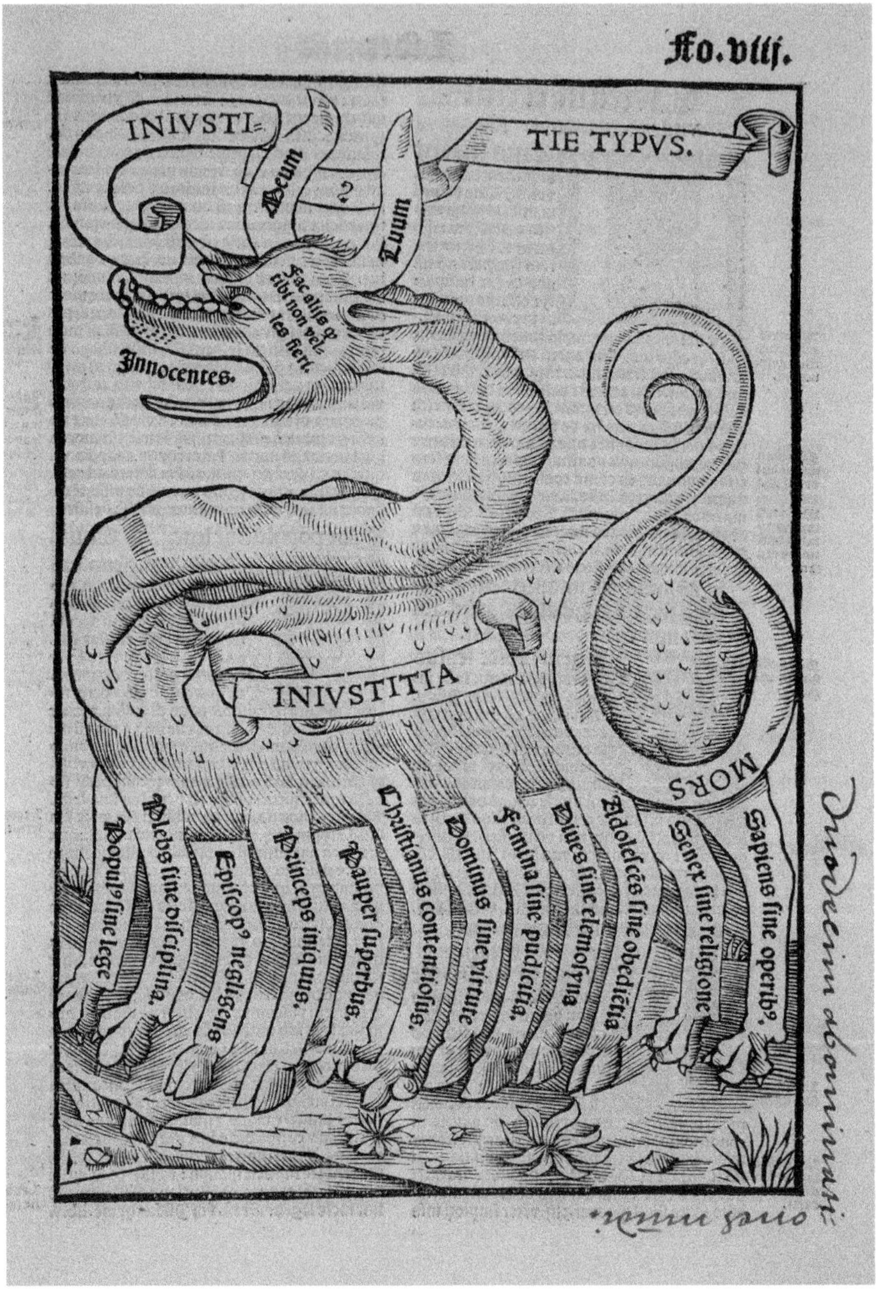

Figure 2.1 From Guillaume Rouille, *Alenconiensis causidici in legibus licêtiati* (1570). Rare Book Collection, Lillian Goldman Law Library, Yale Law School.

reasons—*vividæ rationes*—for obeying law, living with discipline all the way through to the desiderium of putting knowledge to work.

Although the subtitle of his chapter on the topic is 'Reading What Was Never Written', where it should be viewing, the art historian Didi-Huberman makes the key point that the map, or in his case the more poetic atlas, is a visual form of knowledge, a way of seeing that combines two models of knowing: 'an aesthetic paradigm of the visual form, [and] an epistemic paradigm of knowledge', a bifurcation that he claims subverts the canonical modality of both.[10] While the modern map seeks to appear objective and homogenous, it still has colours, codes, text, a grid. Globes even more so. There is a rich luxuriance and persuasive undertow to even the most pedestrian of pictorial representations, as they demarcate, unify, place, and project the imaginal communities that they represent onto a reality that they claim to possess. The map combines the intelligible and the sensible, and in doing so it disrupts the epistemic purity of Platonic knowledge free of all but the idea. The tableau is also a work of art, a fabrication of image-makers occupying a sensible space in which phenomena appear in a visible form. The map thus 'introduces the multiple, the diverse, the hybridity of the montage ... it bursts its frame' by introducing the risk, incompletion, impurity, and disparity of the sensible. In sum, it is a work of imagination, and thus portends the unclassifiable dominion of the imaginal, of sensibility into the reason of law. It looks mimetic but is in fact heterotopic, bringing another order to the otherwise distributed patterns of natural and social relations. It is a coded representation, whose key, however, allows a relatively direct access to the juristic subject matter represented, be it easements, riparian rites, property lines, tracks or traceless navigational routes. It is an image that seems tame, that can be looked at in a seemingly dispassionate manner, in an objective fashion, with a bracketing of the aesthetic or disavowal of the fact that it is indubitably also an image.

Space and time, sovereignty and law are compressed into the geopolitical schematizing of the diagram of authority and ownership. The title page frontispiece to John Speed's well-known chorography of Britain evidences clearly the drive and the trajectory of mapping as a transitive, dialogic, and aesthetic appropriation of a legal fiction of place. What is shown in the frontispiece is a divinely ordained Britannia, peoples and places emblematized in descending historical order, as if on Homer's golden chain, from the divinity symbolized by the lion of the realm of England—*Angliæ*—and the figure of a Briton or Brith, under whom, below right, we see the Goddess Britannia with her trident and staff of office (Figure 2.2 A & B).[11] The frontispiece is expressly *Theatrum Imperii Magnæ Britanniæ*, the imperial theatre of Great Britain, that both ordains and is

[10] Georges Didi-Huberman, *Atlas, or the Anxious Gay Science* (Chicago: University of Chicago Press, 2018) at 3–4.

[11] John Speed, *Theatrum Imperii Magnæ Britannicæ* (London: Sudbury and Humble, 1611).

(a) (b)

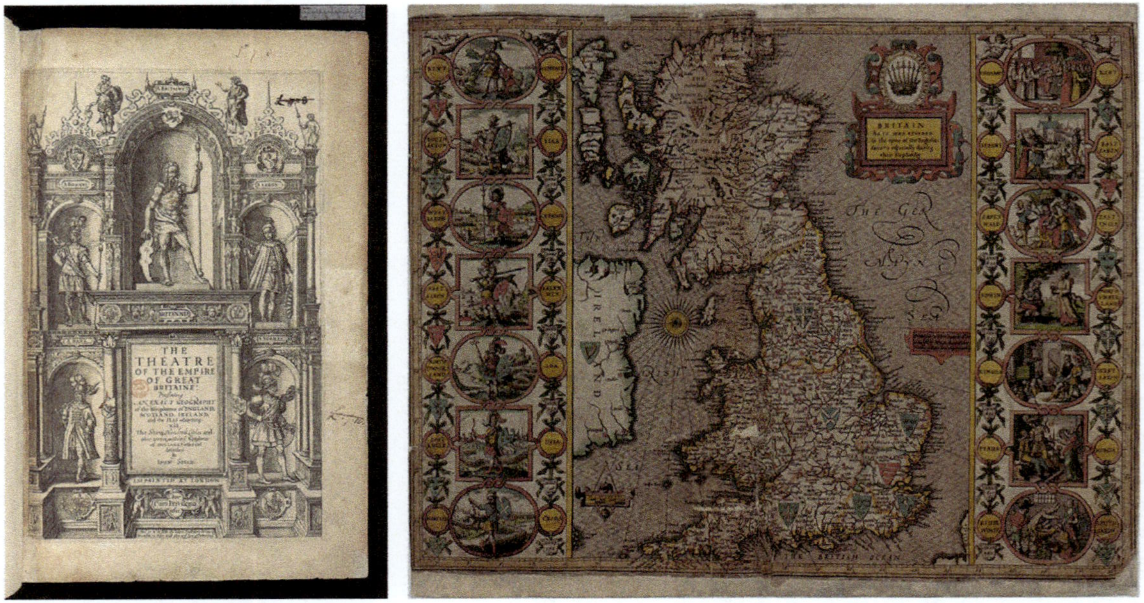

Figures 2.2 A & B From John Speed, *Theatrum imperii magnæ Britanniæ* (1611 & 1612 respectively).

Reproduced by kind permission of the Syndics of Cambridge University Library.

transposed onto the map of the realm. The next page reproduces figures showing the armorial ensigns of all the inhabitants, the royal families and nobles of the kingdoms of Britain, centred upon the throne, theatrically staged, angles opening the curtains on an orb with a lion atop, and then the lion and the unicorn holding up the escutcheon of state, and the royal motto *honi soit qui mal y pense*. The mapping, in the 1612 edition, is explicitly described as being of 'the achievement of our soveraigne King James as he now beareth with the armes of the severall kings which have aunciently raigned within his nowe dominions'.[12] It is in that same vein that it is the glories of Britain that Speed recalls as the record of his eyes having looked, not like Moses upon Canaan from afar, but up close and personal as he travelled through 'this very Eden'. His gaze is that of good fortune and he ends his peroration in praise of England, mimicking the title of John Fortescue's early treatise on English law, *De Laudibus legum Angliæ*. It merits quotation for the sense and aesthetic of the maps that dutifully follow:

> And applying my self wholly to the frame of this most goodly building, have as a poore Labourer carried the carved stones and polished Pillars from the hands of the more skillfull Architects, to be set in their fit places, which here I offer upon the Altar of Love to my Countrey ... whose Womb was my conception, whose Breasts were my nourishment, whose Bosome my cradle, and Lap (I doubt not) shall be my bed of sweet rest, till Christ by his Trumpet raise me thence.[13]

The legitimacy of the lineage of the image is both figured visually and ordained genealogically prior to the viewing of any diagram or chart. For lawyers, historically, the map is thus by precedent an expression of sovereignty, a specific and particular aesthetic of hierarchy and governance whereby the measured space and chorographic description of place is a manner of imposing political power onto the land. The compass rose that Bradin Cormack details, the name Britannia, the crown, faces of the monarch, nobility, administrators all evidence in assiduous form the proximity of measure, of rule and ruler to the realm. The map as legal device is a charter that both inscribes the name of the sovereign or nation on the *imperium*, the parchment empire, and in doing so indicates a measured correspondence of the cartograph to *lex terræ*—the law of nature, custom, and use, inscribed in the very matter of the earth.[14] Juristically the graphic depiction is a code, a device that signals the narrative of governance, the drama of the nation, and, as Siegert allows, 'the marks and signs on a map do not refer to an authorial subject but to epistemic orders and their struggles for dominance over other epistemic orders,

[12] John Speed, *The Theatre of the Empire of Great Britaine* (London: William Hall, 1611) (To the Reader).

[13] Speed, *Theatre of Empire* (To the Reader).

[14] On which point see Bradin Cormack, *A Power to Do Justice* (2008) Ch. 5; and see further Bradin Cormack, 'Paper Justice, Parchment Justice', in Beecher et al., (eds) *Taking Exception to the Law*, at 48–54.

in the course of which marks and things enter a new play of signs'.[15] The map creates an order of representation and constitutes its subject. Despite the nomination of the map in John Speed's case as 'Theatre of Empire', it is treated nonetheless in legal doctrine and practice most usually as a transparent image, as an ostensive and direct representation of territory, place, scene, and property. The atlas is assumed to be a pure image, a geometric device, an index that simply needs to be looked at and then calculated according to the key. It is, in this account, what it shows.

Such is the theory that has operated legally, in what could be termed juristic diagrammatology, as the transparency of atlases and now other topographical depictions such as drones, satellites, and Google Earth.[16] These are images viewed as if they are texts, linear script that is taken to self-evidently enhance the accuracy of location and the viewers' sense of the referent point at which an event occurred, or where a line has to be drawn to demarcate possession. A map will seem to indicate if a curtilage has been infringed, if a truck was on government property when a pedestrian's foot was crushed by a rear wheel, or whether an immigrant was in the United States or still in Mexico when apprehended by a border patrol. The atlas as proof, to take an extreme yet material example, can also be used to signal history, a sense and spirit of place, the intimations of what buildings not only house but ironically also cover over. In the Indian case of *Siddiq v Suresh*, the issue before the Supreme Court was that of an action brought on behalf of the Hindu divinity Lord Ram, an incarnation of Lord Vishnu, in the form of his human representatives, the *shebaits*—the custodians—of a Hindu religious sect.[17] The law suit concerns what is deemed by the Hindu community to be the birthplace of Lord Ram, a religious site that they claimed had been destroyed in 1528 when Ayodhya had been victim to conquest by the Muslim Mughal Emperor, Babur. A mosque, Babri-masjid, had been built on what the Muslims claimed was empty ground.[18] The Hindu community's claim was that under the mosque were the ruins of the temple of Ram. In 1949 the Hindu community invaded the structure for purposes of worshipping and the legal action followed. The plaintiff is the deity Ram—claiming to be the

[15] Bernhard Siegert, 'The Map *is* the Territory', 169 *Radical Philosophy* 13 (2011). For an interesting jurisprudential discussion of mapping as an art form, see Sionaidh Scott-Douglas, *Law after Modernity* (Oxford: Hart Pub., 2013) Ch. 4, arguing by analogy to Bloom's 'map of misreading' that there is no one correct viewing of a map, or here a plan, because issues of scale, projection, intention, and world view will always intervene.

[16] The term diagrammatology is here taken from Sybille Krämer, '"Epistemology of the Line": Reflections on the Diagrammatical Mind', in Olga Pombo and Alexander Gerner (eds), *Studies in Diagrammatology and Diagram Praxis* (London: College Publications, 2010). See also, for an overview of the diagrammatical, Charlotte Bigg, 'Diagrams', in Bernard Lightman (ed.), *A Companion to the History of Science* (Oxford: Wiley Blackwell, 2016) Ch. 39, noting of linear forms of drawing and mapping that they are 'less obvious, or less obviously visual, types of scientific two-dimensional representations. These are not usually thought of as images since they do not follow realistic conventions of representation but rather aim to portray relations, to manipulate numbers and other entities, or to organize, display and communicate information'.

[17] *M. Siddiq v Mahant Suresh Das & Ors* (2019) Civil Appeal Nos 10866-10867 of 2010.

[18] On the archeological evidence, see Supriya Varma and Jaya Menon, 'Was There a Temple under the Babri Majid? Reading the Archaeological "Evidence"', 45(50) EPW (2010) at 61.

presiding divinity of the site—and after sixty-nine years and 4314 pages of lower court judgements, the Supreme Court of India, in a decision that runs to the appropriate length of 1045 pages, the deity Ram won the action and the site has been returned to the Hindu community.

In Indian law, affirmed by decisions of the English Privy Council, deities are juristic persons and have the capacity to sue through their material manifestations: 'A Hindu idol is, according to long established authority founded upon the religious customs of the Hindus, and the recognition thereof by Courts of law, a "juristic entity". It has a juridical status with the power of suing and being sued.'[19] An idol is a vivified image, a consecrated representation of the divinity or, as one court poses it: 'It is sufficient to state that the deity is ... conceived as a living being and is treated in the same way as the master of the house would be treated by his humble servant.'[20] It is not enough that believers have faith in the existence of the divinity; there has to be tellurian presence, an image—statue, painting, relic, or in the present case a marking of archaeological space, a stratigraph—that is in this case the historical subject of ceremonies and rites of worship: 'The vivified image is regaled with the necessaries and luxuries of life in due succession, even to the changing of clothes, the offering of cooked and uncooked food and the retirement to rest.'[21] It is signs of such ceremonies, pieties, flowers, rituals, even sweeping and cleaning around a statue or other emblem of the divinity that were held to be sufficient to found the projected image of the deity Ram as a legal personality. A curtain, a vanishing sign, an altar with an empty space were sufficient references from the image to the thing signified—*ab imagine ad rem significatam*—adequate to manifest the deity as present, enough of a legal persona to constitute a cause of action. While land without any distinguishing feature, absent manifestation of some kind, would be an inadequate apparition of the deity, it is also deemed true in this case that 'the absence of evidence may not be evidence of absence.'[22] The land has, however, to be distinguished from other property for juristic personality to be conferred indirectly on the realty. A mark, a sign, a pattern even on the land would be sufficient, but it is still the case that jurisprudence requires something, be it relic, part object, a circle, a circumscribed empty space to support the assertion of the historical though long-past divine presence and so entitle the deity to juristic personhood. In conclusion, after examining over 300 photographs of archaeological ruins, the products of a commissioned dig, a host of statues, pillars, markings, and emblems, purportedly pertaining to the religious origin of the site as predating the

[19] *Pramatha Nath Mullick vs Pradyumna Kumar Mullick & Another* (1925) LR IA 245. In *Ram Jankijee Deities v State of Bihar* [1999] 5 SCC 50 at 196: 'a Deity being consecrated by performance of appropriate ceremonies having a visible image and residing in its abode is to be treated as a judicial person.'

[20] *Siddiq* paragraph 140.

[21] *Siddiq* paragraph 141.

[22] *Siddiq* at 215.

mosque that now occupied the space, it was decided that the manifestations were sufficient. If the deity is visible in the place, Ram Janmabhumi, then it is proven to the satisfaction of law's 'prudent person' test, that Lord Ram was born there, and the place is sacred. It is not the images, which are secondary, but rather the sanctity of the earth to the Hindu worshippers that confers juridical status upon the idol, Ram Lala Virajman. If the place is worshipped as the site of the deity then the presumption is that the idol has juridical personality and the standing to sue through their human representatives, and the photographic evidence legitimates the decision at which the judgement has already arrived.[23]

The key with regard to the ontography of the image is that, in harmony with the juristic theory of the *sileni Alcibiades*, the image is in appearance the manifestation of nothing, it needs inscription and interpretation so as to speak. The figures found inscribed in the earth have to be opened, not to see through them but to see into them, as bodies, as manifestions. The recognition is that matter is reality and it is the limit of the viewer's capacity to open to it that circumscribes the extent of juridical personality. As remarked at one point, but not followed through, wind, rain, sun, trees, flowers, empty spaces, mountains, dells too can all be deities and increasingly should be recognized and treated as such. Law, however, is moving most slowly towards such recognition, and much of the issue of impediment can be seen in the case at hand. The Supreme Court's extremely lengthy theological, epistemological, and juridical discourse on images is opaque because it is simply discursive and not visual. There is discussion of 315 photographs, detailed review of inscriptions, emblems, carvings, images, smears of paint, but no pictures are reproduced. The judgement, which is surely long enough and detailed enough to include images, the determinative pictures, is in this regard an empty space, a textual site of occlusion. What matters is manifestation and yet come the hour, the image does not arrive, no pictures of the depictions that determined the decision. The deity is legally the incarnation of the divine in an idol, manifest in an image or other distinguishing sign, now archaeologically buried in the earth, but no such apparitions are presented in the judgement. The absence of images is here the evidence of absence, of the blindness of legal reason.

The point can be made directly by reference to the two depictions that do occur in the judgement. These are the plans of the extant building and a map of the site. Two linear, graphic representations, one with vivid colour, the other shaded in parts, but both in their form aesthetic representations and sensible objects of viewing. Here the surface of the sacred buried space—the earth moves on—is delineated, but the map is conclusory, it provides no pictorial indications of the archaeological evidence nor figurative signs of the deity beyond the linear

[23] *Siddiq* at paragraph 197 where the Court rejects the argument that the land—Ram Janmabhumi—could have legal personality. The concept of the land being *svayumbhu lingam*, self-manifesting deity, was refused.

diagram and the merely verbal assertion of presence in designating two squares on the plan as the sites where the deity was born (*Ram Chabutra*) and where his consort cooked for him (*Sita Rasoi*) (Figures 2.3 & 2.4). If we look closely at the plan, it is a partial cartography, a scale has been added and the floor plan has a key, but the only point of historical interest is that the depictions show a wall by means of which the British administration had imposed partition on the two religious groups, Hindu worship to one side and Muslim to the other. It has to be concluded that there are both historical and jurisprudential reasons propelling the assumption that the map is the direct and demonstrative depiction of presence, which is here that of haunting from half a millennium ago. The atlas is presumed to be a rational image, a direct representation of a site, reproduced complete with scale and key, mathematically drawn and free of interpretation. Such is how law has most usually addressed plans, maps, schemata of place. They are taken to be analogous to writing, they escape the sensibilities and affects of aesthetics, they are grounded forms of knowledge, the juridical expressions of Roman alluvion, the earthy property of an epistemology of proximity and a mode of conceptual occupation. For present purposes, however, what is striking about the visual character of the judgement and of its mapping is precisely what it does not show, what cannot be seen, its veiling of the visual basis of the determination. The *sileni* here lack Alcibiades. The box is empty. In holding that the deity had manifested in the archaeological site, the judgement failed itself to manifest the proof of that appearance. The images are hidden from view, and so the probative cannot be probed, the empty plan, diagrams without either reference or link to the signs of the deity, become the talisman and site of power. This is a version of the empty throne, the mystical seat of a potential that is always already invisibly the occupant of the site, the *corpus mysticum* of the divinity itself. Even and indicatively, the plaintiff, Shri Ram Lalla Virajmaan, refers in argument not to the deity Ram per se, but to the Seat of Lord Ram. His passage had left residues and markings, vestiges of prior habitus and habitation, a noseless face indenting the tellurian site.

The Supreme Court reproduces an image that frames the decision by providing a purportedly rational context and sighting of the issue, but it is one that directs attention away from the relevant materiality and the extant signs and images, toward abstraction, textual expression, *ratio scripta* as a mode of absconding from the subject matter of the conflict and the detail of the apparitions in which the deity purportedly manifested as humus, trace, or sign of an absence which in Christian theology was termed an apparition, an aerial and vanishing sign. The diagram can in this sense be taken to represent trauma, the repetition of a prior wound, which is first the conquest of Ayodhya by the Muslims, and second and more directly the partition of the temple which of course invokes the partition of India. To repeat is to avoid, to not look, to act out, and this the Supreme Court achieves with gusto. This is Bataille's desert of words, discourse in its etymological sense of *dis-currere*,

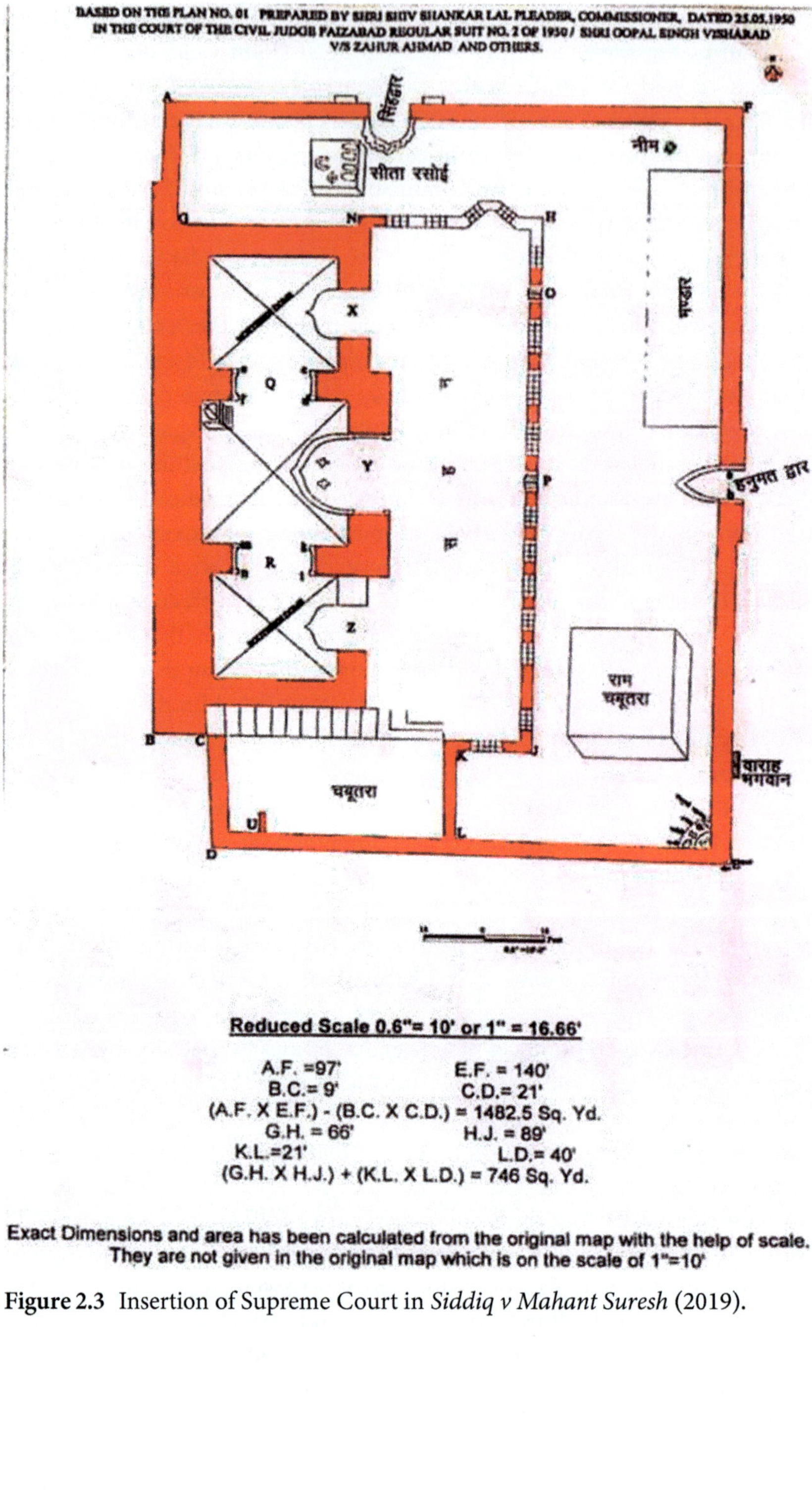

Figure 2.3 Insertion of Supreme Court in *Siddiq v Mahant Suresh* (2019).

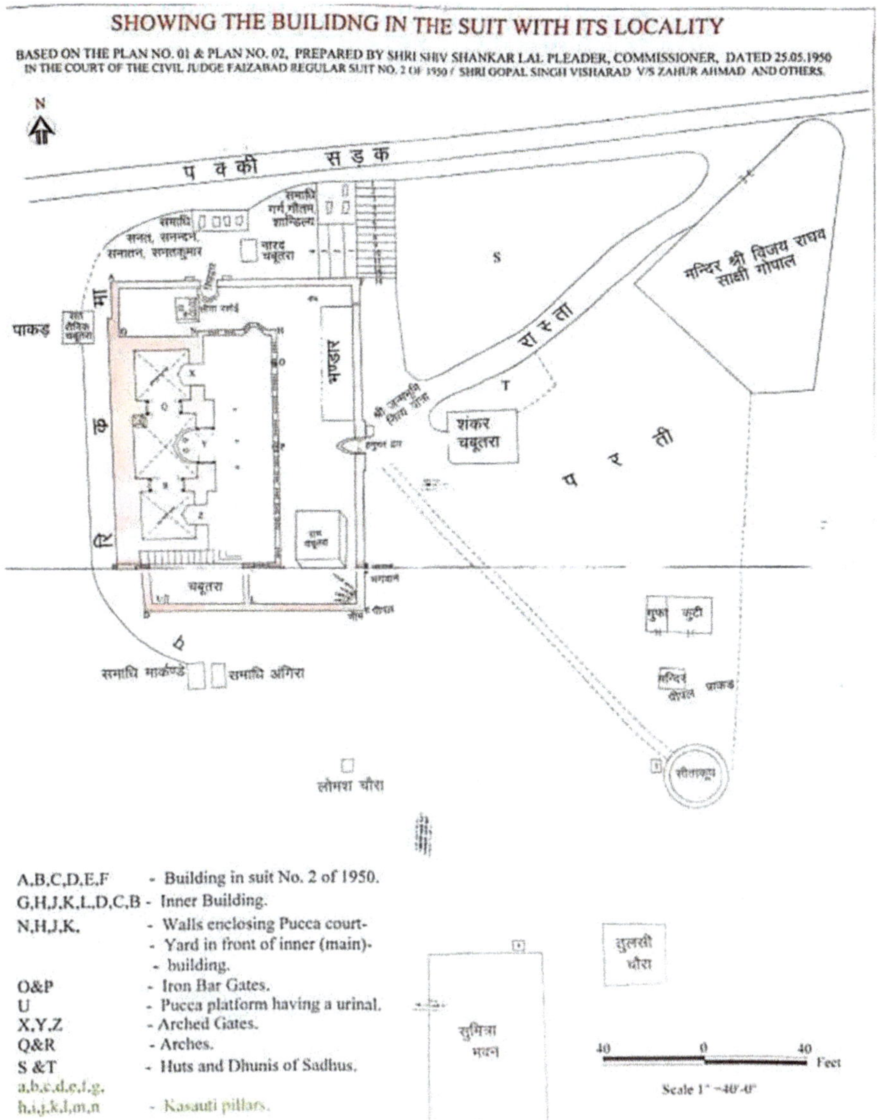

Figure 2.4 Insertion of Supreme Court in *Siddiq v Mahant Suresh* (2019).

of running away, because what we are given by the Court is not matter but abstraction, not immanence but transcendence, even though it is precisely the immanence of the deity, the incarnation in material images that is the proof of possession of legal identity and the jural personality and thence ownership of the place that is in dispute.[24] It would be easy, both incisive of legitimacy and a relief from a prolix

[24] Georges Bataille, *Inner Experience* (New York: SUNY, 2008), referenced by the translator at xxii.

and overwhelming 'verballing' of the decision, the shellac of positivism, to have presented the images that determined the determination.[25] It is frequently done in judgements, the map and the plan are evidence enough that the reader could also be a viewer and see the subject of deliberation. It is impossible to avoid the conclusion that the Court did not wish the images to be seen.[26] It is a marker, of course, of the covertly political character and potentially incendiary consequences of the ruling, but rather than pursue that theme, the map is an insertion of distance, the medium of flight to the text, levitation from matter to the nebulously linear ether of the regimentations of the page.

We are a long way from the matter of the decision, the Court is hiding by speaking too much. Bataille talks of the ostrich burying its head in the sand as a form of discursive escape from seeing, a mode of closing the eyes, an evasion: 'It is through an "intimate cessation of all intellectual operations" that the mind is laid bare. If not, *discourse* maintains it in its little complacency'.[27] It is not the word wind that matters, it is the feeling of the gust, the chill of the draft, the non-discursive sensation that is the goal of the performative utterance, the rhetorical *effectus*. Law is blindfolded by discourse. Consider the 5000 pages that the Indian courts deemed necessary to bury the archaeological question of whether there was visible evidence of a Hindu temple underneath the mosque. The courts dig it up so as to enact a second interment. The photographs, the spectral capture of appearances from the judicially commissioned archaeological excavation site would have sufficed. An extraordinarily extensive discursive divagation was necessary to evade the sensible subject of dispute. Text is here a skin, an outer and ugly face that has to be opened to and opened up for its subject matter to be known. In Biblical terms, *videbunt in quem transfixerunt*, only in breaking the skin, in rending the pages, can one liberate the thought that triggers such non-disclosure. What life does the discourse contain? What ghosts are hidden here? Questions of the eerie and of failed presence, of the haunting of a site and the marks of its agency, if any, that allow for interpretation. The postulated test was that of whether the spirit could be seen, but the Court evades the direct assessment of the optical and imagistic and precludes the subjects of law from seeing the legality and by extension the legitimacy of the jurists' apprehension of the ruins. There is only the diagram and map of the buildings to view, as if these surfaces somehow confirm the subterranean remnants that discourse has so lengthily failed to expose and show. The partition above is verballed into an illegitimate annexation below.

[25] I am taking the notion of verbality and of verballed decisions, meaning the palabras, paraffle and pabulum of positivistic pronunciation from Marret Leiboff, *Towards a Theatrical Jurisprudence* (London: Routledge, 2020) at 64, 80.

[26] Despite promises by the Government to publish the images, these have yet to appear at the time of going to print, June 13 2023, and some four years after publication of the decision.

[27] Bataille, *Inner Experience*, at 13.

What can be seen can be appropriated. The choice of image, of the floor plan of the mosque, is far from accidental. The use of the diagrams most strikingly indicates the Supreme Court's vision of a divided space, a partitioned building, a history that, even though it comes much later, in the colonial era, impresses and quite possibly motivates the Court while having no direct visual relevance to the somewhat metaphysical question of the subterranean signs of the archaeological presence of the divinity in the form of prior worship. What is visually probative yet crucially and epistemically uncertain is excluded from view, while what is safely linear and fairly directly representative of the current site and structure, while making no pretense of any signification of prior shrines, altars, and vivified *emblemata* of worship and occupancy of Lord Ram, is reproduced as comfort for the decision. It provides an air of legitimacy via the representation of a real place, technically the chorography of its tellurian occupation by guardians, custodians, and worshippers of an idol. This distant diagrammatic surface stands in for the sensibility of the visual and for the archaeological matter that the Court will judge.

The cartographic jurisprudence in *Siddiq* is novel for its associative object, that of indexing the site of subterranean presence, and the markers of spectres. To borrow from Başak Ertür theorizing a different case, '[t]he figure of the ghost determined not only the legal outcome of the trial but also its legal and political afterlives'.[28] Time is thrown out of joint. Past and future intermingle. It is after all an abstraction, a diagram of the mosque, putatively marking a buried past, that indirectly lends legitimacy to the judicial discourse that it instigates and dissolves into the text in a legally unexceptional or self-evident manner while in fact functioning to displace and obscure the absence of images of the archaeological patterns and other relics that purportedly indicate the early history of worship, without being shown or seen. The salient point is that we are witness in very striking form to the effect of mapping, and to the inventions of cartographic jurisprudence.[29] It is juristically common. The diagrammatic is ironically the mask of the *certum* of visibility and is the earliest form of juridical image, what the humanists termed *veritas falsa*, the false truth of the picture, and here the particularity and materiality of depiction displacing the object viewed with an imaginal schema. The diagram is not what it shows, and such is peculiarly true of the floor plans reproduced in *Siddiq* which, while they can rapidly be reduced to the literal, a line that marks division

[28] Başak Ertür, *Spectacles and Spectres: A Performative Theory of Political Trials* (New York: Fordham University Press, 2022) 128.

[29] I am borrowing the term from Sabarish Suresh, 'Cartographies', in Goodrich et al. (eds), *Research Handbook on Law and Literature* (Cheltenham: Elgar, 2022) at 175, arguing that '*cartographic jurisprudence* refers to the study of the ways in which law is inscribed through cartography, and how law, in turn, makes use of cartography to reinscribe and reproduce its power, territory and sovereignty. There is a double movement in this operation: first, the cartographic delimitation of law and territory, and second, law's adoption of cartography to sustain, legitimate and justify its force'. See further Sabarish Suresh, *The Traumatic History of Constitutions: The Partition of India and the Laws of Repetition* (forthcoming 2024).

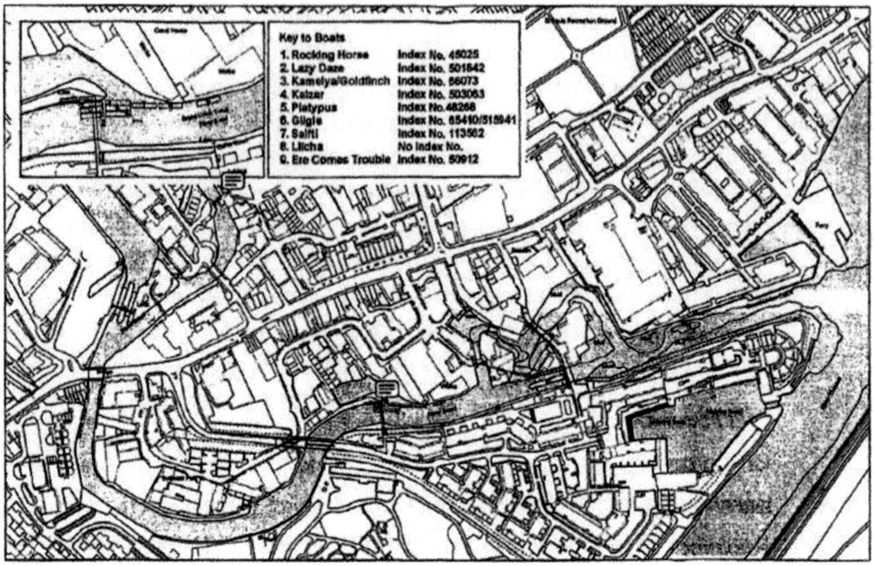

Figure 2.5 Insertion of Justice Mann in *Nigel Peter Moore v Brent Waterways Board* [2009].

between religious uses of the building and indirectly the history of British presence and compromises, are far removed in time and space from the object of decision, which is the buried use of the site some 500 years ago.

Moving from earth to water, a further indicative example can be taken from an English case involving a claim to riparian rights. Nigel Peter Moore, who lived on a houseboat appropriately, as it turned out, named Platypus, challenged a British Waterways Board notice of removal. Moore's claim to moor the boat was not only phonetic but a form of adverse possession based on membership of the Brentford Yacht and Boat Club which had occupied the bank for sixty years. This gave him, he argued, *locus standi*, or more properly *locus fluitem*, and the ancillary right to mooring. The High Court of Chancery rejected the claim on the basis that under section 43 of the Grand Junction Canal Act of 1793, the public right to free use of the waters for purposes of navigation did not extend to permanent mooring unconnected with navigation. Platypus was history.

The judge in rejecting the claim for declaratory relief provides a picture of the river and the site of Platypus and eight other boats moored with Moore's. The diagram of river and bank includes an inset, a flag, a legend, and a key (Figure 2.5). The map does not show any probative facet of the case. It does not evidence the use of the water for free navigation, it cannot represent the length of time that the boats have been moored, it does not provide any significant indication of other users or adjoining properties; it simply purports to show where the boat is moored in relation to the other boats, and that it is on the river Brent and so subject to the 1793 Act. Beyond that, the judge notes that in fact 'the boats are moored somewhat differently today ... [and] there have been other changes but these are immaterial'.[30] Ironically the diagram transpires to be confessedly inaccurate, in part immaterial, and not of the moorings as currently in dispute. The mapping provides a particularly ironic reality effect, a cartographic *causatum*, but it is not an accurate image of the circumstances of the case. It deserves further analysis precisely because its place, status, reason, and role in the judgement are far from self-evident. It appears on the one hand that in the eyes of the judge this is simply a picture, a scaled manifestation of the site and subject of dispute. Assumed to be self-evident, a pure image, an incidental and purportedly linear representation, no further comment or analysis of the image is to be found in the decision even though the diagram is in the record and part of the judgement, a demonstrative dimension of the precedent. On the other hand, Mann J. does note that the real differs from the picture but goes on to assert that such changes or, to be blunt, such misrepresentations are immaterial.

Visually the particular map is a somewhat strange image, appearing tilted, almost falling out of the page, it can be immediately observed that it is neither properly aligned nor well executed. Poor presentation, a lamentably haphazard aesthetics, as already adverted, are common features of judicial imagery and symptomatic both of a lesser status and minimal attention given to the non-textual, and simultaneously of an unconscious or structural carto-juridical function that is asserted. Here the mapping of the river and the moorings not only provides a reality effect, the appearance of substance, but also institutes jurisdiction. What is mapped is putatively measured, controlled, visible, and justiciable. The freedom of the waters is subjugated to the scale, key, and geometry of the cartograph. It is a power to judge that is so easily assumed and so obvious to Justice Mann that it does not even require alignment, colour, or a vexillological symbol of authority, as opposed to a sticky note indicating the site of the riparian dispute. Detail and additional ornament are absent because the representation is deemed direct and purely indicative. It proffers an aesthetic of the inaesthetic but of course that defeasance is a species of denial, and if we interpret the stated immateriality of Judge Mann's pictorial insertion as a slip—it cannot in reality be immaterial, it matters sufficiently for inclusion, it is there in the precedential judgement—then it creates an atmosphere of authority and of knowledge of a particular kind. The slip, in its dual sense, slips into the text. The depiction of the river and docks literally places the dispute into a mapped box, seized by cartograph and the *quo warranto* or lack of authority generated by the absence of a charter. It provides a dull, black and white, linear schema, a monochrome geometrical mapping without figures, without boats, without persons. It reduces the dispute to the monochrome of a linear page and to a series of coffin shaped lots, plots, slips, and berths. The sensibility is one of rigidity, of linearity and law composing and containing the nautical in the normative. The floating signifier lands berth-less, asphyxiated on the page.

[30] *Nigel Peter Moore v Brent Waterways Board* [2009] EWHC B12 (Ch) para. 7.

The aesthetic, even in this inaesthetic or casual mode, nonetheless transforms the dispute, abstracts the issues, and displaces persons in favour of the schema of things. Boats become boxes, geometric patterns on a page. For the purposes of analysis of the judicial image, the key point is the incidental, non-problematic, correspondence theory of transparent visibility, of being able paradoxically to read the real in a confessedly inaccurate depiction. There is, in addition, also the subordination of the image, its displacement and misrecognition, the historical inaccuracy of deeming the map a part of something read and not viewing it as a device, emblem, or picture to be opened to and sensuously apprehended. The map expresses visibility as power, and law as schematic and linear, a matter of boundaries, spaces, and properties measured, scaled, and coded. No Moore the Platypus, Mann is the law and while what is shown is not accurate, it is true—*verum*—a linear universality representing the misaligned cacophony that is the particularity of common law jurisprudence. This same point could be made from an analysis of the profusion of maps, diagrams, pictures of place in decisions. An air of control and of classificatory reason seems to accompany, for example, in a tort case, the Google Map street plan on which there is a penciled square and circle indicating the site of the plaintiff's accident—he tripped—and latterly the employer's parking lot to which Workers' Compensation would apply. The depiction acts as an abstract illustration, it is what it shows within the plan of power, it authorizes and legitimates without being in any sense probative as to the position of the plaintiff at the time of injury (Figure 2.6).[31] What is on the map is somehow true and dispositive, legally placed to the satisfaction of the judge and manifested in the record as illustration and proof of the verballed decision. Obviousness here takes the form of a hand-pencilled square and circle specifically intended to indicate the relevant jurisdiction and the place of injury. The insertions show a square of included jurisdiction, the right angles of justice, the symmetry of law, in contrast to the circle of individual and accidental human presence. The sensibility of the map is that of purportedly demonstrating what the judgement states, but it remains a visual 'as if', *Non-Entia imaginaria*, a fiction of placement, in that neither the parking of the car, nor the tripping that resulted in injury, can be seen on the crudely inscribed map, save as the handiwork of the judge *in abstracto* but visually keyed and presented.

In a slightly later case, in a peculiar contrast, a Google Earth satellite shot provides a meaningless but admissible photograph of where the defendant, allegedly an illegal immigrant, had been apprehended. The Border Patrol claimed that Pasiano Tirado was apprehended well inside the US and stuck a pin in the map along with GPS coordinates that they purported to have recorded at the time of

[31] *Kruge v Workers' Compensation Appeal Board* 2014 WL 273809.

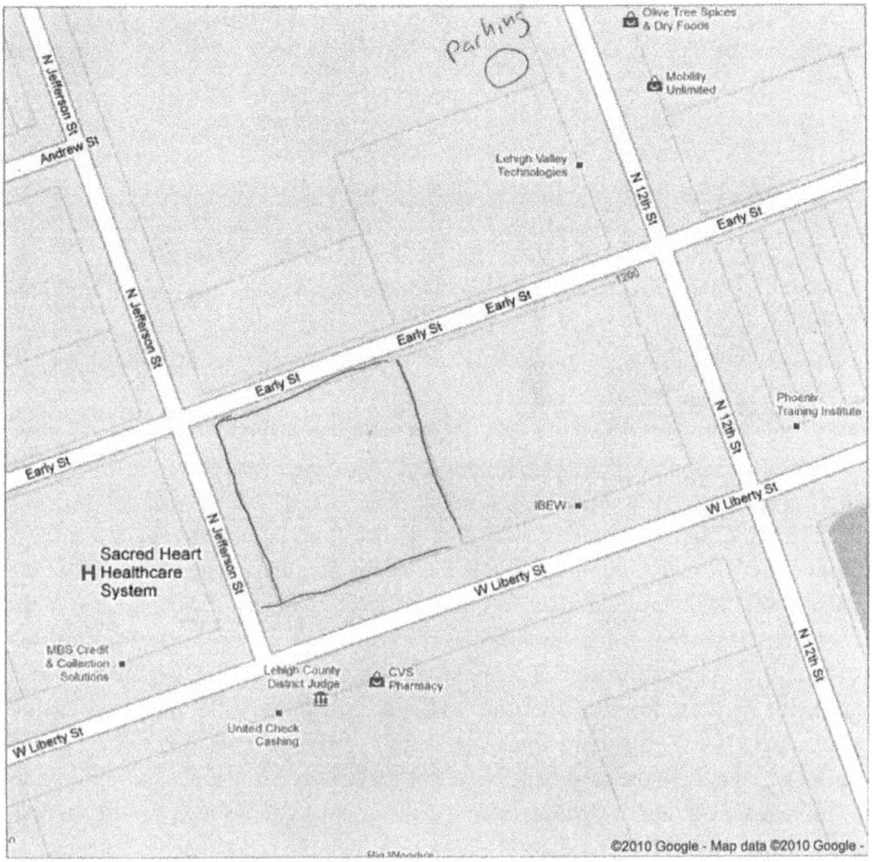

Figure 2.6 Insertion by Judge Patricia McCullough in *Kruge v Workers' Compensation Appeal Board* (2014).

apprehension (Figure 2.7).[32] The pin, a digital tack, purportedly represents the defendant, no more than a prick on the map because he was arrested at night and the satellite shot is taken during the day. The colour version of the image, submitted as 'Government Exhibit 1' in the filings is a picture produced by a third party map preparer, and is a daytime shot taken in 2011, two years before Pasiano was apprehended. The preparer was never cross-examined, and Agent Garcia who arrested the defendant could say no more than that the tack corresponded roughly to the area where Tirado was apprehended.[33] What the Google Map satellite image, the supposedly indisputably accurate representation of a bare

[32] *US v Lizarrago-Tirado* 789 F.3d 1107 (2015). For a further example see *Gilles v Blanchard* 477F.3d 466.

[33] Ibid. Appellant's Reply Brief at 9.

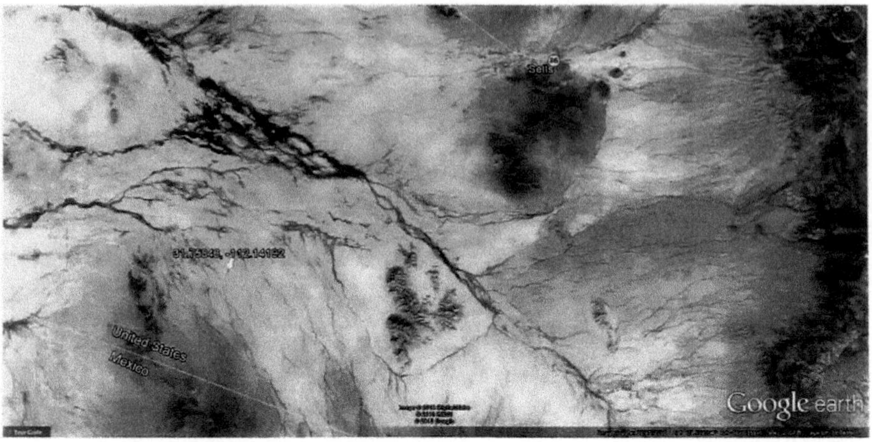

Figure 2.7 Insertion by Judge Alex Kozinski in *US v Lizarrago-Tirado* (2015).

and here quite barren veracity, is in fact showing is the absence of the subject apprehended on a diurnal image that precedes the nocturnal date of the encounter by two years. Where the judge states that the satellite image 'makes no assertion', that is that 'it merely depicts a scene as it existed at a particular time', it in fact not only asserts measure, tone, boundary, possession, projection, perspective, and placement, but also implies a relation to the scene of the crime, the illegal crossing into the USA. The satellite image gives the appearance of reality to the Border Patrol claim because they have the power of surveillance, the ability to see and, as the French scholar Paul Virilio has long argued, what can be seen can be owned, destroyed, or in this instance captured, even though the image itself paradoxically shows that no one is there, only a tack, a digital illusion, a probability, a guess.[34]

In *Tirado* the image enacts an imaginal presence and seizes a place for law. As Andreas Philippopoulos-Mihalopoulos defines it, spatial justice is 'the conflict between bodies that are moved by a desire to occupy the same space at the same time'.[35] By instituting an image of the space, by inserting the digital tack as if it were a place, an atmosphere and intersection of several bodies, the scene has been arrested, controlled, subjected to an abstract law which both eviscerates and eliminates the geo-scape, the terrain and corporeal inhabitation of places and things. The map is indicative of a modern political space and so of sovereignty, a notion that 'refers to the fact that within [these] specific boundaries there is just one supreme power that does not recognize any superior within its territory ... the space of the sovereign state is, tellingly, empty'.[36] So too in the case

[34] The theme of Paul Virilio, *War and Cinema: The Logistics of Perception* (London: Verso, 1989/2009): 'what is perceived is already lost'.

[35] Andreas Philippopoulos-Mihalopoulos, *Spatial Justice: Bodies, Lawscape, Atmosphere* (London: Routlege, 2015) at 5.

[36] Bottici, *Imaginal Politics*, at 94.

under discussion. No Tirado, no Border Patrol, no visible persons, just a staffage digital digit that marks sovereign possession of everything this side of the line. The imperialism of mapping, manifest in this case in the utter abstraction of the monochrome Google image, which like the frontispiece to Hobbes' *Leviathan* contains no life, neither subjects, nor persons that matter.[37] Beings become the subalterns of diagrams, the staffage is suffragan, the absent key to a map view that lacks colour and content, neither affect nor sensibility of any human form. It is treated purely as a vehicle, a transparent medium of locational deployment, even though, even here, there is tone and materiality, form and depth to the picture of the landscape which in the law report is indicatively altered from colour to monochrome image.

In a more recent decision, also concerned with territorial jurisdiction, the defendants were arrested and convicted of drug offenses.[38] The prosecution was brought in Maryland and the issue on appeal was whether the defendants had in fact been in Maryland when apprehended, because if not, if they were in the District of Columbia, then the Court lacked jurisdiction. The question of the situs of the crime, the *locus in quo*, was a question for the jury, a matter of fact and of feet. The appellate Court produces several Google images of the location and adds red pointers to boundary lines, and also puts on view cars, activity, people captured in dashcam photographs. The evidence of life tempers the abstraction of the monochrome images and allows for contestation of the police report, and specifically of the depiction of the place of apprehending the defendants, marked here with a black line and a circle made on the photograph by one named Officer Murray (Figure 2.8). It transpired however that the place of arrest was not in Maryland, or at least that it appeared not to be as represented by the police diagram if this was transposed to a map with a more cartographically accurate depiction of the boundary line between the State and the District. The Court corrects the map and uses a large red arrow to indicate the actual boundary (Figure 2.9). The case is sent back for a jury to decide where the defendants were on the map both literally and metaphorically. One cartograph displaced the other in the hierarchy of place settings and we are witness to an instance of what used to be called the *ius submovendi*, or the power of removing from the map.

With the insertion of arrows and colours, from monochrome to polychrome, the daylight image with a passerby, trees, buildings and their shadows, cars, and telegraph poles, the map becomes a more obviously contestable representation because more manifestly a picture, an aerial view of location without the defendants present and so with only the testimony of the arresting officer, and this undermined by an incorrectly drawn boundary line. There is nothing necessary

[37] One can note, for the sake of completeness, one never knows who will be looking, that the landscape of Hobbes' much discussed frontispiece has two staffage figures but is otherwise deserted of human forms.

[38] *Nikki Shivone Long v State of Maryland* WL 4898877 (2019).

Figure 3. The circle and arrow in this Google Street View image of Blair Road, marked at trial as State's Exhibit No. 2, were drawn by Officer Murray. The markings show where, he testified, he saw the Long sisters' truck was stopped during the alleged drug sale. During cross-examination of Officer Murray, defense counsel's questioning revealed the car was at least partially off the roadway, bringing the events closer to the boundary between Maryland and the District of Columbia.

Figure 2.8 Insertion of Judge Christopher Kehoe in *Long v State of Maryland* (2019).

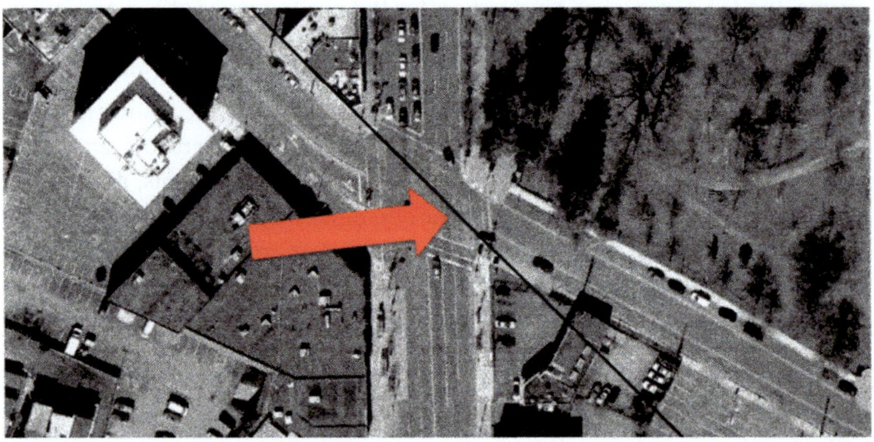

Figure 2. This aerial image was submitted as an appendix to the State's brief in this appeal. The line indicated with a red arrow represents the actual boundary between Maryland and the District. It was drawn using data from a GPS resurvey of the District's borders by the District's Office of the Chief Technology Officer. The line lies about 60 to 70 feet north of the line shown to the jury at trial and bisects the sidewalk on the south side of Blair Road, within feet of where the alleged drug sale took place.

Figure 2.9 Insertion of Judge Christopher Kehoe in *Long v State of Maryland* (2019).

in the map precisely because the issue is that of who occupied it, when and where, and this is quite clearly now drawn onto the image by the arresting officer who inscribes a line and a circle, a black arrow and a black noose, while the appellate Court, in corrective mode, inscribes a red arrow, a *flèche* of blood, signs of life. As intention and technology combine to facilitate the population of the map, the possibility of apprehending its sensible, aesthetic and material character is enhanced. Even the simple use of colour to highlight and enliven is sufficient to signal both the element of interpretative judgement, of hermeneutic intervention, and the affect and atmosphere of inhabitation. The photographic representation has to be constructed and configured to satisfy the particular import that the viewer is to construe from the visual depiction. It is not enough to say that the map is an argument, a mode of advocacy, although such is unquestionably the case. It is necessary to expand the point to an aesthetics of judicial advocacy or proof of decision, which is that the striking use of colour, the *flèche*, the inserted fingerpost signals in the manner of a blazon, inserting a lineal division which purports to indicate the controlling side of the boundary line as definitive and so also as the mandatory mode of viewing the cartograph. The text prejudges the optics and provides an *ex post facto* reconstruction of who was where and when. The red arrow does not prove anything, but it does signal force and danger, affecting a mood and insistence that correctively distinguishes the judicial satellite image from the police officer's picture.

The satellite image provides a new technology of mapping that permits a higher degree of verification. The drawing of the boundary line provides an empirical basis for overruling the police officer's determination, but it bears note that the images here are not probative of what took place or of where the relevant bodies were at the particular time of arrest. What it does allow for is the recalibration of the image used by the police and so can indicate to corrective effect that if the police image and inscription is accurate, as claimed, then the plaintiffs were not in the jurisdiction of Maryland law enforcement but rather in the District of Columbia. The second point to stress is that the digital image, light and shadow, the drawings on the exhibits, the red arrow, all generate a sensibility and stress that intervene in the interpretation of what is seen. The map becomes a material place which is overwritten by the state, police, and judiciary. A demarcating line is superimposed upon the picture, a selective chromatic is used by the judge, and with it is introduced not only a signalling function, but an environment and habitude in which the interventions of the law actively and visibly encounter the lawscape with the colour of force and exsanguination. This is the site of critical inquiry because here satellite imagery generates an affective image of encounter, a viewing of the contested space of an event. What can be missed in these initial forays into Google Earth, but will be of increasing importance, is precisely the dimension of the tellurian, that the earth itself, organic and transitional like all life forms, is part of the law suit, and that the ground—the environment—is necessarily made visible so as to participate in the reason of judgement.

A final and not irrelevant feature to the case is that the dissent also uses a map, a brightly coloured cartograph of the question of interception (Figure 2.10). It is again different by virtue primarily of its abstraction. It is vivid but non-figurative, proceeding in the juristic manner, *more geometrico*, and hence colourfully, in part irately, in part comically, dismissing the appellant's case on the ground that 'Even if the truck had been "straddling" the roadway and the sidewalk, slip op[inion]

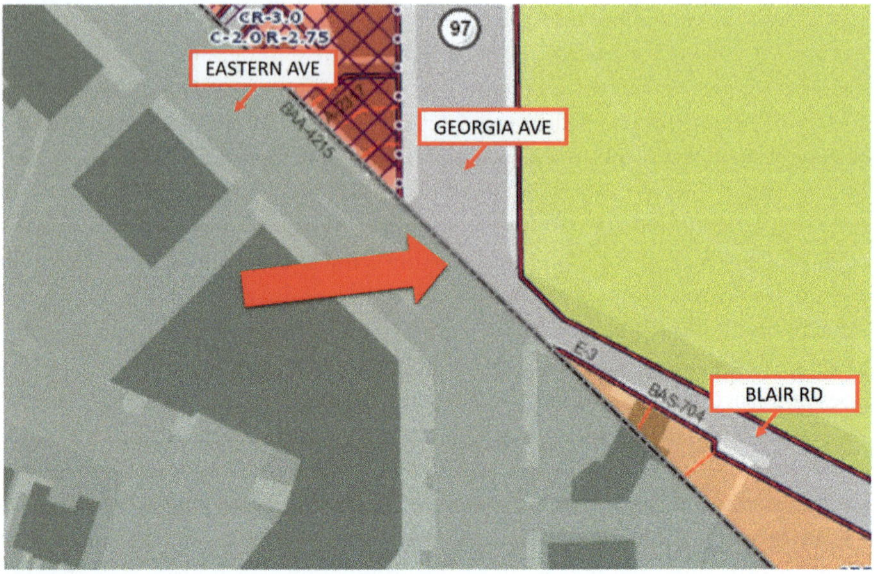

Figure 2.10 Insertion of Judge Daniel Friedman (dissenting) in *Long v State of Maryland* (2019).

at 20, the whole truck was, to my eye, still entirely in Maryland'. The dissenting eye reads the cartographic image differently, but rather than reproducing and commenting upon the figurative representation mentioned in slip opinion 20, and so detailing the optics of this distinct viewing, Judge Daniel A. Friedman chooses to insert a coloured isolarion, a small and abstract detail of the map that excises the law from the lawscape and removes the figurative environment, the trees, the footprints of buildings, houses, automobiles, park, and street that are visible and visceral in the snapshots from the electronic zoning map used by the majority. The dissenting judge does not even comment on the map that is reproduced, but rather tacitly implies that it is irrelevant, both because nothing is said about it, no analysis is proffered, but also because, on a different depiction, his eye sees the plaintiffs as being in Maryland. Whether or not such is the case, the issue for the dissent is one of fact that is properly determined at trial by the judge and should not be reversed. In other words, no maps are necessary, no issue has been raised, and yet he nonetheless inserts a cartograph, an eviscerated depiction of the scene of arrest, as if to reprimand the majority and its use of snapshots rather than the bare map. The colour representation, however, is hardly meaningless. It introduces a vivid visual spectrum, tone, tint, tincture, temper, and mood that not only reformulate the environment of the event but also convey the affect of dissent as vivid and vexed.

Colour and the environmental consequences of development as represented through the life of plants are the subject of an instructive and lengthily litigated

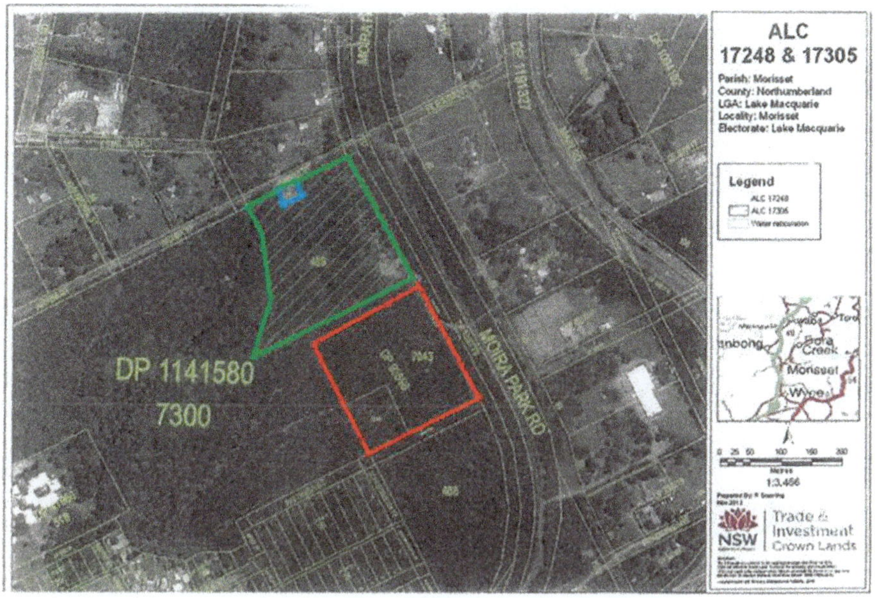

Figure 2.11 Insertion of Associate Justice Moore in *New South Wales Aboriginal Land Council v The Minister Administering the Crown Lands Act* (2015).

New South Wales, Aboriginal land claim case from 2015.[39] The Aboriginal community brought an action to take possession of two parcels of Crown land under the *Aboriginal Land Rights Act* 1983. The Minister charged with determining such claims under the Act had refused the petition on the basis that:

1. The land shown by red hatching and green hatching on diagram 'A' is needed or likely to be needed for residential land;
2. The land shown by blue hatching on diagram 'A' is needed or likely to be needed for the essential public purpose of sewerage reticulation.[40]

Slightly later the judge, Moore AJ, in responding to the Crown Minister's grounds for refusing the claims, observes that '[t]o understand precisely the nature of the recommendations at 1.1 and 1.2 in the briefing note, it is appropriate to reproduce a colour version of the plan that shows the areas hatched in green, red and blue. That marked-up air photo is reproduced below (with the boundaries re-marked by me to make them clear)' and the pictures follow in the online report but not in the downloaded file version of the decision (Figure 2.11).[41] Twenty paragraphs

[39] *New South Wales Aboriginal Land Council v The Minister Administering the Crown Lands Act (Moira Park Road No 1 and Moira Park Road No 2 claims)* [2015] NSWLEC 179.
[40] *Aboriginal Land Council,* para. 26.
[41] *Aboriginal Land Council,* para. 27.

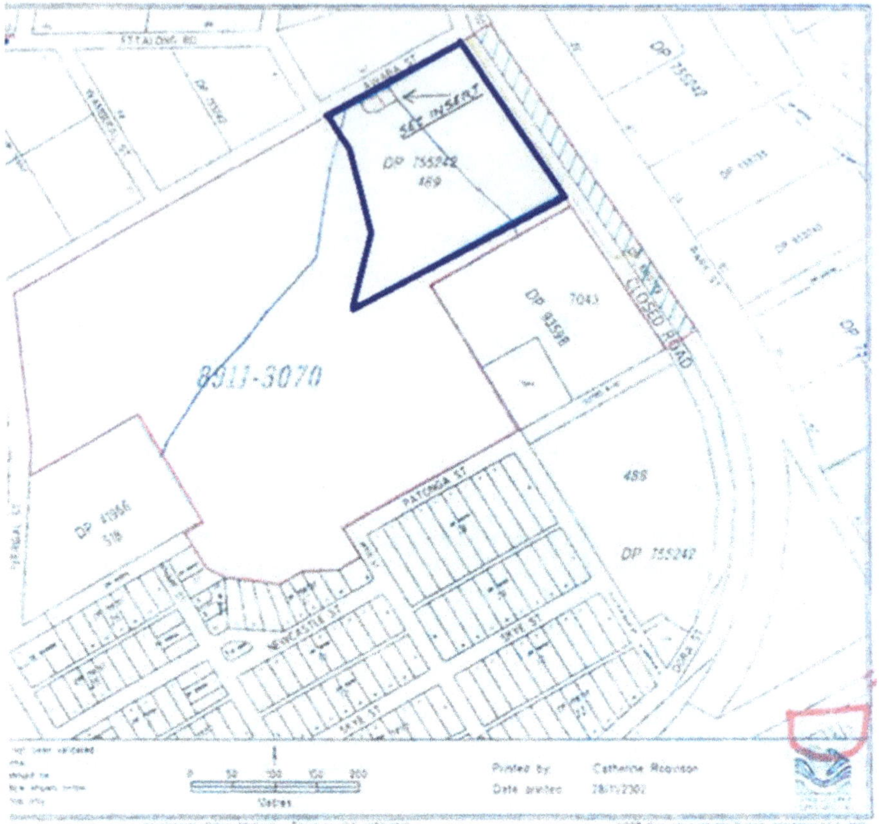

Figure 2.12 Insertion of Associate Justice Moore in *New South Wales Aboriginal Land Council v The Minister Administering the Crown Lands Act* (2015).

further on the judge returns not just to the cartographic image, but also to the colours and specifically to Lot 489, and relays that it 'has been re-marked by me in heavy blue' (Figure 2.12).[42] The red, green, light blue, and heavy blue are inscriptions upon the map which, in the second image, it should be noted, takes on its weightier signification as a diagram marked with emphatic blue. Something is done, a matterphorical incision, an assertion of juridical proprietary interest by what is often termed blue-pencilling. What is shown in colour on the map and in the judgement matters and is also material. The tinctures that appear in the reasoning of the determination and give a distinct form, hue and visible spectrality to the literal, concrete, and organic floral ground of decision require analysis.[43] The

[42] *Aboriginal Land Council,* para. 47.

[43] For definition and expansive elaboration of the concept of matterphor, see Daniela Gandorfer, *Matterphorics: On the Laws of Theory* (Durham, N.C.: Duke University Press, 2024), elaborating on matterphorics as resistance to abstraction and all putatively transcendent or escapist thought.

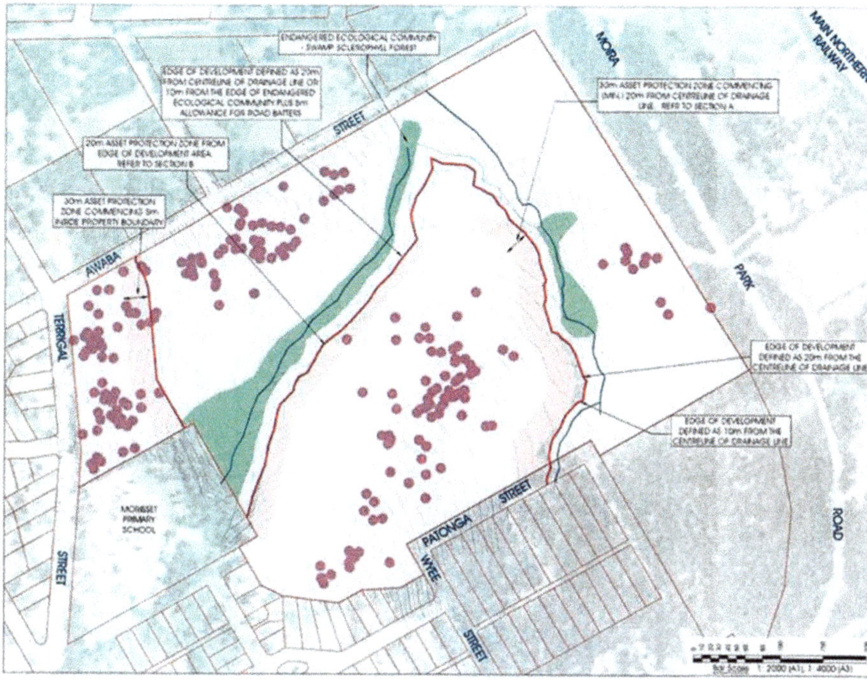

Figure 2.13 Insertion of Associate Justice Moore in *New South Wales Aboriginal Land Council v The Minister Administering the Crown Lands Act* (2015).

judicial remonstrances are based on the diagrams of place and are directed to the Minister of the Crown who is held to have failed to justify his claim, under the Statute, section 36(1)(b)(1), that the lands are needed or are likely to be needed as residential lands. The decision is predicated upon a review of the denial in which it is 'necessary to consider the Minister's opinion in some cartographic detail'. This transpires to be a question of correspondence, of the relationship of the charter to 'the precise terms of the Minister's instrument of refusal being a letter signed by the Minister addressed to the claimant Land Council'.[44] The terms, it turns out, do not cover an intervening ecological impediment to residential development, protected fauna, the rights of flowers, a specific colour on the map, which Moore AJ inscribes as follows: 'The plan of site constraints ... (attached to this business plan) shows clearly the various constraints but, particularly, the GPS-recorded location of occurrences of *Tetratheca juncea* in the context of the combined DA1 and DA2 proposals envisaged at this time. The figure[d] ... plan—showing the *Tetratheca juncea* clumps as purple dots—is reproduced below' (Figure 2.13).

[44] *Aboriginal Land Council*, para. 60.

In an augmenting excursion into wild jurisprudence, the land seen from the perspective of earth jurisprudence, that of a rare, low, shrub flower, also known as black-eyed Susan, precludes development. The colour purple prohibits planning permission, and here again the heavy pink accentuates and manifests a floral presence and the literal colour of judgement.[45] The diagram, because here the satellite image has been scaled and digitized on a grid system, is a plane of inscription allowing for the visual instigation of intellection, or to borrow from the diagrammatologist Sybille Krämer, it 'creates a space for the movement of thought in which theoretical entities are made visible and thus manageable. The perceptual nature of this act may be described as suddenly being able to see a nonempirical state of affairs within empirical arrangements. With regard to tactility, it means that operations of configuring and reconfiguring graphical markings simultaneously carry out ideal/intellectual operations'.[46] The Minister's signed letter is enfolded into a digital diagram, the black and white of ministerial epistolarity suddenly gets juxtaposed with a map of colours, of red, orange, brown, pink, green, purple, and turquoise. The colour purple, inscribed and installed in viral circles and clusters of intensity, provides an array of hues, tints, tinges, and tinctures that spring from the screen and give sensible life to a rare and threatened fauna, *Tetratheca juncea*. The move from monochrome linear diagram to colour and the circular representation of flowers is a move towards the figurative, to putting a face upon the abstraction, a persona, which is to say a potential right to the rule. The colour and the flower matter, they are present in the case, flashes of wild law in the heart of decision.

The argument is both that colour and inscription, code and key, the presence in *Long v State* of a passerby, the light and heavy colours, the shaded dots, the frames and markings in *Aboriginal Land Claim Council*, all shift the abstraction of the diagram with its incorporeal rules and notational patterns towards a more sensible and aesthetic appearance of subjectivity and intervention as mattering both to those affected, the indigenous community, and to the earth. The trajectory of the inscription of colour, the painting of the map, is towards the figurative and living, to matter and incorporation, and with it comes an imaginal impetus and corresponding recognition of the decisional and inventive character of the diagram and the map. The making visible and visceral of the juristic claims, depiction in colour,

[45] There are numerous other examples of colour persuading. In *Animal Welfare Institute v Beech Ridge Energy LLC* (2009) 675 F.Supp.2d 540, eFigure 5, the plaintiffs sued for an injunction to protect the Indiana bat under the Endangered Species Act, a case of bats, wind turbines, and two Federal policies. A map depicting the location of the bat in yellow for summer, blue for winter, and purple for summer and winter was particularly visually persuasive, the only and uncommented picture in the judgement. In *Courtland v Union Carbide* 2022 WL2392871, the map of toxic waste movement views rather like an encoding of threat levels, in red, orange, yellow, green, purple, and blue. All of which colouring is again part of the unsaid of the judgement.

[46] Sybille Krämer, '"The Mind's Eye": Visualizing the Non-visual and the "Epistemology of the Line"', in Elisabeth Nemeth, Richard Heinrich, and Wolfram Pichler (eds), *Image and Imaging in Philosophy, Science, and the Arts. Preproceedings of the 33rd International Wittgenstein Symposium 2* (Frankfurt: Ontos Verlag, 2013) 275–295, at 278–279.

with figures, nature, and things visible, works to sensualize thought on the cloth of the map, on the digitized page, or now in images on screen. After a long era of pure and purely lineal graphics, of graphs, monochrome schemata, genealogical trees and other stemma, equations, tables, and models, the Google satellite image, the photograph, with life and colour, increasingly propels the trajectory of mapping into an animated depiction of control and possession, of markings and inscriptions that mimic John Speed's vivid theatre of empire in clearly demonstrating the colours of law and the arrows of power. The map is the motile and mutable, mobile perception of what is there for the purposes of the case, and whether it is drawn by the cartographer or by the lens of the camera, it is matter that is seen according to the grid and inscriptions of our contemporary practices of retinal justice.

That the diagram or map involves selection and interpretation, that it reflects imposition and insertion, and bears both atmospheric influence and sensible inscription, can be further enhanced by considering the diversity of appearances and uses of maps and other diagrams in judgements. The haptic and material force of the image is nowhere better visible than in a roughly comedic juristic use. A somewhat ludic and more direct expression of similar cartographic sentiments of control and its absence can be taken from the decision in a long-running litigation over home appraisals, mortgages, lending, and trade secrets.[47] The parties' representatives had irked the judge. The pleadings were a litany of 'dirty lawyer tricks', the record replete with complaints about stalling, non-disclosure, failure to attend meetings, abusive language, 'Rambo tactics', and vexatious filings. In brief description, only one of four images appears in the signed text of the decision in *HouseCanary*, and this is significantly not a picture but the more conventional and juristically acceptable diagrammatic form of a map (Figure 2.14). The cartograph or charter shows the borders of the state of Texas, North and West, and portrays forces intruding into the state from Mexico—'foreign'—and adjoining states—migration. It is lawyers from out of state, Northerners, non-Texans, who are lowering the Bar in San Antonio. For the moment, however, the key is that the map is the only image that makes it into the text, as opposed to into the appendices where the other images, an evolutionary clock of world history, the judge's own set of rules of conduct for litigating attorneys, and a picture of Abraham Lincoln are lodged.

The use of the map as the first depiction, as part of the text, reflects its diagrammatic character and putatively schematic role as a rational representation that charts a real geography and so is presumed to escape the aesthetic and sensory qualities of images, even when, as here, it is festooned with arrows and their insinuations. It is nonetheless the legally preferred use and the most familiar and acceptable mode of depiction, even though it distorts and invents quite as much as photographs and other pictorial presentations. The history of the earth in a

[47] *HouseCanary, Inc. v Quicken Loans, Inc.* Civil Action No. SA-18-CV-0519-FB (2018).

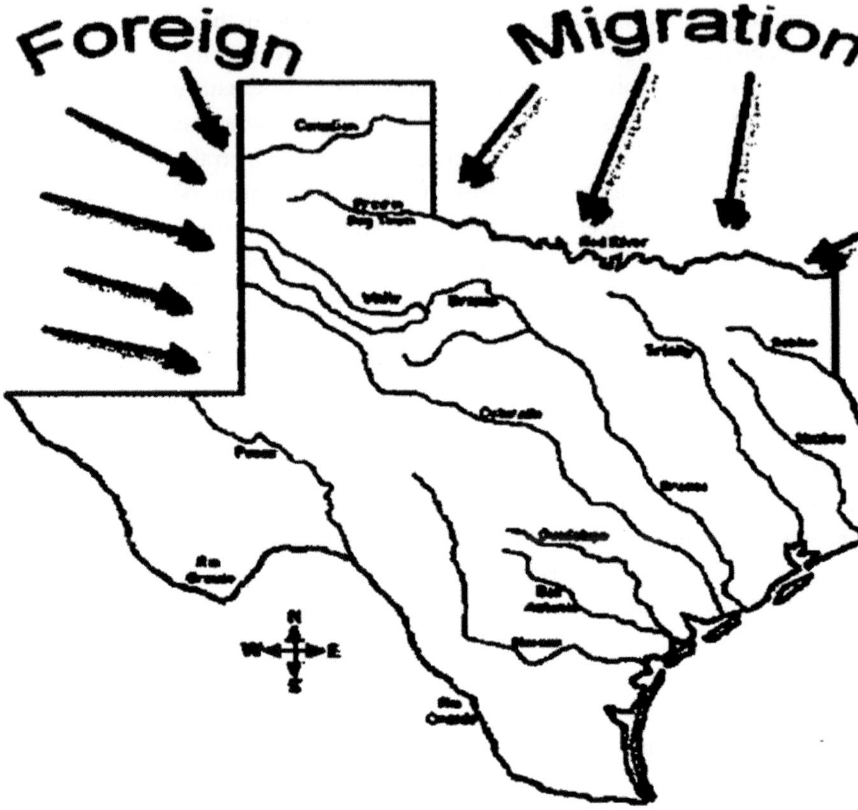

Figure 2.14 Insertion by Judge Fred Biery in *HouseCanary, Inc. v Quicken Loans, Inc* (2018).

24-hour clock and the cliché image of Lincoln dourly discouraging wasteful litigation do not have the same privilege of access to and concurrence with the legal text, and so are cautiously secreted at the end of the judgement as appendices. Be it noted, however, that they are there, extant and visible in the order handed down. They are inserted into the literary pickle jar of precedent and comprise part of a rapidly increasing corpus of visual reasons for decisions that require excision, classification, exposure, and analysis.

The image covers over a void, a gap in reason and text that necessitates a novel form and alternative expression. It shows what cannot be said. Most obviously the map that Judge Biery inserts introduces a series of affects and signals a distinct set of reasons for the decision and order. The map is in this context, as a facet of the precedent, on its surface, a jointure of irony, comedy, and remonstration. It used to be, the judge opines, that lawyers in San Antonio all knew each other and resolved disputes with handshakes but now counsel 'immigrate into Texas, as shown in this illustration'. To this he adds 'Texans you are guarding the wrong river'.[48] The reference mixes nostalgia, melancholy, and humour with frustration and an element of satire which is accentuated by a rather self-conscious quotation from the movie *Star Wars*.[49] The reference to the extra-terrestrial is also a signal of the alien and the theme of the movie, which is of opposed warring forces, darkness encroaching upon and threatening the existence of the good, the white, the Texan, the South. It is still the case, visually, in racial terms, that there are more arrows descending on Texas from the foreign than from the Northern States. What is shown is never exactly what is said.

Rhetorically an enigma, a reference to external and unacknowledged sources, the diagram, like all maps, creates a subject and stakes a claim. The depiction is in the shape of Texas and evidences a jurisdiction, possession in a somewhat retro form of actual as distinct from virtual geography. It makes, however, the jealous point that this is, as stated, ours. Foreign and immigrant forces press upon 'our' sovereignty and intrude into 'our' state, threatening the standing of Texas and the proprieties of the bench and bar. The image delineates an imaginary jurisdiction, a space of disparate identity, and an isolarion is inserted that wills itself pure and free of external threat, resistant to incursion. The diagram shows more. The foreign and the immigrant are imminent, pressing against the borders, about to invade. The nine pointers, the foreigners being a greater threat or at least more numerous than the immigrant attorneys, represent war, the arrows are the mode of belligerent communication, the messengers of the enemy that pierce the skin and kill, or break through the border and overrun. That was the fate of King Harold at the Battle of Hastings, 1066 and all that, and such seems to be the judge's fear for the fate of Texas, not the belligerent Normans but the ill-mannered Normativos.

The image expresses a sensibility and shows an apprehension of siege and invasion which recalls directly the separation of the South from the North, the American civil war being referenced as well by the figure of Abraham Lincoln that is reproduced in the appendix. It is significant, however, that it is the diagram of Texas, a jurisdictional portrayal, a linear graphic representation of a place that inaugurates the other text, the visual depictions that differentiate and diversify the rhetorical force of the decision. There is the appearance of reason, the schematic modality of the diagram is transitional in being linear but figural, verbal and visual, containing the rational instruments of names of places and a compass if not a coda or key. Reason is mixed with the aesthetic of a picture, juvenile though this cartoon figure may seem, the visual with the verbal, and so a third epistemic space and rhetorical illocution of possibility is created, an interruption—a *metastasis*—of the textual relay necessarily occurs.

[48] *HouseCanary* at 4. The image is also used, but in the earlier instance with the addition of some colour, in *Aquifer Guardians in Urban Areas v. FH.A* 779 F. Supp. 2d 542 (2011).

[49] Ibid. at 4: 'A long time ago in a galaxy far, far away'. A footnote is appended to reference the source.

Judge Biery, as we have seen, is certainly not alone in the trend of using maps, granted the ease of reproduction and the familiar and comforting character of these diagrammatic, emblematically viserbal insertions. The immediate point is that the map in the text of the judgement gives the chart a precedential status and weight of legal reason as an acceptable image, a permissible figure, rhetorically an icon, that is licit, more than anything else by virtue of the limitation of its aesthetic and its linear sensibility. The other images, the photographs and pdfs of texts, are placed below the reasoning of the judgement in footnotes and appendices. Only the map is in the text, but does not itself generate any textual discussion qua image. It retains its classical legal status as a depiction that is not an image, or at least it is one that is only part portrayal, and so only very marginally transgressive of the *litera mortua* of strict law. The map renders the spherical flat and reifies boundaries from the Euro-American perspective of the Texan judge. The lines become absolute. The incoming arrows are visible threats to the arbitrary borders, viewed through the unifying gaze of judgement. The image of us, the fiction of the state, has to be maintained, the inhabitants inside the lines have to be protected from foreigners and immigrants, each of whom is potentially *flèche* or arrow that pierces and may kill the native flesh. What the map depicts most clearly is what Judge Kozinski in *Tirado* only shows, namely that the cartograph as homogeneous and objective insertion is actively projecting a bifurcated world trapped in a hierarchical logic that opposes self to other, superior to inferior, continuum and rupture drawn onto the dematerialized plane of the map.

The other key feature to the decision in *HouseCanary* is that the non-linear depictions, the photograph of Abraham Lincoln, the picture of the 'History of Earth in a 24 hour clock', and the judge's humorous assertion of 'The Rule for the Practice of Law' in the form of a pdf, all appear subsequent to the signed judgement. They are paradoxically present yet excluded, a footnote and appendices that both support and destabilize the judgement. It may be that the judge includes these marginalia as paratexts because he views them as incidental and only loosely related to the logic of judgement. Such a perception has a surface appeal, but it ignores the more important feature which is that these are pictures, not linear modes of mapping. It is the photographic, prosopographic, and screenshot character of the insertions that distinguishes them and unsettles the form as well as the logic of the decision. The photograph, as with the satellite Google earth images in the earlier cases, is not a map, it is not a monochrome linear depiction or diagram and, as argued above, it exponentially expands the scope and scale of the investigation. The technology makes the earth, the face, the corpora, and the materiality of the decision appear. Initially, as in *HouseCanary*, in footnote and appendix but increasingly the photograph and various digital images take over and supplant the map, just as the black-eyed Susan in *Aboriginal Land Claim* emerged in colour in the judgement and provided the ground of decision, the real of the environment stalling the epistolary inscription of the Crown Minister's arguments for denial.

The collision of the graphic with the photographic is juristically perceived initially as a confrontation between the linear and the figurative. The map accedes to the logic of textuality, to *ratio scripta*, but the photograph exceeds and intervenes in that logic. The satellite image of the earth brings the world into the text and disrupts the complacently literal view of the cartograph. The intersection of the map with the photograph is the next stage or moment of development in the passage of images into judicial precedential decisions, and so I will move to two examples of such an interface of modes of representation as a key to understanding the emergence of judicial imagery into the light of day—*in piena luce*—and in formal contestation of the text. Thus, in *Chan Chuen v Forestside Ltd*, the claim was one of adverse possession, here of coastal land that the defendant sought to develop.[50] The plaintiffs claimed ownership by exclusive occupation of three lots of land, against the Company which had obtained paper title to the land in 1992. Heard before the High Court, Judge Kwok began with the question of maps: 'at my request the parties produced a sketch for the purpose of showing the relative positions of the lots in dispute. Image C below is a reproduction of the agreed sketch' (Figure 2.15). The judge then acknowledges that 'the parties stressed that [the] Images do not show the precise demarcation of the lots in the Disputed Land'. The map is in other words ambiguous, or, given the number of lots, enigmatic. It does not show the relevant land except indicatively and in relation to other land, and even the colouring is disputed, as what is described as coloured in pink is corrected by the judge who stipulates that 'the actual colouring ... is in red instead of pink'.[51] A map without defined contours, blurred lines, shading whose colour is judicially redefined, suggests that the map is more an object of attachment, a therapeutic device providing a sense of reality than it is a demonstrative reason or correspondence to any concrete actuality. The sketch is sketchy, destabilized already by the Judge, a peripheral item and lot. The images are haphazard, incidental, of poor quality, shaded and then agreed by the parties only to be abandoned as irrelevant when Judge Kwok announces that the plaintiffs are lying and their claim is based on fraud.

To prove ownership by exclusive occupation requires proof of *animus possidendi*, which in essence means use and management of the land manifesting intent to own. The plaintiffs endeavoured to prove such by asserting cultivation of the land, farming, and rearing of ducks along with the erection of a gate to keep others out. The claims made were repelled by the judge as blatantly untrue, disproved by witness testimony but also by a photograph, Image 4, of one of the lots that she claimed to own by extended occupation (Figure 2.16). It appears as an addendum to the report, as an incidental addition, an appendix, even though it is stated to show proof positive of non-occupancy and the falsity of the plaintiff's claims:

[50] *Chan Chuen v Forestside Limited* High Court of Hong Kong HCA 2055/2011 (2016).
[51] *Chan Chuen*, para. 32.

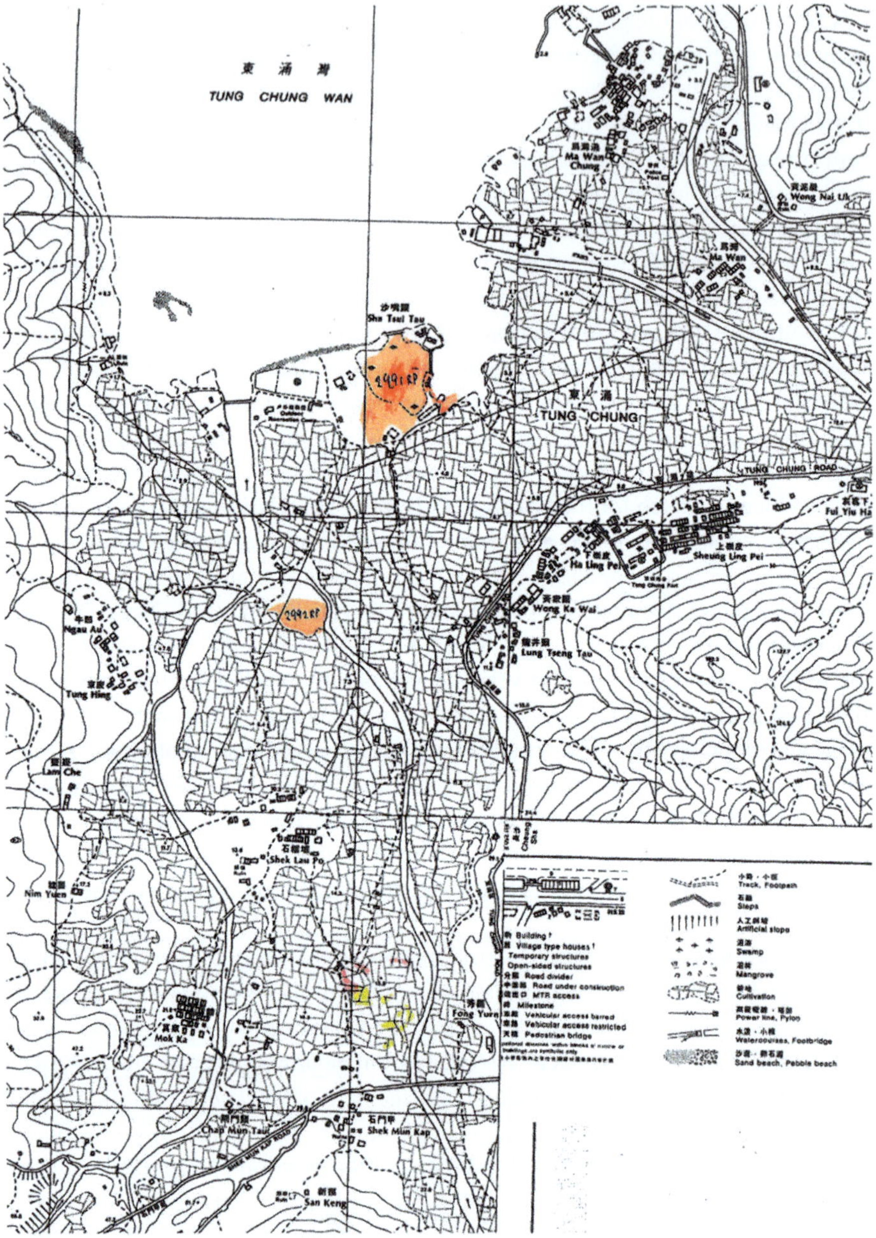

Figure 2.15 Insertion by Deputy High Court Judge Kwok in *Chan Chuen v Forestside Limited* (2016).

Figure 2.16 Insertion by Deputy High Court Judge Kwok in *Chan Chuen v Forestside Limited* (2016).

'The following is an example of blatant lying by Tang ... she was shown page 1703 of the hearing bundles, a photographic image of Lot 2991 (RP)'. That is all. No further analysis, no need for explanation or interpretation. The photograph shows the real, it is what it represents. We can note, however, that the photograph is reproduced sideways in the appendix to the decision, standing on its head in the papers. Significantly, it is not a photograph at all. It is a collage of five photographs with annotations indicating Lot number, construction site, and football ground. The image has been pieced together to show us what we know already and to give the judgement the appearance of reality and the veracity of seen facts. A viserbalizing of the lot and of the judgement. The reality effect is a first impression, a cursory viewing, a unitary and unifying approach to the object shown as if it were a singularity made visible by map and photographs and quite distinct from how it was fabricated, who it was that made it, and the fashion or fiction that presented it in the form used in court and incorporated into judgement. What is key, however, is the transition from graphic, shaded map to photographs of place. The new technology of visual depiction of place as a complement or here a substitute for the map, a picture taking the place of graphic linearity, signals a transition in the medium of decision from the atlas to the photogram, line to image and text to picture. The visible displaces the verbal but it does so in an unthought manner, so far emerging without critical apparatus, scrutation of composition, or apprehension of colour and annotations, sources and perspectives.

The incidental or secondary character of the image is paradoxical. The map, being diagrammatic and lineal, is an acceptable image only insofar as its imagistic character can be ignored and its significance aligned in advance through the presuppositions of the textual analysis. The photographic image too appears here to matter only insofar as it does not matter, or more directly, to the extent that it does not challenge the discourse that precedes it. The installation of the image, the aesthetic act of picturing place and placing depictions in the decision, is largely by means of methodological stealth, covert operations, and the fiction so common to common law that this is already the case, the custom and practice whose reasons are so familiar as to be forgotten. This is not to say that the image is immaterial, quite the opposite, it matters in multiple senses and the plural role that it plays in motivating decision, in demonstrating judgement, in materializing the corporeal and tellurian sites of events and encounters requires skill in aesthetics, a knowledge of legal history and a critical conception of the remediation of law in the affective relay of images.

A concluding example can be extracted from a further instance, a decision in which the judge inserts both a map and a photograph, in the juristically intriguing Australian case of *Clare and Ors v Bedelis.* The issue was one of a restrictive covenant upon land, by which purchasers of property were prohibited from 'erecting any dwelling house other than one having walls of brick or stone and being not more than one storey in height'.[52] A fifty-two-page judgement ensues, primarily on the question of what is a storey, and latterly what is a brick front – cladding or solid brick. It follows in a lengthy line of cases of ontological as well as epistemic definition of issues such as what is a roof,[53] what is a building,[54] what is a 'building site',[55] what is a 'dwelling house',[56] what is a floor,[57] and similar architectural conundrums. The answer comes with a judicial excursion both literal and metaphoric: 'An image of a subject often conveys a meaning more effectively than a description. The picture below was taken by me on Friday 17 June 2016. The house depicted is, in my view, not more than one story [sic] in height' (Figure 2.17).[58] The story at issue in the case is one of height and dimension as well as of interpretation of the purpose of the covenant, and in that context the picture is somewhat surprising. It is not that the judge himself took the photograph. It is not that the judge, having taken and placed the photograph in evidence, simply says that, 'in my view', according that is to the photograph that he took, the *plan subjectif* of the camera eye, it is not more than one storey, although the insertion of my view and my picture does personalize the perspective. What is significant and all too common is that there is no further analysis of the image. Here the house photographed is

[52] *Clare and Ors v Eva Bedelis* [2016] VSC 381 p. 4 para. 17

[53] On what is a roof, see *Health Service Executive v Brookshore Ltd* [2010] IEHC 165, at para. 1.

[54] On what is a building, see *R (on the Application of Ghai) v Newcastle City Council* [2009] EWHC 978 (Admin).

[55] On what is a building site, *Clark v Wodehouse* 669 P.2d 101 (1983).

[56] On what is a dwelling house, see *Downie v Lockwood* [1965] VR 257.

[57] On what is a floor, see *Leichhardt Municipal Council v Daniel Callaghan Pty Ltd* (1981) 46 LGRA 29 (holding that a floor is a storey).

[58] *Clare and Ors* p 34 para. 84.

Figure 2.17 Insertion by Associate Justice Derham in *Clare and Ors v Eva Bedelis* [2016].

the issue and so the story of whether it is one storey or not requires, if it is to be visually determined as the judge evidently desires, some account of what is seen, as opposed to the bare assertion that 'he', His Honour Associate Justice David Mark Brudenell Derham, views it as one storey when what he has photographed is clearly, as digitally captured, on the right side, two storeys, albeit on an incline. The photograph transpires in fact to be entirely misleading, and his perceptual remark unhelpful in deciding because it shows an irrelevant view and perspective upon the house.

Tucked away, secreted, almost hidden at the end of the judgement, is a plan of the properties subject to the single storey restrictive covenant, the lots being outlined in blue (Figure 2.18). The house at issue is shaded in yellow and is on the incline which the photograph indicates as sloping down from Yvonne Court toward Halcyon Drive. What is significant about the plan shown is that it indicates what the covenant is to protect, namely the view from behind the building so that Waverly Glen retains an unimpeded vista of a panoramic horizon. The photograph from the front of the house thus provides no direct evidence of whether one or more storeys are visible from the rear. A picture from the rear of the house, or a map with contour lines, tabulation of elevation, and view would be necessary for a properly visual and adequately depicted representation of the issue to be determined. There are other questions raised, such as whether the garage is within the definition of a dwelling house and so to be counted in the vertical ascension of the property. The judge also poses a hypothetical, that of whether the property would

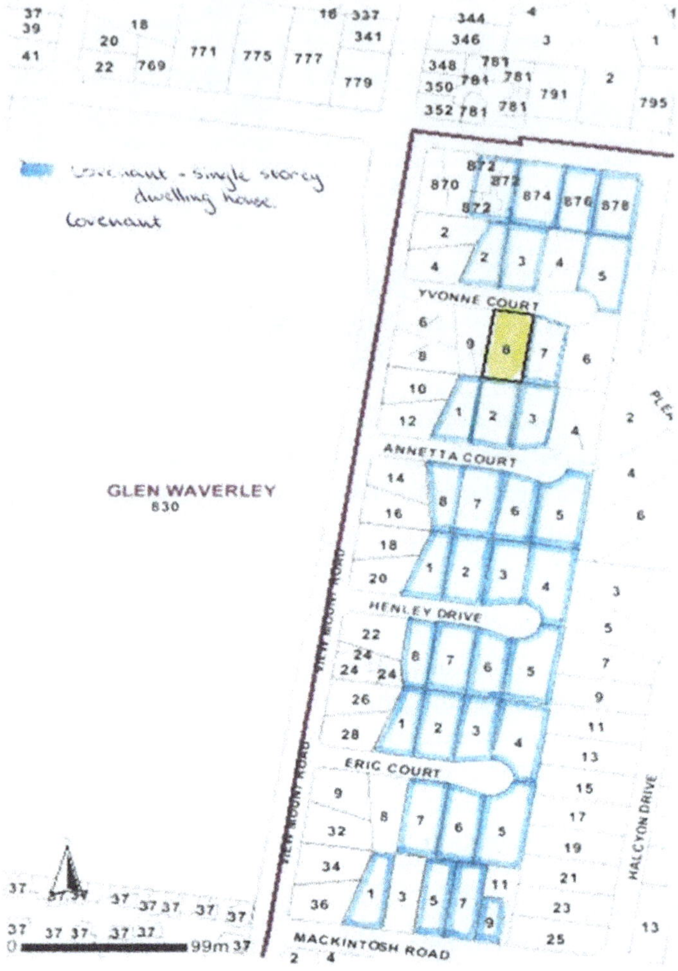

Figure 2.18 Insertion by Associate Justice Derham in *Clare and Ors v Eva Bedelis* [2016].

be deemed two storeys if rather than a garage there were simply piers or pillars without walls and open to the elements holding the latter portion of the property level with the rest of the dwelling.

The judge, to his credit, or by inadvertence, we cannot say, shows the photograph of that aspect of the house least favourable to his determination and most likely to be viewed as two storeys. More to the point, however, the photograph is viewed as transparent, it is simply deemed to be what it shows without any account of apparatus, perspective, choice of exposure, focus, resolution, field of view, angle, height, and all of the other facets of framing, scanning, and locating that make up the composite of this *dispositif* or close up of the facia of a house. This, however, is to date the most usual judicial method of apprehending, proffering a reading of the surfaces of images, the story they wish to tell, and in this case also the storey that has to be counted. Returning to the judgement, the judicial apprehension of the purpose of viewing is significant: 'It is impossible to construe this, or any, covenant, in a completely abstract way'. In a spirit not far removed from the new materialism, the approach is one which refuses to countenance an abstract or in jurisprudential argot 'purely' theoretical analysis. 'It cannot be done in the abstract', the judge reiterates, it is a question of construction that requires context, factual assessment, purpose, topograpy, lie of the land, neighbourhood, the nature and physical characteristics of the housing in the vicinity, and most important of all, the repeatedly used term, 'my view'. Part of the question is posed as that of how these factors will impact 'any dwelling house that can, sensibly, be built on the Land'.[59] There is, in other words, no literal meaning to the word storey in the covenant. The decision has to be particular and the word read in light of the end for which it was designed.

The photograph then is a very partial view of the building and offers no dispositive information as to whether the restrictive covenant has been breached. The judge in fact acknowledges that it is not directly pertinent to the questions to be resolved: 'the house under construction on the Land, and the house it replaced, has only a single level in [the] part of the house to the rear, on the southern side, of the lot. Thus, whether or not there is a sub floor at the front of the lot facing Yvonne Court will not have any impact on the properties to the south'.[60] There is acknowledgement as well of another apprehension and inspection of the property and its context in relation to the meaning of 'brick or stone': 'In my unaccompanied view of the Land and neighbourhood, it became apparent that the bulk of the houses were constructed with an external appearance of brick ... the overall appearance of the neighbourhood was that the houses were substantial in size and built of brick whether that was solid brick or brick veneer could not be seen'.[61] In both cases, what is seen is not what is at issue and in dispute. The subject of determination is

[59] *Clare & Ors* para. 69
[60] *Clare & Ors*, para. 36 d.
[61] *Clare & Ors*, para. 112.

invisible. Impressions of adjoining or tangential aspects are figured in the images and stipulated to be all that can be visually evidenced. The height of the building is of relevance only from the rear, which is not photographed, and the material used for construction of the building, which is also not photographed, although the judge does indicate that he has, in an unaccompanied manner, conducted a visual inspection of the neighborhood and buildings but cannot discern if the brick used is veneer or solid. So why report viewings that provide non-probative impressions, and why post a photograph that is of something other than the view necessary to deciding if the restrictive covenant has been infracted?

The answer lies in the legal history of the image, the *ius imaginum*, which dictates that the pictorial depiction is an end point, the *non plus ultra* where questioning terminates in the screening of the void with an image. This is why Justice Twinfeet in Flann O'Brien's narrative wants a guard for the maps. They are precious images, arcane juridical figures, legitimatory depictions into which genealogy of validity the photograph is inserted. Borrowing from Pierre Legendre, 'the image is the dogma' because it is that which requires no authorization beyond its own manifestation. This means that the image represents what is not there, it is in theological terms the trace of an absence, the materialization of an immaterial being, the manifestation of the invisible cause. The classic trinity is that of *vestigium, imago, similitudo*—vestige, image, likeness.[62] The paradox of the judge's inquiry into the height of the house is thus twofold. First, he inserts a photograph that he has taken on an excursion. The photograph is a vestige of the building, a materialization in a virtual form of something that is not present. The depiction presences absence, manifesting what the judge cannot formulate in words. The photograph is thus a materialization but in the form of a trace of something that cannot be seen in court. It is matterphorical in the alternate sense that it matters to the decision and provides a material presence of the structure, albeit as a vestige, in the forum of the text. In this instance it is the map, the plan of the lots covered by the covenant, that is the most probative picture, but it is the photograph and the sense of place, the ambulatory viewing of the neighbourhood and property that drives the decision. The vision that precedes the photograph is what seems to have been most determinative. It is the feel of the place, the affective apprehension of the neighbourhood, the extancy and environment of the property that motivates the decision. Second, in being a photograph of something other than the view of the house from the rear, the aspect that is covered by the restrictive covenant in the interpretation adopted by the Court, the picture repeats the essential invisibility of the ultimate source of decision, providing a symptom or clue rather than the drive of judgement itself. There is only the plan of the subdivision

[62] Pierre Legendre, *God in the Mirror: A Study of the Institution of Images* (London: Routledge, 2019) at 79. The sources return to Bonaventura, *De Potentia* 1.9 art. 9 c; through Thomas Aquinas, *Summa Theologica* q. 4 a. 3; q. 45 a. 7; q. 93 a. 2, 6.

that will show the rear of the property, but the judicial eye, the sensible body, the skin that touched the surfaces and apprehended the atmosphere of the vicinity is what moves the decision. The photograph thus represents a trace of the structure that is the object and projection of the judgement. What matters to the decision, however, is not that this is a trace, not even that the image is a likeness, but that it marks the judge's presence and embeds both photograph and photographer in the matter of judgement. David Mark Brudenell Derham was there and in being there, in empirical experience, as witnessed by the photograph of what the judicial eye saw, can act as a legitimation, supported juridically by the insertion of an annotated and coloured map of the location in question.

The other image, for the plan is clearly a depiction, with a handwritten note and color scheme, is only referenced directly in a footnote. It is a sensible diagram that maps the location of the property, provides a scale, the names of the roads, the numbers of the plots, and a compass indicating north. The diagrammatic plan can render the problem of storeys part of a numerical collocation: 'The plaintiffs ... claim to have the benefit of a covenant burdening the land owned by the defendant at 8 Yvonne Court, Wheelers Hill, being Lot 46 on the plan of subdivision 26647 and the land more particularly described in Certificate of Title Volume 8131 Folio 781'.[63] The problem remains one of visibility. Can lots 1, 2, and 3 of Annetta Court to the south, and lot 7 of Yvonne Court to the north east, view over the yellow shaded lot 8, the house photographed by the judge from the north side on Yvonne Court, or could they be said to impede the view? The plan is composed of lines, colours, numbers, compass points, street names, with an annotation or key as to the significance of blue shading. It shows no houses, no heights, no view, but rather flattens the dispute, turning lawscape and geography into text, as the judge lengthily expounds on the angles, directions, viewpoints, and construction of properties that exist only as numbers and two-dimensional geometric shapes on a flat page. The map is reduced to being a vehicle for text, its aesthetic and sensible qualities subordinate to the drive of an enumerated linear scriptural judicial description of terrain from a viewpoint neither depicted in the photograph nor available from the plan.

The story of the storeys is multiply pertinent and leads to the inclusion of two images, plan and photograph, to subtend and screen the subject of judgement. There is an appearance of the real as the end point and last ditch of decision. This is the point of dogma. One cannot go through the images, they are presented as last instances, points of conclusion that are equally vanishing signs giving way to the text of the precedent. The image as dogma is apodictic, meaning that whether in the form of a maxim, a custom inherited from time immemorial, or an image and similitude, it is a given and is not to be challenged. There is a point where

[63] *Clare & Ors*, para. 2.

reason runs out and, as the early lawyers were wont to say, authority is more important than truth. This is because the sovereign, or the judge as the delegate of the sovereign, as the case may be, has to see what is not there and can only represent this in the form of image and faith. The closest we can come to the ground of a decision is that aspect of the earth that appears in the judgement, the image as the vision and invention of determination. It takes us closer, as near as it is possible to get to the visceral, incarnadine source of deciding. The picture of the storeys is the start of the story, the narrative, metonymically conveyed through the plan, and the photograph, inserted in the judgement. Vision generates decision and the novelty of technologies that now facilitate placing images into precedent judgements allows for a much more direct and material analysis of the role of these visual fictions, of the unaccompanied view, of photograph, or emoji, meme, gif, and other Instagrams, screen captures, and animatrix in the triggering of legal reason as if they are maps of the subject of judgement.

The building is a structure and has a façade, a face, that can be photographed. This provides a sense of the real and a mask for the judge to wear. What can be seen hides what is unseen and so allows for the staging of the drama of the case, which is itself, ironically enough, about vision and the ability to see over buildings but not being able to see though them. The element of staging is the key to apprehending the significance of the advent of pictures in judgements. It indicates the series of performative moments of enactment that the law engages. The movement from map to diagram to photogram and satellite digital relay tracks a trajectory from partial approximations of place captured in cartographs and, on occasion cartouches, to the contemporary imaginal replications of the real which more affectively and effectively insert the participants into the sensible space of decision. The judge goes to take a photograph and to perambulate in the neighbourhood, amongst the buildings, to get a sense and to relay a sensibility, lawscape and atmosphere. The judge steps out of their office, enters the world, returns with it, *in imagine*, to the court. The image is proof of having looked, of having faced the abyss of the real and covered the infinite regress of origin with a trace of what was seen. The depiction is in this sense a skin, an integument that closes off any further discussion because 'here it is', the house, the issue, the one storey, although of course it isn't there, merely the trace, the covering of what cannot be seen. To borrow from Ovid and the myth of Narcissus, 'he thinks he sees a body, which is but a shadow' and yet while this trace lacks substance, it nonetheless inflames and is the object of desire.[64] The image introduces affect both in that it identifies through vision and in that it projects the viewer spectrally into the viewed. The depiction, flat, prosaic, cluttered, ordinary, nonetheless excites the senses and triggers the desire of both seeing and being seen in the judge and in the

[64] Ovid, *Metamorphoses* Bk 111. at 417–419.

viewer of the judgement. The image becomes the coda of decision, the identifiable and transferential—technically tralatitious—point of judgement in which we are drawn to see what the judge saw and attach to the principal and the principle the visual axiom and depicted dogma that founds the reasoning that supports the verdict.[65]

The examples of diagrammatic forms and maps used in this chapter are intentionally extreme so as to accentuate the principle of translation from one medium to another and the diffraction of media that they imply. There are numerous examples of remediation that can be adduced of maps and Google Earth pictures, plans, and schemata that are used to show a boundary between properties, the site of an event, the point or intersection where collision or contretemps took place, the route of delivery or possibilities of access. The point to be stressed is that these images seem to be, and are presented as if they are simply denotative, the equivalent of linguistic signs which reference a cartographic reality and a familiar linearity that prompts an ease of insertion into judgements and unquestioning viewing of what is deemed a mere illustration of the textual argument. The form of the map or satellite image does not generate discussion, the emergence of the imaginal in the judicial awaits its proper cross examination.[66] The apparent self-evidence of depiction is the conduit for unexamined arguments and affects, epistemic contraband instigated by sight. The familiar appears to be obvious but it is useful to recollect that the etymology is *ob viam*, that which is in the way, impeding and exposed, something that is as likely to trip up as to accelerate or facilitate. The notion of illustration belies the change of medium and the unthought quality of obviousness, the fact that the image lustrates, it shines and introduces a vivified depiction, a material revision of the subject of judgement.

The image, as Ovid also points out, is always more than it seems. This, in contemporary terms, is because the image is apprehended distinctly and viewed differently. It is not text, and indeed from the perspective of reading, the words float in the space of the image because what is seen is subject to spectral modes of viewing. The ambulation of the eye in looking is non-linear, it wanders, traverses, darts in and out, moves laterally, changing focus, scotomizing, registering, glancing, blinking, thinking in its own figurative form. The principle of looking is in many respects sciographic, a dance of shadows, a play of concentration and relaxation, an associative flitting across surfaces, an oneiric modality or thinking in reverie that Bachelard delineates in terms of the imagination of matter.[67] A body

[65] Tralatitious, from the Latin *tra[n]latus*, is the term used in scriptural exegesis for knowledge handed down or passed on from generation to generation. It shares its root with translation and is cognate with tradition. The image is peculiarly tralatatious in that it transfers and translates from one medium to another while maintaining the appearance of tradition and of handing on.

[66] See Jessica Silbey, 'Cross-Examining Film', 8 *University of Maryland Journal of Race, Religion, Gender and Class* (2008) 17–46, and also Silbey, 'Persuasive Visions: Film and Memory' 10 *Law, Culture and the Humanities* 24 (2014).

[67] Gaston Bachelard, *Earth and Reveries of Will* [1943] (Dallas: Dallas Institute, 2002)

looks at a material form, in an atmosphere and environment of sensible impressions, of insufflation and exhalation, both viewer and viewed alive and mobile in their lawspaces, within a scopic regime and sensibility, opening and closing as does the body, human, non-human, transhuman, viewed and looking back.

Retinal justice, the equity of the eye, proposes a distinct and different avenue of apprehension and analysis into the juridical text. It draws upon a separate gallery of images and relays a visual trajectory and imaginal sense of the subjects of doctrine and dispute. Where previously the jurisprudence of precedent distinguished *ratio decidendi* and *obiter dictum*, the binding rule of judgement from the observations made along the way, the novel transition to imagery suggests that the accompanying and in some cases determinative distinction is that between the *imago decidendi* and *obiter depicta*, the vision of decision and things seen along the way. Here the apparatus of decision operates in a necessarily aesthetic and imaginative ocular modality because the introduction of pictures inserts sense and sensibility into the epistemic paradigm and narrative form of the juridical text. Poetic justice is subtended by the retinal apprehension of subject matter, and by the affect and imagination of seeing, accompanied as it is by colour, where clips and links are inserted, by sound and motion as well. These are not incidental, nor are they irrelevant either to the legal value of the precedent or to the allure and attachment that the text can promote in persuasion.

The path charted is that of the persistence of the plan, the longevity of the cartographic in the textual as the covert model, first historical and then theoretical, of the sensible depiction of the real in graphic, diagrammatic, coloured, and coded form. The map is the dogma, the originary ontographic picturing of scene and event in what law takes to be a final and unassailable mode. The roots of the judicial use of images in the earlier form of mapping presume a correspondence theory of truth in which the presence of the image is predicated on the lineal representation of an external reality, an empirical actuality which is certain because it is now depicted in diagrammatic form. Obviously such certitude has come increasingly under critical scrutiny and challenge, but it is essential to recognize the epistemic roots of the judicial visual *certum* in the charter of proprietary rights, territory, and jurisdiction, in plans of buildings, in the quasi-textual presumptions of lineal depiction that particularize the subject matter of the case. The contrast of *certum* to *verum* is somewhat lost in law, insofar as the spiritual truth of legality is presumed to underpin and support the fabrication of the *certum*, in the form of the visualization or in Kelsen's earlier language the concretization of the norm in the territory. Against such cartographic and proprietary presuppositions, a critical curation of judicial imagery has to start from the acquisitive drive of the imaginal inscription and its motivating endeavour, which is that of screening and controlling the object viewed. To map is to make a claim, to shade and figure an encounter, and not simply to reproduce an externality. It is with such a genealogy in mind that the surprising path of the decisional uses of images moves next to the unwittingly affective propensity that the remediation that advances from maps to pictures introduces in their initial precedential instigations. As the pictures that judges increasingly insert are not cartographs, warrants, or maps, and are no longer simply lineal, but figural representations, they are introduced incidentally, as nosegays and flourishes, as epistemic ornaments and most frequently as persuasive surplusage, as depictive pabulum in the textual judgement.

3
Surplusage
Out of an Abundance of Words

The surprising feature of the morphology of the judicial image from cartographic to diagrammatic and schematic to ever more figurative pictorial visualizations is the ancillary and often non-probative if not directly misleading quality of the images inserted into judgements. That is the cautel, the stringent caution with which the investigation of retinal justice has to proceed. The reality effect is precisely imaginal rather than real. This is not to say, as adumbrated earlier, that the depictions do not exist or lack ontology, but only that their status is a floating and plural one, neither real nor merely imaginary but extant spectrally and diversely between, and independent of, any direct embedding in the methodologies of knowing and being as textually governed. The reality effect is a marching order, a motivation and legitimation of a judgement whose principal manifestation or direct exposition is presented as taking place discursively, elsewhere and otherwise. The visualization, the putative *certum* of seeing, is in excess of the text and seldom discussed in detail, as opposed to being presented as mute eloquence or silent testimony as incidental proof in the form of the self-evidence of reference because in the last instance you show what cannot be said. The image is then a clue, a symptom, or using the Morellian method it is precisely the incidental and accidental features of the work, the marginal image, inserted or equally frequently appended or hyperlinked to the judgement, that provides the best clue as to the ground of decision, the *inventio* of the determination.[1] Paradoxically its relevance is its apparent irrelevance, its role as symptom and index, as clue. Juristically, used often enough in early case law in relation to the proper construction of causes of action and statutory phrases, the appellation for such ancillary features of judgement is surplusage *ex abundantia*, or superfluity out of abundance.

Starting from the common law principles that define the doctrine of *stare decisis* and the interpretation of precedent, it is the textual analogy that binds subsequent courts as the rule of law to be derived from the case. As was evident with maps, the methodology of interpretation by textual analogy—*procedere ad similia*—meant that the charter or cartograph was present simply to provide an element of further definition and demonstration in graphic pictorial form to the inaesthetic or strict

[1] The coining of the Morellian method of detecting art forgeries as a fitting description of Freud's approach to analysis comes famously from Carlo Ginsberg, *Myths, Emblems, Clues* (London: Hutchinson, 1990).

Judicial Uses of Images. Peter Goodrich, Oxford University Press.
© Peter Goodrich (2023). DOI: 10.1093/oso/9780192848772.003.0003

reason of scriptural elaboration.[2] The linear representation of the territory was aligned with and reduced to the discursive designations, and so was a matter of abundance but not of superfluity. The marginal depiction added reinforcement to the literal definition without producing any change or variation. This leads to the principle of precedent, and to the path to be followed here, that if images are to be included in judgements then it is to prior case law, and more specifically to the rules that govern additions to the text in the form first of verbal surplusage and now extra pictorial insertions.

Analysis should begin with the legal concept of textual excess. In historical terms the reference is to the juristically ambiguous in the sense of words that have two meanings, distinguished from the plurality of meanings which was defined as enigma. In early case law, *ex abundantia* is often similar to *ex gratia*, signifying that a promise was made without anything being given in exchange. Thus in *Sydenham and Worlington's* case, Justice Rhodes disallows an action in contract, stating 'but if the servant hath wages given him, and the master, *ex abundantia* ... promiseth him ten pounds after his service ended, the same promise shall not maintain an *assumpsit*'. Justice Periam confirms the point, namely that 'contract is derived *con & trahere*, which is a drawing together', whereas *ex abundantia* involves a benevolent gesture or gratuitous act.[3] What is intriguing from the perspective of images is that the gesture *ex abundantia* is as much disassociative as conjunctive; it indicates largesse and extension rather than incorporation or contraction. The new mediatized environment of exponentially accelerating images and their availability to court personnel and judges precisely suggests a plenitude and plethora of accessible images, the smash and grab of screenshots potentially constituting a one-way street, a unilateral expansion rather than a concordance or a critically examined and deliberatively measured exchange of media or remediation.

In its broader sense as an interpretative principle, in construing documents and statutes, the courts favour constructions that exclude surplusage, excess of words, and so find a nuance of meaning that the abundant word proffers. For reasons not dissimilar to those that refuse legal enforcement to promises of payment *ex abundantia*, the extra words are either taken to coalesce with the judicial construction of the clause, adding no variance of significance, or they are excluded as superfluity. Thus in *Marriot and Pascall's Case* from 1588, the addition of the Latin *nuper*, meaning recently, to a lease reading *Hospitalis Henrici septimi Regis H. 7* did not invalidate a lease that read *Hospitalis Henrici septimi nuper Regis Angliæ*. The variance was without substance, and so 'this word (nuper) is surplusage

[2] For an extended recent discussion of the same as the different, and an emphatic refusal of the *præsumptio similitudinis*, see Pierre Legrand, *Negative Comparative Law: A Strong Programme for Weak Thought* (Cambridge: Cambridge University Press, 2022) at 232 et seq.

[3] *Sydenham and Worlington's Case* (1585) Godbolt 32, 78 Eng. Rep. 20.

ex abundantia'.[4] Where meaning is augmented—specified—rather than changed, then surplusage is construed as a synonym. As it is formulated in *Croft v Howel*, in relation to the word craft in a conveyance, 'the abundance of the word craft' which was not in the original document is 'only matter of surplusage, for (Craft) and (Mystery) are all one, and of one sense, &c'.[5] While it might seem that the prolixity is nugatory, the opposite is the case, and it is only if the word adds definition that it can be incorporated into and included in the proper document as a synonym that adds precision but not difference to the instrument. The symbolæograph, to use the correct term, has to be precisely worded without significant variance, addition, misprision, or omission. What that means for proper construction is that in the overwhelming bulk of cases, the judge seeks to find a meaning in abundance and to incorporate that term, thereby extinguishing the surplusage which is otherwise viewed as illicit extension and ground for invalidation in the strict reading of early instruments.

In more modern case law, surplusage is to be avoided wherever possible, as a matter of principle. If a word has been used, or in our case an image inserted, then there is a reason for that, and it cannot properly be construed as juristic surplusage. In *Reg. v Morris-Lowe*, the issue was whether it was sufficient to constitute a woman a 'common prostitute' if she indulged in sexual activity with one man on one occasion. Lord Lane C.J. determines that '[it] is clear to us that the word is not mere surplusage and we do not pause to consider whether the performance by a woman of a single act of lewdness with a man on one occasion for reward constitutes the woman a prostitute. But we are of the view that it does not make her a woman who offers herself commonly for lewdness'.[6] Avoidance of surplusage means finding a reason for the abundance in a text, so that, to quote a Delaware Court, '[w]e will read a contract as a whole and we will give each provision and term effect, so as not to render any part of the contract mere surplusage'.[7] The presumption is that there is a reason and pertinence to the use of a word, that it provides definition, avoids ambiguity, adds to the text even if such is sometimes an excessively timid approach, or as Morton J puts it in a case concerned with whether the word 'debts' included both criminal and civil debts: 'I think it may well be that certain provisions in the regulations in question were merely inserted *ex abundantia cautela*, because those responsible thought that there was a chance that X might be construed as

[4] *Marriot and Pascall's Case* (1588) 74 Eng. Rep. 147. The Latin *nuper* (recently) is in law something of a floating signifier: '14 years shall be said to be nuper, as in the case of sale of land, and 20 years shall be nuper in the tenure and occupation of land'. Whether ten years was *nuper* in land laid down for pasture was moot. Clearly whether a monarch's reign is *nuper* is a delicate (and in part predictive) question. *Genner against Lucking* (1614) Hill. 11 Jac. B. R. Roll. 499.

[5] *Croft and Howel* (1578) 20 Eliz. Plow. Com. 537.

[6] *R v Morris-Lowe* [1985] 1 W.L.R. 29, at 32; cited with approval in *R v MacFarlane* [1994] Q.B. 419.

[7] *Kuhn Constr., Inc. v. Diamond State Port Corp.*, 990 A.2d 393, 396–397 (Del. 2010); and reiterated in the remarkable decision of *Vintage Rodeo Parent LLC v Rent-A-Center, Inc.* (2019) WL 1223026, discussed in Goodrich, 'Against the Spirit of the Age: The Rationale of Relational Contracts' (forthcoming).

meaning Y'.[8] The presumption against surplusage, however, is 'not a hard-edged rule' in contemporary transactional law, precisely because of increasing abundance of media, words, and modes of distribution. Thus, in a recent construction law decision, the position of current commercial law is that 'the court should strive to give meaning to every word in the contract ... But at the same time, the court should guard against giving such a rule too much prominence in circumstances where, as we all know, some tautology, some overlapping terms, some surplusage, will often be found'.[9] Commercial contracts, another court observes, 'will often merely state the obvious', and to this one can add that increasingly they will show the putatively self-evident in the form of an image.[10] It is a short step, one may surmise, from the abundance of words to the incursion of decisional pictures.

Reviewing the curious legal history of surplusage, even as briefly outlined here, it transpires that in parallel to its ambiguity, abundance or excess is doubly meaningful. It is in principle significant because if included in the document it is presumed to have a meaning, to offer the cautel of stipulative definition. It is matter that matters, according to the wording of *Marriot and Pascall's* argument, because the addition of a word must necessarily alter the sense, and that variation of meaning is either legally cognizable or it is superfluous and extraneous to the juridical interpretation of the document. *Nuper*, as in recently, King, was allowable and so too 'craft' to further define 'mystery', but 'vocat. le Savoy' for 'de Savoy' invalidated the lease in *Marriot and Pascall's Case* because it provided an alternative designation of the same property. It did not allow for X rather than Y as the proper construction. The distinction to be made is that surplusage *ex abundantia* falls foul of the presumption when it constitutes an addition to the text and changes the meaning, whereas the synonym is treated as refining and, in its abundance, further specifying the sense. What we can now add, had such been technologically possible, is that photographs or other depictions might well be surplusage that help refine. In another early case, the omission of the words *collegii beatæ Mariæ* from a lease which should have been in the name *Præpositi et Collegii regalis beatæ S. Mariæ de Eaton juxta Windsor*, made by the Provost of Eaton College, Sir Thomas Smith, resulted in the lease being deemed utterly void.[11] A photograph of the Provost, standing outside the hallowed portals, would be surplusage *ex abundantia* that would help further specify the identity of the lessor, and so

[8] *In re Pascoe* (1944) 170 Law Times 171 [Ch. Div.].

[9] *Mutual Energy Ltd v Starr Underwriting Agency Ltd.* (2016) 165 Con. L.R. 220 at 232.

[10] Gross J. in *Ener-G Holdings plc v Hormwell* [2012] EWCA civ 1059. Another intriguing instance is provided by the Seychelles election case *Popular Democratic Movement v Electoral Commission* [2012] 5 LRC 109, where the term 'valid' in 'total valid votes cast' was surplusage because it went without saying that votes cast meant valid votes and did not include spoiled votes whose inclusion in the tally had precluded the PDM from being allocated a seat in the National Assembly.

[11] *Eaton College Case* (1557) 73 Eng. Rep. 327. Ironically, Sir Thomas Smith was a lawyer of some distinction and author of *De republica Anglorum* and worse still of *De recta & emendata lingvæ Anglicæ scriptione, dialogus* yet here the reality of parchment outweighed the dignity of the person and misprision corrupted the deed and the day.

too, and with greater potential for clarification, a picture of the Savoy hospital—*de Savoy*—would distinguish the subject matter of the lease from the inscription of a mere name—*vocat. Savoy*. As Cormack so persuasively argues, law's 'parchment technologies' generated a documentary reality, creating persons, properties, maps, and things as textual substitutions for the real: 'under a documentary order, the real itself begins to lie in documents, with the thing that the document subtends beginning to disappear into the aspect of its own vehicle'.[12] If the deed stated 'de Savoy', and the lease stated 'vocat. Savoy', then the place leased did not exist in the deed, the relevant instrument or indenture, and so lacked legal reality through the inadequacy of the writing. What fails to mirror the juridical writ, literally does not exist. With the passage of time and the invention of new visual technologies, the photograph, the imaginal in its varied visual forms, becomes the new vehicle of ontography, the novel legal real. The graphosphere, as Debray argues, is displaced politically by the videosphere, and in time law will follow this technological declension.[13]

Parchment technologies, as adverted in tracing the legal genealogy of maps, are the model that will initially determine the judicial apprehension of the new imaginal surplusage *ex abundantia*, if only because the two technologies share the essential property of lineal signification. Both are relays of signs, diagrammatological expressions, and law proceeds always *ad similia*. The earlier system of writing, the symbolæography of the lawyers as interpreted by Cormack, treats the document as the reality that adjudicates any external truth, and so the significance of materiality. The image purports another truth, a different mirror, an alternate relay of dissonant and diffractive signs with a distinct history and archive, a gallery of their own. Their surplusage is likely temporary, and indeed, as already shown, images are frequently enough part of the documentation even if legal judgement is as yet a long way from starting to treat pictures as precedents, for fear of subverting the precedency of texts. The question of incorporation, of legal recognition of the image, remains that of an uneven juristic balance between linear and lateral, discursive formulas and visual figures, books and bites, paper and pixels.

Moving forward to the second category of images, one which evidently enough overlaps in positive and negative senses with the more familiar maps, diagrams, and schemata reviewed in the last chapter, is to propose the extension of the concept of surplusage out of abundance from words to the uses of images. It has already been argued that cartographs are frequently of liminal literal significance

[12] Bradin Cormack, 'Paper Justice, Parchment Justice: Shakespeare, Hamlet, and the Life of Legal Documents', in Donald Beecher et al. (eds), *Taking Exception to the Law: Materializing Injustice in Early Modern English Literature* (Toronto: Toronto University Press, 2015) at 50.

[13] Régis Debray, 'The Three Ages of Looking', 21(3) *Critical Inquiry* 529 (1995). The translation is extracted from Debray, *Vie et mort de l'image: une histoire du regard en Occident* (Paris: Gallimard, 1992). Also important for an understanding of his thesis is Debray, *Cours de médiologie générale* (Paris: Gallimard, 1991). For one application of such ideas to law, see Julie Stone Peters, 'Theatrocracy Unwired: Legal Performance in the Modern Mediasphere', 26(1) *Law and Literature* 31 (2014).

in judgements, elements that add in a persuasive but non-probative manner to the formal explanation of the outcome, the reasoning of the decision, and the manifestation of jurisdiction, which is to say the power to decide. The *imago decidendi* is ironically a persuasive device, the visual equivalent of the rhetorical figure of icon, something seen as crucial to judgement, the picture as the reason for deciding.[14] The reality of the image as the affective source of decision, as the motive cause of rhetorical *inventio*, allows a more radical formulation. The theory of judicial surplusage is one of reversal: the significance of a judicial image is most often in inverse ratio to the attention paid to it in judgement. Lacking a conceptualization of the relation of text to image, failing as yet to develop a methodology for inclusion and exclusion, bereft of critical apparatuses for viewing and apprehending the visual, the old law of surplusage operates unwittingly. Imaginal abundance is thus best approached as a symptom, and the less conscious the insertion the more indicative the content.

Why did Judge Kozinski use the Google Earth satellite image in the immigration case of *Tirado*? The answer is not that it shows anything definitive about where the immigrant was at any particular time in relation to the border, nor that it provides any further definition of an ambiguous point, that X is X and not really Y. There is no X in the case, and so it is rather a map that creates its subject, a Google Earth satellite image that provides a panoptic aesthetic and indicates the power of the judge and the omnipercipience of the law. The image is cautionary as well as prohibitive in that it explicitly shows the full military might of the United States; it exemplifies Leviathan surveilling a previously porous border, and allows for a purification of the map, a greater geometry and definition of the purported reality of the boundary lines. Marking a divide, drawing a line in the sand as a barricade, the symbolic import of the image is that of signalling that the impure is kept out.[15] The law is the law and visibly so. It is jurisdiction manifest through vision, even though the snapshot actually shows very little. The surplusage is thus arguably the most important feature of the picture, the clue that unravels the affect of decision, the reason and the purpose of judgement. It does not need saying because it is shown, seen, visible, and indeed more powerful than words, even if nothing is in fact indicated beyond the assertion that there is a border, and that it may be crossed. It is surplusage, visual abundance, that is both central to the

[14] On the rhetorical figure icon, or resemblance by imagery, see the lawyer George Puttenham, *The Art of English Poesie* [1589] (Ithaca: Cornell University Press, 2007) at 329.

[15] See Michelle Castañeda, 'Virtual Judges in Immigrant Detention: The Mise-en-Scène of No-show Justice', in Delage et al. (eds), *Law and New Media: West of Everything* (Edinburgh: Edinburgh University Press, 2019); and expanded in Castañeda, *Disappearing Rooms: The Hidden Theaters of Immigration Law* (Durham, N.C.: Duke University Press, 2023). Purity and danger, of course, is a much more venerable anthropological theme and is the architectonic of positivist legal theory since the publication of Hans Kelsen *Pure Theory of Law* [1934] (Berkeley: University of California Press, 1960).

drive of decision and extraneous to any logic of judgement in that, as said, it offers nothing by way of confirmation of where Tirado was at the time of apprehension.

In the disturbing decision of *Jackson v Beasley*, a version of the U.S. Supreme Court's more famous but now well-travelled judgement in *Scott v Harris*, the plaintiff arrestee was rendered paraplegic when, in attempting to escape from a courthouse, he jumped full tilt into a plexiglass window. One of the plaintiff's arguments was that the window posed an unreasonable risk in that it made it appear as if the hallway of the courthouse was open to the outside. To refute this: 'A photo of the plexiglass panel or stationary window in question, measuring 3 feet in width by 12 feet in height ... is reproduced in the next section of this opinion' (Figure 3.1).[16] Chief Judge Martin goes on to comment that 'the risk of injury from a stationary panel is minimal'. Such may be true, but the question is that of the function the image actually serves, granted that a photograph of a pane of transparent plexiglass is likely going to show everything except the pane of plexiglass. Such is the case here with a mechanical reproduction from the late 1990s. What is visible is an opening and an outside, a hedge, cars, a parking lot, trees in the background, but for the purposes of the reproduction of the image the one thing that is not shown is the single rectangular pane. What appears is an opening that on scrutiny seems to beckon exit, an aperture into the world, whereas the judge is claiming to present a closure. It is surplusage, it remains and it is excess, and thus the image out of abundance, the multiplicity referenced, is that the image opens onto others, a shadow gallery, a rhizomatic plenitude of images and windows that in very similar fashion gesture to opening, to nature, to bucolic escape. Thus, just one example, from the *ius imaginum*, in this instance from Père le Moyne, a prolific seventeenth-century Jesuit whose work on the art of devices is in essence a lexicon of images and opens with precisely such an image, lacking only the plexiglass but in visual quality identical as a sign and invitation of passage and in this instance, to make it clearer, the helmeted guide (Minerva) points out through the opening towards the woods and sky (Figure 3.2).[17]

The point to be made is that the overexposed monochrome photograph in *Jackson v Beasley*, as with other images, brings its own historical gallery of prior perceptions. Previous depictions will act as a reservoir and positive unconscious, or lexicon of looking. The window, in aesthetic and architectural history, is an opening, and a frequent symbol in theological and legal imagery. It is as a window that the image comes to text and law. Here the division between interior and exterior, the window onto the domain of nature and natural forces, is particularly evident. The emblematic gesture in the earlier image is towards the outside scene, pointing through the window precisely so as to indicate the realm of natural law and the embodiment of divine power as signalled by the sun's rays traversing

[16] *Jackson v Beasley* 712 So.2d 162 (1998).
[17] Père le Moyne, *De l'art des devises* (Paris: Cramoisy, 1666) frontispiece.

Figure 3.1 Insertion by Chief Judge Charles Marvin in *Jackson v Beasley* (1998).

Figure 3.2 Frontispiece from Père le Moyne, *De l'art des devises* (1666).
Permission by P. Goodrich.

the image. The tableau, the frontispiece, here shows a lucent opening onto the world. This dual meaning of tableau, as surface and frame of a painting, also has an architectural meaning as the window in the wall, which opens onto the world.[18] The two senses complement each other.

[18] The history of windows is well expatiated in Gérard Wajcman, *Fenêtre: Chroniques du regard et de l'intime* (Paris: Verdier, 2004).

In his study of *homo fenestris*—humanity at the window—Wajcman borrows the architectural sense of tableau as opening, *quod quidem mihi pro aperta fenestra*, as that which is an open window for me, and applies this meaning to history and interiority.[19] Two senses of this elision are important for understanding the frontispiece emblem. First, the tableau, the picture, can be apprehended as an open window, as a hole through which the subject is drawn into the imagery, into a viewed and imagined exterior, while also opening inwards both to allow the apprehension of the image and to let the interior, the soul, *anima* and reverie or invention, to come out. The image too, as the art historian Didi-Huberman has expansively elaborated upon, should be opened. The viewers have to draw themselves out so as to enter the picture just as much as the depiction has to open to the viewer to generate the interior experience: 'To open signifies to enter into a role. The word contains a birth, the concrete image of a body that opens so as to give birth'.[20] In juristic terms, the image opens up and opens into the subject. It is the mode of incorporation, of the obligation entering the living subject and becoming the mirror of the *corpus iuris*.

The second feature of the image as opening is that it leads to what Freud terms the other scene, the unconscious, the body. The image is the medium of dream work and the avenue of corporeal action, which leads to the point that images do things differently and inhabit another scene of motive and affect. Here the crucial question of the importance of the legal history of images, the *ius imaginum* and its *emblemata*, comes to centre stage. We can now build upon the observation that the image, as figure, trope, and tableau, derives from architecture. Buildings have windows before, by *catachresis*, persons do. Buildings are enduring, they are monumental and survive. That defiance of history and death in its human forms is precisely what allows those at the window to look onto history and to view an atemporal and transhistorical, if not eternal, scene. The images that emblems relay do not share the temporality of the quotidian or of current events and practices. The surplusage of the image is as much to do with visual history, the anachrony that Nagel and Wood discuss in terms of the plural temporality of images, and that Manderson depicts and relays as trans-historical materialities of law.[21] The spectral haunts, and the manner of that haunting is the surplusage of the image, especially where the image shows nothing directly probative of the case. It lingers, it persists, it returns—or, in Huberman's phrase, it opens, commences, and founds a continuity, a series of associations that long outlive intention and the time of their fabrication.

The image carries a heavy surplusage of abundance, and, returning to the case and image in *Jackson v Beasley*, the photograph reproduced in the text brings

[19] Wajcman, *Fenêtre*, at 21.

[20] Georges Didi-Huberman, *L'Image ouverte* (Paris: Gallimard, 2003) at 37.

[21] A. Nagel and C. Wood, *Anachronic Renaissance* (New York: Zone Books, 2010); Desmond Manderson, *Danse Macabre: Temporalities of Law in the Visual Arts* (Cambridge: Cambridge University Press, 2019).

with it a shadow gallery, an array of prior images, the rhizomatic structure of the visual. It suggests pictorially, not out of caution but due to abundance, that the visible hedge can be vaulted over, the car park entered, and that the apparently halcyon outside is but a leap away. The judge focuses on the context of the aperture, remarking that 'the window is encased by a frame that extends from each wall of the hallway and a few inches above the floor level and below the ceiling of the hallway. This frame is easily distinguishable from the adjacent walls and floor, being darker in color. The panel also extends much higher toward the ceiling than the doorways on each side of the hallway near the plexiglass. The framed window shows no handle, doorknob or other ornament to indicate that it is even a door which allows outside ingress or egress. See photo, supra'.[22] Slightly later the judge again references 'the frame surrounding the panel distinguishes it from the adjacent doorways and defines the fixed panel as a fixed window'.[23] What the judgement is most at pains to stress is thus principally what is not visible, absent from the photograph, namely a door, a handle, a doorknob or ornaments, and of course plexiglass as a visible item, presumably because the purpose of glass is to be looked through. There is nothing said about the allure of the outside, the visibility of externality and freedom, the lucidity of the path to escape, the transparency of the window and the apparent accessibility, as well as the inviting allure, of the outside scene. What the picture shows, the surplusage of the very visible exterior, the car park, nature, egress, is ignored, overlooked in favour of the peripheries of the window, the wall in which it is installed.

Viewed as an element of judicial reasoning, the picture is both poorly reproduced and visibly fails to further specify the scope of the duty of care owed by the police to the plaintiff, or why it appears to the court self-evidently not to have been breached. The depiction introduces an entirely new element into the decision, and it is one that divagates in an extreme manner from the discourse being elaborated. The surplusage of a picture of an entirely luculent, crystalline see-through window, lacking doorframe and doorknob, indeed, as reproduced in the monochrome photograph, missing any indicator of restraint or impediment, leads the eye directly to the outside and away from the building. It is the allure of escape, the visibility of nature and world, that is most immediately on view, to which one must add the connotations reviewed above of freedom. Windows and openings, as also sun and nature in the gallery of cultural imagery, relay unconscious, anachronic possibilities of exodus to the eye. The image indicates that what the court is stipulating to be X is, as depicted in the judgement, something else, Y. Such a formulation, of course, again abstracts and renders the corporeal alphabetical, the flesh becomes an algebra and we risk losing touch with the atmosphere and visceral feel and sense of a particular place, its inhabitation and

[22] *Jackson v Beasley* at 167.
[23] Ibid., 168.

rules for living which, in confusion, terror, or inspiration, the defendant had so unfortunately broken.

The point can be elaborated even more directly by returning to the images used in *HouseCanary v Quicken Loans*. At the end of the decision, not making it into the text but rather inhabiting a strange internal *hors-texte*, the fallen footnote becomes an appendix and appendage. Here, enraged by the dirty lawyer tactics used by the litigants, the judge places an image, a pdf screenshot of rules of conduct, and then a photo-portrait of Abraham Lincoln. The images are now deep in the textual unconscious, coalescing in a depiction of words, a table of rules, a crescendo picture of commandments. After the insertion of a footnote picture of an historical clock of the world, resident visually just under the judge's chirographic ownership of the order announced, comes Appendix A. This takes the form of an image of a text, a tabulation, no less, of Biery's own nine commandments: 'The Rule for the Practice of Law', inclusive of instructions for implementation and penalties for non-observance. He echoes Robert Burton's *Anatomie of Melancholy* and its raillery at lawyers as the cause of most of the unhappiness in the polity: 'where a population be generally contentious, where there be many discords, many laws, many law suits, many lawyers ... it is a manifest sign of a distempered, melancholy state'.[24] Whatever the status or originality of these rules—the Texas Lawyer's creed—presenting them comedically as a table, as an image, a Diet of Worms, in an appendix, both dislocates them and distances the table from the case, but also authorizes and legitimates the rules by rendering them as a tabulation, a flyer or posting that is theatrical, simultaneously parodic and pompous (Figure 3.3). All of this, recollect, is in a judgement issuing an order which is followed by the image of Abraham Lincoln, the President who saved the Union, who brought peace, who sits now, dour, unsmiling, waistcoat and fobwatch chain, as if a judge, as if holding a hearing, and about to pronounce judgement on the lawyers today (Figure 3.4). Lincoln's view, cited below the photo-portrait, is an irenic one, urging compromise, communication, comity, and community. Make peace not law. But why show the portrait, the all-too-solid, sedentary figure, *ex cathedra*? Granted that the image comes after the historical clock of the world and the rules of irenic legal practice, the answer has to be that this is firstly a history lesson, part of the blinking of the eye, a reminder of the communal civility of Texas and of what it means to practice law. More than that, however, the portrait, *haec imago*, is a sledgehammer image of authority and foundation used here to authorize 'The Rule' and bring *gravitas* to the *levitas* of the nine tables of the law. The civil war was won, the Union persists, and keeping the peace means following the time honoured and genteel traditions of specifically Texan lawyers, so that the North does not come down again. More

[24] Robert Burton, *Anatomie of Melancholy* (Oxford: Cripps, 1628) at 69, continuing: 'a purse-milking nation, a clamorous company, gowned vultures ... a company of irreligious Harpies, scraping, griping catchpoles (I mean our common hungry pettifoggers ...) without art, without judgment, that do more harm ... than sickness, wars, hunger, diseases'.

Appendix "A"

The Rule

For the Practice of Law

Treat others (including lawyers, parties, witnesses and Court staff) as you would like to be treated.

***The Implementation of* The Rule**

Our goal is the fair, peaceable and efficient resolution of disputes, and to seek the truth within the bounds of the rule of law.

There is a difference between advocacy for the sake of prolonging advocacy and serving the best interests of clients in bringing litigation to closure.

The law is only a part of life. It is easier to abide by The Rule if one occasionally breaks bread with one's adversary.

Abide by the Texas Lawyer's Creed.

***The Penalties for not abiding by* The Rule**

The loss of respect and goodwill from one's professional colleagues, thus making the practice of law much less enjoyable.

The writing of The Rule in multiples of fifty on a Big Chief tablet with a Number Two pencil.[1]

The donation of numerous pictures of George Washington to deserving charitable organizations.

Others within the discretion of the Court.

Fred Biery
United States District Judge

[1] This penalty is reserved for those whose conduct is particularly childish.

Figure 3.3 Insertion by Judge Fred Biery in *HouseCanary, Inc. v Quicken Loans, Inc* (2018).

Discourage litigation. Persuade your neighbors to compromise whenever you can. Point out to them how the nominal winner is often a real loser–in fees, expenses, and waste of time. As a peacemaker the lawyer has a superior opportunity of being a good man. There will still be business enough.

Abraham Lincoln

Figure 3.4 Insertion by Judge Fred Biery in *HouseCanary, Inc. v Quicken Loans, Inc* (2018).

than that, it appears *in ludo veritas*, an instancing of the playfulness of truth as in the old genre of *serio ludere* to which, historically, the tradition of legal emblems, of pictures in law books, belongs. The judgement seeks to be visible and accessible, a bite, a meme, to circulate *in imagine*, while also conveying serious social speech. This is *lex populi*, law *a comicis*, for the laity, the picture on the street, or at least in the Bar of San Antonio.

The ironically irenic figure of the preserver of the Union, Inserted as a full-page image at the end of the judgement, coming after and under the signature of the judge, is entirely surplusage *ex abundantia*. The presumption against surplusage means that it be given significance, that the image is not redundancy to be jettisoned from the interpretation of the case, but rather it allows for further definition. The office of the lawyer and the channels of juristic communication are staged so as to signal that bad things can happen to the lawyers and the lawsuit if duties incumbent on members of the bar, the community of jurists, are not observed and the proprieties of procedure are disregarded. It is indicative also, in a very direct manner, of judicial identification with the patristic icon, an emblem of action whose presence in the text evidences the fact of sovereignty and that the judge too can do what he lists in the judgement. As to variance or simple excess of meaning, the image of 'The Rule' as a table of nine commandments immediately followed by the portrait of the leviathan statesman, all of this as a visual compilation appended after the judicial signature, indicates a dramatic desire to expose the non-juridical, socio-political roots of the conflict and the white hot disaffection of the judge when faced with the melancholic litany of pettifogging trickery. It adds nothing directly or doctrinally to the decision in the case, which concerned procedural issues, but as a symptom of the ground of judgement and as a point of entry into the interior world of the judge, the affect of determination, the vision in decision, it gestures directly to a heterotopic space of mosaic proportions. Biery is sounding the law, posting the tables, invoking the sedentary *imago* of a gargantuan political figure as ground and justification for a ruling that covertly—though ironically visually—states far more than law.

The surplusage of the image indicates a spectral left field, an oneiric or preconscious imagination, hypnopompic reveries transferred into a pictorial form in a field of judgement that resists the actual depiction in the very instance of inserting it, refusing aesthetic analysis and treating the pictorial as literal, as read. Surplusage incorporates the image so as to overlook it, slipping the image to the eye like a shark aesthetic moving past the barrier of doctrine and the resistance of words or overlay of reasoned justificatory discourse, reducing the surplusage to the textual meaning, insisting that it shows that X is X, while deflecting or ignoring any contrary or closer viewing. The point can be expanded by way of a negligence case. The plaintiff, Michael Dick, tripped and fell in a truck stop bathroom.[25] He

[25] *Michael Dick v Pilot Travel Centers, LLC* 2018 WL 2761407.

sues the operator of the facility on the basis that the manager should have known of the 'slippery stuff' or substance that he suggests he had felt underfoot before falling and injuring himself, and his memory. What we see in the two photographs reproduced in the judgement is the *locus in quo* but out of use and free of slippery substance, soap, or other lubricious or unctuous conditions (Figure 3.5). That two toilets were necessary, two shots from different angles of what someone looking into the shower unit would see as opposed to the perspective that the complainant would have had from the inside looking out. Whatever the focus and camera angle, what is shown is not what was seen, nor does it attempt to approximate to the scene of the slippage. But expand the analysis only very slightly and the image of toilets, of what in German is termed *scheisenhausen,* lends an air of austerity and effluent to the suit. Introducing pictures of the latrine has zero probative value and misleads the eye at least in the sense of drawing it away from the shower and its floor, the subject of dispute, and towards the adjoining cubicle, as the only available image of what went down, as the impertinent but persuasive reality effect that surplusage promotes. There was a room to let, a toilet, but besides prompting the fact finder to see the scene, the images serve to remind the viewer of the animal in the human,

Figure 3.5 Insertion by Judge Michael Walker in *Michael Dick v Pilot Travel Centers, LLC* (2018).

the bestiality of the body that, as Judge Schreber was fond of pointing out, has to shit. It is a reminder as well, in the terms of the civilizing process, that law is also, as here, addressing itself to pathology.

The toilet provides a Duchampian style of the surreal, a dadaist air of the anachronistic to the event and suggests, although very indirectly, a comedic 'anything is possible' depending upon one's perspectival point of apprehension, and that is indeed what the court held in the case. Maybe there was soap or something slippery on the floor, the court does not know and so sends the case for trial. The trucker slipped bare by his bathroom. Again, however, the key doctrinal issue is the image of what is juristically nothing, the unstated relay of the picture, the rhizomatic lure of the visual juxtaposed with the putatively rational determination of the law of negligence and the docrine of 'obvious hazard' in dispute. The image is surplusage *ex abundantia* because of what it introduces, the scene and sense of place, ablution and excretion, bodies and nakedness, bare life in the distinctive sense of inhabitation, bodily function, skin, limb, touch, and tile is precisely what the court does not wish to view or examine in its specific detail and architectural context. The decision wants to come after the cleansing, as a pure rule, but the image belies such pre-conscious, affective drive. The pictures suggest Y not X, they lead away from the abstract positivity of legalism towards materiality and movement, sites and sights of action and environment, atmosphere and world, that law here hesitates to encounter.

Certainly, the decision can be portrayed as poetic, which is frequently an accurate declension of the determination and a proper presentation of the power of the imaginal, but the opportunity staring back at the court from the photograph, inaccurate though it may be in perspective and focus, is not taken. The poetry of the image, its creativity as depiction and insertion in a judicial text, is motivated neither by an abundance of caution nor generosity, though these are nonetheless implicit potentials of the portrayal of place. We are shown a picture of an empty space, free of any indication of slippage, lacking any inhabitant, a pristine shower and toilet, not in use, that are all in this context indicative of a dutifully kept and well cleansed space, an image that catapults the claim into the further reaches of surplusage and of juristic implausibility. Had the court looked and opened to the picture, then a material sense of the image, a haptic feel of the confinement, of openness and closure, of what was possible in such a space, could have added significantly to the decision, offering augmentation and specification of the range of possibilities and constraints of such a bathroom. In simple functional terms, an image of the shower, showing the showerhead, the placement of the soap dispenser, the site of the drain, would have been relevant. The photographs used, somewhat less so. There are multiple meanings to the matterphor of walls talking and yet none of these were noticed, none taken up. If this is poetic justice, it is blank verse offering no more than the trace of a reality effect that pertains, if at all, to a different space and another occasion. The image is here a generosity that is legally known as an *ex gratia* offering, *nudum pactum*, naked in the shower, and the bare promise of visual apprehension without direct force or effect. The image, however, as surplusage, as the trigger of an abundance of words, still bears a significant and enigmatic undertow of unconscious meanings from surrealist art to the intimation of exclusion, to evacuation, as in getting rid of it, flushing it away in the mode of beings born *inter faeces et urinas*.

The relevance of the image is paradoxically its irrelevance to, and potential contestation of what is stated, its centrality to what Derrida termed 'the said of the unsaid' and which here can be formulated as the scene of the unseen.[26] It proves for the court that there was nothing to see. A wall, a frame, a window onto the frame, but not the scene of what had happened. Something to see through but not to pass through. That sense of superfluity, however, is true of all symptoms, and is precisely what instigates closer viewing, stricter scrutiny. In a Freudian sense, the surplusage is central, it explicates the drive and allows another sense of the meaning of the decision in its imaginal form. There could hardly be a more vivid instance of surplusage than that of the introduction of an image culled from *Our Texas Magazine*, Winter 1995, in a case brought by an adult entertainment club to challenge a city ordinance requiring exotic dancers to wear bikini tops.[27] The plaintiff, 35 Bar and Grille, claimed that nudity should be protected as freedom of speech under the First Amendment. In a judgement that is a tour de force of punning, the indomitable Chief Justice Biery is constrained by appellate precedent to hold that the ordinance applies to the plaintiff club. The relevant prohibition on human display, deriving from, because lawyers write like this, Ordinance 2012-12-06-0934, amending Chapter 21 of a 2005 Ordinance, defines semi-nudity as:

> a state of dress that fails to completely and opaquely cover (a) human genitals, pubic region, pubic hair or (b) crevice of buttocks or anus, or (c) *any portion of the female breast that is situated below a point immediately above the top of the areola*, or (d) any combination of (a), (b) or (c).

The club had sought to limit dress to a g-string and a pastie covering the *areolae* of the breasts and this, in the appellate court reading, infracted subsections (a), (b), and (c). In disagreeing with the defendant's justification for enforcing the ordinance, on the grounds of secondary adverse effects of the sexually orientated business' failure to require more attire, the judge puns his way with bravado. He starts as he intends to continue: 'An ordinance dealing with semi-nude dancers has once again fallen into the Court's lap ... the age old question before the Court, now with constitutional implications, is: Does size matter?' (708). The judgement then proceeds on rhetorical lines of erotic innuendo and *double entendre*. This

[26] Jacques Derrida, *Negotiations: Interventions and Interviews 1971–2001* (Palo Alto: Stanford University Press, 2002) at 158: Everything took place underground, in the said of the unsaid.
[27] *35 Bar & Grille, LLC et al. v City of San Antonio* 943 F.Supp.2d 706.

is not entirely uncommon in the case law, where rhetoric will on occasion mirror the subject matter, though seldom with the high spirits, the perseverance and dubious élan of CJ Biery, stating 'to bare or not to bare, that is the question' (712 col. 2). The plaintiffs' aim to clothe themselves in the First Amendment, 'seeking to provide cover against another alleged naked grab of unconstitutional power'. The court then goes on to infer: 'Plaintiffs fear enforcement of the ordinance would strip them of their profits, adversely impacting their bottom line', while the city believes that these businesses 'need to be girdled more tightly' (709 col. 1). Reaching an early climax, the judge then expostulates that '[p]laintiffs, and by extension their customers, seek an erection of a constitutional wall separating them from the regulatory power of City government' (709 col. 1). After denying judgement to the plaintiffs, the judge offers the envoi that '[s]hould the parties choose to string this case out to trial on the merits, the Court encourages reasonable discovery intercourse as they navigate the peaks and valleys of litigation, perhaps to reach a happy ending' (712 col. 1–713 col. 2). The citations are necessary as context for the seemingly random insertion of the image of Miss Wiggles in a leotard, gyrating on her head. On page 2 of the judgement, in setting out the initial facts, before even arriving at the section headed 'Background', where the course and cause of litigation is delineated, Judge B. remarks, seemingly quite impromptu, as if it just slipped out, an ironic aside, that visitors to the location 'would have enjoyed far more the sight of Miss Wiggles, truly an exotic artist of self-expression even into her eighties'.[28] Biery then inserts the photograph of said Miss Wiggles on her head. A search of YouTube will further uncover a clip of Miss Wiggles performing energetically in the 4th Annual Useless Talent Competition.

The image borrows from a lengthy visual archive of a topsy turvy world, of reason turned to folly and the natural order of things inverted as in the land of Cockaigne where abundance and an alternate hierarchy reign. Whether consciously or otherwise, the judge has invoked a domain of madness and profligacy, of disorder and illicit actions *contra naturam* and in defiance of both goodness and godliness. Early emblems are replete with many instances of depiction of such insane performances, as in John Taylor's 'Mad Fashions', whose frontispiece tells a story that persists over time, anachronically, through many instances of human folly and of the world going backwards (Figure 3.6). The horse pushes the cart, the mouse chases the cat, and the head appears out of the arse in a variation upon the normal depiction in which the subject stands on their head. Top left corner of the image, however, note that the visually determinative scopic point, dexter chief in the heraldic argot from which emblems devolve, is a church upside down and that, in nuce and eggshell, is the message that the judge likely wishes to convey. It is encapsulated in the final lines of Taylor's verse, which ends, last lines for style:

[28] The image of Miss Wiggles is from *35 Bar & Grille, LLC et al. v City of San Antonio* (2013) and is linked here: https://larc.cardozo.yu.edu/faculty-online-pubs/61/, eFigure 6.

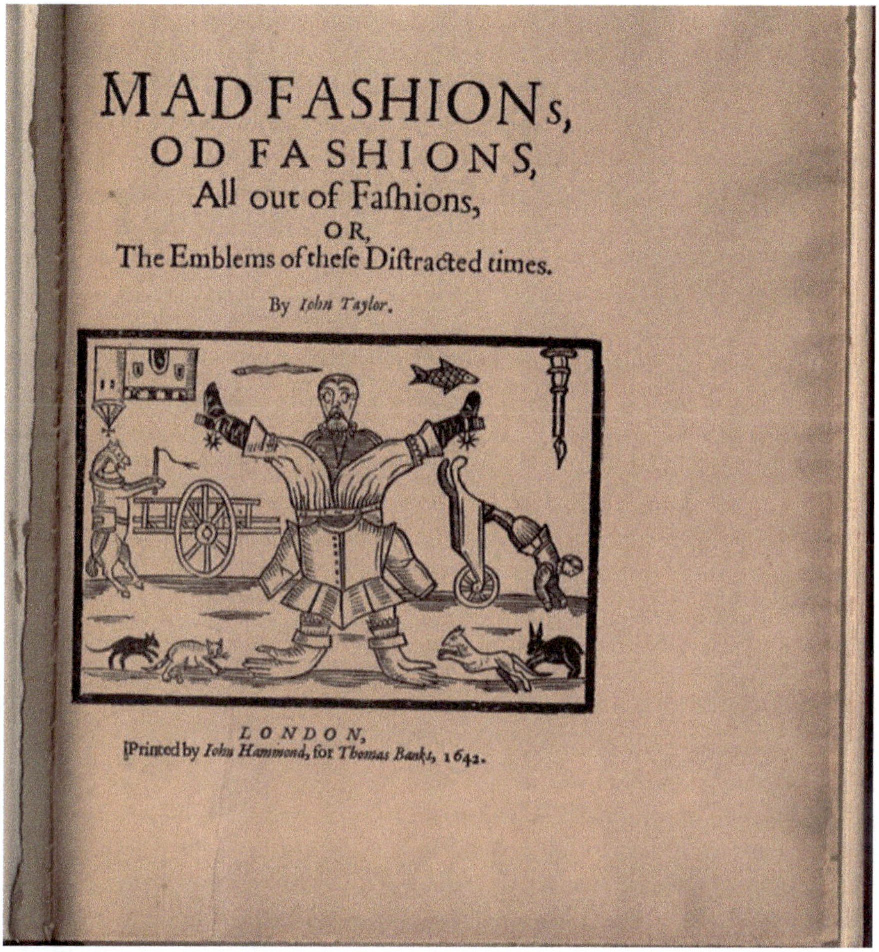

Figure 3.6 The world upside down, from John Taylor, *Mad Fashions* (1642).
Permission by P. Goodrich.

> Meane time, till wee amend, and leave our crimes,
> The Picture is the Emblem of the Times.
> FINIS.

The image, in other words, is rhizomatically connected to an imaginal history and album of such depictions and they bear a heavy visual signification of right and wrong, an undertow of a religious and sartorial hierarchy of meaning that distinguishes in a judgemental form between clothed and naked, costume and body, civility and savagery, in the relay of a Christian law that returns to the myth of Eden which tells us that it is the privilege of the Gods to be naked and that humans must be clothed to remember their original sin and, in Freudian argot, their primal scene. Here the invocation and depiction of Miss Wiggles, fully clad, as far as can be discerned, and swivelling on her head provides the appropriate key to the drive of the judgement. As the harm of the club's erotic activities seemingly does not, for Judge Biery, lie in adverse secondary effects—it is not nudity but alcohol, testosterone, and the availability of guns that causes the harm—the issue must be closer to home and primary. The judicial selection of imagery explains, where words have simply skirted, that it is the aesthetic of semi-nudity, the palpable lack of art, the obviousness of being bare that has offended. The club offers nothing beyond brute bodies. Miss Wiggles, he suggests, provides both spectacle and propriety. The fact that she is dressed, and that she dances on her head, also provides a superlative image of *détournement*, of the visual taking up and changing how we think an issue or decide a case. The referent is ultimately biblical, and it is dogma and scripture that determine that 35 Bar and Grille have exposed too much. They have forgotten the root of sin in the Garden of Eden, they have ignored the expulsion from the terrain of primordial innocence. It is in their oblivion to sin that they have sinned. More simply, in depicting a dancer on her head, the judge has invoked a heathen world, a globe upside down, topsy-turvy times, in which evil is confused for good, harm for benefit, crudity for art. The image of Miss Wiggles has a strong symptomatic significance, signalling the judge's latent anger at an improper lack of dress, an inartistic and graceless aesthetic to which Judge Biery responds with an ethically driven desire to ridicule the plaintiff club's artlessness and, by extension, godlessness.

The surplusage thus comes to indicate another scene of judgement, a nuance or specification of meaning by other media, the intimations of affect arriving by imaginal means in the text of decision. The image is doctrinally extraneous but hermeneutically pivotal, the royal road to the motivation of determination. In *Grayson v Schuler*, to take a reasonably well-known instance, the judge includes an iconic yet extraordinary photograph, culled using Google images, in the judgement (Figure 3.7).[29] The picture is of the late Bob Marley and is taken, unacknowledged, from 'The Cannabis Social Network' website. The lower third of the photo on the relevant web page states 'The Real Reason Bob Marley is a Marijuana Icon—High There!' None of that appears in the judicial record, but the image does. The photo is of the Rastafarian composer and lead singer of 'The Wailers', the harbinger and scion of reggae music which swept the pop scene in the late 1960s and 1970s. The image conveys the Rastafarian propensity for dreadlocks, a sense of concerts, pop festivals, musical escape, a sensibility of freedom and the spiritualism and connectivity of those that are stoned, as in high. It connotes a musical sub-culture and lifestyle, an Afro-Caribbean ethos, leisure and sun: 'don't rock my boat', as one lyric goes, 'because I don't want my boat rocked'. What then is the case in which the image is inserted? A civil rights action by a prisoner against a

[29] *Omar Grayson v Harold Schuler* 666 F.3d 450 (2012).

Figure 3.7 Insertion by Judge Richard Posner in *Omar Grayson v Harold Schuler* (2012).
Photo © David Corio.

correctional officer for forcibly shearing his dreadlocks as a 'security risk'. The prisoner in question is neither a Rastafarian nor a musician but rather a member of the African Hebrew Israelites of Jerusalem and had taken the Nazarite vow not to cut his hair. The picture of Bob Marley is then explained as indicating that dreadlocks can attain 'a formidable length and density as shown in this photograph'.[30] From this the judge infers that 'a shank or other contraband could be concealed in an inmates dreadlocks' to which he adds: 'Short hair is also more hygienic than very long, braided hair'. It is, one must confess, a rather opinionated opinion, although the judge as hair stylist, the legal expert in coiffure, goes back at least to the Order of the Coif and thence to the peruque and the wig and might merit jurisprudential discussion. Here, however, the judge is excited by recognition of the image of dreadlocks and thus is driven to dealing with them not *in abstracto* but *in capitis*, on the head, except that it is the wrong head, not the imprisoned body, but the liberated Bob Marley. Eros will out.

The judicial smash and grab of the photograph, by way of a screenshot, is highly reductive and even the barest of contexts, as adumbrated above, is lacking from the insertion of the image. What is shown is asserted to be simply and only what the judge sees and in this particular case his evident ignorance of reggae and

[30] *Grayson* at 452.

Rastafarianism leads him to misinterpret rock and roll, rhythm, dance, the peaceful and festive, with threat, and so to conclude absurdly that the photograph of a lead singer in concert shows that dreadlocks are in essence a mode of concealment, a covert weapon. It appears to be misrecognition of the worst sort, a mislabelling, a fact-finding rampage, but the image is always more than it seems. Rastafarianism is a philosophy of freedom and Bob Marley a species of liberation theologian advocating 'do what you will'. In such light, it is genuinely symptomatic that while the judge says that the image is of danger, that the hair is both unhygienic and potentially a weapon, the decision concludes that because the corrections officer justified shaving the prisoner's head on the grounds that he was not a Rastafarian and so not entitled to dreadlocks, it was religious discrimination. Freedom, it seems, will out where Bob Marley appears. In this instance, to borrow a phrase, the unconscious too is a Rastafarian.

At a jurisprudential level, it is again the rhizomatic character of the image that is most in play. The linearity of the text is disrupted by the discordance and remediation of the photograph, and the imaginal economy of depiction subverts the linear logic of the rule. The image carries its own morphology and multiplicity, it brings music to the judgement if not to the judge, and libidinal liberation to the closure of the precedent. The weight of affect that the image carries overrides its conscious or surface presentation and signals the intrusion of Jah, of an Afrocentric Rastology, and the positive assertion and vindication of the prisoner's rights. This in a sense despite the judge. The surplusage of the image here provides the elliptic reason of determination, the vision in decision, meaning here a fissiparous indeterminacy of judgement. The logic of the deliberation comes close to inverting the traditional juristic hierarchy of text then image, the literal rule of reading law with downcast eyes. Inaccurate though it may be, the sense that dreadlocks equate with Rastafarianism and that freedom from religious discrimination should protect the plaintiff from the correctional shears has a degree of poetry, an affable equity to it, a surplusage that adds a degree of unintended nuance, which is to say, an extrinsic affective relay, in its purest form.

The poetic, the unspoken visual force of affect, of corporeality and materiality entering into the invention of decision, can be seen more directly in a negligence case where a teacher slipped and fell on a wet school floor (Figures 3.8 A & B).[31] Here the reality effect is augmented by CCTV colour video stills, the teacher standing, the teacher prostrate. Again, the immediate impact of the pictures is indicative of *casus*, the case, the fall, having happened in the context of yellow signs warning that the floor is wet. To show stills of before and after, however, does beg the question of why the still or, better, the video of the incident itself is not shown or linked to the text. The image, in other words, is again surplusage out of abundance in the exact sense that the issue is not that she fell, which is not contested, but

[31] *LaSonya Robertson v Clarksville-Montgomery County School System* 2018 WL 3199219.

Figure 3.8 A & B Insertion by Judge Arnold Goldin *Robertson v Clarksville-Montgomery County School System* (2018).

rather whether the school had acted reasonably in its placement of warning signs of wet floor, while the custodian mopped away in the rear of the second still. Here at least the warning signs are visible, the site of the fall is shown and the trajectory that the teacher took from classroom to corridor to collapse can be mapped. In this instance, the images could offer precision, a specification of X meaning X, the spot where the event took place, and not Y, but the court does not take that opportunity. The issue is not that she fell, but where she fell and what she was warned of by way of visible danger of wetness prior to falling. To this end, the court adds two picture stills of the yellow warning signs, the second of which I reproduce here for a sense of the scene and signage (Figure 3.9). The mop is now leaning against the lockers and the depiction is evidently of some other time than that of the accident, but it undoubtedly provides an indication, proximate in time and place, of the means and the look of the corridor that the plaintiff encountered. It helps, in other words, to specify in greater detail the *locus delicti* or scene of the tort, yet as in *Tirado* it is of indirect relevance because it is evidently not of the signs at the time of the event.

Probative though the second image of warning signs, of floor, lockers, and mop, could be for the decision, the court again is not concerned to offer a critical viewing or material analysis of the pictures. Are the signs sufficiently compelling, one facing, one turned away? Is the floor visibly wet, shiny, and obviously slippery? Is the placement of the signs such as to suggest that it is only the floor by the lockers and not on Ms Robertson's route that is wet and dangerous? It is the dissenting judge, Brandon O. Gibson, who makes the point and reproduces the images used at trial, who looks for himself and uses the pictures to visualize and sense the scene of the fall, concluding 'I fail to see how the placement of two wet-floor signs, as depicted in the photographs above, is unreasonable. The trial court and the majority determined that the absence of a wet-floor sign on the right side of the hallway was not a reasonable implementation of the mopping policy. The policy, however, does not require signs on every square foot of the hallway, nor should it'.[32] The pictures add precision and specification to the analysis, adding, for the dissenting judge, a variation on the trial court's view, namely that if there is contributory negligence

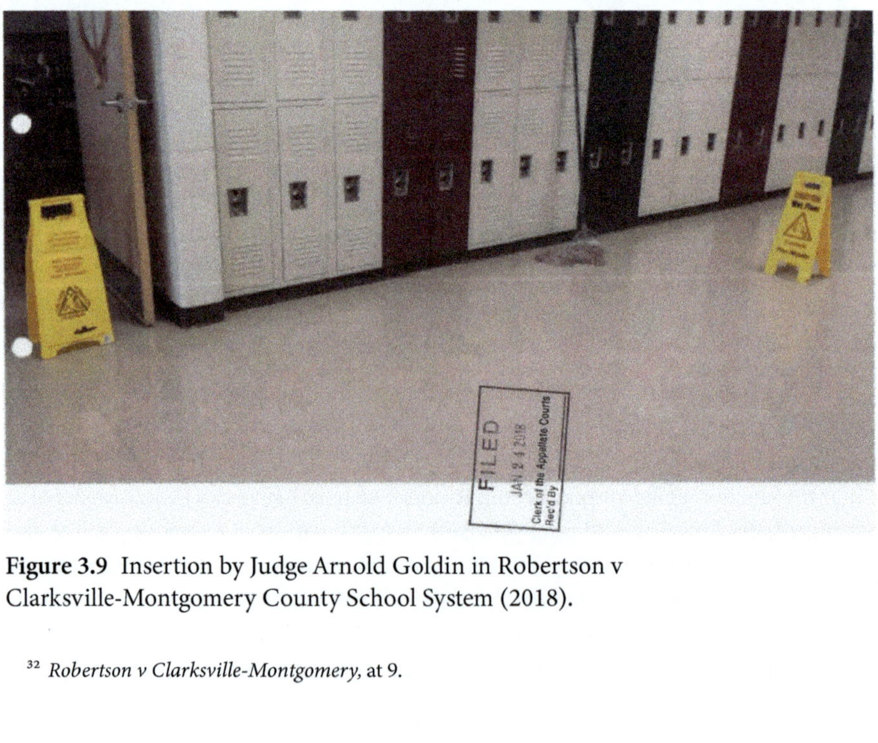

Figure 3.9 Insertion by Judge Arnold Goldin in Robertson v Clarksville-Montgomery County School System (2018).

[32] *Robertson v Clarksville-Montgomery*, at 9.

it is that of Ms Robertson and not that of the school district. The dissenting judge does not linger to scrutinize the pictures very closely, nor does he address the fact that the still pictures of the warning signs, and included in the judgement, are taken at a different time and form a distinct angle to that of the plaintiff's presumed viewing. Equally importantly, the warning sign by the open door has been moved slightly to face the door out of which Robertson had emerged, whereas in the CCTV stills it is actually turned somewhat towards the corridor and does not directly face the egress of the plaintiff from her classroom. Again, for the point cannot be stressed too often, the looking appears to be secondary to the discursive presupposition at which the judicial viewer has already arrived and now wishes, *ex post facto*, to prove with pictures. Progress is textual and *ad similia* as opposed to being visual and *ad apparentiam*.

For the majority, showing the picture of the fallen plaintiff, the pedant felled by a mopping, has other purposes, affects, and effects. The force of law becomes momentarily the farce of law, the slapstick of a banana peel upending a protagonist, the prostration of the pedagogue. The unexpected capsizing is a common enough comedic figure, but in the context of trial it is viewed in stasis, a still frame of a fallen faculty member which picture will likely generate empathy after the humour has evaporated. The image of the prostrate pedant in the melancholic blue tone of the footage evokes sympathy, it draws attention to the wound and impels the eye to the victim rather than to the cause, which being water, being transparent, is not visible in the picture. As any advocate would inform you, the moment that the court is looking at a video of collapse, it is being persuaded not only of the reality of the event but also of the legitimacy of the cause. It really happened, we can see it in its visceral, visual intensity and humiliation of the didact. It must have hurt. It is beyond dispute, a visible *certum*, which is indeed exactly how the court determined this case, and on appeal enhanced the responsibility of the school from 75% to 100%. The image ruled the majority judgement, even though it is not shown in their deliberations.

Taking stock, following in large measure the logic of spatial justice, the image appears first in judicial texts, most comfortably and easily, in the form of graphic depictions, charts, graphs, plans, diagrams, and maps. These are surplusage in the sense of visual synonyms, confirmations and sometimes clarifications of arguments made discursively and so they augment, providing proof that X is X. The images are deemed and treated as optical aids, illustrations of deliberative argumentations, often numerical depictions that swell words with numbers, and appeal in large measure as disembodied, abstract representations of shared and familiar perspectives upon a bifurcated world. The image as picture, first graphic and then increasingly photographic and figurative, as tracked in this chapter, follows a comparable and equally dismissive trajectory. The imaginal depiction is surplusage and has either to be reduced to the logic of the text, subordinated to words, confirming and detailing while generally being overlooked as mere incidents of proof, or it is excluded as ludic, excessive, and irrelevant to the strict discursive logic of the judgement. The vision in decision goes ironically unseen. It is included so as to indicate the obvious, previewed so as to provide a scenography, to demonstrate place, persons, or purposes in a visual mode that augments, that gives a reality effect to abstract legalisms that might otherwise pass unnoticed and so improperly apprehended. It is this dimension of surplusage that is of greatest significance to the interpretation and critical apprehension of judicial pictorial insertions.

In incorporating the image, in including the visual abundance in the text of the decision, the picture brings much more than the discourse can either relay or easily accommodate within the methodological norms of precedential reasoning. The image is more than a norm and tends to rule without being a rule. The image impacts as more than and other than reason, and it is this advent of affect, of aesthetic and material sensibility into the judgement, that is of greatest import. The image brings with it a world external to the abstract reason of law, an imaginal community and its shared reveries of coexistence. More than that, as Coccia argues, the imaginal is in this materialization the other life of law, a sensible existence that becomes visible, sensory, and material in its embodiment in images.[33] When pictorial depictions emerge in judgements, they render the haptic performativity of legality visible, they destroy the boundaries drawn by words, confronting verbality with the viserbal, an embodied sociality and disciplinarity exterior to any strictly discursive legality now present in precedent. The abstraction of the rule is brought back to earth by the medial space of the imaginal, a mediality that, as argued at length here, is surplusage *ex abundantia*, part of law and more than law. It is what Coccia terms an 'objective unconscious', meaning something external to the subject and extrinsic to the discipline of law as a textual endeavour: '[the image] is a form of objective unconscious because it does not represent a mode of subjectivity; despite defining the virtuality of every subjective perception, it is the actualization of a sensation that takes place outside the organ of perception'.[34] In other sounds, and despite the emphasis upon common law as an unwritten law, this visual surplusage opens up the interior of judgement to the externality of its founding perceptions.

[33] Emanuele Coccia, *Sensible Life: A Micro-ontology of the Image* (New York: Fordham University Press, 2015) at 8.

[34] Coccia, *Sensible Life*, at 52. At 97: 'The image captures the real (whether this be psychic or object), and transforms it into something that is able to exist beyond itself, or beyond its nature and individuality; the image multiplies the real and renders it infinitely appropriable'.

4
Comedy of Eros

There are occasions when the force of law slips into the farce of law. In the last example of the prostrate pedagogue, there is an element of slapstick, banana skin and laughter, that should not escape the observant viewer. It could be a meme. When a judge places a picture of Miss Wiggles upside-down on a chair, gyrating on her head in a leopard skin leotard, in a judgement relating to the administrative application of zoning regulations, there is equally an unmistakably humorous aspect to the image. Judgement stands on its head. This also implies another scene, that of the unconscious economy of the psyche. As Freud puts it 'a new joke ... [is] an event of the widest interest ... ' and by close analogy the visual quip, the trompe l'œil, the surprising picture in a legal decision are all significant indicia of law's psychic, and in this instance specifically comedic and libidinal economies.[1] In psychoanalytic argot the joke is a condensation that compresses and disguises an unconscious thought process. The joke escapes the repression barrier, but it does so in a displaced form as the point of intersection of several different chains of association. As a nodal point, the condensation is marked by intensity of energy and excess of meaning, which is itself the result of displacement and the sign of latent content. Thus, in *Gonzalez-Serv*in, reviewed in the Introduction, the judge includes a photoshopped picture of an ostrich with its head buried in the ground, next to a besuited figure with their fair aspect and snoutfig also interred, the rear raised but not gyrating. The picture materializes the vision of the judge in what is a comic and corporeal image that also bears an ineluctable erotic sense. In visualizing his critical point, the judge exposes a latent content, a psychic economy that includes burial and birds, blindness and insight, narcissism and superiority. Similarly, the teacher who slips, the inverted dancer, the disfigured ostrich, and defaced lawyer are all dispositive, comic and erotic inventions and incursions that bring the body into legal judgement, and manifest flesh in the face of written law. The incongruity, the surprise, and the physicality of these corporeal manifestations materializes the subject of law looking back from the text, acting as incongruous to the literal and surprising to the judgemental, and so generating laughter.[2]

[1] Sigmund Freud, *The Joke and Its Relation to the Unconscious* (Harmondsworth: Penguin Books, 2002) at 7. On libidinal economy and bodily tensors, the source is Jean-François Lyotard, *Libidinal Economy* (Bloomington: Indiana University Press, 1993).

[2] The linkage of comedy to eros goes back to Roman law and the ban on citizens appearing on stage, because theatre was foreign and immoral, the histrions being Greek players who would walk amongst the audience semi-naked, arousing physical reactions. See Florence Dupont, 'La scène juridique' 26

Judicial Uses of Images. Peter Goodrich, Oxford University Press.
 DOI: 10.1093/oso/9780192848772.003.0004

The body is funny, particularly the nose, but the unexpected apparition of persons in their corporeal matrix, the comic and erotic dimensions of these images, has generally been overlooked, deemed peripheral, *sotto voce* asides at most, and yet as Freud points out at length this negligible quality is of prime interpretative significance because the marginal is of hidden yet central importance.[3] The comic, manifest in visual jokes, is symptomatic or at the very least merits some analysis as relating to the unconscious sources of law's psychic economy. I will not digress into Freud too far for fear of slips, but a few preliminary words on the significance of comedy, the force of laughter, the eros and morphosis that these visual *scintiallae juris* portend must meet the eye. The *jus* in justice, the sauce of law, is a primary facet of the retinal equity that this work seeks to deliver. And it is an old topic, from the Roman jurist Valerius Flaccus' imaginary cases, to Quintilian's declamations, to the mock trials of the Basoche, to Inns of Court revels, to the curious customs and courts collected in Blount's *Fragmenta antiquitatis,* to the collections of *facetiæ iuris, Lawyer's Merriments,* the *Comic Blackstone,* the *Green Bag* and other less diverting *ludi liberales.*[4] Just some examples from a vast array of literatures and comedic performances to whose visual features and histrionic forms I will direct attention.

The tradition of visual comedy in legal texts stems principally from the legal emblem books which were in significant part humorous, serious playfulness—*serio ludere*—being their genre and intent. The visual form developed out of the Erasmian tradition of the recollection and relay of adages, of classically derived epithets, apothegms, maxims, dogmas, brief sayings, which were now used for didactic emblems with ludic as well as juridico-political purposes. It was a lawyer, the Italian jurist Alciato, who added woodcut pictures to the adages which blossomed into the genre of legal emblems which Hayaert discusses at length as *mens emblematica* and which transforms later into the comic cartoon and other instructive humourous didactic devices that lead from laughing to teaching through pictures: *ridendo ad pigendo docere.*[5] I will not repeat that history here save to note

Communications 62 (1977); and for discussion in English, see Goodrich, 'Law', in Tom Sloane (ed.), *Encyclopedia of Rhetoric* (New York: Oxford University Press, 2001).

[3] Freud, *The Joke*; Erica Weitzman, *Irony's Antics* (Evanston: Northwestern University Press, 2016).

[4] Stephanie Lysyk, 'Loving the Censor: Legendre, Censorship and the Theatre of the Basoche', 10 *Cardozo Studies in Law and Literature* 113 (1999); Thomas Blount, *Fragmenta antiquitatis* (London: Atkins, 1674 edn); John Willock (ed.), *Legal* Facetiæ: *Satirical and Humorous* (London: Literary Society, 1887); David Murray, *Lawyer's Merriments* (Glasgow: MacLehose, 1912); Gilbert A. A Beckett, *The Comic Blackstone* [1869] (Wentworth Press, 2019). I review the literature in Goodrich, 'Satirical Legal Studies: From the Legist to the *Lizard*' 103 *Michigan Law Rev.* 397 (2004). Peters, *Law as Performance*, 280–295 provides a bravura conspectus of the force and importance of the revels or, as she coins them, 'law-sports'.

[5] Valerie Hayaert, Mens emblematica *et humanisme juridique* (Geneva: Droz, 2008), and for a brief version of her thesis, see Hayaert, 'Emblems', in Stern et al. (eds), *Oxford Handbook of Law and Humanities* (Oxford: Oxford University Press, 2019); Anne Teissier-Ensminger, *Fabuleuse juridicité: Sur la littérarisation des genres juridiques* (Paris: Garnier, 2015) especially 816–823, pays considerable attention to the ludic and comedic dimensions of jurisliterature. See also, Goodrich, *Legal Emblems and the Art of Law*: Obiter depicta *as the Governance of Vision* (Cambridge: Cambridge University Press, 2014).

the adage that I see and I laugh—*video et rideo*—being the Latin mode of apprehending that the imaginal is the most prone to the ridiculous and risible because what we see reminds us inevitably also, as Norbert Elias so fondly explained, of our bestial character, the explosiveness of the body, and the wifty waftings of the jurists' proboscis. The comedy of manners is joined to the buffoonery of body parts. Where, however, is the judicial in the imaginal of manners, where the affect of the agelast? The answer lies in practice, *a comicis,* and the frequently remarked uses of comedy in advocacy and in judicial responses, in their dictats, fiats and fuits from centre stage.[6]

For purposes of classification and analysis of the uses of humourous images in decisions, three categories are important in defining the relation of wit to judgement, and thence to the reasoning of jokes.[7] First is *hauteur,* meaning hierarchy and the expression of superiority as Hobbes and others have depicted the phenomenon of laughing at something or someone.[8] This is ontological and political in the sense that it places the subject laughed at and so re-establishes the superiority of the judge in the corpus of images viewed here. Second is insight, the humorous image that sees and sees through the subject viewed, as in *video et rideo*—I see and I laugh.[9] This is epistemological, the vision leading directly to decision, the seeing through constituting an uncovering and revelation of the clue that determines the verdict. The third criterion is ethical and political, meaning that humour and eros, comedy and the desire that it manifests and incites, is potentially transformative. The power of humour lies in the physical shaking of the body, the visceral incorporation of laughter, the convulsion of the diaphragm, the breaking up of the face as brilliantly discerned in Parvalescu's treatise on the topic.[10] Here the question is one of *détournement,* of transformation through the matterphoric power of humour both to explode the complacency of the established and familiar, and to transport meaning to new spaces.

[6] Quintilian, *Institutio oratoria* (Cambridge, MA: Harvard University Press, 2001) §36.431–436: ..., *ego dicam: a comicis* ... Meaning learn Latin from those that speak it, and common law too, by extension, from common use.

[7] On wit and judgement, see Laurence Sterne, *The Life and Opinions of Tristram Shandy, Gentleman* [1759–1767] (Harmondsworth: Penguin, 1978); and in juristic terms, see Laura Little, *Guilty Pleasures: Comedy and Law in America* (New York: Oxford University Press, 2018). For accessible analysis of humour as the bestial in the bodily, see Simon Critchley, *On Humour* (London: Routledge, 2011); and for a general survey of the politics of comedy, see Terry Eagleton, *Humour* (New Haven: Yale University Press, 2019).

[8] Contemporary lawyers, on those rare occasions that they turn to questions of humour, have a tendency to start from and privilege the Hobbesian theory. See, for example, Little, *Guilty Pleasures,* at 9, and most recently Rachel DiCioccio and Laura Little, 'Comedy Collides with the Courtroom', 92 *Temple Law Rev. Online* (2020) at 4.

[9] The maxim is given in various emblems, although for ease of reference I take it here from the frontispiece of Lenton's *Characters: Or, Wit and the World in Their Proper Colours* (London: Samuel Speed, 1563): *Dum vivio video, & Dum video rideo.* Other editions have variant forms of this inscription.

[10] Anna Parvulescu, *Laughter: Notes on a Passion* (Cambridge, Mass: MIT Press, 2010); and before her, the immortal Laurent Joubert, *Treatise on Laughter* [1560] (Tuscaloosa: Alabama University Press, 1980).

In the latter sense of transformation, the comic image is latently or projectively an act of morphosis that shifts and changes the subject viewing and the substance, legally the conflict, being viewed. It presents, as Professor Peters so ably recounts in her history of law as performance, both the appearance of reality and the illusion of the real: 'The advocate's artful reality effect, heightened through *actio*, did not offer a mere illusion of reality (as the actor's did): it made reality appear as real as it really was.'[11] The ludic in the illusory is in her account central to the theatrics of law and takes up what the barrister Blount, in his *Glossography*, terms comediography, namely the staging of a fable 'as in a mirror, the similitude of civil and private life, beginning with some troubles, but ending with Agreement or joy. These plays are called *comœdia* ... '[12] The explicit staging or theatrical import of introducing depictions, figures, pictures, scenes, and sketches into judgements to 'show' the resolution is to provide a visual ending, a putatively happy climax and outcome. The morphosis or shift in significance is a remediation of the legal conflict and stages entry into both civil and private change of key. The image in the judicial determination is in this sense a species of what Debord terms metagraphy, the shift of an item and here an optic into a novel context thereby revising both the significance of the image and the meaning of the discourse into which it is inserted.[13] Humour, the comedy of the staged trial, is here an implicit attack upon solemnity and a challenge to anterograde conceptions of objectivity because it is everywhere evident that the order of things, denotation, reference, and meaning, are not simply what they seem.

At the risk of being heavy-handed, the orchestration of the juridical comedy, the hierarchical placement of those appearing before the law in their varied superior and subordinate positions, has an ontographic role to play as is suggested by the glossographer's use of the term mirror to describe comedy as 'a kind of fable, representing as in a Mirror, the similitude of a civil and private life, beginning for the most part with some troubles, but ending with Agreement or joy' and one could add concluding with social contract and legal promulgation.[14] The mirror identifies, it subjectifies and in a spatial sense it marks the place of the person before the law. It is closely related to Freud's concept of narcissism. It is true that the image is necessarily marked by narcissism, the myth of seeing oneself as another that Ovid relays and which Lacan reformulates as the mirror phase of subjective development. For Freud, as already adverted, humour has a specifically narcissistic aspect which he depicts in the essay on 'Humour':

[11] Julie Stone Peters, *Law as Performance* (Oxford: Oxford University Press, 2022), 87.

[12] The definition of comedy (*comœdia*) is from Thomas Blount, Glossographia*: or a Dictionary, Interpreting all such Hard Words, Whether Hebrew, Greek, Latin, Italian, Spanish, French, Teutonick Belgick, British or Saxon, as are now used in our Refined English Tongue* (London: Newcomb, 1656) s.v. comedy.

[13] Guy Debord, 'A User's Guide to Détournement', in *Situationist International Anthology*, trans. Ken Knabb (2006), www.bopsecrets.org/SI/. There is fine discussion in Keston Sutherland, *Stupefaction: A Radical Anatomy of Phantoms* (London: Seagull Books, 2011).

[14] Thomas Blount, *Glossographia* s.v. comedy.

> Like jokes and the comic, humour has something liberating about it; but it also has something of grandeur and elevation ... The grandeur in it clearly lies in the triumph of narcissism, the victorious assertion of the ego's invulnerability. The ego refuses to be distressed by the provocations of reality, to let itself be compelled to suffer. It insists that it cannot be affected by the traumas of the external world; it shows, in fact, that such traumas are no more than occasions for it to gain pleasure.[15]

Hauteur inflates the superego and in doing so diminishes the ego and the circumstance that confronts the judge. It is lesser and deluded if there is any indication to the contrary. Thus the brown suited lawyer, next to the ostrich, both with their heads in the ground, is ironically exposed and belittled. It is a distancing technique in which both judge and viewer differentiate themselves from the subject viewed. They look at rather than with, closing and not opening the image to its own responsiveness. The subject becomes an object, and the strictures of legal logic produce absurd results through masochistic attention to detail.[16]

Back in the trial, in the court room from which judgement still emanates, the picture brings with it the lure of ludic desire and the prospect of an element of comedy, occasioned by satisfaction of the scopophilic drive, the longing to see, to make evident and visible the matter and material of trial. Escape from abstraction, from relentless verballing as Leiboff coins the drone of advocates and precedents, is another prompt of surplusage, as a remedy for attention deficit, as desire for action.[17] Make it vivid is a primary rhetorical rule and judges are not immune to such affectations. The body and part objects appear in staged and demanding forms in the reasoning of decisions, as excitation and excess, as well as supports of outcome. This is not, of course, to dismiss the element of Eros, or the force of laughter, but it is important to defining a third phase in the judicial circulation of images which is that of the appeal to comedic affect and the optical drive to persuade the audience of the force of decision. This is not to say that the images are persuasive, and especially not to critical analysis, but they do tend to open up the decisional process and betray what is generally the restraint, or simple conservatism of the judicial eye to popular perception and, frequently, approval. The last laugh, the rendition of judgement, is the longest, meaning that the judge's height, the looking down, the provision of resolution fosters a comedic and to some extent participatory sense of superiority. To borrow from an unlikely source,

[15] Freud, 'Humour', [1927] in *Complete Psychological Works* (London: Hogarth Press, 1961).

[16] See, for example, the cases provided by Judge Charles Darling, *Scintillae juris* (London: Davis & Son, 1879), an early humorist writing imaginary cases in comic style, later made famous by A.P. Herbert. See, for instance, *De Fraude v Snafflebit*, a case of warranty, in which the defendant warranted that the horse was 'quiet in harness'. Purchased on 29 February, a 'leap year', when the Plaintiff's groom tried to put the bridle over the horse, it bit his ear, kicked him, and then galloped away and has not since been discovered. As the horse was not harnessed, the Plaintiff could not prove that it was not *quiet in harness*.

[17] Marett Leiboff, *Towards a Theatrical Jurisprudence* (London: Routledge, 2019) at 62.

Charles Lamb on 'Stage Illusion', where he remarks that it is 'a proof of the highest skill in the comedian when, without absolutely appealing to an audience, he keeps up a tacit understanding with them, and makes them, unconsciously to themselves, a party in the scene'.[18] The judge too is also a player, a comedian, and the comic image, the surprising optical turn, is one device that they can use to garner approval and imply legitimacy. Thus Judge Posner ridicules the attorney who has failed to cite earlier precedent, with an image of an ostrich. Judge Biery pillories the nudist bar with a figure dancing on her head, or laments the lack of civility in the San Antonio Bar by reproducing a map of northern incursion upon the Great State of Texas. Chief District Judge Walker, in a fractious litigation concerning administrative delay in providing court filings, inserts a meme from Marvel, two cartoon spidermen pointing at each other. The judge views this as a salutary corrective to litigants who are simply blaming each other so as to take none themselves.[19] It is also, though this is not analysed, a cartoon meme, a children's comic book figure and image, a regression and populist expansion of the tone and modality of judgement, which is here expressly *a comicis* or in a common manner.

Instances of judicial comic eros are more often less explicit, if no less unconscious. An example can be taken from the Federal Court of Australia, where Justice Steven David Rares favoured feminine dishabiliment.[20] It was a trademark case, in which the respondent argued that their registered trademark 'Centrefold Entertainment' was infringed by another party, Metro Business Centre Ltd, using 'Centrefold Strippers'. The complainant, Centrefold Entertainment, comprised solely of one Mr Prendergast, brought the action on the basis that the word centrefold was sufficiently distinctive and unique to his business to be infringed by the appellant. The doctrinal issue was lexical: did the word have a sufficiently distinct meaning to be infringed by others using it? At the end of a judgement of two score pages, the conclusion that Rares arrives at is:

> I am of opinion that the word 'centrefold' is not allusive or metaphorical of the services supplied by Entertainment ... The word is not inherently adapted to distinguish any services that Entertainment provides from the services that others, such as the Metro parties, Ms Scott or Ms Jones, provide ...[21]

No image is necessary to support this conclusion, and yet two images of Centrefold models in bikinis are reproduced in the judgement, and one screenshot of an advertisement for escort services which latter I will reproduce shortly, alone,

[18] Charles Lamb, *The Essays of Elia* (New York: Putnam, 1845) Series 2, at 21.

[19] *Courthouse News Service v Brenda Forman* (2022) 606 F.Supp.3d 1200 at 1216 reproducing the image and providing the link that follows: https://screenrant.com/spider-man-pointing-meme-cartoon-origin/, and eFigure 4.

[20] *Metro Business Centre v Centrefold Entertainment Pty Ltd* [2017] FCA 1249 can be accessed at https://larc.cardozo.yu.edu/faculty-online-pubs/61/, eFigures 7 and 8.

[21] *Metro Business Centre v Centrefold Entertainment Pty Ltd* [2017] FCA 1249.

as the bikini clad centrefold models are beyond the ken and spectral permissions that the Press lawyers demand. The images used are important and distinctive for their salacious intimations of flesh, or soft-core erotic character, and, to reiterate the point, they are included in colour, full frontal, in the decision.[22] The insertion of such images is stipulated as being to evidence the meaning of a word, which the judge concludes is not distinctive of any specific use. The pictures of centre page models, as well as a screen capture of an erotic webpage image of rouge lips and white teeth nibbling the end of a finger, may seem as opaque legally as they are ribald, raunchy and raucous in their rendering of visual judgement. As Judge Rares formulates it: '"Centrefold" is an ordinary English word that is apt to describe the kinds, qualities and characteristics of performers, models and others, as persons who appear, or have appeared or are prepared to appear, nude or scantily clad before strangers and in pages of magazines'.[23] This does not suggest that the verbal reasoning, the etymology, or socio-linguistic features of the word require the insertion of pictures of their use and denotation, yet there can be no question but that the judicial atmosphere of the case, the perceived sensuality of the referent of the word and the judicial sensibility at issue and at stake in the case, are materially augmented by the relay of pictures.

There is a certain honesty, a degree of freedom, an insight of a unique kind into the judicial sense of the word, of what the judge imagines, as one that long predates Mr Prendergast's claim to have invented it for his own business purposes. It evidences or perhaps better exposes a certain worldliness in the judge, that Rares is common, but more importantly it visualizes the affective substrate of the decision and puts on view the internal imagery of judgement, the play of themes that constitute its undercurrents of desire, exploitation, objectification, titillation, tumescence and prurience, comedy, and manners, as the marks of arbitrium and decision. Here, in the eros of its imaginal relay, one can see the site of affective determination, both the common character of the images and the judge's view that exploitation of women is linked to inexactitude with words. The models are histrions, fleshy reminders of worldly lures and distractions, of materiality that the judge will rise above. It is an admission, nonetheless, that where there is a body, there is sex, if only in designation, and where there is gender and performativity there is also comedy, and the full panoply of *la comédie humaine* in the images. The website commendations of the services of Entertainment are on view and incorporated into the vision in decision. It is in one facet an instance of judicial lexitainment

[22] In support of this viewing, I can note that when I sent these images as separate files for publication in an article in the academic journal *Critical Inquiry*, I was twice told by the managing editor that my transfer had been hacked and that I must send the correct images. The article and images eventually appeared in Goodrich, 'Retinal Justice: Rats, Maps and Masks', 47 *Critical Inquiry* 241 (2021) at 258. The images are posted on the following link: https://larc.cardozo.yu.edu/faculty-online-pubs/61/, eFigures 8 and 9.

[23] *Metro Business Center v Centrefold*, para. 102.

or of law going pop.[24] It matters more, however, that the insertion of bodies in bikinis, of lips caressing fingers, is accompanied by a judicial discourse that treats Prendergast as a mendacious, unreliable, and incredulous witness who lies in his words and in his images. As with the earlier adverted decision on the minimum attire required of sexually orientated businesses in *35 Bar and Grille*, the substrate of judgement, ironically captured here in the repetition of centrefold images, is that of implicit moral condemnation, a puritanical censure of sorts that also, in its very repetition, relays an imaginal attachment to them, an elliptical sensibility and desire. What is supposed to be abstract as opposed to conceptual *hauteur*, legal sovereignty rather than fleshy incorporation, is confused by the mingling of erotic images in a text that is concerned with verbal strains of reference.

The disapprobative drive of the judgement is thus most evident in the second screenshot of Centrefold, in which the centrality of the depicted body displaces the words, and the trademark asserted is only marginally visible whereas the model is all that is fully in view. The word Entertainment, in caps, is seen but Centrefold, the appellation in issue, is cut off at the knees. Below, the model, named Chrissy Teigen, is on full display, legs akimbo, triangulated to mirror the bikini, on bare rocks, with water as the backdrop to her windswept hair. Chrissy, however, was not one of Entertainment's 'hot models', nor was she on its books at all, the picture having been taken from 'a 2012 edition of the well-known Sports Illustrated magazine'.[25] This behaviour on the part of Prendergast is 'unscrupulous', 'misleading or deceptive', and so leads to a general discounting of his testimony. Words slip into images, discourse into bodies, and texts to acts. The image is the other scene of the text and, in this instance, the texture of decision. The libidinal economy of the determination is played out across the tensor of the pictures, the skin of the histrion displacing the tympanum of the text to provide an image of an emergent model only partially restrained by trademark or words. The excessive quality of the pictures is precisely their point. They are more real than the claim to trademark property, and they are equally visceral, the *vividæ rationes* emergent out of the judgement, comedically undoing the verbal locution of reasons. The judge is stretching, in the rhetorical terms adverted earlier, *a comicis*, to the comedians but also to the common, acknowledging the reality of the erotic and the expansiveness, the human allure of desire.

The severed head of the page, the decapitated logo of Centrefold, becomes a part object of judgement in the third visual insertion, that of a screenpage of advertisements for strippers, which includes, as mentioned earlier, in the top left, sinister chief in the heraldic argot, an image of lips and teeth biting the tip of a finger (Figure 4.1). Next to this, following the legally required textual line of vision from

[24] Lawrence M. Friedman, 'Lexitainment: Legal Process as Theater', *DePaul Law Review* 50 (2000), 539–558; Richard Sherwin, *When Law Goes Pop: The Vanishing Line between Law and Popular Culture* (Chicago: Chicago University Press, 2000).

[25] *Metro Business Center v Centrefold*, para. 80.

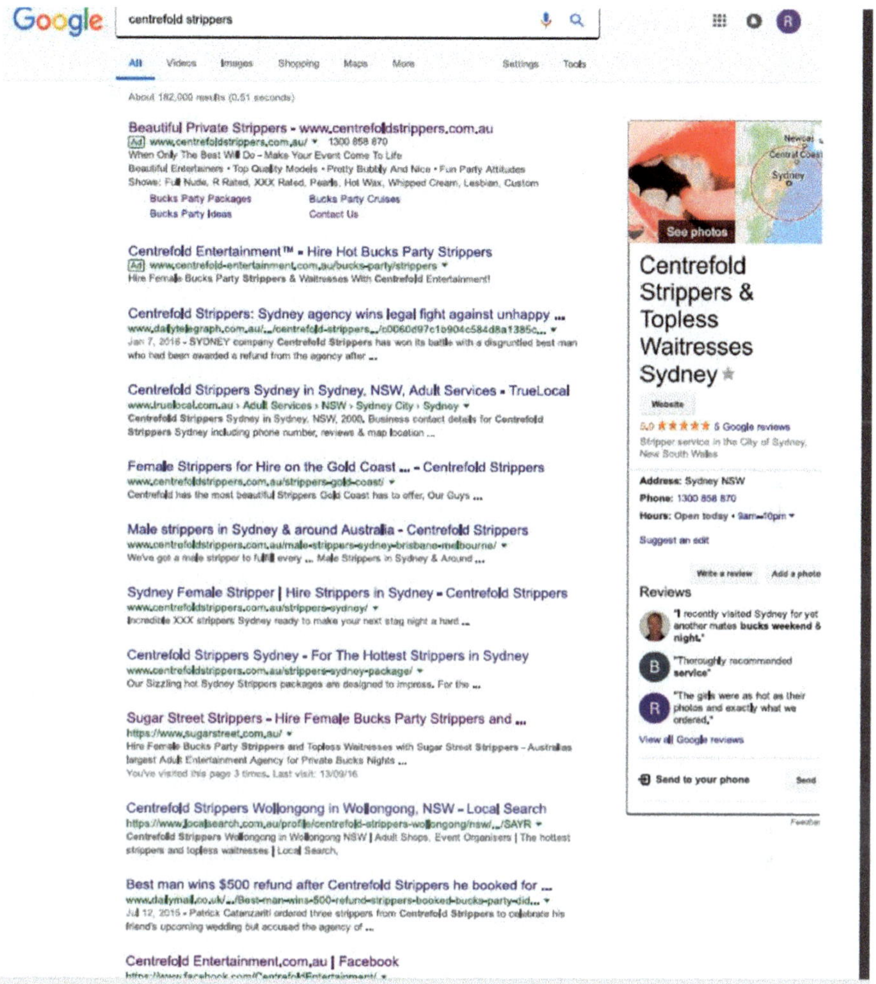

Figure 4.1 Insertion by Judge Rares in *Metro Business Centre v Centrefold Entertainment Pty Ltd* [2017].

left to right, is a segment of a map of the East coast of Australia, an isolarion of sorts, which draws a red ring around the capital of New South Wales and its environs. It seems visually to suggest that the lipstick labial aureole is implicitly encircling Sydney. The red of lipstick desire, of fleshy labia, becomes the sanguine sign and bloody mark of danger. The teeth here playing out Freud's fantasy of *vagina dentata* imply in the adjoining map a cordon rouge of threat, a target, a virus to be contained or eradicated. Ironically, which is to say comedically, the screen page is inserted for its thirteen websites advertising sexual services using the header or name Centrefold, except for one which references Sugar Street Strippers. This in itself was sufficient to eliminate the trade mark because it clearly lacks distinctiveness, whereas the image suggests a certain contradistinction, showing as it does Centrefold but with no accompanying Entertainment.

Do we need such explicit visuals? But that is simply to ask if repression is preferable to expression or if judicial divagations are to be ignored due to some transcendental privilege appurtenant to a hierarchy long since demised and defunct, at least in scholarly terms. It is not a question of right or wrong in relation to the determination so much as it is an issue of visual apprehension and of recognition also of the body that judges. There is in the determination of Rares J. a dimension of disapproval of the activity and the testimony of Mr Prendergast. It is the banality of the photographs, the lack of art and aesthetic novelty in the pictures, their purloined quality, that as much as anything else denudes the claimant of success. Words will apparently not capture the full extent to which Prendergast is ghastly, his advertisements misleading, his claim not simply insalubrious, but conniving, manipulative, and perilously close to fraud. The pictures are not accidents, the figures are metonyms of a lack of scruples and of exploitation, save that Rares J. cannot say that; he needs to show it for there to be adequate force and affective power in what is already a lengthy written and revised decision. There is, in sum, an openness, an exposure of judicial affect that is rare and in itself probative of the incalculable force, the justice of decision as inhabitant and relay of the imaginal, now captured in the insertion of pictures as the appearance of the subject of judgement far below the vantage point of the judicial throne.

There is an element of the classical histrion, of the erotic comedian, the body of the actor circling amongst the auditors, to the vision in decision. Take the analysis a step further and it is Rares who ambulates amongst images and exposes the comedy and the common character of the centrefolds and strippers. It is the judge who screengrabs the pointed red tipped finger caressing lip-glossed labia. In doing so, the judge expressly places the subjects of judgement, and specifically Mr Prendergast, as being in this instance the generator of purloined images of a young woman in 'a suggestive pose in what usually appeared to be lingerie or a bikini'.[26] These images are false lures, deceptive and misleading suggestions, lies perpetrated by Prendergast who is visibly exposed in the imaginal insertions placed in the judgement. He is within the danger zone, trapped in the red circle, part of the virus or contamination of the regional capital. It is that latter sense of the image as a mode of marking and placing the subject of judgement in vivid visual context that constitutes the immediate comedic role of the image in the decision. The judge, in a rare and explicit exposure of the subject who is to be dismissed, stands high above, reproducing images from popular illustrated magazines, porno pulp, sexploitative pictures that are by implication demeaning and specifically denigrate the overblown claim of the litigant to own the Centrefold logo.

[26] *Metro Business Center v Centrefold*, para. 24.

Adopting again the argot of spatial justice, Judge Rares cannot be in the same place as Prendergast but rather enfolds or centrefolds his claim into a populist genre and demotic demographic that is considerably below the refined language and lofty principles of the Trade Mark Act of 1995, section 7(1), and in infraction of Australian Consumer Law section 18. The wit of the decision is not evident in the fairly standard forms of judgemental evaluation of the respondent Prendergast's performance as a witness, but in the visual excoriation of two digital centrefolds and a Google search splash-page with a salacious image in the top left of the screen. What is significant is the juxtaposition, the mingling of partially clad female models and a picture of an open mouth and gleaming teeth in a judgement, semi-bare life on the page of decision. It is rare to encounter soft porn pictures in a law report, but there they are, extant, vivid, luring images, and they are inserted to place the subject as well as the subject matter of decision. The law is above, the populous and populace are below, ironically both distanced and included by pictures, mapped with a circle of red quarantining them and their behaviours, Prendergast quoted and quipped.

The Australian case is an extreme one, allowing for a clearer perspective upon the most usual function of affective images, erotic and comic, which is first to humour, to give appearance to a bearable lightness of being, to the human comedy, and to dismiss it in the discursive juristic substrate of the pictures. Second, the subject placed by the depictions, materialized associatively or directly in the inserted image, is at the same time evaporated by the visual association. Ontographically, by association, Prendergast is a fool, a lascivious businessman, a slabbering subject and an *in vivo* disgrace, defined out, disapproved. The implication is that his was the unspeakable act of exploiting these women, these images, these malversations that cannot be said but can only be shown. Innocence has been corrupted. Insofar as *hauteur* is a physical feature of being a judge, the throne upon which they sit being generally above the court on a raised tier, and protected by clerks and bar, with their own entrance and exit separate from the other protagonists in the pit of the court, it is not so surprising that humour will often be pitched against those that appear 'before' the judge and their elevated and protected architectural site.[27] This will be translated into a visual comedy of juridical manners in which the litigant is put back in their place, in the pit, prendergasted by pictures. To which one must add that in addition to *hauteur*, a feature that accompanies all three genres of the comedic eros of imagery, there are also implicit epistemological, ethical, and political implications to the depictions that are circulated.

[27] See, for example, Christie Davies, 'Judges and Humour in Britain: From Anecdotes to Jokes', in Jessica Davis and Sharyn Anleu (eds), *Judges, Judging and Humour* (Cham, Switzerland: Palgrave Macmillan/Springer, 2018) 53–58. On gender dimensions to superiority, see Les Moran, 'What's a Box of "Bakewell Tarts" Got to Do With it? Performing Gender as a Judicial Virtue in the Theatre of Justice', in Davis and Anleu (eds), *Judges, Judging, and Humour*, at 211.

The pictorial joke, in the second genre, has a strong epistemological role to play. In *Metro Business v Centrefold* the picture of Chrissy Teigen has the ostensive purpose of showing a model advertising Prendergast's Company, despite the fact that she did not work for Centrefold Entertainment, and was not available via that website or organization. The picture is evidence of duplicity, but it is important to note that such an epistemic function is not elaborated upon nor referenced as part of the visual impact of placing the scantling costume colour picture in the text of the judgement, honouring Chrissy while belittling Prendergast. *Hauteur*, with its implications of pride and narcissism, may appear to play the role of the superego and of normative regulation but the image is not a norm, it is an intimation of affect and of thought streamed associatively in the preconscious mode of reverie, as play and exploration of the associative chains that the picture, as remediation, introduces. The comico-erotic image puts the body into the text, and while on the one hand the legal judgement endeavours to clothe the body with the discourse of doctrine, it is equally the case that the image strips the text of its words.

The image is not a norm, and so a degree of autonomy and a distinct economy of the judicial psyche needs to be pursued. Rares writes to the accompaniment of imaginal insertions and, in presenting the photographs of centrefold subjects, also and necessarily exposes himself and the intimacy of reasoning. The pictures are the vanishing point of his discursive logic in the translation of imagery, in the visualization of the unsaid. Wit in the form of the image can be more subtle, but the same principle of addressing the meaning that escapes discourse in the modality of the visual insertion carries its own epistemic force, the picture as a vehicle of a heterotopic, affective, and sensible mode of knowing. In a UK case involving a claim of patent infringement by the European Central Bank, the role of visual humour is supplementary and epistemic.[28] Document Security Systems Incorporated claimed that the European Bank had infringed their patent, EP UK 0 455 750. It brought similar claims against the Bank, based on 'sister' patents, in Germany, France, Netherlands, Spain, Italy, Luxembourg, Belgium, and Austria. The English first instance Judge Kitchin had held the patent invalid, as did a French Court, while the German and Dutch courts had held it valid. The Court remarks 'that [i]n sporting terms, the score is currently 2-2 to the ECB at first instance level'.[29] This leads the court to descry the plurality of venues for patent validity and patent infringement claims, which in its view should be heard by the same court at the same time.

On the patent validity issue, Lord Justice Jacob indulges in a moment of levity, referencing Professor Mario Franzosi, who 'likens a patentee to an Angora cat. When validity is challenged, the patentee says his patent is very small: the cat with its fur smoothed down, cuddly and sleepy. But when the patentee goes on the

[28] *European Central Bank v Document Security Systems Inc.* [2008] EWCA Civ 192.
[29] *European Central Bank v Document Security*, para 4.

attack, the fur bristles, the cat is twice the size with teeth bared and eyes ablaze'. But then he observes: '[s]o much is by-the-by'.[30] This is presumably because humour is marginal, although it has to be pointed out that the cat that bristles to twice the size is creating an illusion, it has not increased its stature by a single cubit and the court goes on to hold the same of the patent EP UK 0 455 750. It has not patented, as is claimed, the moiré effect that the European Bank has used, nor is that printing mechanism implicit in the patent. The claim, when read closely, is all bristling fur and no substance. A cat fight and not a real dispute seems the most likely connotation.

The move is then from felines and fur to pixels and moustaches to explain the method of halftone printing and its combination with moiré effects to produce bank notes that cannot be counterfeited, even on the most sophisticated laser copiers (Figure 4.2). To explain halftone printing the Court inserts an enlarged image of halftone dots and then one seen at normal size. The Court reproduces two pictures of Albert Einstein, one from a few metres away, and one from close up. The Court does not name Einstein—jokes are worthless if explained—and in the second image, Einstein loses his moustache. Note first that the Court reverses the previous image of halftone dots, the close up on the right becomes the normal sighting, whereas the normal viewing becomes the pixelated image without the definition of the moustache (Figures 4.3 A & B) A little quip to ensure that the reader is awake and adept enough, like 'the skilled addressee' who is the notional reader of the patent application, to understand that the image of Einstein is an inverted instance of the previous depiction of dots. You don't have to be Einstein to understand the process, which is then explicated further by an image of a moiré grid and then a colour depiction of a grid overlaying coloured halftone dots, all reproduced in black and white.

The polka dots are not quite a bikini but the selection of Einstein as the image does humourously raise the question of the level of expertise expected of the skilled addressee. The inventor of the theory of relativity, a synecdoche for genius, and the playful inversion of the image of dots and the photoportraits, serves the purpose of visual allegory, again reversing what is necessary for patent validity: the application does not include the bristling feline fur, nor does it include the famously wild hair of Albert Einstein. And the best feature of the visual jape is that it does not have to be said, it is simply there in the judgement for all to see. The obviousness of the implication is the implication of obviousness into the patent application and specifically its determination of the CGK—common general knowledge—that our skilled addressee will possess. The photoportrait suggests an aspiration and a standard that Document Security Systems had failed to meet, their patent application

[30] Lord Rodger of Earlsferry, 'Humour and Law', *Scots Law Times* 20 (2009) at 2, for brief discussion of cats and humour; see also Lucas Hori, 'Bons Mots, Buffoonery, and the Bench: The Role of Humor in Judicial Opinions', 60 *UCLA L.Rev.Disc*, 16 (2012).

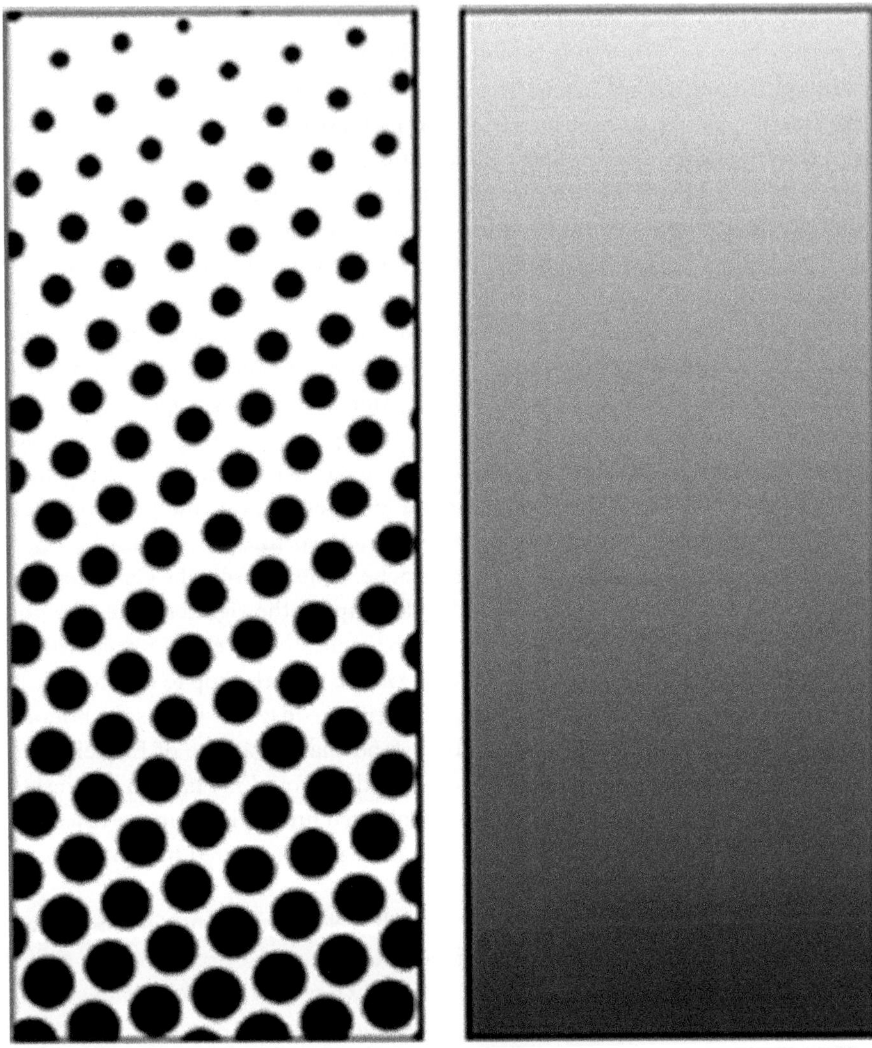

Figures 4.2 A & B Insertion by Lord Justice Jacob in *European Central Bank v Document Security* (2008).

lacking the requisite detail, and so failing to provide a valid description and proprietary claim to the system of moiré that the European Central Bank had been utilizing. If an image were to be taken from the practices of European banks, then the 'screen trap' picture of a snipe on the Dutch 100 Guilder note, discussed with reference to the prominence of this picture of a bird, would have been the obvious choice. And again, Einstein is significant as the selection in its implication of relativity, the warping of space by the size of the object suggesting that pragmatic concerns might also favour the megalithic, multi-state, Bank. It is tempting

(a) (b)

Figures 4.3 A & B Insertion by Lord Justice Jacob in *European Central Bank v Document Security* (2008).
Photo by Philippe Halsman © Philippe Halsman Estate.

again to suggest *in ludo veritas*, that this is an instance of comedic truth, *serio-ludere* providing access to the reasoning of the judgement and easing the path of following the very complicated deliberations as to the techniques of securitizing banknotes and the details of the patent which even the expert witnesses had trouble understanding.

There is a pleasing economy to the subtle visual deliberation and its silent humour or mute wit. Einstein too can be made to disappear, even the genius is relative, pixels consume us all. The image of judgement lingers not merely as a mnemonic but as an instance of contrast and analogy that indicates how the image is not entirely what it seems, it requires cross-examination to show that the humour is significant and symptomatic, the facilitation of reasoning important. It is comedic without being comic. The playful use of the serious looking photoportrait has explicative value as well as humorous effect. The comedy, the joke, as noted, is for Freud the contribution made to the comic from the realm of the unconscious.[31] There are elements of identification in the use of the depiction and the implication that even the most complex of phenomena can be broken down into constituent parts and can then frame a solution to relativity or here the grave and engraving issue of protecting European currency from counterfeiting. The image is an instance of *elegantia iuris*, of a humorous supplement that enlarges and appears as a conduit for the reasoning of judgement, the depiction acting as a totalizing representation, only slightly askew, of the decision. Einstein,

[31] Freud, *The Joke*, at 163: 'Let us now draw together those characteristics of the joke that can be referred to its formation in the unconscious. There is above all its peculiar brevity …' which is taken as a sign of the unconscious revision that it has undergone.

as an emblem of science and of genius, appears in the judgement as a symbol of didactic correction and humorous remonstration, apparently offering epistemic visual evidence of the logical slippage of the claim being made according to a trajectory that moves from the exaggerated fur of fighting felines to the halftones that the claimant has inflated into the assertion of infringement of a patented effect.

The epistemic import of the visual quip is indirect, affective and lateral rather than direct and demonstratively probative. This is because the comedic pictorial instances are brief and bound to the surface to the text, but in terms of emotional cognition and pleasure, their source is unconscious, for here, in Freud's formulation, '[t]he thought plunging into the unconscious to form the joke, is only revisiting the ancient home of its erstwhile play ... '.[32] The visual jape and feline figures access and invoke an alternate scene and body, a remembered sense of infancy, of feeling, and the ludic logic of desire. The comedy can be interpreted as having a dual function in both the relay and reasoning of decision. As a feature of transmission of the judgement, the image is impertinent and surprising in that it is not of a banknote or of figures on bank notes, snipes, for instance, on Dutch 100 Guilder notes. It signals a moment of introspection and didacticism, in which the instance of levity, the *fort-da* of the depiction mirrors the appearance and disappearance of the desired object, generative respectively of pleasure and disappointment. The Court is thus appealing to the viewer, playing with the image, reasoning visually not only to indicate the ludic character of counterfeiting, but also to demonstrate the classical figure of forgery as a trick that the law can unveil and expose. Consequent upon this entry into the realm of magic deconstructed by way of the prosopopoeia of the theory of relativity, the second role of the image, conscious or otherwise, is that of expanding the medium of deliberation, a remediation that signals a desire for the *certum*, the particularity of the instant case, in the humorous knowledge that all certainty is relative. In this instance, where the issue is of counterfeiting, of passing off notes as authentic, the question is necessarily a visual one and the Court responds in the appropriate performative vein, in the mode of poetic justice, by inserting images that demonstrate that the complaint is unfounded, that you don't have to be Einstein to understand and use the moiré effect.

On occasion, the comical is itself the subject matter of the case and it would be wrong to leave the epistemic value of the comic and erotic without a brief account of a case involving a cartoon character. In *Hearst Holdings* the issue related to the use of the cartoon character Betty Boop and claims of trademark infringement and the tort of passing off (Figure 4.4).[33] The trademark is of the 'device' and words, meaning the cartoon image of the 1930s character, a sketch at best of the animated figure, and of the words Betty Boop, however reproduced, whatever the

[32] Ibid., at 165.
[33] *Hearst Holdings v A.V.E.L.A.* [2014] EWHC 439 (Ch).

Figure 4.4 Insertion by Justice Birss in *Hearst Holdings v A.V.E.L.A.* [2014].

typography, or swashes, tittles, and tapers, under the image of the graphic heroine. The device and on occasion the device and the words have been trademarked, as listed in the Schedule to the judgement, where an additional six images of Betty Boop are reproduced. The seven images of Betty Boop suggest a certain luxuriance, a play of similarity and difference, although it transpires from the judgement of Mr Justice Birss that for the purposes of trademark '[i]t is the character Betty Boop herself who is recognised by the average consumer. It is the character who acts as a sign. The character is recognisable in different ways, but she is the same character. The words BETTY BOOP have this effect as do pictures of her' (Figure 4.5).[34] The test for trademark is whether the 'average consumer who is reasonably well informed and reasonably circumspect' views the Betty Boop character as a brand and so indicative of origin. The sign must be distinctive, recognizable, and convey the message of origin.

According to Birss, who does not at any point analyse the seven Betty Boop images that he reproduces in the judgement, 'the key visual sign is her head. It is instantly recognisable whether on its own or with a more or less visible body'.[35] Usually the name appears with the head but 'either alone is sufficient to convey the message'. Later Justice Birss notes in terms of the distinctiveness of the brand that she can be portrayed in many ways, 'including the pose with the leg raised but

Figure 4.5 Insertion by Justice Birss in *Hearst Holdings v A.V.E.L.A.* [2014].

[34] Ibid., para. 101.
[35] Ibid., para 101.

also all the other numerous depictions either of the head alone or of the character in a myriad of styles and poses. These are all recognisably Betty Boop due I think really to her head.'[36] This leads the judge to conclude that even where the head is surrounded by red roses or has a heart shaped tattoo on her shoulder, where the font is different, and where the words 'I ♥ ME' appear above the character, on clothing, the brand and origin have been used. The average consumer would identify this as the Boop character and the merchandise as being of that origin. And if it is the head that is the sign, the visual indicator of the trademark, the carrier of the history and goodwill associated with the cartoon, then why reproduce the cluster of Boop figures as reproduced here? Why not compare the authentic Boop figure with the logos on clothes that have been sued for passing off? The answer has to be that the images are different, that there are subtle distinctions, including the barely visible uses of the words Betty Boop in the figures.

Degree of definition, size of reproduction, the hair, the curls, the eyes, the index finger pointing, the balloon heart around the head, the accompanying words or their absence would all seem to be relevant facets of the figure, of *caput*, *chef*, and head as marking the trade item. What is surprising and comedic is that the reproduction of the seven cartoon figures effectively turns the depiction into a nascent cartoon, which is after all the drawing of the same figure with slight variations to signal, when reproduced in sequence at twenty four frames per second, movement and animation. The cartoon of the neotonous amorous and erotic pop character of Boop, a flirtatious figure of a starlet caricaturing a Jazz Age flapper and doo wop style. During the mid-thirties the character had to be toned down for fear of moral censorship by the puritanical Hays Code. The cartoon indicates desire, mixing innocence with sexuality, a compulsive coiffeur, a heart shaped bust, a small body, a thigh garter all lend an air of eroticism to the character who is famous for singing 'Minnie the Moocher' and 'Don't Take My Boop-Oop-A-Doop away'. It is enough for the judge in an early copyright case involving Betty to conclude that 'the result is very taking, and the cartoon, shown all over the world, presented a strong temptation to an infringer ... '[37] Inserting seven images of Betty Boop is Justice Birss' way of invoking the cartoon, of animating the issue and suggesting that eros sells and thus that use of the figure should be paid for by the infringer, which is not incidentally what the New York court cited from 1934 also held. The judges are seduced by the figure, and in the case of Birss, the sevenfold pleiad portrayal indicates that number of times that the head is constant in its difference, that it is the sign of signs of Boop, the look of the trademark and an erotic figure as well as a mark that should not be infringed in any sense. In juristic provenance, the number seven also has a certain constitutional significance, as humanist lawyers

[36] Ibid., para 151.
[37] *Fleischer Studios, Inc. v Freundlich, Inc.* 5 F.Supp. 808 (1934) at 809.

liked to note.[38] Seven is the number of harmony, of musical modes or rhythms that found the commons upon which the polity is based. Seven is also the number of intervals of the spheres, and thus of days of the week and divisions of the *Digest*, and, according to Sir Edward Coke himself, of the ideal number of judges on any given bench.[39] It is in a dual sense that the visual depiction of the comic character becomes the law.

In traversing the comedic and erotic qualities of judicial images, their unspoken eros, the comedic effect of their gaze, the insight they offer into the logic of judgement and the motive of decision, the picture provides a location for determination, it places the judge in relation to the subject of dispute. The cartoon image in fact is peculiarly pertinent in that the comico-erotic picture blends words and images in a depiction of desire that straddles text and the visual. As Giddens puts it:

> the in-between status of comics exposes the complex boundary regions where text and image, rationality and aesthetic sensuality, meet. Engaging with these borders encounters the limits of law's dominant ways of knowing (the textual, the rational) with respect to the fluidity of the visual and the aesthetic, and the complexity of life more generally.[40]

Legal reason is placed by the image of Betty Boop, just as much as law materializes her as form and subject of conflict. There is also, however, in addition to the panoptic gaze of the law, the levity of the cartoon, the moment of fun, the feeling of eros or at least of play in the repetition of the image in the judicial text. The lines of the letters bend and snake into the figure of a cartoon character, a balloon heart appears as a halo around Betty's head, the text becomes image as if the words have fallen from the line, concertinaed and kaleidoscoped into the figure.[41] One form mutates into another, the text becomes labyrinthine, the linear becomes lateral, a judge meets a comical character in the course of a case and just as he judges, the cartoon sketches him. It is comedy which turns the judgement around, the depiction is in one admonition 'very taking' and the question is where

[38] Etienne Forcadel, *Sphaera legalis* [1549], reprinted in Anne Teissier-Ensminger, *La sphère du droit* (Paris: Garnier, 2011).

[39] Sir Edward Coke, *Reports*, Vol. 4 Preface, in Steve Sheppard (ed.), *The Selected Writings of Sir Edward Coke* (Indianapolis: Liberty Fund, 2003) Vol. 1, 101, arguing that the decisional deity likes uneven numbers.

[40] Thomas Giddens, 'Comics, Law, and Aesthetics: Towards the Use of Graphic Fiction in Legal Studies', 6(1) *Law and Humanities* 85 (2012) at 108. For further on comics and law, see Mark Giancaspаro, 'Picture-Perfect or Potentially Perilous? Assessing the Validity of "Comic Contracts"', 10(1) *The Comics Grid: Journal of Comics Scholarship* (2020), 1–27, and Michael Murray, 'Toward a Universal Visual Language of Law', 46(1) *Law & Psychology Rev.* (2021–2022) at 86–103.

[41] As happens, for instance, in Keith Aoki and Garrett Epps, 'Dead lines, Break downs & Troubling The Legal Subject Or "Anything You Can Do, I Can Do Meta"', 73 *Oregon Law Rev.* 551 (1994). The inspiration for this can be found in Keith Aoki's 'Casual Legal Studies'. See my 'Satirical Legal Studies: From the Legist to the *Lizard*', 103 *Michigan Law Rev.* (2004) 997, and also Thomas Giddens, *On Comics and Legal Aesthetics: Multi-modality and the Haunted Mask of Knowing* (Abingdon: Routledge, 2018) preface.

it takes, and what it takes or takes away from. In epistemological terms, Betty Boop inserted seven times into a judgement is a significant *détournement,* upending or turning around, of the trajectory of decision. It has changed form, it has engaged with a cartoon character, it is viserbal as opposed to monotonously verballed. The affect of deciding, the being 'very taken' by Boop comes into play, signalling the revenge of form upon content, of aesthetics upon the norm—*pigendo et ridendo docere,* picturing joins laughter and critique. It is what Abby Warburg termed a dynamogram, the survival of the aesthetic form, of the body of Boop, as the force behind the judgement. She must be saved, kept pure, and not exploited.

The ethical and political role of comico-erotic images, their dynamographic force, flows easily and directly from their ontological and epistemological features. Boop is placed and she has an explicatory role to play as well as a ludic affect to introduce into judgement. There is also, of course, an element of ethical and political evaluation connected to the reasoning relating to the image. She has, for Birss J., a significant head, to which he adds the evaluative opinion that the 'average consumer will see the image of Betty Boop as being attractive and in that sense aesthetic or decorative. After all, they will not want to buy a product which does not look good'.[42] So Betty looks good to the judge, she was very taking for the US judge, and so both good and a good. The moral is evident in the heart-shaped kiss of the image as a species of authorization of the product that it is attached to and helps to sell. The epistemological role of the cartoon in the judgement, as a novel and comic dimension of the normative reasoning, merits further viewing.

There are differences in definition and size to the lineal representations and it would seem arguable that a weakly pixelated Boop was not much of an endorsement and so a weak claim of infringement. The images, however, are not used for scrutiny or detailed viewing and examination. It is their presence, their immediacy and visibility that seems to be the reason for inclusion. The cartoon figures in the judgement provide the *certum* of being seen and so of particularizing in the cause of demonstrating a degree of likeness as well as the distinctiveness and repeatability of a brand. The role of the depictions is not, however, merely probative or evidential. It is also histrionic. The judge acknowledges the affective lure and visual appeal of the image, although without any supporting analysis because, presumably, it is there to be seen and the judge is assuming that he is 'one of us', a reasonably well-informed and reasonably circumspect consumer. The circumspection is a significant clue as to the illocutionary force and epistemological function of the figures in a dual sense. First, circumspection, looking around, heeding the visual insertions, is indicative of what Sir Edward Coke termed a 'visial line', a genealogy and lineage of the image as a sign, a specular intervention and difference. Betty Boop signals jazz, an era and style captured here in a fleeting static form, the mute intellection of a radical and coloured genre that the

[42] *Hearst Holdings* para. 110.

judgement seeks to contain and control. In its secondary sense, circumspection is wariness, caution, and takes the form of placing comico-erotic cartoon figures, as an appendix and appendage, in a judgement, so as to show without saying or at least without any extended analysis or discussion.

The ostensible purpose of the cartoons is that of demonstrating recognizability, but at the same time as the reasonably informed viewer acknowledges the familiarity of the figure they also feel, in the judge's opinion, the attractiveness and allure of the depicted cartoon of a stylized femininity. The drawing breaks out of the text and relays affect and emotional recognition, the comic again performing as an unconscious symptom of childhood, of play and pleasure in earlier years, a libidinal drive that is fleetingly acknowledged in the judge's approbative aside. He likes the image. He sides with Boop, and with this recognition comes the form of the visible, of the unsaid, of the image that escapes the repression barrier and flirts with the judge at the same time as it generates a palpable juristic desire to protect the vulnerable, scantily clad, delicate, feminine figure. When the judge admits that he is 'taken' by the cartoon, the confession should be interpreted analytically as a displacement triggered by the comic drawings. The affective associations are to an emotional history and patterns that draw the judge out of the textual and its normative deliberations into the realm of the imaginal whose roots lie in the corporeal, the oneiric, in childhood patterns and the ludic origins of desire. The visual figure in a juridical text is in Freudian terms a condensation, a mark of intensity and energy, the compressed point of intersection of several associative chains. It is precisely this affective dimension of judgement, the unsaid of the said, that also generates the protective armour of the decision, the determination in favour of the brand and against its imitators. It is as if Birss had thrown a juridical cloak over a scantily clad woman encountered on a dark and stormy night.

Eros is constantly engaged with the superego, fighting the law that generates desire, and while the cartoon figure motivates and relays another scene of judgement, an extra textual knowledge and decision, it also necessarily connotes an ethical and political judgement. The point can be expanded by looking at another conflict in which the judge actively engages, one that incorporates a comic, feminine, libidinal figure into the judgement together with a hyperlink to a video of the performance from which the still is taken. In *Conrad v AM Community Credit Union*, Catherine Conrad brought an action against the defendants for infringement of her intellectual property rights in her act as a singing telegram: she calls herself the 'Banana Lady' and performs wearing a costume in the shape of a giant banana. You can watch her dancing the 'Banana Shake' on YouTube, at www.youtube.com/watch?v=DG-QJWW6w5c. There is a still photo, which is in the record, of her performing in her costume.[43] Nothing more. Just a figure of

[43] *Conrad v AM Community Credit Union* 750 F.3d 634 (2014) at 635. https://larc.cardozo.yu.edu/faculty-online-pubs/61/, eFigure 9.

interest. Then the judge goes on to describe how, proceeding *pro se*, Conrad sued the defendant Credit Union for copyright infringement. Contrary to her express instructions to the Union, she alleged, attendees had recorded her performance and then posted photographs and videos online.

Deciding that her dance routine was not copyrightable, having no written dance notation and so lacking 'fixed or tangible means of expression' that could be infringed, the suit was dismissed as frivolous. This, however, was not before the judge had reproduced the photograph of Banana Lady and provided the link to a video of her act, thereby presumably exacerbating the complainant's perceived injury and multiplying the audience of the disputed images that had been posted. The judge's implicit logic is that as the act was definitively non-copyrightable in its evanescent performance, neither the photograph of the plaintiff nor the video clip of the act were protected, but nor then were they legally relevant to the decision. The childish image simply sits in the judgement as a cipher of the complaint in the amusing and absurd figure of Banana Lady, a performer wearing party gear, a fairly common body suit, fancy dress for children's parties and, or so it seems, for corporate revelry. The YouTube clip is not discussed at all, although it shows the entire dance routine performed on stage at what would appear to be a children's party, including jokes such as 'I have a peel'.

As the judge does not indicate any reason for inserting the picture or providing the hyperlink to YouTube, the inferences have to be by implication from the text. Obviously enough, a woman dressed as a banana has some degree of sexual connotation and paradoxical phallic visual reference. The clip of the dance, of shaking it about, also has a degree of erotic valence, although neither aspect is directly implied in the judgement but is rather present in its absence, as an unspoken negation. The image and the hyperlinked clip tell another story, a judicial digression in mute eloquence but one which is ontic and evaluative, a narrative of superficiality, frivolity, lack of tone and depth. The act is not discussed, it is shown, and what is demonstrated affectively and elliptically is an inartistic, underdeveloped, juvenile, and in sum and judgement an irritating performance. The image, with its wide eyed, Cheshire cat grin is jejune. It is also decidedly and intentionally frivolous. So too, of course, by association, the referent emerges in the judicial text and makes its reasoning also lacking, deficiently serious, ill-considered, and so more revealing. The less that is said, the greater the weight and the visual implexity of the unsaid, of the unconscious significance of the depiction and video to the precedent. It stands out in the judgement, an eyesore, a singular figure or finger, and it transpires, upon close viewing and critical reading, that it ends up being the judge's version of giving the finger to the complainant, *bananam impudicum*, or flipping the banana at Catherine Conrad with all of the expansive and erectile, comedic and irascible, absurd, and equalizing connotations that flow from such a gesture.

The insertion of the picture is indicative of a character that the judge deems to be of deplorable shallowness, and of an act that he views as an anti-aesthetic.

Picturing here marks an inclination of hostility towards the plaintiff that carries the judge on to castigate Conrad for abuse of the legal process, non-payment of court ordered damages and costs, for making deranged accusations, and bringing numerous vexatious lawsuits. Divagating into the complainant's history, Judge Posner recounts an earlier case against one of the defendants whom she described as 'armed and dangerous', Conrad apparently 'compared him to the Unabomber, and suggested that "someone from Homeland Security or Fort Know" (she must have meant Fort Knox) should take his "threats seriously". She didn't specify what those threats were, or whether she meant that he had made threats or that he posed a threat'.[44] She also, we are told, sued her web host for taking down her web site after she had failed to pay the bill, even though it was down because she had failed to pay. The web host paid her $4000 for loss of business while the site was down. 'She pocketed the $4000 and sued in state and federal court anyway'.[45] On another occasion she sued event organizers who mailed an invitation postcard with a picture of her in her banana costume on it, while in another instance she sued a videographer who declined to post the video of her performance on their website. Point made. Frivolous and vexatious lawsuits, though she made a considerable profit from them, as she never paid court ordered expenses or damages.

The judge's opinion was thus that 'her suit has no merit. But we cannot end this opinion without remarking her abuse of the legal process by incessant filing of frivolous lawsuits. This is at least the eighth case she's filed in federal court since 2009, and she has filed at least nine cases in state court just since 2011'.[46] The picture is by implication the sign of an immoral actor, a lady who conflates banana suits with lawsuits, acting with legal action. She is, at least juristically, a comedienne without a cause. The photo and the linked clip are expressions of judicial *hauteur* and superiority, but the key feature in this context is the ridiculing of the complainant, the ethical judgement that subtends the insertion of a meiotic, diminishing depiction. The image is being used in effect to satirize and punish a litigant who otherwise seemed most adept at evading court orders and escaping the reach of the civil arm of justice—she owed something in the region of $140,000. She even litigated, salt in the juridical wound, *in forma pauperis*. Powerless Posner, for it was he, opted for a symbolic punishment in the mode of *meiosis* or mockery of the plaintiff for her low-brow performances, lame lyrics and execrable act. The comic figure is a disapprobative sign, a metagraph for frivolity in the face of the *gravitas* of the juristic text, a revel too far in the eye of the law.

The caustic and perhaps vitriolic view of the judge as expressed overtly and optically in the judgement, the severity of the satire in the context of the reasoning of the decision, might seem to place the image in *Conrad* in the first, ontographic

[44] Ibid., at 638.
[45] Ibid., at 637.
[46] Ibid., at 637.

category of a *hauteur* and simple placement of the litigant below and diminished by the judge. There is certainly an element of that comic semiotic in the insertion, but the textual context makes it clear that Posner is concerned primarily to manifest an ethical denunciation of the plaintiff and seemingly to raise an alarm, to warn against this illicit bilking of state and federal funds and the misuse of the action *in forma pauperis*. Banana Lady takes the judge to the end of his tether. He fears her and feels powerless to prevent further abuses of process and obliviousness to court ordered payments. She shows that the system doesn't work, and the response is a species of visual snicker, a disrespectful, indeed satirical laugh, *risus sardonicus*, that includes insertion of picture and link. These, however, are hardly innocent. They may indicate ethical failings on the part of the plaintiff, but again the image has a history and the performer on stage is a competitor with law, a differently costumed player wearing a distinctive mask. The optical indication of the image is somewhat other to the judge's intention, suggestive as it is of play, of theatre rather than court, of revel as opposed to law term, of festival and carnival where social norms are suspended or transferred to other jurisdictions. The masked player is a sign of *dies nec fasti*, non-law days, and of alternative forums, the court of piepowders, *risus paschalis* or the laugh of dust, of the fair and of travellers. Here then the image also bespeaks of the limits of law and not least its failure to recognize humour and the comedic dimension of its own practices. Conrad is faulted in this regard, her image displayed to try and dissuade the histrion from competing with the legal forum or putting it to theatrical use.

Comedy threatens law because, like Banana Lady, it cannot be governed, it unsettles the complacency of the norm and suggests the madness of the future as well as the wreckage of the past. It also reminds the jurist of other stages, different players, alternate causes, or what historically might have been termed *ius quaesitum alteri*, another law. The comic, *serio-ludere* in the form of an image touches a nerve and unsettles a boundary and in this and other instances elicits a moralizing response.[47] The minor jurisprudence of travelling theatre, the masks of entertainers, the banana shake, revels, and other carnivalesque forms of inversion of hierarchy and anarchic disarray are too close to law to be easily accepted. In a Georgia case, *Gates v Khokhar*, the question concerned the Anti-Mask Act.[48] The facts were relayed as follows. The plaintiff joined a march in downtown Atlanta against the grand jury decision in the Ferguson police shooting case. During the protest the plaintiff was given a 'V for Vendetta' mask by another protester. 'As the

[47] In *Schwartzwald v Oath* (2020) US Dist. LEXIS 165641 the plaintiff had photographed the actor Jon Hamm apparently in public not wearing underwear, just pants, as trousers are called in the USA. It is a ridiculous picture for star watchers and the lewdly inclined, which image the Court does not reproduce in the decision, but rather the supposedly infringing image which had a black box with the words 'image loading' over the offending nether region. A judicial jape in visual form, image and words, optical *meiosis* of both cause and subject complained.

[48] *Austin Gates v Hassan Khokhar* 884 F.3d 1290 (2018).

image attached to the complaint shows, the mask is a stylized image of the Guy Fawkes character from the movie "V for Vendetta". It is designed to cover the entire face'.[49] He wore the mask both to express disagreement with the grand jury decision 'and to maintain his anonymity during the protest. Plaintiff claims he never intended to threaten or intimidate anyone by wearing the mask'. The defendant officers at some point during the march ordered the protesters to remove their masks and subsequently ordered the arrest of anyone wearing a mask. The plaintiff claimed he had not heard the warning. He was arrested, handcuffed, shoved in a police car and eventually told that he was being arrested for wearing a mask. The District Court held that the officers lacked even arguable probable cause to arrest the plaintiff for violating the mask statute, and so were in violation of the Fourth Amendment. The instant case before the US Court of Appeals, Eleventh Circuit, overturned that decision.

In upholding the legality of the arrest, the Court addressed its reasonableness in terms of the purpose of the Anti-Mask Statute, which according to precedent required that the defendant '(1) intended to conceal his identity, and (2) either intended to threaten, intimidate, or provoke the apprehension of violence or acted with reckless disregard for the consequences of his conduct ... '.[50] On the facts as viewed by the majority, the mask gave the arresting officer reasonable grounds for inferring that the plaintiff intended to intimidate, rounding out their opinion by observing that 'a nameless, faceless figure strikes terror in the human heart'.[51] That said, the Court does discuss the image, in this case the mask and references, as adverted, the black and white photograph of the mask which is contained in the docket but not inserted in the judgement. The Court also twice provides a link to numerous pictures of the *V for Vendetta* mask taken from an article on Guy Fawkes which is hyperlinked in the judgement. Specifically, it is stated that

> although not outcome-determinative, we also note that, in explaining the origins of the Guy Fawkes mask, Plaintiff implicitly acknowledges that the mask could be perceived as celebrating violent protest against the government. Specifically, the complaint links to an article that describes Guy Fawkes as "an infamous insurgent who tried to blow up the British Parliament in 1605. See http://theweek.com/articles/ 463151/briefhistory-guy-fawkes-mask".

The Court then goes on to discuss the *V for Vendetta* mask and its association with 'vigilantism and the violent overthrow of the government'.[52] In a footnote to the point, the link to the article is repeated and the text is cited to the effect that '[o]ver the past decade, dissidents across the globe have appropriated the visage of

[49] Ibid. at 1295; https://larc.cardozo.yu.edu/faculty-online-pubs/61/, eFigure 10.
[50] Ibid., at 1299; citing *State v Miller* 260 Ga. 669, 398 S.E.2d 547 (1990).
[51] *Gates*, at 1301.
[52] Ibid., at 1302. The link to the Guy Fawkes article is also provided in footnote 4 of the judgement.

Guy Fawkes, the infamous insurgent who tried to blow up the British Parliament in 1605, warping the once-reviled fringe rebel into a widespread symbol of resistance'. Reference is then made to the graphic novel and the film of *V for Vendetta* and, depending upon one's perspective, its vigilante or liberatory hero.

The comedic image par excellence, the mask, is introduced three times into the judgement, twice by hyperlink and once by reference to the Docket. The image of the actual mask worn is not shown but rather the putatively non-outcome determinative link to the mask article and its necessary inference, according to the Court, that the Plaintiff 'implicitly acknowledges that the mask could be seen as celebrating violent protest against the government'. Thus, the questions arise of what is introduced by hyperlink, why is it inserted if it is not determinative, not part of the reasoning of the decision, and how can the expressed 'association of the "V for Vendetta" mask with vigilantism and the violent overthrow of government' not be veridical and a driver of outcome? At a visual level, the article on the mask, incorporated by reference into the precedent, shows a picture of Guy Fawkes, and then four further photographs of anti-globalization and Occupy movement protests or installations involving individuals wearing the Guy Fawkes mask. The visage is placed in significant contexts and in one image is shown as part of an inflammatory crowd of Egyptian protesters during the Arab Spring. Eight masks and a portrait of Guy Fawkes are shown in the article, and of the depictions, only one is implicitly violent. Even in that case, there is no visible violence, and the protest in question is against a repressive regime, and a corrupt dictator, the Egyptian Morsi. Looking closely at the images, which the Court appears not to have done, they are far from supporting the completely generic argument that the majority is seeking to make by innuendo or at least without discussion of the specific visual support being invoked. The article and its images are neither neutral nor balanced, and the journalist's focus is specifically concerned with the mask and dissidents. It then has to be pointed out that this focus is one of many, the use of the mask in dissent is only one face of a theatrical and filmic device, a prosthetic that has a range of other connotations, including those of freedom of thought, the power of ideas, the collectivity of intellect, self-determination, adherence to principle, denunciation of systemic injustices, and the enduring force of comedy, both satire of the false and humour, the dance of truth.[53] The singular mask has many faces, of which the Court addressed only one and even in that case by way of presupposition.

[53] On the connotations of the mask in contemporary movements, see Sofia Alexopoulou and Antonia Pavli, '"Beneath this Mask There is More than Flesh, Beneath This Mask There is an Idea": Anonymous as the (Super)heroes of the Internet', 34 *Int. J. Semiotics of Law* 237 (2021) https://doi.org/10.1007/s11196-019-09615-6; Lewis Call, 'A for Anarchy, V is for Vengeance: Images of Guy Fawkes and the Creation of Postmodern Anarchism', 16 *Anarchist Studies* 105 (2008). For further discussions of the mask and of *V for Vendetta*, see Vladislav Maxsimov, 'Politicization of Life and Auto-Thanatopolitics in V for Vendetta', and Goodrich, 'The Mask as Anti-Apparatus: On the Counter-*Dispositif* of *V for Vendetta*', both in Thomas Giddens (ed.), *Critical Directions in Comic Studies* (Jackson MS: University of Mississippi Press, 2020).

The Court raises the question of the mask only to gloss it over without any comparative or theatrical discussion, interpretation, perspective, or context but rather the simple and simplistic view that it is a sign of violence and intimidation. It is, however, a complex issue visually, conceptually, and legally. The image of Guy Fawkes, his vizard as Hobbes would say, is but one instance of the mask or *imago* as the sign of a juristic entity, as a *persona* that is recognized by law. The attribution of violent characteristics to the mask, and a specific identity to a generic and exponentially replicable theatrical device is a projection of an extreme kind. The Court has strong feelings and a distinctive vision of this piece of attire, affects that lead to multiple indirect representations of the mask in the judgement. If 'all the world's a stage' and we but players on it, then Austin Gates, who had been walking peaceably, without threat or menace, did nothing wrong except for wearing the device. How then does a story that in contemporary versions is one of high principles and transcendent justice become, in the figure of a face, a legal symbol of riotous intentions for the Georgia Court?

The answer is plural. As the Renaissance constitutional theorist Guillaume Perrière comments in his study of good government, 'you shall find in any place / few that do not carry a double face'.[54] It is not the wearing of a mask that is the problem, for everyone has a *persona*, wears a painted cloth and face, the vestments and accoutrements that fit their mood or role. The issue is one of juridical personality and control of juristic recognition of legal entities. The same issue arises in court when witnesses, whose faith so requires, wear a veil, mask, or niquab while appearing. In *R v D (R)*, a witness appeared in court wearing a burqa and niquab. She declined the court's request to reveal her face and it was held that when giving evidence she was required to remove the niquab 'for purposes of identification'.[55] That the persona required for testing evidence in court is the bare faced appearance of the witness imposes a particular species of image upon the participant and player. It is not that the appearance of the actor is neutral, but rather that a shift is demanded which is here from theology to jurisprudence, from one monotheism to another. Each has their element of the histrionic and of the comedic, of staging and performing the real. Theatre and law share a propensity for the stage with the singular difference that too direct a viewing of the thespian dimension of legal performances threatens the juridical as being no more than an alternative play upon the social boards. To create a persona and to claim a social space for that entity is to challenge the legal monopoly upon the casting of the mask and the identity of the social subject. The comedian at large, the joker with a mask proclaiming freedom, generates an unbearable tension with the legal identification of the subject via their face which is defined in Christian terminology as *haec imago*,

[54] Guillaume Perrière, *Le Thëatre des bons engins* (Toulouse: Janot, 1540) fol. Biiii.

[55] *R v D (R)* [2014] 1 LRC 629. See further *AAN (Veil)* [2014] UKUT 00102 (IAC). For the views of the Canadian Supreme Court on this issue, see the extensive deliberations in *R v NS* [2012] 3 SCR 726.

the likeness of the divinity and so not to be casually altered by burqua or niquab, Guy Fawkes mask, or indeed a fully painted face. To wear a mask is theologically to follow another God and while the Court does not explicitly travel that path, it is evident that the wearing of the device is viewed as radically disruptive of the order of appearances. The unity of the subject is infracted by the comedic public performance of an alternate identity, and unauthorized *persona*. The juristic entity is hidden by the theatrical presence. The threat does not lie in the behaviour of the masked subject, but rather in the conceptual challenge that the mask poses to the panoptic vision of the social. It is the idea and not the flesh that constitutes the intimidation that the Court fears.

The argument can also be inverted. We can note that the image is denied twice. First, it is not reproduced directly in the judgement, but rather is proffered by hyperlink to an article which reproduces a number of potentially inflammatory photographs of protest and *V for Vendetta* masks. Then, second denial, the court disavows the importance of the image to the decision, even though it is precisely and immediately after incorporating the hyperlink to Guy Fawkes into the record that the legitimacy of the police perception of the violent implications of the mask is positively and approbatively asserted by the majority. The dual denial ironically unmasks the reasoning of the Court as negation, negative incorporation of the mask into the logic of decision: the device undermines the authority of law by questioning the juridical monopoly over all aspects of identity. Costume and custom conflict in the comedic apparition of a masked demonstrator demonstrating too much: another face, a different play, a taking to the social stage improperly dressed for the symbolic. *Haec imago* in this instance becomes for the judges an idol, an alternate vizard, a comedy in one act, a plethora of players where what is demanded is the unity of monotheism and the singularity of legal responsibility. Hence the hyperlink, hence the disavowal and the willingness to treat the peaceful use of the mask, as statement and as dress, as communal sign and collective representation, as freedom of expression, as choice of appearance upon the social stage, as a threat of violence. It is paradoxically treated as undermining law at the very same moment that the Court hesitantly and yet nonetheless on the record introduces that self-same image into the judgement.

The clash of cultural symbols, of uniformed officials with masked demonstrators, police with players, robed judges with defaced defendants, suggests both the proximity and the parallelism of law and comedy, magistrates and manners. Returning to the broader question of comedic and erotic images, the comic visual insertion is of greatest ethical significance where law is most challenged. The threat of the mask was to the institutional order of the law, to the hierarchy and definition of persons, and so elicited the most extreme ethical and political judgement, which is that simply wearing the device and peaceably walking down the street is violent, intimidatory, vigilantist, and by extension threatens to overthrow the government. All that in a playful, comedic mask. It can lead to the conclusion that the comico-erotic image, the theatrical performance of everyday life in the mode of a mask, an item of apparel, ironically materializes the subject and the subjectivity of decision. The scopic regime or control of the soul takes the body as its point of governance and here arrests the visage of public speech, the face of freedom, as disorder, as uncontrollable, and as a mutely eloquent representation of the overthrow of government.

In incorporating images, the Court shows what it sees, and so exposes the vision in decision to analysis. The affect of the visible necessarily also enlivens judgement and proffers a sensual dimension, a distinct material and sensible form to determination. It manifests and unleashes an emotive aspect to the reasoning of the precedent. The erotic and the comedic variously excite, that much is obvious, but they have the further facet of constituting the most directly performative of images in that comedy and eros can arouse and impact both subject and object, transforming how we see and how we apprehend what is viewed from the unsettled, diaphragm shaking, and tumescent spaces of humour and lust. As Virgil notes and Lacan reprises, *trahit sua quemque volutpas*—we are bound to follow our desire and in the hidden spaces of that authenticity signal with images the fantoms of affect and drive.[56] Complacency, the norm, the routine patterns of practice are disrupted, novelty of form and substance emerges and bears noticing. The theatre of law becomes present and visible in the insertion of comic images into judgement, and it is this thespian sensibility, the corporeal sketched, the body dressed with a mask, a costume, with eros or polka dots that impacts decision most directly. Changing the form and aesthetic of judgement also necessarily alters how the subject matter is viewed. This exposure may not always be to the advantage of the legal institution, but the principle of honesty that it incorporates is of value, while the recognition of the ontological, epistemological, and ethical features of comic visual insertions can do much to invest the juridical with a sense of the multimodal and plural forms of contemporary legal transmission.

It is in some senses obvious that erotic and comic images inserted in judgements are subject to strictures of caution from a juristic perspective, even where judges engage liberally and preconsciously with the shadows and associations that such pictures trigger. The capacity of such images, and of the theatrical more generally, to transform the subject have been viewed legally as histrionic, alien, and dangerous. Theatre has frequently been banned as voluptuous and distracting, and comedy too, conceived in its modern sense as play and as jocastic, has also often been the butt of legal censure and exclusion. The border between law and dramaturgy, *gravitas* and *levitas*, serious and playful is one of the most opaque and hard to delineate, generating an obscure object of desire, an alluring yet forbidden affectivity on the borders or in the minor jurisdictions of legal practice. As the practice increases and images proliferate in decisions, the judiciary owe a duty of

[56] Virgil, *Eclogues*, 1.65.

care in utilizing such imagery precisely because the comic and erotic engage the unconscious and repeat patterns that, as Freud demonstrated, bear serious and repressed yet decipherable significances of which the judge is frequently unaware. The comic insertion will tend thus to distract from the interpretation of the plurality of meanings of the pictorial intervention, which is to say that the symbolic dominion of law is frequently a distortion and deformation of the real, a flight from materiality, and passage to abstraction. Humour is rebellious and a sign not only of conflict but of crisis which legal decision making is most often directed at containing and controlling. The force of humour, the laughter of critique just as much as the farce of law, deserve both introspection and analysis as objective facets of judicial decisions that can be and should be scrutinized, viewed and contextualized as well as analyzed as symptoms of unconscious sources of judgement. For Freud the joke is hard to judge, and in juridical forms it is tendentious, generating uncertainty because of the indeterminacy of meaning that generates variously enjoyment, confusion, transformation and new forms.[57] The comic is in this theory produced by the degradation of the 'ought', the norm, the law, by 'what is'. It condenses and transforms, and it is this function and effect of comedy that makes it significant in its judicial uses, indicating a complicity between judge and audience, the expression of decision and the common, Quintilian's *a comicis*, which here and most directly renders the juridical as interrupted by and invested in communal thought.

[57] Freud, *The Joke*, at 85–88; and see also Lisa Trahair, *The Comedy of Philosophy: Sense and Nonsense in Early Cinematic Slapstick* (Albany: SUNY, 2007) at 105–106, 122–123.

5
Evidential Expositions

The insertion of images—humorous, erotic, cartographic, or identificatory—into judgements brings the world into the courtroom. It crosses the line, the threshold that separates law and event, and in that transgression introduces a different dimension, an aesthetic sensibility into legal reasoning, affect into the aspirational interstices of a putatively objective law. It is not that such sensory facets are lacking in the scriptural forms of written reason, but rather that they are not generally viewed or apprehended as such. The words are signs, painted cloth or tattoos on parchment and paper, colours, emblems, typographies, fonts, tactile vellum, sibylline leaves, and soft leather bindings, as the case may be, but the juristic propensity, from the glossators onwards, has been to read rather than to view even the most beautiful of manuscripts and illuminated scrolls in their sensible qualities.[1] The familiarity and discipline of reading, the controlled and scripted logic of the anglophone eye moving from left to right in linear and legal fashion, is taken for granted as being too well accepted and too long confirmed to be excavated as sensual modes of apprehension and transmission. Typography is deemed a transparent vehicle, text and tympanum, paper and binding, format and layout, are legally legible and scanned rather than visually imbricated or viewed aesthetically. The lawyer reads with incredible intensity for the insensible, for what isn't on the page: the referent, the denotation, the message, and not the medium of its material transmission. With the ease of advent and insertion of imagery, the unquestioned unilinearity of access to the referent is increasingly stalled—obstructed or subtly deflected—by pictures. The imagined object of reasoning is interrupted by the image of that object. The immediate judicial response is denial. Proceeding by analogy, the tried and tested approach is to disregard any novelty of form or meaning, and so to endeavour to reduce the depiction to a lectoral content, to read 'as if' it were a text.[2] The recourse to a concept of visual literacy,

[1] The exception is the late Pierre Legendre, who both in his films and in his scriptural contributions paid close attention to the haptic and aesthetic quality of the legal text, the hermeneutic of what he termed 'a montage of aestheticized writings' which made possible, 'the artifice of being face to face with the alterity of the *Corpus iuris*'. Legendre, *L'Autre Bible de l'Occident: le Monument romano-canonique* (Paris: Fayard, 2009) at 345.

[2] This point is well made in Christina Spiesel, 'More than a Thousand Words in Response to Rebecca Tushnet', 125 *Harvard Law Forum* 40 (2012), arguing, at 46, that 'Pictures leap across linguistic barriers ... The law, if it is not to be muddled, needs to understand pictures, if only because otherwise the meanings they import will be missed and good judgment diminished'. Michael Murray, 'Towards a Universal Visual Language of Law', *Law & Psychology Rev.* 46:1 (2021–2022), at 86–103, makes a similar argument, although even his title betrays the reduction of the visual to the linguistic and textual.

Judicial Uses of Images. Peter Goodrich, Oxford University Press.
 DOI: 10.1093/oso/9780192848772.003.0005

embedded as it is in the drive to order images by way of analogy to language, by reduction to texts, strongly suggests that pictures, like words, are initially apprehended as additions that self-evidently support, demonstrate, and prove what the verbal argument defines.

Obviousness is the primary category of judicial vision. What is seen is believed and shown so as to manifest a linear truth. One of the most famous and frequently discussed of examples in the academic literature is the US Supreme Court decision in *Scott v Harris*.[3] In brief, the majority judgement linked a video collage to the opinion, in a footnote, with the immortal words that 'it speaks for itself'. Specifically, and a little cantankerously, the majority opinion dismisses the Court of Appeal's viewing and that of the dissenting Justice Stevens on the Supreme Court by saying that '[he] suggests that our reaction to the videotape is somehow idiosyncratic, and seems to believe we are misrepresenting its contents ... We are happy to allow the videotape to speak for itself. See Record 36, Exh. A, available at http://www.supremecourtus.gov/opinions/video/scott_v_harris.html and in Clerk of Court's case file (Figure 5.1).[4] The denial of the medium, of the movie, of sound, motion, and vision is immediately apparent: the video is 'speaking' for itself, exuding language, verbalizing, becoming linear and univocal, unitary, and unequivocal in its demonstration of what the justices see.[5] Ironically for such a putatively rational and irrefragably verbal apprehension of the clips, the filmic character of the video and the affective bodily responses of the judges are much in evidence in the oral argument as well as in the focus of the decision upon the putatively obvious effects of the visual. Justice Breyer simply but significantly notes that '[b]ecause watching the video footage of the car chase made a difference to my own view of the case, I suggest that the interested reader take advantage of the link in the Court's opinion, ante, at 1775, n. 5, and watch it'.[6] Justice Breyer is at least consistent and does not bray but rather lets the video appear for itself. Justice Scalia, writing the majority judgement, is much more loquacious.

The case involves a car chase—watch the video—that is captured by police dashboard cameras. The pursuit ends with deputy Timothy Scott ramming the fleeing Victor Harris's car with the result that it was tipped off the road and crashed so

[3] *Scott v Harris* 550 US 372 (2007). Discussed, as adverted earlier, in Dan Kahan et al., 'Whose Eyes are you Going to Believe? *Scott v Harris* and the Perils of Cognitive Illiberalism' 122 *Harvard Law Rev.* 837 (2009). There is extensive discussion in Richard Sherwin, *Visualizing Law in the Age of the Digital Baroque* (Abingdon: Routledge, 2012); and in Peter Brooks, '*Scott v Harris*: The Supreme Court's Reality Effect', 29 *Law and Literature* 143 (2017).

[4] *Scott v Harris*, at fn.5. Justice Stevens had concluded: 'In sum, the factual statements by the Court of Appeals quoted by the Court ... were entirely accurate'.

[5] For further instances of the juristic yet inaccurate cliché, see *Kochanski v Speedway SuperAmerica LLC* 356 Wisc.2d 1 (2014)—'But if a picture says a thousand words, then a video speaks volumes'; *A.D. LLC v 2004 Partners LLC* 860 N.W.2d 341 (2014): 'A picture (or two) can be worth a thousand words'; *Milatz v. City of Cincinnati* 145 N.E.3d 1117 (2019): 'Because sometimes a picture is worth a thousand words, we include a photo below'.

[6] *Scott v Harris* at 387.

Figure 5.1 Still from video clip posted by the Supreme Court in *Scott v Harris* (2007).

violently that he was rendered paraplegic. The 'Precision Intervention Technique maneuver' that deputy Scott utilized was deemed by the Court of Appeals to be unnecessary and illegal. The Court of Appeals had watched the video of the chase composed from the dashcams of two police cars and concluded that being at night and on fairly empty roads, the force of the intervention was excessive. To this, Justice Scalia responds by stating: 'The videotape tells quite a different story. There we see respondent's vehicle racing down narrow, two-lane roads in the dead of night at speeds that are shockingly fast ... what we see on the video more closely resembles a Hollywood-style car chase of the most frightening sort, placing police officers and innocent bystanders alike at great risk of serious injury'.[7] The video apparently can only be viewed in one way and this leads Scalia to chastize the lower Court, remonstrating that adopting the victim's version of events was an untenable position, the appellate division 'should not have relied on such visible fiction; it should have viewed the facts in the light depicted by the videotape'.[8] That said, presumably because it is somehow speaking for itself, no viewing of the video, no critical frame-by-frame analysis of the composition, cutting and quality of the collage of clips is proffered beyond the very brief observation that the (in this

[7] Ibid., at 379.
[8] Ibid., at 381.

instance) inaptly named Victor's car swerved, at times drove on the wrong side of the road, and ran multiple red lights. Granted that the video is black and white and of low quality, the apprehension that multiple red lights have been transgressed is telling for its inventiveness, it was at most two and that is uncertain even on careful viewing. When Harris went on the opposite side of the road it was to go around stationary vehicles. The speed of Harris' car is also undetermined, but appears cautious and is unknown although it could have been fairly easily calculated by dividing the distance travelled by the time taken, as indicated on the dashcam. Beyond that it is simply the emotions that govern: it is 'shocking' and it is 'frightening', it is 'dangerous' and it is 'reckless', purportedly posing a high likelihood of serious injury or death, causing the Supreme Court majority justices to flee their seats rather like early cinematic audiences scurrying from a screen image of a train coming towards them. Any other viewing would be 'fiction', despite the optical fact that any label of make-believe attributed to the dissenting judge and to the Court of Appeal is both wholly assertive in epistemic character and analytically an exercise in projection. It is at the very least peculiar for the higher court to conclude that the Court of Appeals judges fall into the category of viewing in a manner that no reasonable person could see.

Turning next to the oral arguments, Justice Breyer famously remarks of the video and the plaintiff's claim, quoting Chico Marx, 'who do you believe, me or your own eyes'. Justice Scalia, for his part, references the Hollywood movie that he associates with the car chase and which he alludes to in his judgement, saying in oral argument that 'this is the scariest chase I ever saw since the *French Connection*'. It has been pointed out by others, and at length, that the Justices' opinion of the video is far from objective and their viewing of the footage is not one that is shared perceptually or conceptually by other demographic groups. Their vision in decision is distinctively dogmatic. From the perspective of retinal justice, the equity of the eye, they have fallen prey to a species of shark aesthetic, meaning that they have reacted before thinking. The images hitting the thalamus prior to any rational filter have determined judgement.[9] The video appears to have had a high cathartic impact and so suggests a limited judicial repertoire of chase movie viewings. To the point, however, which is that the two Justice's in the majority who focus on the video and link it to the decision do so because they believe that it unquestionably demonstrates the accuracy of their opinion and so supports their judgement. They believe their eyes, they feel fear, they experience shock, and, critically, they project these sensations onto the car and driver of the crashed vehicle. At a guess, the Justices were impacted by a species of reverse causality. The effect became the cause. The crash determined the chase. That, however, is not the immediate issue, but rather the retinal point that the link is posted because it is obvious. What one sees

[9] For discussion of 'The Aesthetic of the Shark', see Gabriele Pedullà, *In Broad Daylight: Movies and Spectators after the Cinema* (London: Verso, 2012) at 79ff.

is what is there, in an unmediated fashion, and it becomes part of the judgement because the Justices believe that it is the effect of the real, the visible truth of the determination, the *certum* of imaginal apparition in all its particularity.

Bodies view and apprehend, and in this case the judicial corpora share their sensorium discursively, and it is the emotional impact of the visuals that governs their judgement. We could digress at this point into film studies, and look at the composition of the clips, at camera angle, perspective, aspect ratio, sound, frame, quality, and the fact that two dash cam's footage has been silently combined, and all of this will be necessary for the curation of precedential images, but at present what attracts attention is the notion of obviousness. Bodies trip and fall. The obvious—*ob viam*—is that which stands in the path and in the way of progression. The obvious is an obstacle, something visible, an impediment that can trip one up, and that is arguably what happened here. The assumption is of transparency and yet to see through something is not necessarily to pass beyond it, or as Nietzsche formulates the conundrum:

> Surprise at resistance: because we see through a thing we think that in future it will be unable to offer us any resistance whatsoever - and we are surprised at finding that we are able to see through it, and yet unable to run through it. This foolish sensation and surprise are similar to the sensation which a fly experiences before a window pane.[10]

The Supreme Court being the highest court in the US, its presuppositions and perceptions are exemplary and cannot be discounted, whether empirically accurate or not. It is the starting point for doctrinal analysis in the jurisdiction and proffers the first and dominant category of judicial insertions of depictions in judgements as evidence of their opinion, the visible proof and ocular testimony evidencing and supporting the verdict.

Optical obviousness is close in doctrine to both sensibility and truth. For Justice Scalia the Court of Appeals had relied upon a 'visible fiction' because they had not relied upon the 'different story' that the videotape 'tells' or the facts that it throws 'light' upon. The eyes will have it. From the perspective of retinal justice the key point is that both Scalia and Breyer treat the scopic as unidirectional and as unmediated either by the technology and choices of visual relay, or by the perception and preconceptions of their viewing. They look, as lawyers, for a narrative, a discursive documentation, an instrumentalizable non-fiction, but nonetheless a story that throws light upon the facts. The language of description indicates that the Justices read and verbalize, rather than viewing or, even better, watching with its implications of chariness and caution. Claiming to apply a test of 'objective reasonableness', the majority is persuaded by a low-quality video according to what in

[10] Friedrich Nietzsche, *The Dawn of Day* (London: Allen and Unwin, 1903) aphorism 444.

French film terminology is the *plan subjectif,* the point of view of the police vehicles pursuing the respondent. Adopting uncritically the point of view of the pursuer, the subjective perspective of following the camera allows only one specific scopic gaze, it restricts but at the same time it creates a sense of obviousness, of being there, identified with the lens and apprehending the scene in the comfort and familiarity of its visibility from the front windows of the pursuing police vehicles. To follow the camera is the obvious and unreflective viewing, and it introduces into the record evidence from outside the record as if the court had entered the world and gone back in time to see precisely, unequivocally, directly, and unquestionably the circumstance or event under review. It is as if the event is made obvious by the images. The picture is made to speak at the same time as the images collapse into the uncritically apprehended affects of viewing. These unreflective sensations are then verbalized as the reason of judgement without any attention to perspective, editing, framing, absence of sound, colour, and video quality. The *imago decidendi* is here far from being a *ratio decidendi,* not because it is not written but because what is unwritten is not viewed through any critical analytic lens. The evidence of the unseen, of the partially viewed, of judicial blind spots, SCOTUS scotomized, as it were, dominates the bench which sees itself more as camera lens than as subjects viewing the screen, or active and impactful participants in the reconstruction of the events. Incertitude, the vagaries of vision, transpire paradoxically to be the immediate medium of visibility.

The epistemic of obviousness develops out of the juristic desire to view the image as evidential, deeming it to be the most directly probative indicator of what happened. Maps provide a reality effect, comico-erotic images provide moral contexts, but it is in tort and crime that the *locus in quo,* the visualization of the place, scene, and sometimes the persons inhabiting events is most often inserted. Where what occurred can apparently be seen, the probative value or *certum* of visibility edges closer to centre stage and scope of judgement. Juristically the category of the obvious is far from obvious, indeed it is much litigated, and not infrequently judges will include pictures to evidence their conclusions on such self-evidence, most usually in negligence cases where an open and obvious hazard vitiates the duty of care. The theory is that if one can see the obstacle or danger, if it is not hidden or secret, then it does not obstruct or occlude. Thus, in *Milatz v City of Cincinnati,* during Oktoberfest, Margaret Milatz fell over a utility box that had been used to cover loose wires. She returned the next day to photograph the box in daylight, and the Court reproduces the image, stating 'Because sometimes a picture is worth a thousand words, we include a photo below' (Figure 5.2).[11] The photograph is not discussed beyond a cursory remark that it is 'an incorrectly assembled safety utility box' and then that '[t]hese boxes consisted of raised, elongated rectangles with sloped edges which allowed the power cables running along the ground to fit

[11] *Milatz v City of Cincinnati* 145 N.E.3d 1117 at 1119.

Figure 5.2 Insertion by Judge Pierre Bergeron in *Milatz v City of Cincinnati* (2019).

safely underneath (to prevent tripping). Covered in bright yellow to attract attention, the top of the box also contained an anti-skid, texturized surface ... '[12] The picture actually reproduced in the judgement is not discussed, beyond its generic incorrect assembly. The effect of the uncorrected, of the sinister snakes of wire that protrude and pass alongside the curb, gain no mention. The key question in the case, that Margaret tripped, is relegated visually to a parenthesis wherein tripping is said or at least implied to be prevented by safety utility boxes. This is an aside presumably because it is obvious and indeed the judgement goes on to spell out at various points that the danger is open and obvious and defines this as 'one that is not hidden, concealed from view, or undiscoverable upon ordinary inspection'.[13]

The Court repeats that the box was incorrectly assembled, which does indeed appear to be the case from the photograph selected. Nothing is said about this uncorrected incorrectness, nowhere does the picture in fact get discussed. It was taken the day after the accident, in daylight, by Milatz. It does not indicate when she tripped and, more significant evidentially, it does not show where she tripped. What it does show are serpentine wires that are visually snaking out of the incorrectly assembled box and running partially hidden along the street below the curb. The picture may save a thousand words, but it raises a somewhat comparable number of questions of perspective, lighting, expectation, circumstance, and event. The Court may somehow, by visual intuition, because they have not explained this nor detailed their vision of the encounter between box and tripper, assume that because it is visible to the sedentary Court, in broad daylight, it must have been so to the plaintiff, even though the fact of her tripping means it was self-evidently not obvious to Margaret. Such viewing as there is takes the form of verballing,

[12] Ibid., at 1119.
[13] Ibid., at 1120.

of a substitution of words for the image, the rhetorical figure of *synecdoche*, and the implication is that the literalism of legal interpretative method applies just as much, by analogy, by presupposition, but certainly not by any pronounced aesthetic reasoning, to the perception and reduction of the picture to plain meaning.[14] Having indicated that the picture tells a story, the Court declines to even discuss the plot, the verbal narrative and fiction of the event, let alone the implications of the image. The obvious is lost in its obviousness, indeed it is obviated by the lack of viewing and obscured by discussion that avoids any sensible apprehension and attendant critical implication. To simply reiterate that the obvious is not hidden, that it is open and not concealed, is to treat tautology as reasoning.

The variety of obviousness cases, of tripping, slipping, falling, and injuring preclude any complete survey, which is in any event unnecessary in that the issue raised by the images is interpreted as being one of the immediately apprehensible, of the *certum* of visualization, and so precludes any extended critical analysis. The point can be made by reference to the fact that frequently these cases are decided by summary judgement. Thus, in a case against Home Depot, there was a nylon strap loose and lying across the floor (Figure 5.3). 'After the incident, Rincon's son went back and took the following picture of the location where Rincon tripped (and in the direction they had walked). Rincon and his son testified that this photograph is accurate for the time and conditions of the aisle when Rincon fell ... '.[15] The next reference to the image of the nylon strap is simply and solely to ask the rhetorical question of whether it was open and obvious, 'in the photo above'.[16] Summary judgement is awarded to Home Depot, primarily on procedural grounds because Luis Rincon had failed to file a response to the defendant's motion for summary judgement, but the Court does add that 'reasonable minds' could not differ on the obviousness of the nylon strap. The photograph is, in the repeated words of the Court 'accurate' and: 'These facts regarding the nylon strap make it akin to the edge of a fountain or a patch of ice—both open and obvious conditions that courts have held no duty for in the past'.[17] The surprising analogy to highly dissimilar sights and circumstances can be accentuated by viewing the photographs, in which the image of a fountain is the precedent picture for the circle of

[14] Stanley Fish, 'The Law Wishes to have a Formal Existence', in Austin Sarat and Tom Kearns (eds), *The Fate of Law* (Ann Arbor: Michigan University Press, 1991) deals excellently with the literalist view of documents that assume an obvious 'plain' meaning, using *Trident Center v Connecticut General Life Insurance* 847 F.2d 564 (9th Cir. 1988), making the point at the outset that Judge Kozinski's claim that the language of the contract at issue leaves no room for any other construction is 'a judgment belied by the fact that Trident's lawyers managed to make room for just that construction in their arguments ...' (at 163) or in our case that the plaintiff fell. The same point, of course, is made by Justice Stevens in his dissent in *Scott v Harris* where he treats the Court of Appeal's viewing of the video as accurate, whereas the majority view as irrational, as projecting a prior disposition and apperception in the face of the visual story, the facts relayed by sight.

[15] *Luis Rincon v Home Depot USA* 2019 WL 6118406 (2019) at 2.

[16] Ibid., at 4.

[17] Ibid., at 7.

Figure 5.3 Insertion by District Judge Brantley Starr in *Rincon v Home Depot USA* (2019).

nylon strap. In the fountain scene, Y marks the spot is the implication, and above the Y, a slip of the pen is showing, but this is pure Rorschach, a miniature dolphin leaping (Figure 5.4). The circled Y in fact obscures the site and sight of the incident and intriguingly the Court notes that it does not know the exact height of the fountains and continues to note that 'the photograph reveals that the fountains stand more than a couple feet above the height of nearby dining tables and chairs'. Optical revelation, the evidence of the obvious, the visual testimony and here ocular argument are an inexact affair. The proof by photograph is at best extremely casual and at worst misleading. A fountain's edge is not a strap of nylon, a restaurant is not a hardware megastore, boxes are not dining tables, aisles in a warehouse are not dividers of a hotel eatery, and family shoppers are not coworkers taking a meal break. The event has been transformed into an abstraction, and in the latter case, *Culotta,* it even takes the algebraic form of X, Y, Z.[18] The relevance of the lateral comparison of images cannot be as precedent, the images are too distinct and different, and so the only plausible reason for insertion would be as the basis for developing a method of viewing, protocols of scrutiny, yet not only is such

[18] *Richard Culotta v Doubletree Hotels LLC* 2019 Tex. App. LEXIS 5272.

Figure 5.4 Insertion by Justice Sarah Beth Landau in *Richard Culotta v Doubletree Hotels LLC* (2019).

entirely lacking, but the images themselves are given only the most cursory and cursive (lectoral) of viewings.

The judgement proceeds in stages, in inquisitive rather than probative mode. First, is the photograph of the strap accurate? In juristic argot that is usually a question of whether it has been manipulated digitally, edited or altered in any way. The Court holds that it has not, but that is hardly a definition of accuracy. The etymology, ironically, is *ad curare*, to take care over, to be precise, and that is an exactitude that is distinctly lacking, if the purpose is to ask whether the loose noose of nylon on the floor is a hazard. The picture shows the nylon after the event and with different people and trolleys or carts visible. The individual who has just walked past has avoided the nylon trap, perhaps because they have their goods to their left and so are walking in full view of the nylon. Accuracy would require knowing whether Luis was pushing a trolley or carrying goods that precluded view of the hazard, the lasso of manufactured fabric. Where other family members and shoppers were located would also impact scopic scope or point of view. Depending upon the circumstances, the nylon strap could easily have been hidden and obscured from sight, and accuracy would require a photograph of the encounter of plaintiff and strap, and, failing that, a careful reconstruction of the occasions and persons, boxes and carts in play at the time of the event. The 'photo above', already truncated verbally, referenced informally, is accurate of something else, a different scene, and so it is necessary, for the sake of accuracy, to look beyond the inaccurate photographic representation to precedent, but such prior imagery would at best open the eyes of the judge to the manner and patterning of their looking as opposed to offering any precedential picture that could resolve this particular instance of hazard.

The nylon strap is held to be 'akin to' the edge of a fountain or a patch of ice. No image of the ice is provided in the decision in *Netherly v Turco* and so no visual precedent is available.[19] Taking into account, for accuracy, that ice is frequently invisible, the Court perhaps thought that a photograph would be unhelpful, or it is possible that the ice melted before there was any thought of capturing it on camera. As for the fountain's edge, with its X, Y, Z markings, it could hardly be more dissimilar visually, in circumstances, route, occupancy, and function than the photograph from the hardware store. The image of the fountain, said by the Court to add an aesthetic dimension to the restaurant, sadly lacks its aesthetic in the monochrome and scribbles of the photograph.[20] It also lacks sounds of water and occupancy of the restaurant which borders both sides of the waterfall. The scene of the event, the encounter between shin and fountain's edge, are not on view. The actual description the Court prescribes is that 'the photograph reveals that the fountains stand more than a couple of feet above the height of nearby dining tables and chairs. The fountains have tiers that allow water to cascade down the various levels until it reaches the matching pools below. The walkway to the back dining area is situated between the two pools. The water fountains add an aesthetic element to the restaurant'.[21] After such largely unnecessary editorializing on the part of the judge, the next step in reasoning is then, in summation, 'the record does not support any inference that the fountains were concealed. Instead, the evidence supports the conclusion that the fountains were objectively observable to a reasonable person'. The record is the picture, and this shows a deserted, empty, closed restaurant, without diners, trolleys, staff, *maître d'hôtel*, disc jockey, bar tenders, parties, Culotta's coworker, or any other sesquipedalian potential impediments actually present at the waterfall scene of the tripping. Suffice to say that the picture is only precedential in its inaccuracy, particularly as this photograph, as reproduced, has been altered by the drawing of letters on various parts of the image, both distracting from and altering the scene being represented.

That the Court allows a picture with additions is not unusual, and indeed where scales, rulers, keys, and codes are provided they do so in the expectation of significantly enhancing the visual apprehension of the scene. Here, however, and also not unusually, an altered image is introduced without analysis of the augmenting, chirographed signs, and so obviousness again is the epistemological criterion and constitutes the sum of the viewing methodology that the Court is using.

[19] *Jeannie Netherly v Martin Vincent Turco* 2017 Tex. App. LEXIS 6053, 2017 WL 2774448.
[20] *Culotta*, at 2.
[21] Ibid., at 4.

This becomes even more significant of its evidential practices in the judgement, when the Court not only, as adverted, indicates that there is nothing available to determine the exact height of the fountains, but also when it adds that 'the co-worker stated that the "sound of running water" could be heard in the area of the walkway'. It is open and obvious, so much so that the Court references, presumably as authority, another case which held that skylights through which someone fell while working on a roof is a similar instance of such overt and conspicuous hazard. Ice, a fountain's edge, and a skylight are a strange trinity of affinities to a noose of nylon strapping, which seems in one aspect to be standing up as a species of trap. But the question is that of how the judge uses the images, two photographs and two internal pictures or imaginations. It is the very informality of the depictions, the casual character of the markings and drawings that makes them so important as symptoms of how the image is internalized judicially, what the picture as montage and collage means as evidence for the reasoning of legal doctrine in which projection and presupposition allow the photographs to provide what seems to be deemed an optical demonstration or visual evidencing of the view of the court that views. The picture is paradoxically the sign of what is not known, an ocular testament to an oblique heuristic and non-knowledge whose extra-textual and remediated value in law is that of an uncertain obviousness that unconsciously or at least with limited scrutiny facilitates transmission of the decision rather than more directly validating or proving judgement. The theory seems tacitly to be that what is shown does not need to be said but rather is simply there to illustrate the theme of the decision, to provide a context but not to form the subject of decision which lies with the legal category and not with the real.

Take a very simple further example, from a case where a sidewalk crack injured a visitor to a Christmas craft fare in the Drill Hall at a Naval Air Station (Figures 5.5 A & B). 'The weather was clear and sunny, and Mrs. Schaefer was wearing tennis shoes'.[22] Ambience set, the Court then describes the issue as one of degree and visibility of the cracked concrete: 'At its worst, the misaligned pieces created a lip with a depth of about one to one-and a-half inches, as depicted in the photos below'. There is no discussion of any depth of crack or misalignment as evidenced in the photographic images, only a repeated reference to not knowing the exact size or length of the gap. Repetition compulsion perhaps in the face of not knowing because the depth of the crack, and its misalignment, was precisely what is not visible in the pictures. The photographs do not show any crack in the concrete because, according to a footnote, '[t]hese photos were taken in 2014 after the sidewalk defect had been repaired. The black lines are the sidewalk defect as best remembered by Mr. Schaefer'.[23] In the unaltered black and white photograph, taken after the event and after the path had been repaired, there is no

[22] *Sheryl Lynn Schaefer v United States* 2017 WL 2506174.
[23] Ibid., at fn. 2.

(a)

(b)

Figures 5.5 A & B Insertion by District Judge Paula Xinis in *Schaefer v United States* (2017).

misalignment, crack or defect in the concrete on view. In the colour photograph the visibly new rectangle of concrete has a zigzag black line and an X drawn onto it. It is essentially the feel of the scene, the imagined crack, the look of the path that is introduced by the Judge to show that there is nothing there, that all is open and obvious, that there is neither hazard nor danger here. Only the altered image, taken from the street and not from on the path, with its snake of black suggesting a rather abstract or two-dimensional threat, is provided. It is hardly more obtrusive or obstructive looking than the shadow of the wooden pole that also falls across the path and, as an imaginal impediment, it is equally unlikely to trip a visitor to the craft fare.

Prior disposition, extant sympathy, identification with the camera trajectory, the unacknowledged persuasion of the *plan subjectif* adverted to earlier, all fuel the conception of obviousness while silencing description or actual viewing and critical analysis of the complexities of visual context and composition of the images inserted. As the metaphor of the value of images in part suggests, the picture acts ironically to silence discourse, to suppress verbal elaboration, to show rather than to tell, save that the demonstration by image is in a conclusory and secondary form as an illustration of discursive descriptions that precede it conceptually if not textually. To the legal humanists' concept of the picture as *veritas falsa*, we can add a later soubriquet, which is that the image is *muta eloquentia*. It arrives without voice, its affective impact precedes discourse, it pierces—gets under—the skin, and is only later, if ever, tamed with words and then represented in the text as if it is the product of the verballing.

In a Wisconsin slip and fall case, it is the dissenting Judge Ann Walsh Bradley who seeks to wield the weapon of obviousness of images. Channelling *Scott v Harris*, she begins: 'A picture says a thousand words and represents some of the best evidence'. She continues, '[b]ut if a picture says a thousand words, then a video speaks volumes', which in turn suggests a flooding, an emotional deluge or submersion in cubics.[24] The majority in the Wisconsin Supreme Court had sent the case back to trial because the Circuit, in their view, had erroneously given an absent witness instruction to the jury and so prejudiced the Defendant's case. The conditions before and after the fall were recorded on Speedway's surveillance cameras and 'provided a wealth of information' on which the jury could base their decision, an award of $317,545.58. She then makes the visual obviousness argument: 'It is only by refusing to acknowledge what is depicted in this video evidence presented to the jury that the majority is able to discard the jury verdict ... '. The Judge then moves to discussion of the video surveillance footage, which shows clearly that there was snow outside the store and that the snow was visible from the cash register. The video pictures 'revealed that the outside snow conditions were in plain view'. A picture of an individual, the plaintiff presumably, walking upright towards the store is then reproduced and even in the poor quality of CCTV stills, shows not inconsiderable snow outside the shop. Tension is building, and we are then told that Speedway employees saw the fallen Kochanski prostrate and 'writhing in pain ... but they did nothing to assist him. The video picture below shows the two Speedway employees looking out the window at Kochanski during the time that he is lying on the sidewalk' (Figures 5.6 A & B).[25] A footnote to that point helpfully explains that '[t]his image is from 12:54:57 of the surveillance tape. Again, the online version of this opinion is displayed in color and more clearly shows the images'.

Examination of the image, in text and online, black and white and in colour, enlarged, highlighted, scrutinized, does not show employees 'looking out the window at Kochanski ... lying on the sidewalk'. According to the previous image and the description provided by the judge, Kochanski was walking into the store and so should be visible through the glass of the door. He should be on the pavement

(a) (b)

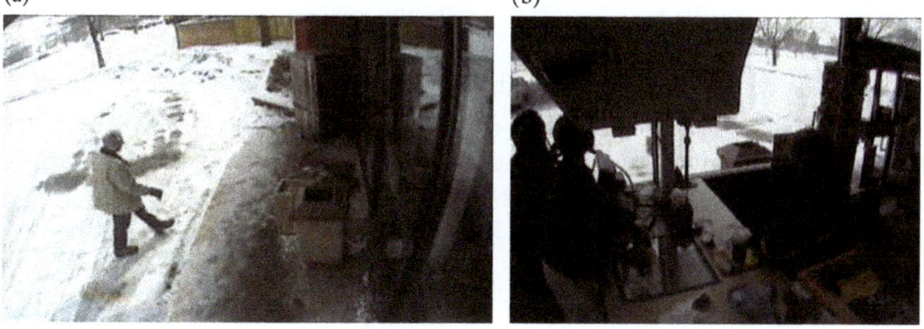

Figures 5.6 A & B Insertion by Judge Ann Walsh Bradley (dissenting) in *Kochanski v Speedway SuperAmerica LLC* 850 N.W.2d 160 (2014).

[24] *James and Cynthia Kochanski v Speedway SuperAmerica LLC* 850 N.W.2d 160 (2014) at 175.
[25] Ibid., at 178.

outside the store, having tripped on the snow-covered curb. But he is not. Perhaps the barely discernible customer at the counter is looking at the felled Kochanski elsewhere and out of view, but whatever the case, there is no picture of any supine subject or recumbent individual on the street outside. The picture is placed in the judgement as evidence of visual obviousness but ironically it does not depict what the judge describes, it does not show what is 'revealed' to the retina of this particular Justice. The elaboration of a narrative of slipping and falling, the plaintiff ambulant and then being watched passively writhing in pain, provides strong affective, graphic discursive, contextual support, as in X marks the spot, for the argument that the dissent is making, but it does not provide any direct visual evidence of the actual scene described. When the judge proceeds to lambast the majority for 'ignoring evidence of record' and for turning 'a blind eye to pivotal parts of the record', it is possible that in castigating the mote in the eye of the majority she has missed the beam in her own. Scotomization or blind spots are common knowledge and empirically now well evidenced and mapped. We only see a portion of what we view, and we fill in the rest.[26] Everyone misses things scopically, but the image is inserted precisely so that careful scrutiny, detailed apprehension, a course and ambulation of an optical ilk, and deliberation over time are possible. The picture is a sensible visual mode of evidencing the judicial reasoning and so careful curation of these depictions of obviousness and truth, critical analysis of composition and evidential content would appear to be both possible and most necessary. The dissenting judge, Ann Bradley, has made here a commendable but untutored attempt to analyse the visual evidence, and its retinal apprehension, but common sense is not aesthetic acumen, nor does it proffer any critical curation of the image qua image and as part of the growing gallery of judicial depictions.

If the picture is the evidence of obviousness then some calculus of what is obvious needs to be coordinated, tabulated, connected to the aesthetic, material, and sensible qualities of the image and linked to the archive of such images of obstacles or visual obstructions to ordinary progression. The judicial decision and reasoning is composed of text and image, the legible and the visible, the linear and the sensible. The enhancement of judicial discourse with the addition of retinal justice requires of inserted depictions not only accuracy and authentification, but also examination of context and composition, analysis of perspective, calibration, and calculation of grid—distances, heights, foreground, and background—provision of codes and keys for scopic review. This would potentially form a start to apprehending what the image is evidence of, and why it is deemed to be obvious in the specific context of its manifestation in the imaginal of law. The more subjective category of judicial reception of the visual, retinal justice in its most basic form will often determine criminal as well as civil liability and necessarily does so by

[26] On scotomization, see, for instance, *Berkson v Gogo LLC* 97 F.Supp.3d (2015) 359 reproducing a graph of blind spots at 379.

engaging with the aesthetic sensibility, the haptic and hepatoscopic or divinatory aspects of pictures, the unconscious relay and relations of the image to a history and sensorium of other and connected images, the 'shadow archive' as Pugliese terms it, although I would rather a gallery, a term less suggestive of enclosure and archiving, and more redolent of openness to the collectivity, the *zoē* or communal life of imaginal sensibility.[27] Law moves slowly and changes seldom, or at least more covertly than overtly where possible. It is thus with classification, calibration, codification, and calculation that the effloresence of deconstruction of the obvious should begin.

In an Australian case concerned with speeding on the Caloundra Road in Maroochydore on the Sunshine Coast in Queensland, video footage was used to review the magistrate's decision. Aaron James Ring was convicted of riding his motorcycle in excess of 70 kilometres per hour, the speed limit in the relevant section of road. In upholding the conviction, despite some errors in the proceedings at first instance, the determination was held to be sound. Judge Cash begins with a reference to Galileo and a short lesson in the science of measurement of velocity which could have usefully been provided to the US Supreme Court in *Scott v Harris*. He begins: 'Since at least the early seventeenth century it has been understood that the average speed of an object during an interval of time can be calculated by dividing the distance the object travels by the length of the interval. Commonly expressed, the mathematical formula is $v = d/t$ where "v" is speed, "d" is distance and "t" is time. If any two of the variables are known it is possible to calculate the third'.[28] Using CCTV footage of the road travelled by Ring, police investigators were able to identify two frames, numbered 884 and 929, in which the motorcycle is seen (Figures 5.7 and 5.8). These frames are reproduced below and allowed police to calculate the speed of the motorcycle from the distance travelled and the time elapsed. This required taking into account the frame rate of the video footage and measuring the distance on the road, while allowing for fluctuation in the position of the motorcycle in the lane in which it was travelling. Taking all this into account, the speed was between 85 and 102 kph. To determine the speed from the video required a calibrated measurement of a scale map, ascertainment of the frame rate of filming, sequential numbering of each frame, identification of the motorcycle, identification of the place occupied by it, and taking into account the 'parallax error' when the footage of the motorcycle was compared with a staged reconstruction using a police car and a different camera position. Taking

[27] Joseph Pugliese, *State Violence and the Execution of Law: Biopolitical Caesurae of Torture, Black Sites, Drones* (Abingdon: Routledge, 2013) usefully develops a sophisticated conception of shadow archive, the real mirroring fictive and filmic imagery of abjection and death. Such imagery may well merit archiving—imprisonment, punishment, stasis—but for most images mobility, willingness to trace their movement over time and context, is both epistemically liberating and intellectively appropriate. Georges Didi-Huberman, *The Eye of History: When Images Take Positions* (Cambridge, Mass.: MIT Press, 2018) also makes this point with force.

[28] *Aaron James Ring v Commissioner for Police* (2019) QDC 32, para. 1.

Image 12: Frame number 884 of the CCTV footage showing the front wheel of the motorbike alongside the start of the broken white centre.

Figure 5.7 Insertion by DCJ Cash QC in *Ring v Commissioner for Police* (2019).

Image 13: Frame number 929 of the motorbike, with the front wheel emerging from the left side of the Bob Jane T Mart sign.

Figure 5.8 Insertion by DCJ Cash QC in *Ring v Commissioner for Police* (2019).

account of these factors, and explicitly treating the camera as 'silent eyewitness', the judge concludes that '[i]t follows as a matter of physics that the average speed of the appellant's motorcycle was more than 70 kilometres per hour'.[29] It is 2019, and the Court was willing to adopt a scientific methodology for determining

[29] Ibid., at para. 38.

speed of locomotion and to scrutinize all features of the inferences made from the images. It also admits that variables such as position in the lane, the time interval between frames, the exact distance travelled all render the video imprecise but can calculate speed within verified parameters, a minimum of 85 kph and a maximum of 104 kph.

In similar fashion images can be used to demonstrate visibilities and digitally altered representations, computer generated models and schemata can indicate in a verifiable form through a visual calculus. In a case from Western Australia, *Sanders*, to take a simple instance, a resident sought judicial review of an administrative decision to grant planning permission for a neighbour to construct a house that would block the plaintiff's view of the river Canning. The decision involved analysis—review—of the existing view, compared with future vistas of the river from the affected property, to determine whether lines of sight were 'significantly obstructed'. It might seem obvious, but in fact determination of significance and extent of any blocking of view depends upon the position of the viewer and the direction of their gaze, whether looking south, south-east, or east and from what point in the house will alter the extent of the vista and the place of the impediments. This question is evaluative as well as measurable but, as the Court frames it, the concern is 'with actual, rather than theoretical, views'.[30] Thus a photograph of one view from the property is juxtaposed with a digitally configured image which measures the impact of the proposed construction upon the view. Plans allow for

Figure 5.9 Insertion by CJ Quinlan in *Sanders and Others v City of Perth* [2019].

[30] *Helen Sanders and Others v City of Perth* [2019] WASC 226 at 42 and 43.

Figure 5.10 Insertion by CJ Quinlan in *Sanders and Others v City of Perth* [2019].

measurement, and the digitally altered image can demonstrate effects upon the vista visible from the balcony (Figure 5.9). Pictures were also inserted that showed other views of the river still available from the house (Figure 5.10). The calculus of impact, however, does not take into account the different sensibility, the disparate depth and shades of the photograph in comparison to the digital image and its tonally distinct quality. The table and chairs on the balcony have gone, trees have been excised, the opposite river bank and its foliage is missing, the colours are shallower, digital effects. The affective and aesthetic remain the unspoken volume that the picture conveys, the unconscious undertow of inference, the affective coil of mute deliberation.

Other examples of calibration and calculus of the content of the image can be expanded upon briefly. The size of a vehicle, the width of a boat, the speed of an automobile, the position of an actor, the width of a lane, the markings on a road, the condition of a drainage pipe, the boundaries of a property, the proximity of neighbours, the warnings on a water-vehicle, the consent icon on a splashpage, the colour and lettering of an advertising hoarding, are all verifiable visually and so have an epistemic value as well as an aesthetic force.[31] The numerous instances of

[31] *Ausbal Pty Ltd v Grandsea Holdings Pty Ltd* [2014] VSC 625 (height of a truck); *Emprja Pty Ltd v Red Engine Group Pty Ltd* [2017] QSC 33 (width of a boat); *Ring v Commissioner for Police* (2019) QDC 32 (as above, the speed of a vehicle); *David Jeans v John Varga* 2019 U.S. Dist. LEXIS 171,401, 2019 WL 4,857,720 (2019); *Roy Ruffino v City of Puyallup* 377 F.Supp. 3d 1205 (width of a lane); *Carmen John*

images that can be measured, however, does not address the affective and sensible dimensions, the feel and aesthetic of the multimodal reasoning that provides a visual identification, photograph, digital image, videoclip, animatrix, or graphic depiction of the subject matter, scene, or parties to a dispute. The point is that even the calibrated and calculative presentation of an image as evidence carries with it an affective charge and aesthetic sensibility, the rhizomes of other views and earlier depictions, that need to be accounted and worked through if retinal justice is to play a conscious role in reasoning as opposed to having an unconsidered visceral effect, for good or ill, upon the elaboration of argument and the verdict arrived at by the judge under the influence of imagery—not DUI but JUII. Consider a digital image from an extremely lengthy class action, a negligence case against the manufacturers of medical mesh. The plaintiffs had all suffered extensive injury from surgery involving the transvaginal implantation of synthetic mesh. The case contains fifteen images of medical devices and diagrammatic representations of procedures used in the various surgeries. These are loosely evidential as explicating the modes and risks of medical procedures using such devices, and the meshes utilized are reproduced in colour in the online version of the judgement. One of the offending synthetic substances was Gynemesh PS, 'which is made from Prolene Soft mesh. The "PS" in its name is an acronym for Prolene Soft. It consists of rectangular sheets of mesh that may be cut as desired by the surgeon. This is what it looks like' (Figure 5.11).[32] In this instance the reason for the depiction is usefully enigmatic. It is presumably a visual device for identification of the substance under contention, and Judge Katzmann, author of a judgement which runs to 1536 pages, is describing the composition of the mesh and the history of its uses and abuses. It was used here for purposes other than those for which it had regulatory clearance and was the cause of considerable injuries yet, as pictured, it 'may be cut as desired', and, in effect, here it is, 'this is what it looks like'. Lacking only music, it manifests as if the wavy, flexible, patterned, and coloured translucent mesh fabric is held softly by the thin fingers of a sensuous cyborg hand in a surreally alluring rose-coloured virtual screen environment. It both is and is not Gynemesh PS, more an advertising image than a reconstruction, it is the very definition of an imaginal depiction, neither real nor imaginary but lodged, in limbo ontologically and epistemologically, between those old and discarded binary categories. The mesh is the dash, the possibility that the phantasmograph, here an advertising picture, holds as a sensory compendium, as an image and vision that the judge chooses

Perri v Public Storage et al. 2019 WL 7,881,617 (disabled markings); *A.D. L.L.C. v 2004 S.C. Partners L.L.C.* 860 N.W.2d 341 (2014) (condition of drains); *Ben Pelech v Royle* [2019] WASC 297 (boundaries of a property); *New South Wales Aboriginal Land Council v The Minister Administering the Crown Lands Act* [2015] NSWLEC 179 (boundaries of properties); *Dariana Mizrahi v Yamaha Motor Corp.* 2019 WL 3,890,311 (size of warning signs on watercraft); *Australian Competition and Consumer Commission v Viagogo* AG [2019] FCA 544; *Melbourne's Cheapest Cars PTY Ltd v Melbourne Street Cars* [2004] FMCA 606 (advertising hoarding's colour and typeface).

32 *Kathryn Gill and Others v Ethicon Sàrl* (No 5) [2019] FCA 1905, para. 138.

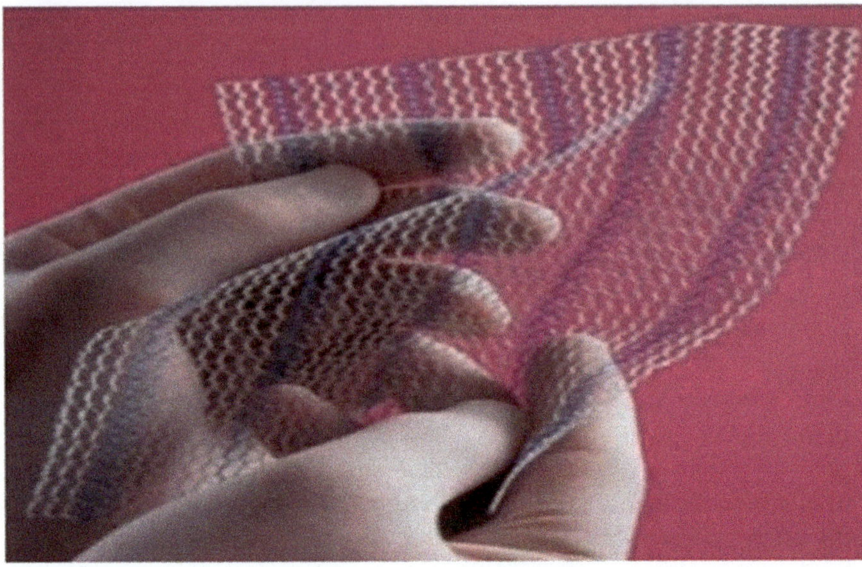

Figure 5.11 Insertion by Judge Katzmann in *Gill and Others v Ethicon Sàrl* (2019).

to relay without critical tools, constraints, or channels of viewing.[33] It is evidence, which is to say it is apparent, obvious, but what is obvious is a much more complicated question and one which entails an apprehension of colour and context, of the hand that holds, of the positioning and the folds of the improperly used, virtual gynemesh. The image is striking, alluring, and is even described judicially as being subject to the surgeon's desire. It is significant in contrast to other images used of Gynemesh PS, such as the Prolift device made of the mesh which, according to the Judge 'looks like this:' (Figure 5.12).[34]

The monochrome, diagrammatic representation is no more accurate or free of affect than the colour depiction, but it is certainly different in its apparently neutral, scientific aura of measurement, lettering, and graphic design. A distinct imaginal relay is not somehow more real or less affective, but it does convey a visual sense of numerical precision, of surgical dissection and of abstract designation, inclusive of the boxing in of the Prolift product. As was argued in Chapter 2, this diagrammatic representation, even if consciously addressed as an image, is likely to be viewed as juristically better evidence in that the aesthetic is easier to

[33] I am borrowing the concept of phantasmography from Robert Desjarlais, *The Blind Man: A Phantasmography* (New York: Fordham University Press, 2019) at ix: 'It is not enough to stick with empirical studies of apparently real things, for life is much more than that. Nor can one contend that there is a strict divide between what is taken as the perceived and the imagined, or the actual and the virtual, for these forces are closely intertwined. What is implicit in this, though not acknowledged in the text is that phantasmography, the 'writing of phantasms ... graphic inscription of the flows and currents of fantasy and fabulation', as Bottici cogently argues, is of a suspended ontological status.

[34] *Gill v Ethicon*, para. 173.

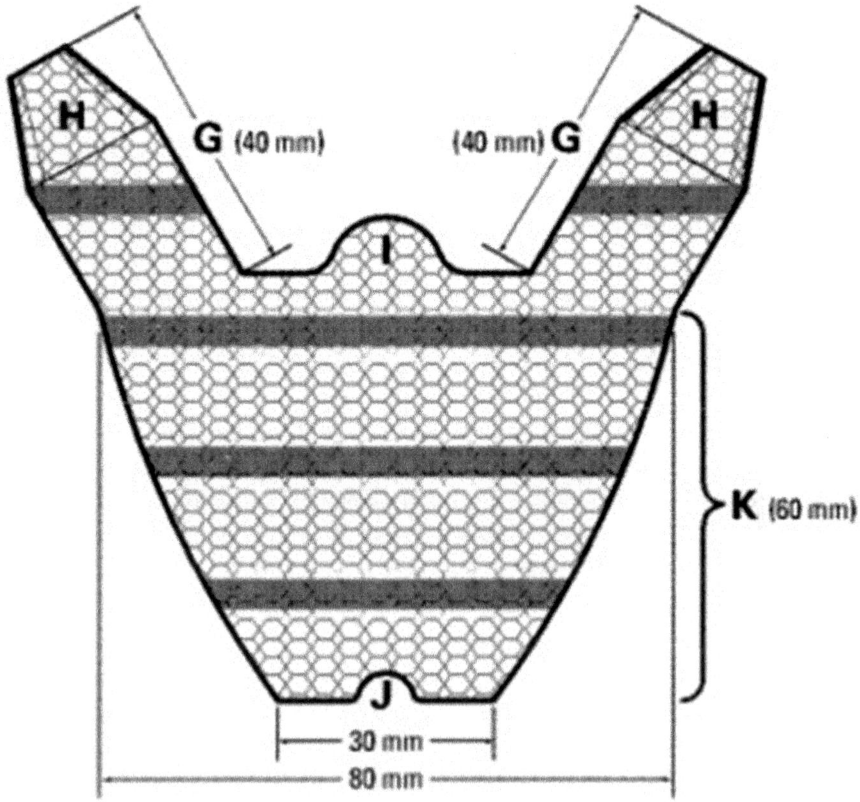

Figure 5.12 Insertion by Judge Katzmann in *Gill and Others v Ethicon Sàrl* (2019).

ignore and oblivion to affect can be presumed. It is visually similar to an identikit representation, not that this would be recognizable on the street, but the evidence of identity would allow for apprehension in surgical settings. Whatever the purpose, the indicative statement is ostensive and directional, it is said repeatedly to look 'like this' and no further explanation is deemed necessary, although of course being 'like this' does already and inexorably indicate that it is not this and therefore some account of mediation and viewing is logically and legally necessary for this to be evidence in any veridical form. Even so, the Court does not take the position that the digital mesh requires description; the bars, measurements, indicators, and the monochrome, apparently, are in no more need of deliberation than the rose-pink background of the image of the fabric Gynemesh. We see what we see, but for that to be true would require a complete cessation of intellectual activity, erasure of the patterns of memory, as well as quieting of thought, openness to the sensory that the court is determined to prevent through a return to discourse and the linear directionality of prose.

The self-conscious evidential use of imagery in judgements is most often used to support identification of subject matter to be determined, the ostensive vision in decision. The Court in *Gill v Ethicon* was attempting in a rather indirect fashion to provide a visual designation of products, patents, and uses, even though the issues related to the internal, post-operative decomposition of the mesh in dangerous and painful internal forms that presumably could not be viewed and certainly were not shown in x-ray or decision. No speculum was offered to the fact finder. Identification by means of camera and picture, by means of a purported yet prior and non-dispositive depiction of the fabric in its pristine state, asserting that this is what it 'looks like' is positively misleading if not critically curated and contextualized visually. The picture as evidence, not only of Gynemesh, but as visual testimony in similar terms is common in criminal cases identifying the accused by photo-portrait, usually a CCTV capture, aimed at objectifying the determination by visual demonstration of the accuracy of the verdict.

In the well-known Canadian case of *Nikolovski*, the question on appeal was whether it was safe to convict solely on the basis of a videotape picture of the accused. The answer was that the picture was 'real evidence' and 'to a certain extent testimonial evidence as well'.[35] The Court set out rules, including that the video has not been altered or changed, and that quality of tape, degree of clarity, and the duration of accused's appearance on the video are all to be given weight.[36] Cory J goes on to substantiate the value of video as evidence by observing that robberies are traumatic and then, taking up the filmic references so fond to courts looking at video: 'Not every witness can have the fictional James Bond's cool and unflinching ability to act and observe in the face of flying bullets and flashing knives'. The Court continues to opine that not even James Bond could live up to the sang-froid of film: 'The video camera on the other hand is never subject to stress. Through tumultuous events it continues to record accurately and dispassionately all that comes before it. Although silent, it remains a constant, unbiased witness with instant and total recall of all that it observed'.[37] The appellate Court confirmed the clarity, quality, and strength of the video in *Nikolovski*, but exact criteria for viewing are lacking from the rules set out. Recourse is again made to the simple and directly ostensive quality of viewing, and the trial judge concludes: 'I cannot ignore what my eyes tell me, and my eyes tell me, and there's no dispute this isn't a video tape of the robbery, that the person who committed that robbery is Mr. Nikolovski', and then a few lines latter, summing up, 'I think we've beaten this to death ... I'm satisfied that the robbery was committed by your client. I'm satisfied on looking at that tape that that's him'.[38] The multiplication of negatives in the statement of the authenticity of the video blending into the obviously visible

[35] *R v Nikolovski* [1996] 3 RSC 1197.
[36] Ibid., at 1215–1216.
[37] Ibid., at 1209–1210.
[38] Ibid., at 1204–1205.

Figure 5.13 Insertion by Justice M. Wong in *R v Shaun Burgher* [2016].

already belies the certitude purportedly being asserted. Betrayed by syntax, the unconscious glimpsed in the rhetorical form of grammatical error, so beloved by the Vienna brigade, at least suggests a moment of doubt, a condensation, where other factors and causes of decision are laid to rest.

Following the thread of *Nikolovski*, it can be noted that in later cases the issues do get greater deliberation in terms of the quality of transmission. The character of video evidence is sharpened, as also is the willingness to describe facial features and detail the degrees of likeness. In *R v Burgher*, for example, a breaking and entry case, also from Ontario, Wong J provides eight video stills from camera footage in the relevant building.[39] The accused is shown frontally, in profile, close up, and at a distance, singly and with an accomplice. Even taken together the images, while similar to the accused in Court, were not sufficiently clear to convict. Similarities, such as hairline, profile, beard, mustache, height, weight are discussed in detail, but overall the blurry quality of cheap video cameras is insufficient to prove identity (Figure 5.13). The reason is in essence that it is not obvious, although it should be acknowledged that Wong J does spell out the degrees of similarity and of dubiety in visual detail and concludes that '[t]he best I could say is this man looks like

[39] *R v Shaun Burgher* [2016] O.J. No. 2738.

Mr. Burgher'.[40] A low-quality, monochrome still with clear distortion at the sides and lacking adequate pixelation, whiting out and blurring in the background, was simply inadequate to the task of designation of identity.

Visual evidence concerning identity is now usually covered by better quality of digital capture, and supplemented also by DNA evidence. The issues of digital video tend to be more complex and relate to position, attitude, or level of apprehension of threat, contextual factors, presuppositions of the viewer, as well as composition and use of the visual evidence. Thus in *Jeans v Varga* what the video has to identify is the threat level of the petitioner and so the reasonableness of arrest under the Fourth Amendment (Figure 5.14).[41]

The Court reviews twenty-three freeze frame CCTV images inserted into the judgement to determine the reasonableness of the petitioner's attitude, degree of threat to the arresting officer, and the scope of the 'protective pat down'. All of which is to say that there are numerous variables and many invisible facets to the viewing. After careful review the State Appellate Court held the video was inconclusive as to the scope of the officer's pat down of the petitioner: 'at best, the video is inconclusive. Thus, we cannot agree that the video conclusively establishes that the officers exceeded the permissible scope of the frisk'.[42] In reviewing the visual evidence, the District Court offers the following description of the freeze frames: '1. [Petitioner] was at the GoLo gas station ... a number one hotspot for narcotics in the police district. 2. Police surveillance had identified a possible drug sale at the station 3. Police found drugs on Aranjo who had been in the gas station although he had not been seen buying drugs from him. 4. Petitioner did not turn his body towards the Officer, but maintained what is termed a bladed position, as visible in the freeze frame'. The freeze frame reconstruction provides very limited visual evidence of the reasonableness of the police suspicions and the attitude as opposed to posture of the petitioner. He did not change position, but it is the prior assumptions, the unseen testimony as to the narcotic character of the scene and the preceding surveillance of the comings and goings from the site that lead the court to view the interaction as one of threat and response, even though it is admitted further on in the judgement that 'it is true that the gas station's surveillance video does not show Petitioner selling drugs to anyone coming into the store'.[43]

Jeans v Varga makes abundantly evident that the evidence of visuals is never simply a question of looking, and thus never genuinely obvious nor just a question of identification, because even identity is mired in the narrative that seeks it and the context into which it is placed, both visually and discursively. To this one has to add the composition and history of the recording, the provenance of the image which took centre stage in a California case where Sunny Delight

[40] Ibid., para. 28.
[41] *David Jeans (R42876) Petitioner v John Varga Warden* 2019 WL 4857720.
[42] Ibid., para. 5.
[43] Ibid., para. 8.

Figure 5.14 Insertion by District Judge Jorge Alonso in *Jeans v John Varga Warden* (2019).

Beverages were sued for misrepresenting that their drinks contained fruit of any kind. The plaintiffs presented visual evidence to the Court in the form of images of Sunny Delight drink labels, *in situ*, on bottles of the fruity-flavoured concoctions.[44] The picture reproduced in the judgement appears to show two bottles with misleading representations of the fruit from which the drink is made. The argument is that the label is a misrepresentation. A flavour of the complaint can be taken from the pleading: 'As shown in [the image], above, the "Orange Strawberry"

[44] *Michelle Hunt v Sunny Delight Beverages Co* 2018 WL 6786265.

flavor Product's label shows life-like pictorial representations of fresh, ripe, whole strawberries ... The "Orange Strawberry" Product, however, contains no actual strawberries or strawberry juice ... ' It would at first viewing appear that the labels arguably do create a false impression and do not carry any disclaimer. It transpired, however, that Sunny Delight had never sold any products carrying these labels and 'that the disputed images are merely stylized renderings of the labels ripped from Defendant's website'.[45]

In an imaginal environment of digital relays there can be no assumptions about veracity without investigation of provenance, site, rendering. As Jessica Silbey has put it, cross examination of imagery is needed.[46] Viewing, visual prudence, sensible apprehension of the image as the mode of retinal justice must take account both of the technical facets of every representation and of the context of its judicial insertion, as well as the perceptual aesthetic of the picture. In this case, the symmetry of the depiction, the bright colour, the dew of freshness on the bottles, the black background accentuating the definition of the product all suggest an advertisement, a desire to sell SunnyD and more than that, as was the case with the plaintiff, an augmented desire to sell the critique of the manner of sale, a reduplication of the misleading picture's purpose. It was indeed for that reason that the judge did not strike out the key element in the complaint, which was simply that the labels, with or without disclaimer, were potentially visually misleading. The evidence of the image is multifaceted and in this instance of advertising, of sales-orientated visual persuasion, it carries its share, though not perhaps that great a content, of an aesthetic of allure, a sensibility of desire.

The picture is the bearer of a visual velocity, a virtual power that leads from the category of evidential image to that of aesthetic and affective force representing a continuing power, a spectral undertow and sense of the dynamogram. In all of the imagery reviewed in this chapter, there are elements of the emotive both in the context of the insertion of the pictures into judgements and in the images themselves. The prospect of slipping and falling, the threat of a black zigzag snake drawn on concrete paving, the serpents of wire running from a security box, the CCTV capture of a drug bust, the bottles of SunnyD, all, in their variable forms of sensibility, carry with them and so intrude into the case an affective cluster of menace, anger, danger, allure, loss, hope, and desire as palpable facets of the reasoning and its expression. The aesthetic and correlative affect relayed by the images evidencing decisions is the most opaque and least discussed dimension of retinal justice because it is seldom acknowledged juristically and rarely

[45] Ibid., at 3. The image is available at https://larc.cardozo.yu.edu/faculty-online-pubs/61/, eFigure 11.

[46] Jessica Silbey, 'Cross-Examining Film', 8 *University of Maryland Law Journal of Race, Religion, Gender & Class* (2008), 17–46 and Jessica Silbey, 'Evidence Verité and the Law of Film', 31 *Cardozo Law Review* (2010) 1257–1299. See further, Jennifer Mnookin, 'Semi-legibility and Visual Evidence: An Initial Exploration', 10(1) *Law, Culture and the Humanities* (2014) at 43–65.

self-consciously included. Law's resistance to emotion results most usually in the secretion of the felt dimension of decision in the unsaid of judgement, and while images are often not discussed or dissected even when inserted in judgement, the affective force of the depiction is most frequently actively though not necessarily particularly self-consciously evaded as impertinent to the topical structure and logic of decision in cases of delict and crime in particular.[47]

When the affective relay of the image is discussed in these judgements it is most usually for the reason that the sensibility and feeling portrayed is in some measure identified with by the judge. A dissent that includes a picture of a solitary worker, without harness, lanyard, or protective net, walking on a roof girder, as if on a tightrope, funambulously high above the ground, in low quality monochrome, conveys a distinct and vivid visual innervation of danger. The judge feels that the image fully justifies a finding that the plaintiff was in breach of statutory regulations and had placed himself in a perilous and illegal position, concluding that 'The pictures below are, in themselves, "substantial evidence" to support' his finding because the threat posed by the plaintiff can be seen and felt.[48] Distorted images which in the online report cover part of the text, brilliantly and unintentionally prefiguring the viserbal, here the literal imbrication of the visual and the verbal, project a sense of precarity while dark clouds above hint at storm and further ominous portent (Figures 5.15 A & B). In this instance at least the work environment, the scene of the judgement, is cast for viewing although again nothing is said as to the provenance of the pictures or who it is that walks solitary upon the girder

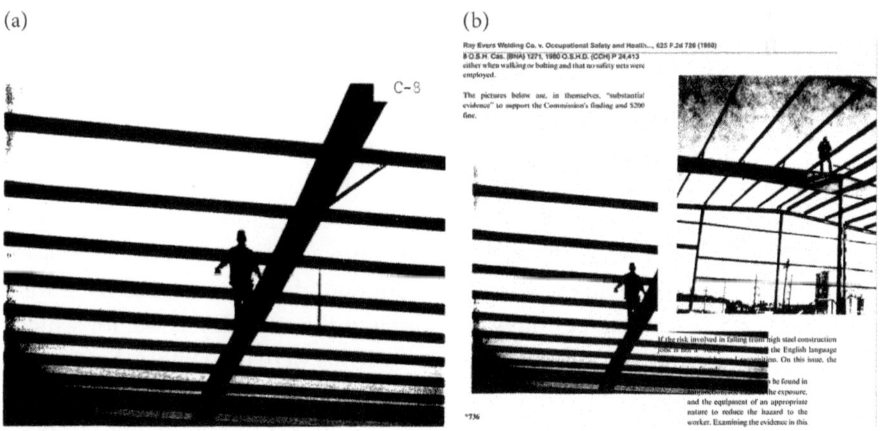

Figures 5.15 A & B Insertion by Chief Judge Edwards (dissenting) in *Evers Welding Co. v Occupational Health and Safety Review Commission* (1980).

[47] On the interplay of robes and lobes, law and emotion, legal sensibilities and aesthetics, see Julia Shaw, *Law and the Passions: Why Emotion Matters for Justice* (Abingdon: Routledge, 2020).

[48] *Ray Evers Welding Co. v Occupational Health and Safety Review Commission* 625 F.2d 726 16 (1980) at 735–736.

towards the lower flanges. It is noticeable, however, that Chief Judge Edwards, in dissent, inserts the images as best expressing his feeling of danger, of darkness visible, but his analysis is no more precise than to say, just visible under the second picture: 'If the risk involved in falling from high steel construction jobs is not a "recognized hazard", the English language has been twisted beyond recognition'.[49] The implication is that the image provides for recognition, it is visual evidence of substantial hazard that the majority decision has not included because they have presumably deemed the affect and aesthetic of danger detrimental to their determination.

The dissenting judge treats the affective force of the visual as obvious, which again raises the question of the role of such an image in the judgement and specifically the force (*vis ac potestatem*) that it carries not only in its presence but in the judicial affect that led to its insertion. The strength of the judge's feelings make an uncharacteristic appearance in the precedential picture to denounce this labour relations practice, and to dissent from the verdict. With nothing more expressed by way of analysis of the visuals, alternative viewings are without question possible. This could be theatre, acrobatics, trapeze, still life, a demonstration of the need for safety equipment, an advertisement for workers protective gear, a costume commercial, and similar. We don't know because we are not told, the etiology and composition of the image remains opaque as to when, where, who, and what is being depicted. The affect that the judge expresses transpires to be the principal import of the visual insertion, along with a sense of incompleteness and indefinition, an identification with the unidentified.

Evidential force, in the specific sense of *potentia* that includes the affective and aesthetic dimensions of the image can range from fear to desire, frustration to confusion, anger to Eros, hope to Thanatos, or, as in the curious case of *Sandifer v US Steel Corporation*, it can include both desire and threat.[50] The case went to the US Supreme Court, but the instance of judgement that I will address is the seventh circuit Court of Appeals. First the prose. In a class action, the employees of the defendant steel corporation sued under the Fair Labor Standards Act for compensation for time spent at work changing into work gear. The Act stipulates a minimum wage for all hours worked but does not define work. The issue was whether the apparel being put on was clothing in the everyday sense, for which compensation was not payable, or whether the items were not clothes, but rather safety equipment, in which case donning the outfit would be encompassed as work, as part of the job and so compensable. As the Act did not define clothes, it was for the Court to determine the propriety of inclusion or exclusion of travel to and from the changing rooms and changing time as work or as being on the

[49] Ibid., at 736.
[50] *Clifton Sandifer v United States Steel Corporation* 678 F.3d 590 (2012).

workers' own time. As Posner J puts it, the failure of the statute to define the meaning of work is 'a critical hole that the courts must fill'.[51]

A critical hole, a blank space, a lacuna, gap, or breach suggests the figural in its classical sense of *fingo*, forming and making, shaping and fabricating a cover, a screen, an image that will veil the void. Already there is a sense of the hole as a trap—it is critical, dangerous, law threatening—while also inviting invention, creation of an argument, the imaginal depiction of a resolution that will efface the deficit and render the hole whole. The exercise in invention begins with a lexical description: 'The alleged clothes consist of flame-retardant pants and jacket, work gloves, metatarsal boots (work boots containing steel or other strong material to protect the toes and instep), a hard hat, safety glasses, ear plugs, and a "snood" (a hood that covers the top of the head, the chin, and the neck)'.[52] As the description covers items of apparel that would never be encountered in any non-specialist clothing store, and as two of the items are so unfamiliar as to require parenthetical definition, the impetus of the description would appear to be towards these items being specifically for work and therefore included in the Act. Surprisingly, that is not, however, how it looks to Judge Posner, or subsequently to the Supreme Court which affirms his decision.[53] The judgement makes a sudden turn, a self-conscious shift in medium and direction of argument with a magnificent apparent non sequitur: 'since a picture is worth a thousand words, here is a photograph of a man modeling the clothes ... ' (Figure 5.16).

The sudden incursion of an image fills the critical hole in the text and at the very least suggests a screening and veiling of the legal lacuna with a portrait of the real. The image is bright and imposing, taking up over a third of a column and in colour, but gains little direct discussion, it speaks or more accurately does not speak but obscurely demonstrates for itself. It is literally the said of the unsaid insofar as Posner J. restricts his analysis to stating that, other than the glasses, ear plugs, and hard hat, 'the outfit certainly *seems* to be clothing ... '.[54] And of the other items, the hat '*might* be regarded as an article of clothing, and in any event putting on the glasses and the hard hat and putting in the ear plugs is a matter of seconds and hence not compensable, because *de minimis*'.[55] It is a matter of impressions, looks, the phantasmography of the image drawing the viewer into a dictated appearance, orange modelled affects represented verbally as clothing to resolve the case. At the same time, however, the judicial sentiment leading to the insertion of that particular

[51] Ibid., at 592.
[52] Ibid., at 592.
[53] *Sandifer v United States Steel Corporation* 134 S.Ct. 870 (2014). Elizabeth Porter, 'Taking Images Seriously' *Columbia L. Rev.* 114 (2014), 1687–1782 at 1696, draws attention to Justice Ginsberg, commenting in a similarly naïve vein in *Sandifer* that the protective gear at issue in the case 'from the picture—it looks like clothes to me'. Transcript of Oral Argument at 5, *Sandifer v. U.S. Steel Corp.*, 134 S. Ct. 870 (2014) (No. 12-417) [Sandifer II].
[54] *Sandifer*, 678 F.3d 590, at 593. (Italics in the original).
[55] Ibid, at 593.

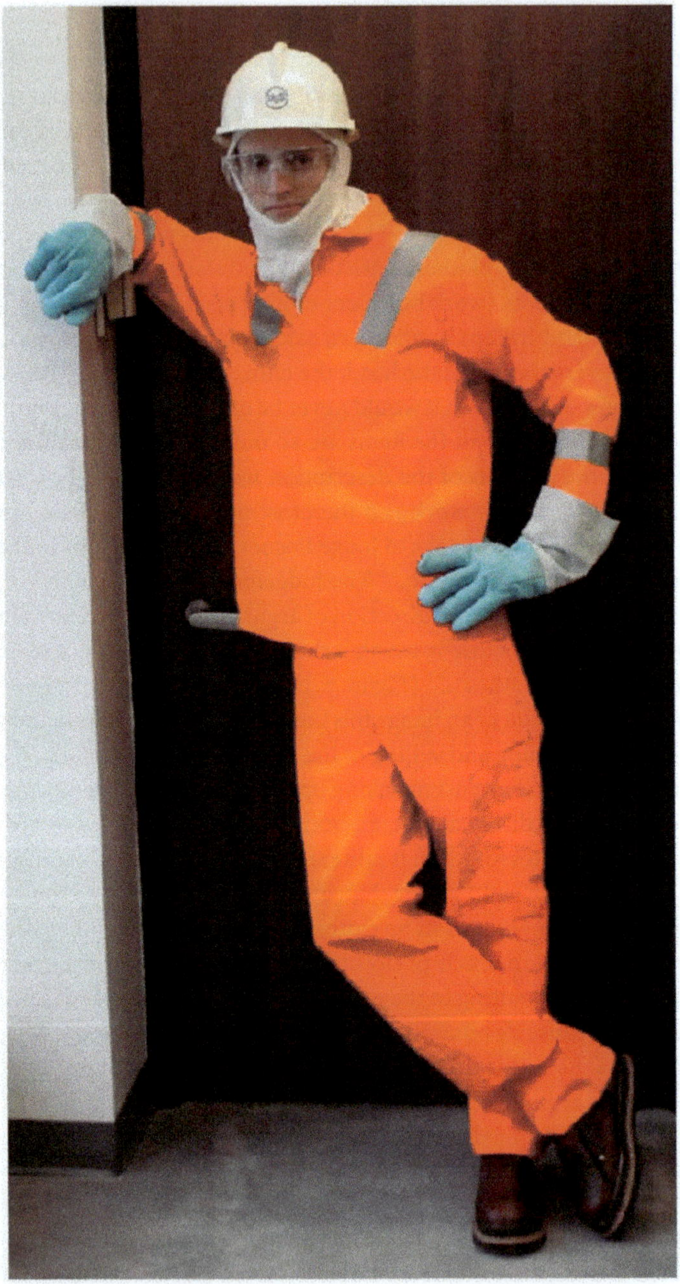

Figure 5.16 Insertion by Judge Richard Posner in *Sandifer v United States Steel Corporation* (2012).
Permission by Timothy Shapiro.

image, the interior of judging a question of danger or dress, is briefly unveiled and can be pursued.

The key term, italicized by the judge, is that it 'seems' to be clothing. The picture is evidential of the identity of the sartorial subject matter of the case. The beseeming of the seams is highly suggestive: the outfit, we are told, has the appearance and feel, the look and cut of clothing, but precisely in seeming to be clothing the judge is arguably betraying the fact that it is not in reality clothing. The image is here a simulation of apparel, a modelling of a costume, but precisely in seeming to be other than it is, in merely representing rather than being clothing, the appearance is arguably deceptive. This quality of simulating is perhaps obvious from the fact, discovered after lengthy investigation, that the costumes are actually modelled and photographed by Judge Posner's law clerks. The vestments in the picture, the habiliments portrayed are presented in the style of fashion and are effectively advertised as a species of clothing whereas their actual function is quite other to the runway and the *beau monde* of celebrity designers, the in vogue and high style. The judge gives no consideration to the fact of the costume being modelled, nor does he appear to proffer any attention or weight to the svelte figure and pose of the model. There is another context to this other scene of the image as judgement. This is particularly surprising in that the photograph shown transpires upon investigation to be the product of work of the highest order by a trinitarian concatenation of Judge Posner's law clerks. The photograph proved dispositive and not only withstood appeal to the Supreme Court but merited positive comment from Justice Ginsburg in the course of argument before the Court. It surely deserves mention that the photograph was taken by Timothy Shapiro; the paraphernalia, snood and all, was modelled by Mark Savignac; the conspectus, event, and entertainment were assisted, singly and severally, by Daniel Siegfried.[56] They merit condign acknowledgement and proper laudation for an imaginative instance of imaging that early augurs a now expansive trend in the remediation of argument and decision. At the same time, however, the miscognition of the image, the willingness to glance at it and infer without further deliberation that it 'seems', that it appears to be clothing, signally fails to address the fact that precisely in seeming, it dissimulates work gear. The barest rudiments of critical analysis of appearances would hasten caution, at the very least in the sense that seeming is simulating, that the image is staged and that the staging is an unacknowledged part not only of what is shown but also of the hidden drive, the desire that opens, and so founds the image as the covert figure of the juridical imagination. There is another scene to this other scene of the image as judgement.

[56] The trio were Judge Posner's law clerks, and the details are as relayed from correspondence with all three, who generously recounted the circumstances of composition and modelling. My thanks to Timothy Shapiro, Daniel Siegfried, and Mark Savignac, graduates of that 'fancy law school' in Chicago and erstwhile clerks to Judge Posner.

Staying with the 'seeming' to be clothing, the image has a dual function. In one aspect, it is there to point, an ostensive reference to an imagined and clearly fictional real. The picture is conjured by law clerks and then judicially inserted, to show that the work costume is clothing, to dispense with argument by means of demonstration, by the visible truth of what is modeled for the viewer to apprehend. The picture, somewhat counter intuitively or at least uncritically, is presented as self-evident, or, to borrow from Saint Augustine, as *vera philosophia, non simulationis*. We are supposed to straightforwardly perceive the picture as clothing, in part at least because clothes are what models don, adorn, and display, and in other part because that is how the image appears to the Judge, because they say so. The disturbing aspect, however, of this emplotment of a picture in the judgement is that it necessarily traduces the argument by introducing a synecdoche, a picture that is expressly deemed a substitute for a thousand words, as if the picture were simply an incursion of the immediate reality, a quicker relay of what the text will bring and thus a reason for brevity of proof or discussion. In treating the image as self-evident, as seeming to show clothes, the Judge also reduces the image to text, the depiction to language, the portrait to a common sense or putatively uncontested, shared perception of common clothes and common law.

It is in the latter aspect, as a simulation of a common sense of clothes, that the insertion of the image has its greatest effect and moves towards dissimulation—the pretense to not be what it is, an image, a depiction, *veritas falsa*. The picture is of a youthful student, dressed up as a steel worker, modelling an outfit. It simulates the apparel that the steel worker has to wear in the precise sense that the model is not a steel worker and is nowhere near the agon, the molten pig iron, the sparks, flames, liquid metal, intense heat and fire of a steel foundry. The simulation, a concept developed by Gilles Deleuze, pretends to something it does not have, a reality that it mirrors whereas, for Deleuze, the simulation 'is the phantasm of itself, that is, the effect of the functioning of the simulacrum as machinery ... By rising to the surface, the simulacrum makes the Same and the Similar, the model and the copy, fall under the power of the false (phantasm)'.[57] This is to say that the simulation announces the emergence of the image in the associative domain of the imaginal, which functions to remove the depiction from any immediate connection with the source or apparent subject of the representation. It takes flight and represents in its own right. The image of the model wearing the workers' gear is thus thrust into an associative chain of images that have no actual reference in the empirical domain in which the disputed apparel is used. The dress that is modelled has no relation to the worker, nor is the image related juristically or otherwise to the gallery of images upon which it is itself modelled.

[57] Gilles Deleuze, *The Logic of Sense* [1969] (London: Athlone Press, 1990) ('The Simulacrum in Ancient Philosophy') at 263.

For the judge, the image appears to be extracted *ex nihilo*, as an autonomous, free-standing, pristine, undiluted, and direct representation of what it is that the workers wear. The inserted depiction, however, proffers the precise opposite of such denotation. It rather channels attention away from the litigating subjects and into an entirely different domain of costume, of 'painted cloth', of livery and coat armor in the classically heraldic terms in which apparel encountered law, and images contested sumptuary rule. Dress has always generated anxiety, in that it expresses spirit and can be variously idiosyncratic, being treated juristically as either excessive, or properly restrained and mutedly fashionable.[58] For the purposes of viewing Posner's image, however, it is the fact that the clothes are being modelled that is most striking and significant. In the world of fashion, *Project Runway*, *Top Model*, and the like, fashion dominates the domain of dress and it is clothes that are the primary object of modelling. The association is thus consistent with fashion and the fashionable, and by extension with the flimsy and evanescent, with changing winds and transient trends expressed in lissome and often emaciated forms. A model is a 'fashionista', a devil wearing Prada, and so to show an outfit being worn by a model is to set up an image that appears to be concerned with clothes, but carries with it an undertow, a vast domain of the unspecified and unsaid lusts and desires, carnal and venal, curatorial and status driven, that fashion imposes.

In *Sandifer* the meaning of such 'seeming' to be dress, the composition of clothes is deflected by way of the image of the clothes, and specifically by virtue of the absence of the persons who wear them and the context in which they are worn. The model is rather a pretty substitute, a false person, an actor pretending, simulating a worker. But the actor is not a steel worker, nor is the protective gear as modelled the same as the protective gear worn by workers in the dangerous context of production. The picture used does not represent the subjects under discussion, nor does it depict the garments *in situ* or *in actu*. The image rather simulates in the strongest of senses because what it represents is itself a simulation, a modelling of a significantly absent worker. The image hides as much or more than it reveals in that it is a copy of a copy. The point, the *punctum*, in semiotic terms is that 'far from being an image without signification, the simulacrum is at the center of an intensification, namely a more sophisticated play of sense, which interpretation should not ignore'.[59] The judge, however, chooses precisely to ignore, to extract and abstract, to avoid and to stupefy. After all, the model explicitly shows a modelling of clothes. Standing in a doorway, in a non-descript environment, the contexts in

[58] Gary Watt, *Law, Dress, and the Naked Truth* (London: Bloomsbury, 2013) at xix arguing for the homonymy of law and dress based upon a territorial similarity between the jurisdiction of law and the jurisdiction of dress. The early modern regimen of sumptuary law, the regulation of colours and cuts of cloth, is sketched in Alan Hunt, *Governance of the Consuming Passions: A History of Sumptuary Law* (London: Macmillan, 1996).

[59] Paolo Bertetto, *Le Miroir et le simulacre* (Rennes: PUR, 2015) at 27.

which the protective gear would be used, the furnaces, the fires, the smelting, the intense heat and danger, that the gear protects against are entirely absent, as are the workers and the smoke and grime, the burns and wounds, that attend such industrial activity. Nothing could be less threatening than the context of the modelling, nor further removed from actual use, and thus distracted by the simulation, the judge can move to ignore the fact that what is modelled is not clothing that would ever be worn outside a dangerous work environment. He refuses to admit that the items are protective in function and specific to the work being done, thus falling into the statutory requirement that work time be compensated.

There is a long history of legal intervention in what can be worn, in how different ranks and genders dress, and that history is the subject of sumptuary law, concerned as it is with the social divisions and statuses, the dignities and honours, uniforms and rites that dress models and expresses. Industrial dress is not entirely distinctive, but being primarily functional it is generally governed by the Factories Acts and by Health and Safety Codes, or by military, para-military, or police regulations. The police officer in the United States and elsewhere may wear a gun, but it is not dress. By extension it can at least be argued associatively, by way of images, that insofar as what is put on is for protection, be it from crime, or fire, or industrial hazards, it is probably not clothing in its accepted contemporary senses. Protection may look like clothes, it may seem to be sartorial attire, when worn by a model or seen out of context, but such modelling and such images are highly deceptive, or in the old language of such debates they are more idols than icons, simulations rather than replications. The image of the protective gear, if uncritically viewed, if judged simply by what the picture seems to show, is a lure, a seduction to fashions and scenes that are not simply non-probative but likely misleading. The picture is in essence here a manner of unsaying, it is the unsaid of the said. It would have been perfectly possible for the judge to insert a picture of workers, single or several, of the steel plant, of furnaces, but he chose not to do this. Posner ignores the subjects and their context, the reality of the dispute. The unsaid here gains expression in the unseen. In political terms it is the who of the case, the human matter, actions, and relations that form the subject of conflict in the context of conflagrations that are obscured by the non sequitur of the image selected. This is judicially, to borrow a phrase, a reckless unsaid, a refusal to address the dress, to engage with the actors, who, in this juridical context, are precluded from appearing and so remain excluded. The picture appears real but operates to screen the real from view, remediating danger into seduction, threat into fashion, the spectre of death into the habiliments of desire. The spirit of costumes is here dispirited by law.

The essential point is that the image, a singular, peculiar, posed representation of the sartorial subject matter of dispute seems to determine the decision as the evidence of the matter in dispute. What is shown but not said, what is presented as imaginal evidence, leads to the verdict that this is clothes, whereas a more considered and extended visual investigation would have likely had other consequences and outcomes. The force of the image, its evidential valence, lies in the affective implications of the pose. Choosing between protective gear and clothes as quotidian costume, the image lures the viewer briefly but effectively into a visual scenario of youth, glamor, leisure, masculinity, sartorial accessories, and in sum of the everyday play of appearances laced as they are with the accoutrements of desire. The force of the image is its divestment of danger. That force is precisely what attracts the judge to order the composition of the image and to insert the picture. The power of the visual, however, can lure and mislead because it is the force of the depiction rather than analysis of the composition that leads the way. The judge says nothing of the making of the image. How come a worker is wearing this pristine, clean, new, unused clothing outside of work? He asks us to look, not to think. To judge by appearance and not examination. Force and affect dominate over analysis and thought. The vision in decision rests on the decision to use vision.

To recapitulate and conclude, the wild disarray of evidential uses of images allows paradoxically for a brief summation. The image appears in decisions as evidencing the matter in dispute—be it the identity of a person, the function of a costume, the hazard occasioned by a skylight, the threat posed by the stance of a filling station patron, or the danger of ice. The concept of evidence, however, is textually dominated such that it is the discursive context that will determine the perception of the depictions used. The evidentiary function is thus primarily predetermined as legitimating the perspective of the judge who inserts it for the purpose of confirming their presuppositions. As with the maps and satellite images of place, discussed in Chapter 2, the principal modality of inclusion is analogical and reductive insofar as the picture diagrams and charts the discursive logic of decision. What has been argued here is that, with all due respect and deference to the pressures of time and rigours of caseload, the remediation of the matter of judgement in the modality of images requires apprehending the difference between the pictorial and the discursive. This means exiting the diagrammatic and linear logic of the textual elaboration of precedent in favour of the novel visual medium and attending to the critical apprehension of the lateral path and affective ambulation of the eye. To look means to silence presupposition and to scrutinize the detail and the aura, the affect and the patterns of association that are embedded in the relationship of viewer to viewed. The image is rhizomatic and multiple, it changes over time and in distinct contexts, and thus the evidence proffered is never simply what it seems.

6
Extispicious Depictures

There is a final feature to the force of the image, the key sought throughout the analyses of this book, and that is the extispicious and liturgical qualities of the imaginal. The image, the medium of aesthetic sensibility, emerges to unsettle the rule of writing because historically it has been party to a power and *potentia* that exceeds the scriptural and always threatens to achieve a greater effect than words alone. Verballing can flatten, abstract, and bore, while images enliven, transport, and transfer. Such is the meaning of the dynamogram, a concept that Aby Warburg devised to describe the aesthetic of a force that allows an image to continue and survive across time and populations. It is for this reason that when law historically sought to lend a greater force to the text, words became images, red letter rules, gothic typeface in heavy print to express the illocutionary force of the words as the signs of normative governance and of sovereign rule.[1] A muted sense of the spectacular, the lurking shadow of leviathan and accompanying nebulous figures of divine authority and liturgical effect are shape shifting and on occasion explicit structures accompanying the volumes of law and inherent in the use of dogma and depiction, staging and performance. The extispicious image is divinatory, in the dual sense of being the object of a legal conflict and containing the potential to be the most direct avenue and medium of its determination. Where a photograph or video clip is the actual subject of judgement, it often plays an extispicious visual role, and the judge as haruspex or extispex, shaman or soothsayer, closely examines the image to determine its significance, what it augurs for both the verdict and the future generality. The image here becomes hepatoscopic save that it is the image rather than the liver that is pored over, touched and moved around in the ambulation of the eye across the surfaces of vision. As Didi-Huberman depicts the process, 'hepatoscopia mixes empirical precision (close vision, grafted onto the entrails) and symbolic proliferation (clairvoyance haunted by a whole dramatic art of far-away relations between the gods)'.[2] The juristic version of the extispicious is one that treats the image to scrutiny and then rather than aligning sidereal connections, relates the haptic picture to the web of law.

[1] The themes and history of legal typography are elaborated skilfully and analysed critically in Thomas Giddens, *Fonts of Justice: Typography and the Common Law* (Edinburgh: Edinburgh University Press, 2024)

[2] Didi-Huberman, *Atlas or the Anxious Gay Science* (Chicago: Chicago University Press, 2018), at 20.

Judicial Uses of Images. Peter Goodrich, Oxford University Press.
 DOI: 10.1093/oso/9780192848772.003.0006

In the last case discussed, *Sandifer*, the two-piece orange, protective outfit, pristine and modelled by a youthful judicial clerk, hid the danger that the suit, along with metal capped boots, hood, and snood, was made to guard against. Judicial vision arguably went awry, not least because the image was abstracted from the context and the fulminations in relation to which it was made to be used. There was a lack of close visual scrutiny, and the image thereby became immaterial in the sense of appearing not to matter to the arc of decision or symbolic proliferation that the Court of Appeal and the Supreme Court imposed upon the outfits, the dress and habits that the steel workers had to wear. Put differently, there was no danger in the context of the costume, what was not shown could not be seen even though the image was purportedly taken to evidence what steel workers wore as opposed to what a Court Clerk modelled in a safely anodyne environment. As detailed in earlier discussion, the pristine garments triggered a proliferation of sartorial as opposed to protective visual connotations, and the symbolic medium of fashion rather than labour. The image had force and what I would argue was an errant interpretation. Apposite symbolic proliferation was absent, the connectivity of the depiction was obscured by a carefully staged yet radically shallow and cursory viewing that remained locked on the immediate surface of the image and the most proximate of symbolic intimations of the modelling. Even the colour, the warning orange, ironically also often the colour of US prison uniforms, was ignored. That said, despite all that is overlooked, the image guides the decision and so also allows for critical and aesthetic reappraisal of the judicial looking that was seemingly the means of determination, the pivot or seamless thread of judgement. What is key to the extispicious is that the visual marks and directs the reasoning of the case, extispicy meaning that what is seen, the entrails, the parts, the track of the eye, are what determine the configuration of elements, the images of invention that trigger the reasoning and the symbolic alignment of the judgement that follows. Here justice or injustice are directly retinal in the sense that the hepatoscopic sifting of the visual evidence is the mode of determination, the viewing is the verdict. Implicit in this formulation is the observation that what is seen exceeds what can be said and determined because the ground of decision is scopic and the ambulation of the eye over the visual materials, the materiality of the image and its plethora of connections to other pictures, to the imaginal relay of the community of intellect, is directly dispositive.

Moving to the final mode of visual reasoning in judicial determinations, the key lies in the sense that the image has to be divined, the scopic elements presented must be sifted, examined, inhabited to extract and accompany a vision that cannot only be said but also requires the extension of looking. In viewing evidential images it was argued that there is an aesthetic and affective force that frequently accompanies the insertion of pictures in judgements and that this surface of visual matter will impact the decision or set the reasoning in emotion. The evidence, what is seen, is folded into judicial discourse to solidify, visualize, and subtend the logic of determination and confirm the verdict. The *certum* of visualization provides the evidential basis for determination, even though the grounds of such apprehensions and inferences are often more discursively asserted than visually explicated. Evidential images refer to and are supposed to denote in probative fashion a reality exterior to the picture, the act, scene, or person of what are most often criminal, tortious and infringing actions or events. The extispicious image differs from the evidential in that the image itself is more directly the referent and subject of legal deliberation and decision. While the extispicious is also evidential it is cumulatively more than mere proof by visual means because it provides a heuristic mode of interpretation or associative chain that both demonstrates and explicates through connection to the dominion of the imaginal or proliferation of the symbolic that Didi-Huberman references. It becomes part of the normative reasoning, a feature of the argument that rationalizes judgement.

The distinction and diffraction that the image as subject of decision brings takes on a greater role and sets judicial reasoning on a different path. A scopic track and viewing juxtaposes aesthetic discrimination and legal determination. There is a sense, of course, in which the image will always twitch judgement to another route, but in the retinal category of extispicy the point is that the visual, as the subject of conflict, necessarily lies at the roots of invention and frequently appears at the origin of decision. As Lyotard put it, some time ago, '[o]ne only has to allow oneself to slip into the well of discourse to find the eye lodged at its core ... The figure is both without and within'.[3] Once the visual is recognized, the scopic aligned, and the judicial eye examined in its practices of viewing, now that the depictions inserted are available to scrutiny, the determinacy of the imaginal can begin to be reconstructed as the other world, the plastic alterity and matterphoricity of the art of law. Here, in the depictions used, it is not only important that a visual record, an album and gallery, is constituted for later normative introspection and reflection, but also that the remediation of law, the image that tears the text, that rips open the page brings judgement to a more vivid and visceral presence; it comes alive, joins the imaginal, and generates an access that has long been missing.

To see extispiciously is to look into, to pierce connections and gaze across and in relation to, so as to divine non-verbal associations, matterphorical and imaginal links to a visual configuration that, once apprehended and scrutinized, can frequently determine the suit or subject of conflict. The gaze of the jurist becomes the visual major premise of an imaginal network and relay. The eye of justice,

[3] Jean-François Lyotard, *Discourse, Figure* (Minneapolis: University of Minnesota Press, 2011) at 237. Noting also that '[t]he position of art is a refutation of the position of discourse ... Art stands in alterity as plasticity and desire, a curved expanse against invariability and reason, diacritical space'. For expanded discussion of the interrelation of verbal and visual, see Laurence Moinereau, *Le Générique de film. De la lettre à la figure* (2009) [*Film Credits: From the letter to the figure*], and discussion in Goodrich, 'Faces and Frames of Government', in Manderson (ed.), *Law and the Visual: Representations, Technologies, and Critique* (Toronto: Toronto University Press, 2018) at 51–74.

retinal review, is an agonistically prompted scrutiny that strikes both denotatively and laterally. As Benjamin so percipiently observed, the unconscious was discovered shortly after the invention of the x-ray and what is in imaginal terms the objective unconscious of law, the sensibility of the judiciary as recorded in precedential imagery, takes a similar path, the retinal spectrum coming to present what is invisible to discourse. Thus, Benjamin writes, 'evidently a different nature opens itself up to the camera than to the naked eye—if only because an unconsciously penetrated space is substituted for a space consciously explored ... The camera introduces us to an unconscious optics as does psychoanalysis to unconscious impulses'.[4] The camera and the x-ray alike introduce what cannot be seen by the eye to a mechanical viewing. The externality of such images makes evident that the medium mediates and also that the existence of imaginal entities is not dependent upon the viewer but rather external to perception: 'It is only by recognizing the non-psychological origin of the image that one is able to grasp the power of the sensible on human and animal life. We live tied to the sensible, not to language ... '[5]. The question of priority, of precedence, is clearly significant for law because if judgement is overdetermined by sensibility, it is to the images and not to the text that one should look first. In which spirit of chimera, a case that inserts x-ray images of a femur and hip is potentially probative. Retinal logic suggests starting with a question of visual methodology, the technique of looking inside.

In a medical negligence case from New South Wales, Ms Kelly Lange sued Dr Timothy O'Carrigan, an orthopaedic surgeon, after two elective surgeries produced what she deemed unfavourable results.[6] The first, a total hip replacement, resulted in the plaintiff's left leg becoming longer than her right. This was the result of an intra-operative error caused by the use of a size 2 rather than a size 1 femoral prosthetic stem. The second operation was conducted to correct the discrepancy. In analysing the standard of care actually used by the doctor, the judge reconstructs both planning and surgery. The planning involves x-rays which are used as templates for the measurement of the prosthetic appliances that will be needed and specifically the femoral and acetabular components necessary. A pre-operative x-ray of Kelly's hip is then inserted: 'The following scanned extract from Exhibit "2", page 3, shows the oblique line that Dr O'Carrigan had marked on a radiographic

[4] Walter Benjamin, 'The Work of Art in the Age of Mechanical Reproduction', in Hannah Arendt (ed.), *Illuminations* (New York: Schocken, 1968) 236–237. See Akira Lippit, *Atomic Light (Shadow Optics)* (Minneapolis: University of Minnesota Press, 2005) particularly ch. 3 on modes of avisuality. Coccia, *Sensible Life: A Micro-ontology of the Image* (New York: Fordham University Press, 2016), at 52–53, develops the thought on the path of exscription, by observing that we should 'not think of the medium as a purely cognitive or noetic space. Every image is the Being of knowledge that acts outside of the subject, a sort of *objective unconscious* ... At the foundation of any psychic movement is something that has no psychic or subjective consistency, nor does it have any objective consistency'.

[5] Coccia, *Sensible Life*, at 53.

[6] *Kelly Lange v Timothy O'Corrigan* [2015] NSWDC 173.

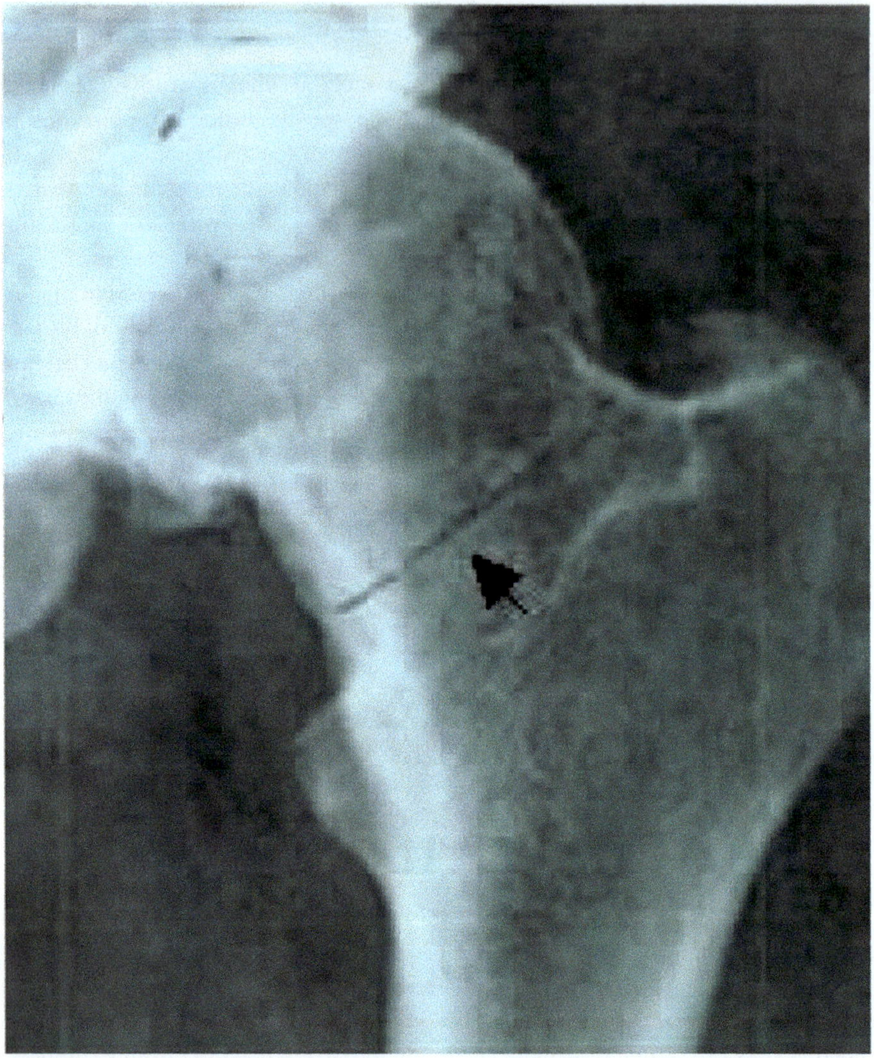

Figure 6.1 Insertion by DCJ Levy in *Lange v Timothy O'Corrigan* [2015].

film of the plaintiff's left hip to denote where he had planned to make the osteotomy cut in order to remove the femoral head of the plaintiff's left hip' (Figure 6.1).

The cursive arrow has been added by the Court specifically to indicate the line that O'Carrigan had drawn. It is the one visual intervention that the judge makes, and while it might appear to be neutral, it acts scopically to suggest precision and planning and so to bolster the defendant's argument that he had not fallen below the standard of professional care required of a surgeon under relevant legislation. When the issue before the Court is taken into account, namely the operation itself and its consequences, the image of the pre-operative hip transpires to be a strange choice of picture, selected from a significant number presented in argument and examined at length by several expert witnesses. There is no probative content to the first x-ray and so it provides background and context to the operation, visual information of a general kind that will not play any direct role in the dispute as to the skill used in the surgery and the actual extent of the discrepancy in leg length after the operation. Discourse and image, text and picture, verbal argument and visual portrayal are so far distinct, lateral rather than conjoint.

The first x-ray shows the ossification operated on, although it could belong to anyone. The sense of the radiological image is that of implication, that the defendant has approached the operation with care. Although it might be supposed that a subsequent x-ray would be compared to the first, what is provided is an inadequate and indeed useless image of the new hip (Figure 6.2). The judge prefaces the image by stating that 'the following scanned extract from Exhibit "2", p 4 shows part of the x-ray image of the plaintiff's left hip taken in post-operative recovery with the prosthesis in place as described above'.[7] Here one might be forgiven for thinking that a visual comparison is the purpose of the image, but it transpires that light reflecting off the prosthetic precludes any measurement of discrepancy: 'Dr O'Carrigan explained that as can be seen from the above image, the nature of that x-ray did not permit fine judgements to be made concerning leg length discrepancy due to the quality of the relatively poor x-ray as it was necessarily taken in less than ideal circumstances ... The purpose of the x-ray was essentially to check the position of the prosthetic components' and could not be used to check leg length.[8] As can be seen from the image, there is a degree of white out to the top of the picture which precludes accurate measurement.

It could be argued that the art of x-ray is inexact and that mobile post-operative x-rays are a poor means of measuring discrepancies, but what is at issue in the case is principally the degree of deviation from prior length which could be measured by means of an erect post operative x-ray. This was done six weeks after the second surgery, on 15 September, and was the image that the expert witnesses debated at length, opinions differing between a 2.8 centimetre and a 1 centimetre discrepancy in leg length. It is in essence the lesser figure that the judge accepts and is grounds for dismissal of the negligence claim. There are other factors contributing to this decision that are less quantifiable or visualizable. Part of the intra-operative skill the surgeon has to use is 'manual "feel" of the placement of the device whilst trialling the prospective sizes *in situ*. That was the final determining factor for completion of the size selection process'.[9] A process of 'trialling' the prosthetic once inserted by means of 'shucking manoeuvres' *in situ*, also required the surgeon

[7] Ibid., para. 104.
[8] Ibid., para. 105.
[9] Ibid., para. 97.

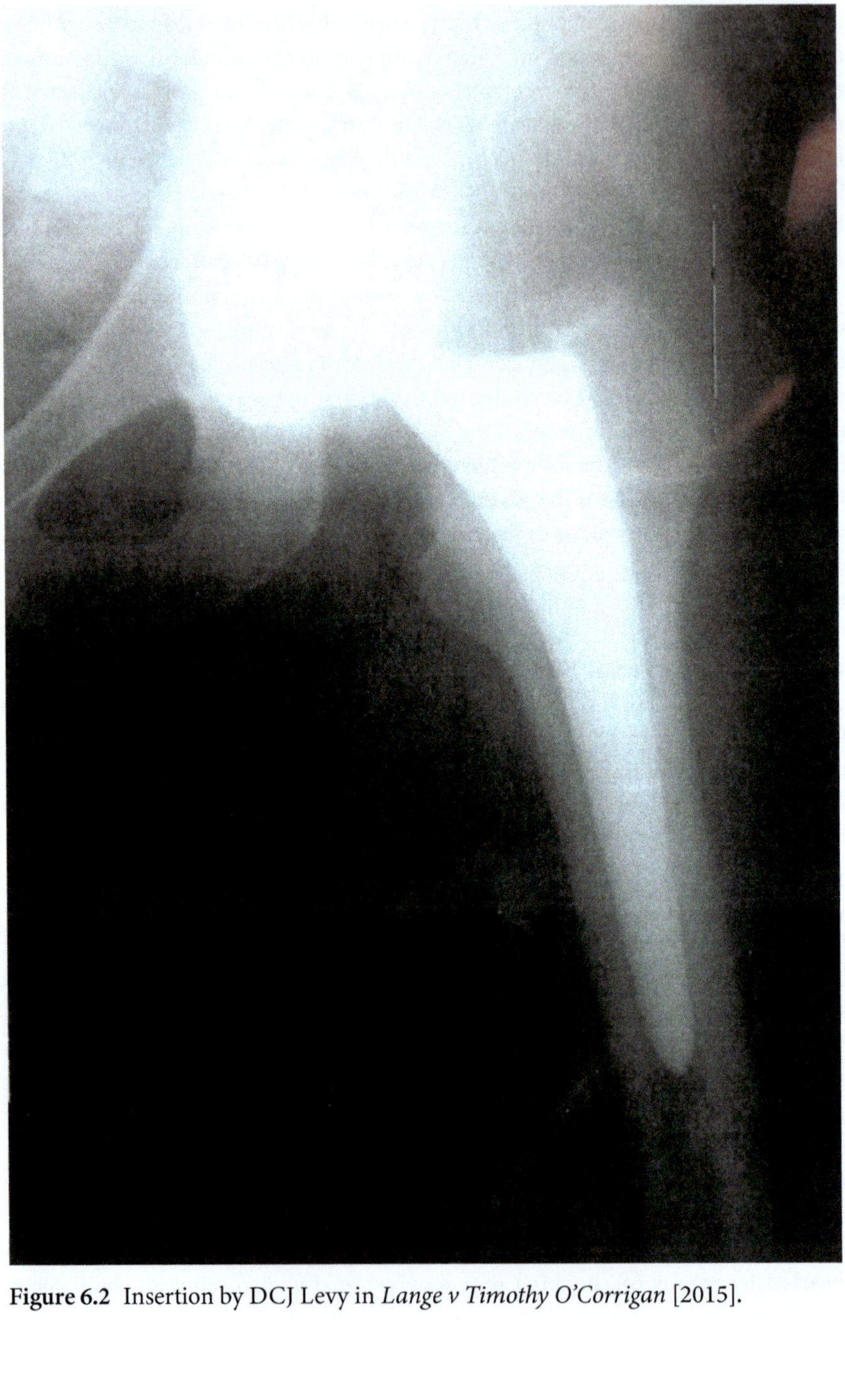

Figure 6.2 Insertion by DCJ Levy in *Lange v Timothy O'Corrigan* [2015].

to decide on fit by means of 'feel'. There was one other factor, that of panic or of pressure at the time of taking and of viewing x-rays which could contribute to poor quality and different measurements: 'Dr O'Carrigan explained that such measurements were best undertaken in quiet time when on his own in the absence of time pressures when he could make the necessary study and identify appropriate landmarks for making measurements'.[10]

The x-ray images cannot show feel, and they are not capable of creating quiet time, but they can generate an aesthetic and sensibility. Whether x-ray or camera obscura, the image of the subject matter both shows and occludes, senses and desensitizes, as here in the monochrome and flash, the stark yet indistinct images of the skeletal interior. The mobile radiographic imaging, taken during the operation, failed to provide clear pictures of placement and effect of the prosthetic. The only images that provided calibrated measurements of the hip discrepancies were taken after the operation as erect images. These are not inserted into the judgement and are not shown despite being, with the assistance of expert witness testimony, the ultimately visual basis of decision. The erect image haunts but does not appear in the judgement. As Benjamin notes, the optical unconscious goes further than the eye, making the skeleton visible on film but ironically in this case not visible to later courts, jurists, doctors, and citizens subject to the precedential value of the decision, engaged in comparative or doctrinal investigation. It provides no guidance as to the status of an x-ray or the requisite methodology and manner of viewing. As to the image provided, the reflection back of the light makes it somewhat abstract, a spectral event with elements of red brown in the right-hand top corner and a metal rod for calibration. These remain unexplained beyond a statement of their thwarted purpose: 'The practical purpose of that x-ray was to undertake a gross check in order to confirm the correct location of the hip prosthesis and to determine whether there were any major complications, such as malpositioning of the prosthesis or periprosthetic fractures. There were no such complications evident on that x-ray'.[11] They were not evident, they could not be evident, because the quality of the mobile x-ray shown was insufficient to allow for either diagnosis or measurement.

In sum, the judge, Leonard Levy SC, adopts the position of the haruspex and examines the x-rays, the visual entrails, in divinatory mode, arranging the elements in novel form to elicit the runes of decision. It is a thorough judgement, running to 114 pages and one in which it would have been easy enough to include the determinative images, to levy the visual evidence, save for a certain diffidence in relation to visual depictions and to the interior, the skeletal unconscious as such. The judge shows two x-rays. The first indicates with clarity the plan that Dr O'Corrigan had formulated for the operation, and the second shows a spectral and somewhat

[10] Ibid., para. 157.
[11] Ibid., para. 103.

ghostly hip with luminously indistinct contours. It implies visual support for the doctor's case in showing nothing wrong or misaligned, but it does so, in the case of the latter image, by inserting a depiction that is wholly indeterminate, that can neither denote accurately nor disprove, except to a divine or divinatory eye. The decision, however, rests on a third x-ray which is not reproduced. It is the absent image that is debated by the expert witnesses and discussed by the judge and the defendant at length. Here we are informed there is a tilt of the pelvis that renders measurement inexact, but the conclusion is that the discrepancy is 1.1 centimetres and within acceptable limits. The x-ray shows the skeleton, it reveals the hip and prosthetics in dispute, but it is not included in the judgement, as if the image shows too much, would be contentious, might undermine the outcome or at least open it to other divinatory procedures and interpretations. It is the irony of the x-ray that it shows what cannot be seen directly, it pierces the body, reveals the interior but it does not reveal all, and far from being obvious requires extensive review and generates competing perceptions. The interior of the body is the unconscious, the skeleton is slow growing muscle with its own memory and patterns, with feel and fascia. There are many senses in which we do not know or are not conscious of what we see in and as the body.

The methodological clue is that the judge includes the x-ray images because there is something to be seen in them that would otherwise not be visible, and while it can be described verbally, it is different in visual perception. The x-ray that the judge does not levy or insert shows visibilities that could mislead the unskilled or that are more than merely apparent. This image cannot be viewed because the juristic methodology of ocular apprehension is more nebulous than precise, more asserted than explicated. There are always further images, other pictures, a spectral realm and gallery of photographs, x-rays, pictures, models, and poses that lure the viewer to other visions and to disputation of the determination, the *incertum* of precedent depictions. The uncertainty of what is depicted, even in an x-ray, becomes a site of judicial anxiety and generates a momentary sense of loss of control. The photograph, in leading also to further albums and galleries of visual record, threatens to escape the law, and hence the move again, in the face of the pictorial, to the text or, as the Reformers were wont to say, *fugiendum ad montes, ad montes scripturarum*—flee to the mountains, the mountains of scripture.[12] The images, shown and described, are subject to writing, to the rules of procedure and doctrine, but their extispicious advenience or juridical effect is one that is deemed necessary to demonstrate that the judge is correct and that the issues are as he decides or liturgically levies them. To show that the law is correct through images is to legitimate optically, and so with putative certainty,

[12] John Favour, *Antiquitie Triumphing over Noveltie: Whereby it is Proved that Antiquitie is a True and Certaine Note of the Christian Catholicke Church and Verity, against all new and upstart heresies* (London: Field, 1618) at 141.

because visualization purports to reveal the accuracy of judgement and here to evince that the very hip and prosthetic are visible, further syllables, photograms, that are known and significant to the law. The x-ray adds an element of the liturgical to the rite of precedent, showing that judgement does what it says, that it effects an otherwise invisible truth and that this is properly an act in law or in the old language *actus legitimi*.[13] The image is both more than and reduced to the written rules because to proceed *ad apparentiam*, according to visual connections, is as yet to exceed the law in a manner that only judges can transgress but that they have as yet to delimit and define.

The question of methodology is greatest where, as in *Lange*, the issue before the Court is that of making sense of the image, a semiotic deliberation on what the vision signals and how it exists within a system of signs that has to be aligned with the rules of law. Here the judge needs to engage in a species of 'exscription' in that providing images inaugurates a figurative relay of judgement and an imaginal dimension to decision that engages in what is properly deemed speculative in both senses of the word. Where Hobbes and the later theological tradition treat the extispicy of images as an angelic—angelological—feature of ideation and intellection, a more direct depiction is that of the speculum, of spectres and the spectral haunting legal discourse and carrying within it the ghosts of precedent, the visions in decisions past that operate as law's slow cancellation of the future.[14] The juridical x-ray and the unconscious, law and psychoanalysis, finally come to share in a 'science of ghosts', 'the study of how reverberant events become revenants'.[15] This is to say that ghosts matter, that the revenant as the visibility of the past now comes into legal view and circumspection. The courts have to look before they write. The x-ray is one more ghost, the visual emission of a figure that is rhizomatically tied to an esoteric and in the main unexamined imaginal relay of legal rules, the precedential past of the visions in decisions now emergent and exposed. The key, *clavis corporis*, that the x-ray passes to the judge is that of an ostensive optics of the case. What was hidden becomes visible, ghosts materialize, the interior is exposed and in the old language of extispicious rituals, the inner organs can be seen, moved around, dissected, and interpreted, which is exactly what Dr O'Corrigan did and that Judge Levy simulates through the use of x-ray images. The Doctor as haruspex is judged extispiciously.

The manner of viewing, the direction of the gaze, the movement of the eye are most directly in issue where the image is the subject of judgement. Such

[13] On liturgy and *effectus*, see Giorgio Agamben, *Opus Dei: An Archaeology of Duty* (Palo Alto: Stanford University Press, 2013); and for detailed exposition, see Nicholas Heron, *Liturgical Power: Between Economic and Political Theology* (New York: Fordham University Press, 2018).

[14] The phrase is taken from Mark Fisher, *Ghosts of my Life: Writings on Depression, Hauntology and Lost Futures* (Winchester: Zero Books, 2013), who in turn borrows the phrase from Franco Berardi, *After the Future* (Chico, CA: AK Books, 2011) at 18–19.

[15] Fisher, *Ghosts*, at 18–19.

was indirectly the case in *Lange* but is more immediately apparent in patent and copyright disputes where judges are inclined to include the pictures upon which judgement is passed in terms of the impression they make, the feel of the image as divined in terms of likeness and difference, simulation and dissimulation. There is also the advantage that in these cases the question is one of comparison, of how one picture looks in relation to another, forcing a deliberation upon the methodology of normative visuality, the scopic regime and sensible life of law. Here retinal justice almost comes into direct expression. Surfaces can be scanned, distances and perspectives measured, colours compared, depth, width and length, material and design juxtaposed and calibrated. The model of extispicious image is the x-ray not only because the lens will always see more and differently to the naked eye, it will mediate, but also in that it provides a view, a return, the material revenant of what is no longer present but rather immobilized by cellular or digital capture and awaiting, in Didi-Huberman's expansive view, the revivification of a new encounter, the event of a novel and distinct relationship with a living viewer in their temporally changed circumstances. The grip of the past lies in the spectral accession to revenants, the visions of precedents of yore stilling the *perpetuum mobile* of the living law until viewing recognizes the mobile and changing character of images in their passage through time. The key, as argued throughout, lies in acknowledging and analysing the imaginative life of the present in the juristic modality of retinal justice. The imaginal is the route to change, adaptation to contemporary and future threat, because the image escapes the dead hand of the text, the pickle jar of precedent. How then does the judge look, what visiocratic gaze governs the retina and produces justice, what is the visual *dispositif* of legal judgement when an image is the direct determinant of decision?

The camera provides a close up of the past. It allows the event to return, the revenant to be seen. The image may only be a radiographic reflection, a thermal or sonic outline, an animated reconstruction, the staging of graphics, the posing of mannequins, or a visual capture, but in each instance it is a reappearance, viscera of the past made visible, the interior of the case exteriorized. A simple example can be taken from a South African case in which the details, the bodies involved in the event, are reconstructed to divine the probable circumstances of death.[16] High Court Judge Makaula was faced with a squalid double murder. Using the medical examiner's report and photographs of the crime scene, Warrant Officer Bekker endeavoured to reconstruct the trajectory of the event and the path of the bullets using two computer generated mannequins (Figure 6.3). As this is criminal evidence the standards for visual reconstruction are explicit, and the officer explains how he uses the doctor's report on the height and anatomical features of the body together with the physical evidence collected from the crime scene to recreate the path of the bullet. He proffers a caution: 'My Lord, please note that this

[16] *State v Redhouse and Another* (CC14/2017) [2018] ZAECPEHC 43 (26 July 2018).

is only one instance, one single event, in a whole series of possible events and this specific event that I have chosen here is the one which I have got the most direct evidence ... ' from which to represent the trajectory of the bullet to the head. Then the judge proffers the image: 'The reconstructed scene is as follows':

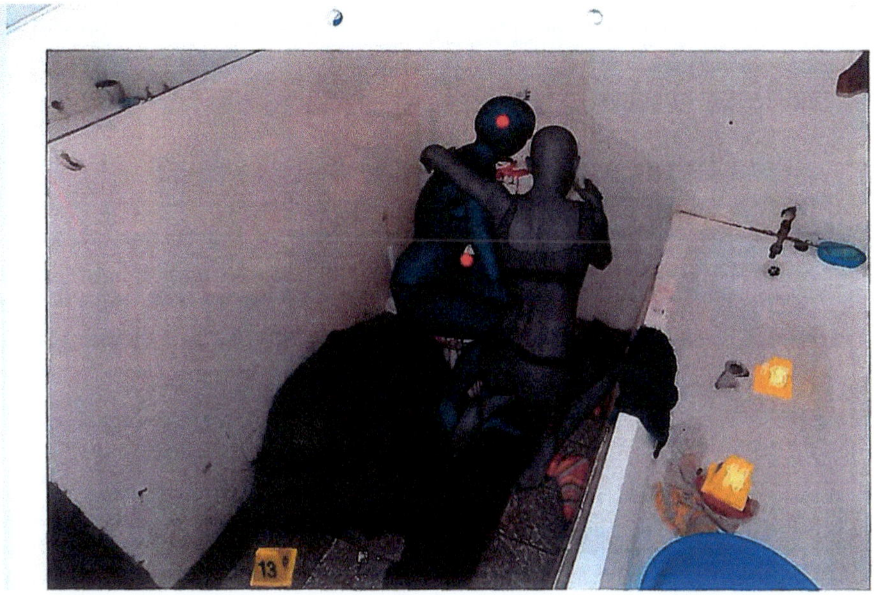

Figure 6.3 Insertion by Justice Makaula in *State v Redhouse and Another* [2018].

The Court is led into the digital recreation of the world and in consequence into the dominion of virtual visibility, the imaginal domain. To judge it is necessary to imagine, to conjure an image, and this visual recreation of the murder scene using mannequins *in situ* gives a tangible sense of the scene of the crime. It also indicates in considerable detail the path and sanguinary effects of the bullets. Red dots mark the entry points of bullets and red daubs reproduce the distribution of blood through 'misting' and through gravity as well as the 'void' where blood should have landed but did not because of body parts covering surfaces. The blue mannequin represents the victim Aaliyah, the grey mannequin Candice who survived and gave testimony. The female mannequins are provided, somewhat strangely, with lingerie. A foot with a brightly coloured sock on it is visible but unexplained, and a hint of colour underneath Candice's knee seems to suggest a further socked foot. These appear extraneous, although they do give a further sense of an inhabited bathroom and likely clutter or detritus in the domesticity. In the psychoanalytic classificatory system used by Henry Bond in *Scene of the Crime*, the reconstruction would fit the psychotic crime scene; the random feet, the disorganized clutter, the figures facing the wall, one seated on the toilet, the other kneeling on the floor, the dump of black material on the left, the clothes in the bath, suggest foreclosure and chaos, the familiar objects of everyday life 'unbonded from the (symbolic) signifying grid'.[17] The Court, for obvious though clearly disputable reasons of forensis, does not view the image as an interpretive scene, but rather as a representation of the ballistic path of the bullets.

The digital photograph of a reconstructed scene portrays forensically what happened to the satisfaction of the judge. It puts the events in pictures and provides a view of what cannot be seen, the past which like the interior of the body requires technology and imagination to reconstruct. It is a juridical 'as if' or *scilicet*, that is neither what it shows—mere simulation in frozen time—nor tracks the path of the bullets, but it appeals to the sensibility of being there, of seeing the situation, of experiencing the sparseness, the scrimshaw free environment, the squalid circumstances, the cramped and lavatorial occasion of death. The image shows the crime and allows the judge to divine, which is here to say to confirm what had happened, but with the additional caution that this is clearly not what occurred but rather one possible version, as the warrant officer had declared initially, and which requires the judge to dissect and then decide by way of confirmation of the reality of the representation. The depiction plays the role of all images as false truths, alternate relays that are both real and fantastical, representations whose epistemic status in the judgement is that of legitimating the effect, trajectory, and outcome of decision. The aim of the judge in describing the imagined scene in great detail is to lend an air of reality and precision to a crude and largely non-probative depiction of the fatal encounter. The image is corralled by words and limited to a legitimating role, although it is also affectively and hermeneutically evidence of much more. The colour and the embrace of the mannequins (femmiquins?), their dress, the pink hue of the wall, the yellow numbers—13, 14, 15—all incorporate an affective and dispositive creation from which the extispex will draw their full conclusion. It is significant as well that the judge introduces only one photograph from an album that the police presented in evidence, as if there is a special status to this singular pictorial reconstruction. There is implicitly a weight to the depiction, a power of the image, which also serves other functions. It is sensory and cathartic, a mode of mourning and release, of seeing and evacuating an event, an anterograde portrayal that allows judge, Court, and reason to move on.

As in *Lange*, so also in *Redhouse*, it is the surface of the image that is scrutinized so as to divine the actual course of events and to decide on the basis of what is seen, inside the body in the first case by means of x-ray, and also the past, as digitally reconfigured, in the second. The aesthetic and affective dimensions of representation are left unconscious and not infrequently to be acted out in the determination,

[17] Henry Bond, *Lacan at the Scene* (Cambridge, Mass.: MIT Press, 2009) at 93. In terms of classification, Bond writes: 'There are two key themes that I develop in order to apprehend evidence of psychosis. First, I propose that visual evidence of fragmentation and chaos may be interpreted as a consequence of foreclosure. And secondly, that visual evidence of a bizarre or incomprehensible organizing logic may imply the presence of a—protective—delusional metaphor' (34).

the judicial reading of the signs in discursive modes that deny the affect and effect of image, context, colour, and visual dramatization, the two female figures in *Redhouse* embracing, comforting each other, turning away from terror in the narrow corridor of the bathroom. This, however, must be acknowledged to be the current judicial method of viewing, proffering a brief and visually vacant account of the surfaces of images, a point that comes more clearly into focus in the well-publicized copyright infringement case of *Samsung Electronics v Apple* in the English High Court before His Honour Judge Birss QC.[18] The issue before the Court and before several European jurisdictions was whether the Samsung Galaxy tablet computer infringed Apple's registered design for the iPad, Design No. 000181607-0001. The judge's starting point, after acknowledging that Apple did not want either the iPad 1 or 2 used as concrete manifestations of the registered design, is that '[l]ooking at the Apple design itself, what strikes the eye immediately is its simplicity. The article is unadorned and tile shaped', as visible in design 0001.3 (front) (Figure 6.4).

Figure 6.4 Insertion by Judge Birss QC in *Samsung Electronics (UK) Ltd v Apple Inc* [2012].

[18] *Samsung Electronics (UK) Ltd v Apple Inc* [2012] EWHC 1882 (Pat). Affirmed by the Court of Appeal in *Samsung Electronics (UK) Ltd v Apple Retail Inc* [2012] All ER (D) 176 (Oct) para. 28: 'The judge had been entirely aware of the need to consider the overall impression of the design as it would strike the informed user bearing in mind both the design corpus and the extent of design freedom' (Sir Robin Jacob).

Birss J. continues 'I start by reminding myself that what really matters is what the Court can see with its own eyes ... The most important things are the registered design, the accused object and the prior art and the most important thing about each of these is what they look like'.[19] The Court will look, the eye of law will survey, to which the judge then adds a reminder to himself that the exercise is a visual one and that what is key is the optics of appearance and not verbal generalities.

The issue is thus defined as that of what the two touch pads look like in comparison with each other and in relation to what is termed the design corpus which includes other pad designs, and specifically featuring the Pepper Pad, the Stevenson (a Canadian designed pad), the Ozolins and Bloombergs, the Viewsonic Airpanel V150, IBM Thinkpad notebook computer, the Flatron and the Showbox, Knight Ridder, and even the Chumby which is very thick. The front is one aspect of comparison, the *dispositif* of the fascia which the judge elucidates by remarking: 'When I first saw the Samsung products in this case, I was struck by how similar they look to the Apple design when they are resting on a table. They look similar because they both have the same front screen. It stands out. However to the informed user (which at that stage I was not) these screens do not stand out to anything like the same extent. The front view of the Apple design takes its place amongst its kindred prior art'.[20] Apple in its arguments relied upon the similarity of the front face of the iPad and it is 'the strength of this similarity that is "the key to the case"'. We are shown the face, as above, sketched, minimalist, low-definition drawing, grey on white, no detail, no colour. The other faces shown are, as listed, diverse and disparate in appearance, design, as well as in mode and medium of representation. The face of the Chumby could hardly be more distinct. A different functionality, a previous generation, a niche role, a forgotten device and a missing image in the present context for copyright reasons but available in the judgement.

A more interesting and probative comparison is to the Stevenson and the AIPTEK (item 35) which indicates the shift to thinner screens, and to the conclusion that 'the appearance of thinness is an expedient found in the design corpus' (Figures 6.5 A & B). Function also plays a part, but the overriding test is that of whether an 'informed user' would view the likeness of the two, the registered design and the accused object, as being so close as to infringe. Long strings of images of design and products accompany the 191 paragraphs of judgement, but it transpires fairly quickly that the test is what the judge sees in the generality of images: 'the outcome depends on overall impression ... For all the similarities and differences, the weighting exercise is concerned with assessing the significance of

[19] *Samsung* para. 9. A test that is substantiated by the UK Supreme Court in *PMS International Group Plc v Magmatic Limited* [2016] UKSC 12 para. 10: 'And the most important thing about each of these [elements of design] is what they look like'.

[20] *Samsung*, para. 189

(a)

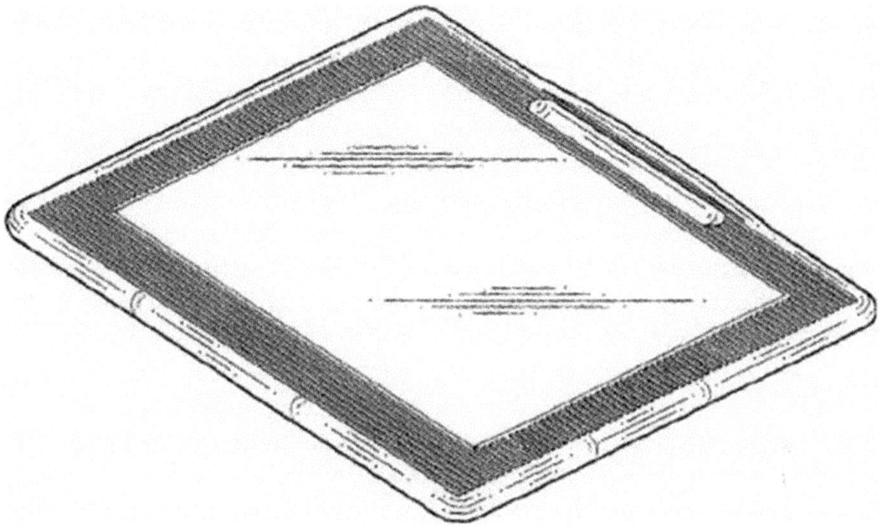

(b)

Figures 6.5 A & B Insertion by Judge Birss QC in *Samsung Electronics (UK) Ltd v Apple Inc* [2012].

the similarity to the informed user'.[21] To offer more precision the judge then specifies, some pages on, that the test is really that of 'different overall impression'. The significant analytic language of being impressed by the designs can be gleaned from the judicial description of the Apple design as 'strikingly' simple, as having 'crisp edges' and concluding 'The design looks like an object the informed user would want to pick up and hold. It is an understated, smooth and simple product. It is a cool design'.[22] As for comparison of the two designs in the context of the design corpus, the judge embarks upon the summation of evidence with the statement, 'To my eye the most important similarities are:' and then the listing follows. Thus, 'the front is really striking', the 'relative thickness' of the designs is hard to judge from drawings and photographs, and attention is drawn next to a variety of visual similarities and differences, and a conclusion that the family resemblances between the disputed designs and the design corpus is sufficiently strong to preclude the claim of infringement of the registered design (see https://larc.cardozo.yu.edu/faculty-online-pubs/61/).

[21] Ibid., para. 32. For further discussion of impression, see *PMS International Group Plc v Magmatic Limited* [2016] UKSc 12, concurring that what matters is 'how those similarities and differences would affect the informed user's overall impression' (para.15), a point repeated numerous times in Lord Neuberger's judgement.

[22] *Samsung*, para. 182.

The judge has an overall impression of the visual significance of what his eyes tell him, and this is essentially that the Apple design, the slim, curved shape as seen from the side, is cool and desirable. The front 'is really very striking'; the edges are 'crisp'. There is of course a history of impressions and 'impresa', *impreses* in the early modern English terminology of heraldic devices, but in modern legal usage the term references visual impact, as in 'one would have to visualize how thick they would be if they were the same length or width'.[23] In sum, visual prominence, visual effect, visual significance, visual similarity and difference are the collocated optical aspects of the case that count 'and not a verbalized list of features'.[24] As in previous cases, the judge is embarking upon an epistemological distinction between the visual and the verbal, what is seen and what is said, but the distinction between the putatively distinct media is not expanded upon and no methodology of viewing beyond seeing, being struck, visualizing, feeling, being impressed by, is elaborated. The judge has set himself up to use the 'informed observer' test for the similarities and differences of the two images. To be visually informed means that the judge, the extispex, should inform himself of the visuals directly, and this he has signally failed to do at any level of historical, geographical, or aesthetic depth. The repetition of the words does not serve any methodological purpose other than emphasis and in time most likely negation of the optical content of the judgement. Judicial lack of visual conusance rules the day.

The most important feature of the judgement is that it recognizes expressly the distinctive epistemological character of visual comparison even if that apperception is not operationalized. The ontology of the scopic, and the life of the sensible, the objective unconscious that is the image outside the viewer, internalized retinally, is not the equivalent, nor reducible to discourse. That is a major step in judicial thinking and method, though a small one in that the viserbal is not accorded a particularly rigorous analysis nor provided with many critical tools of reception or encounter. Nonetheless, to be impressed, to view something as impressive, does start the material ontographic task of treating the image as mattering and so allowing for the synaesthetic character of looking at and comparing the impression of things and, in Lord Neuberger's succinct expression, comparing on a 'like for like' basis that takes account of colour and other features of ornamentation, such as horns and wheels, noses, handles, straps, stripes, and shades of grey in the latter case involving competing children's wheeled cases.[25] The impressing indeed is haptic, sensory and sensible. That the pad is cool, its edges crisp, that the informed viewer would want to pick it up, 'to hold it', that it has allure, is the description of a sensory response and affective approach to the object that is

[23] Ibid., para. 155. On *impresa* see Samuell Daniell, *The Worthy Tract of Paulus Jovius, Contayning the Arte of Composing them, with Many Other Notable Devises* (London: Waterson, 1585).
[24] Ibid., para. 31.
[25] *PMS v Magmatic* [2016] para. 53.

deemed svelte, slim, thin, curvaceous, and striking.[26] The object stands in the path of vision and on the way to decision. It is surprising in this respect that the judge does not compare the registered design to the Apple products or applications as well as to Samsung products, pictured in colour.

The lapsus in the judgement comes from the fact that the terms of visual comparison are never worked through. The overdetermining legal propensity to proceed by analogy—*ad similia*—is undermined by the failure of Judge Birss to indicate the sensible quality of the comparata. The fact that the registered Apple design is a schematic, a colourless diagram of a possible product, undermines any genuinely synaesthetic method of visual apprehension that the judge is suggesting in the language of his decision and applying to the design corpus but not to the Apple product. The reason for this disjunction, for the unhelpful comparison of lateral views, one horizontal, one vertical in the record, and one a diagram, the other a colour digital picture of an actual product, again unsettles the value and ignores the effect of visual comparison and the meaning of impression. The material product, the pad as apparatus, is clearly different from the design if for no other reason than that one is a drawing, the other a colour picture of a plastic, glass, and metal thing. The description of the actual tablet, that it is cool and it is slim and alluring links the product most directly to the other actual products shown in the judgement, the series of colour photographs, including very unlike and unlikely devices such as the Chumby, but nonetheless draws the eye to colours and to actual devices, thus placing the Samsung in a category of homologous objects, yet visibly distinct from and dissimilar to the various black and white drawings that are reproduced in their monochrome tedium. In other words, the absence of any actual image of the iPad effectively and affectively excludes it from the visual field of similarity upon which the eye of the judge is cast and by means of which the decision is taken. It makes a lesser impression by virtue of being a lesser depiction.

The test developed is conceptually and epistemically backward looking. The impression made is to be orchestrated legally by reference to how the object looks to the informed user. The judge starts out the decision by admitting to not being an informed user but then informs himself and applies the test. It follows in a long line of precedents: the reasonable man, the reasonable person, the officious bystander, the passenger on the Clapham omnibus, the denizen of the Philadelphia suburbs who takes the weeklies and mows the lawn wearing shorts.[27] Compare then, at the level of method, the absence of photographs of one of the comparata in *Samsung* to a decision involving two London omnibuses both of which could well be en route

[26] eFigure 12, https://larc.cardozo.yu.edu/faculty-online-pubs/61/.

[27] For a recent discussion of the reasonable man as mentally unstable, see Lucy Jewel, 'Does the Reasonable Man have Obsessive Compulsive Disorder?', 54 *Wake Forest Law Rev.* (2019) 1049. The locus classicus for this view is A.P. Herbert, *Uncommon Law* (London: Methuen, 1935) 1 ('*Fardell v Potts*: The Reasonable Man').

to Clapham in exemplification of the common law.[28] We are back before Judge Birss, and the 'superficially simple question' is whether the defendant, Houghton, has infringed copyright in the plaintiff Fielder's photograph of a London omnibus on Westminster Bridge in front of Big Ben (Figures 6.6 A & B). Mr Houghton's tea company's best-selling tins of the leafy nectar bear images of Anglican landscapes and 'Icons of England' which in this case took the form of the red Routemaster bus on Westminster Bridge in front of the Houses of Parliament. Here the seat of legal reason, the itinerant common sense of the reasonable person, is photographed first by the plaintiff and latterly by the defendant, and Birss J. begins by stating, in rather conclusory fashion, that '[a]t the crudest level the two images in question simply look strikingly similar'.[29] Case closed. But why? The answer is surely that the judge has reproduced two photographs, both in a mix of colour and monochrome, and has placed the two images side by side. The immediate and obvious visual similarities go hand in hand with the obviousness of the visual methodology and mode of apprehension chosen. Leave out the colour, and there would be no case of visual infringement, viewed crudely or otherwise. The Judge does elaborate on similarities and on criteria of comparison: 'What is decisive are the arrangements (motif,

(a) (b)

Figures 6.6 A & B Insertion by Judge Birss QC in *Temple Island Collections v New English Teas Limited* [2012].
By permission of Temple Island Collections.

[28] *Temple Island Collections v New English Teas Limited* [2012] EWPCC 1.
[29] Ibid., para 11

visual angle, illumination, etc.) selected by the photographer himself or herself', but the crux of his viewing rests upon a singular feature, that of the selective chromatic, the monochrome image with a red insertion.[30]

The analysis of the composition of the photograph is relatively sophisticated, with 'specialities of angle of shot, light and shade, exposure and effects achieved with filters, developing techniques and so on', and then foreground, background, and far ground features, the figures introduced, the river and craft on the river all have 'visual significance' and contribute to the aesthetic sense of the photographer and so to the originality of the composition which 'creates the visual effect in question'.[31] What is key to the case, and common law should certainly not be troubled by decisions involving omnibuses caught on camera travelling to South London by bridge, is that here Birss J. compares like with like, photograph with photograph. It is a different number of bus, on a different route, in front of Big Ben displaying a different time, with different figures on the bridge, and no river in view. That said, the judge is persuaded by the selective chromatics, but once again the photograph is taken to be simply what it shows without connection to a visual past or the morphology of photographic techniques. There is some limited analysis of the surface, the appearance, but not of the roots, the multiplicities, the rhizomes that tie images to other images, the symbolic proliferation. The Judge recognizes the specific and iconic character of the image and so intimates at least that there is an established and recognized tradition of such depictions of buses, of Parliament, and of England, our England, the land of lost content, but does not infer from this any optical context and history of similar images or any visual corpus and gallery as the relevant comparata.

The originality of the plaintiff's image is deemed to be the selective chromatic, the red bus strikingly contrasted to the monochrome icons in the background. This, however, is in fact less impressive and potentially misleading as the Court is simply exhibiting a lack of awareness—the observer is uninformed—that there is a considerable tradition of such imagery, from the Spielberg movie *Schindler's List*, which the plaintiff photographer acknowledges as his inspiration, to Leslie Anderson's *If*, to *Don't Look Now*. But ignore the chromatics, the bus and Big Ben with the addition of a London cab is an image used by the BBC in 2002 and has been replicated in similar though not identical forms by other photographers. The judge ignores the morphology of selective chromatics and the specific genealogy of the image itself. Concerned with the immediate and superficial, if detailed, analysis of the two photographs, the viewing is reduced to literalism, to a reading of the photograph as if, *scilicet*, it were a text. This obliterates the autonomy and *dispositif* of images as distinct from words. The connectivities, the rhizomes of the photograph, extend far beyond the plaintiff's image and the differences of angle, exposure,

[30] Ibid., para. 20.
[31] Ibid., para. 34.

illumination, and depth, to a far ground that includes many earlier versions of the selective chromatic and of the staged scene. Whatever the similarities and differences between the defendant's photograph and the plaintiff's, as shown in the case, the underlying issue of the legal methodology of viewing images remains that of synchronicity, obviousness, and immediacy of appearance. The diachronic facets of the photograph, the atlas of images, the public character of the scene and force of repetition in the different genres and occasions of its appearance, the lack of originality in the claimed copyright, are all ignored.

Extispicy requires the judge to connect the visual viscera of decision both to the elements that disparately make up the image and to the symbolic and legal connections that the pictorial matter connotes. Within the latter, the series of apparitional relationships must be included in the eye of the judge and the gaze of law which, in Birss' diction, as noted earlier, allows that 'the Court can see with its own eyes'. It is not a one-way street, the object gazes back, matter moves, the image accosts the eye of the law as much as the gaze of the judge both blinks and wanders. These disparate facets of constructing a diurnally and oneirically lodged visiocracy, a regimen of images, requires a process of excising and exposition, as will be conducted in the next chapter. For present purposes, it is the dim lit eye of the jurist, the fading or inconstant vision of the judiciary, that is called to our attention. The colours of law, the sounds of portrait and depiction, the movement of the players and pictures, pass largely unnoticed, not because the visual is unnoticeable, but because the retina of rectitude, the judicial speculum, sees the print but not the paint. By the same token the sound and motion of film fragments hyperlinked or posted with judgements are deemed at best to be accessories to the drive of the text and the white lines of the page. The phonetics of diction and the rhythm of prose are lost to the an-acoustic practices of transmission, and movement falls prey to the stasis of a law that aspires to being both statute and statuary, solid and sedimented.

The scopic point, repeated here, is that whether filmic, still, plastic, or digital, the image is never singular, its plurality implying the interconnectivity of iconic and familiar, haptic and spectral, sensible and symbolic within the screen and framing of any depiction. This plurality of affects and effects needs to be recognized and worked on at many levels of epistemic, ontic, and ocular impact, as can be gleaned from another cautionary instance. In *Sikhs for Justice v Badal*, the plaintiffs sought to serve an injunction upon the defendant (in absentia), the Chief Minister of Punjab, under the Alien Torts Statute, for extrajudicial killings and torture, in violation of customary international law and the Torture Victim Protection Act of 1991, committed by the Punjab police while he was responsible for overseeing all security services. The judge expresses a certain enthusiasm for the case, a touch of exuberance appearing in his definition of the issue: 'This appeal presents a single issue, which is whether the defendant was served with process; yet the case could be the basis for a novel of international intrigue'.[32]

[32] *Sikhs for Justice v Badal* 736 F.3d 743 (2013).

Judge Posner's remark about the novel should not be viewed as innocent. He was at the time also a lecturer in law, the author of a study of *Law and Literature* as a misunderstood relation, and of many essays on Shakespeare and other literary figures who have impacted legal reasoning and sensibility. He recognizes even in the first edition of the treatise on legal fiction that the study of law 'is undergoing fundamental change', but his thesis is primarily that law and literature is an academic exercise and of marginal practical value, whatever soul-enhancing effects it may paradoxically have on lawyers and critics.[33] The dismissal of fundamental change to the cloistered realm of scholarly elaborations and pedagogic pursuits leads both to undermining the fundamental character of the change, and to ignoring the novelistic character of his own development of the facts of the case. The reference to the novel is symptomatic of the fiction that he is engaged in developing. In the judge's own account, the plaintiffs hired a process server, Christopher Kratochvil, and showed him a video and gave him a picture of Badal: 'The photograph and the video showed a tall, thin, elderly man with a long white beard and a moustache, wearing a turban (mandatory for Sikh men) and eyeglasses', and instructed him to serve the defendant during a ceremony at a High School in Milwaukee that the defendant was due to attend (Figures 6.7 A & B). The process server claimed to have duly served Badal, but the defence argued that he had served another Sikh, a teacher named Kalra. The judge reproduces a photograph of Badal and one of Kalra from the case files and proceeds to elucidate upon the fictive import of the images.

Of the images, Judge Posner states that they support the trial court's determination: 'What makes the judge's finding especially convincing is Kalra's resemblance to the defendant, as seen in the photographs in the appendix to this opinion'.[34] He continues to observe that we tend to look 'unconsciously' at the outer features of a face, hairstyle, and 'one imagines a turban, rather than giving equal weight to everything we see in the face'.[35] To this, the judge adds the flourish that 'people of one race sometimes have difficulty perceiving facial differences in people of a different race'.[36] Such would certainly seem to be the case with the judge himself. The point is not that the two parties look strikingly different, nor that the photographs reproduced are in such poor monochrome quality as to conceal as much as they reveal, but rather that the judge is defining the images reproduced in abstraction, by reading texts into them, asserting in effect that we don't generally recognize difference, we look at clothes, facial attire, rather than the face, as race generates unfamiliarity as likeness and triggers non-recognition. That may be true of the protected social circles and homogeneous peer group in which the judge mixes, but it is an extraordinary projection on to a process server whose job and métier

[33] Richard Posner, *Law and Literature: A Misunderstood Relation* (Cambridge, Mass.: Harvard University Press, 1988) at 362.
[34] *Sikhs for Justice* at 744.
[35] Ibid., at 747.
[36] Ibid.

(a) (b)

Figures 6.7 A & B Insertion by Judge Richard Posner in *Sikhs for Justice v Badal* (2013).

is that of recognizing individuals in all clothes, colours, guises, and disguises. Discrimination in vision means looking more closely, but this is precisely what the judge fails to do, remaining on the exterior even of the visage, looking at costume and follicles rather than at *imago* or the face itself.

The Judge uses the pictures to tell a story:

> Kratochvil is not an Indian, and not a Sikh. To the non-Sikh the salient features of a Sikh man are abundant facial hair and a turban. If the man is elderly, the beard will be white. The photo that Kratochvil was carrying to enable him to spot the defendant showed an elderly man with a long white beard and a turban. Kratochvil had been told that the man in the photo would be at the high school, presumably in a place of prominence since the defendant is a very prominent Sikh (even if hated by the SFJ)—and bingo, at the head of the room Kratochvil sees a man who closely resembles the man in the photo ... So Kratochvil makes a beeline for him, hands him the papers and flees before the man has a chance to ask him what is this all about and to tell him that by the way his name is not Badal.

The images trigger a narrative that would likely not otherwise have emerged in the judgement, evidencing the drive of decision and the latent content of the pictures in the novelistic fiction that the judge uses to describe the imaginal scene of process delivery. The photographs condense affect relating to race, allowing the judge to discourse on facial hair and turbans, beards and colour, similarity and difference of race and identity. The images allow an unguarded glimpse of the retina of judicial imagination because the photographs are there, everyone can see them, and in the mind of the judge they show what he perceives, a unity, identities without significant differentiation—in the Augustinian analysis so foundational for the West—*imago simillima rei*—an image that is in all aspects similar to the thing seen. The juridical viewer, however, is the agent of the unification, and in the mode of projection attributes to the other what he misrecognizes in himself, treating the inability to differentiate Sikh individuals as a feature of the external world. The judge places the stamp of cultural identity onto the other, viewed through the lens of white perception and the narrative of our identity compared to 'their' difference. The desire to be seen is the same as the desire that triggers seeing. The judge in essence sees himself as the proper affect and vision of the world, projecting his perception onto that of the participants in the dispute. That the image is the dogma means that the picture seen, the reflection of Narcissus in the water, is the structuring principle of vision, the desire for the self in the other, a depiction and simultaneous demission of retinal justice. It shows a lazy eye and shallow viewing, prevision that in this case is predicated upon an invented, novelistic view of the circumstances and encounter that is being described.

The retinal compass views the elements of the image but does not make the extispicious connection to the symbolic context and proliferation that the viewing projects. The living actor, *in situ* and in action, in colour, with sound and movement, amongst a number of other Sikhs, is a very different sight to that of the monochrome web captured images whose provenance is neither provided nor analysed. Are these the only photographs available, when and where were they taken, what is the logic of monochrome as opposed to colour, and most importantly why this comparison in this mood and mode? Is it that any Sikh would look the same to the judge or is there a reason for these particular comparata in respect of tone, angle, perspective, and choice of a single subject as opposed to several? Why no image of the context and other participants, including other turbaned Sikhs in the hall? Why two and not five or seven or three? Why in such similar poses, if not to imply similarity? The eye of the judge immobilizes the photo-portraits a second time by means of looking at a contracted scene, an upper body picture without context, and one which fails to take account of the images, photographs, and videos that the process server was using as the visual basis of identification. The low-quality images indicate again that for all the talk of a thousand words or of the value of the picture, it is hardly looked at—because 'they all look the same'—and is of insufficient probative or dispositive importance to merit reproducing higher quality depictions or providing a detailed analysis of what is actually available in visual particularity. The photo-portraits are the proof of the misidentification claimed by the defence. They are what the judge is judging, but rather than an extispicious review of the scopic viscera, the optical arrangement of the visual elements, the magisterial eye slips swiftly over the surface to instantiate an unseen determination, to prove what has never been proofed.

If, to reduplicate the judicially overused phrase, a picture is worth a thousand words, then it merits scrutiny, detailed visual analysis, a scopic account of precisely what is seen and significant of such a significant lacuna of words. It requires staying with the eye, ambulation over the elements of the image, a lateral passage to an optical accounting of the ocular encounter. Viewing should not, as here, be occluded. The image should not be a flash, a mere apparition or spectral presence in an hauntological sense. The composition and the panoply of medial facets of the photo-portraits are to be glossed. The physical context and scene of image capture should at least be adumbrated. The event and encounter of shooting the pictures needs expatiation. The colours, sounds, movements, and contexts of photographer and subjects recorded must be observed. These factors all should play a part in viewing the visual depictions and so also the history of the portrait, the genealogy of the face as identifier, the connotations of persona, visage, and mask. If the picture is of value then it should be valued and that means what I am here arguing for as an extispicious approach to the reconstruction of what is there, the viscera of the image, and then its alignment with the symbolic and aesthetic systems to which the specific pictures belong or relate, the rhizomes of the particular depictions being myriad, varied, and spread across the expanses of time and space as a florilegium of prior mediations. Even a hand signal, a gestural sign, an indigitation or in the old language of chirology, a chironomic expression of manual rhetoric belongs to a lengthy history, and if the sign is the subject of judgement, reproduced in an image, then that genealogy too merits visual consideration.

Staying with the chironomic theme, in a case concerning lawyer misconduct, the issue, in brief, was that of the abusive behaviour of the plaintiff's counsel, Stephen L. Anderson, towards the pro se defendants in a trademark infringement case.[37] Anderson had sought to interview one of the defendants, Maestre, the owner of the restaurant that was using the disputed image. He was told that Maestre was not there and was refused contact information. In the words of the District Court Judge Conrad: 'Notwithstanding the dispute as to what was said, it is indisputable that Anderson approached Garcia at the counter and gave her the middle finger, see the date-and time-stamped image below.' It is an unusual depiction for a law report but is deemed dispositive and sufficiently significant to reproduce in colour (Figure 6.8). It may seem strange to modern eyes to ask the meaning of *digitus*

[37] *La Michoacana Natural, LLC v. Maestre*, 611 F.Supp.3d 87 (2020).

Figure 6.8 Insertion by District Judge Robert Conrad in *La Michoacana Natural, LLC v. Maestre* 611 F.Supp.3d 87 (2020).

impudicus or raised middle finger, but it is an indigitative sign with an expansive history and so requires review of its symbolic proliferations, the connotations, manipulations, and here intercessions that it unfolds. The gesture returns of course to the Greeks and to Aristophanes, but it was the Roman orators who devoted considerable space to hand gestures as a species of universal language—no eloquence it was said, without the hands—*sine manu nulla eloquentia.* Quintillian was long on praise of the digital gesture as a powerful supplementary marker and visual aid to delivery: 'The action of the other parts of the body assists the speaker, but the hands (I could almost say) speak themselves. By them do we not demand, promise, call, dismiss, threaten, supplicate, express abhorrence and terror, question, and deny? Do we not by them express joy and sorrow, doubt, confession, repentance, measure, quantity, number and time? Do they not also encourage, supplicate, restrain, convict, admire, respect? And in pointing out places and persons do they not discharge the office of adverbs and of pronouns?'[38] The oratorical value and theatrical role of gesture, manual rhetoric included, and so also the deliberations of the forensic orators on the appropriate optical signals made by the hands, is important to understanding how a Court should see the raised middle finger.

Moving to the more specific, John Bulwer, in his *Chirologia* of 1644, specifically picks up the theme and provides an extensive set of indigitative canons, of which canon 25 is 'The Middle Finger put forth, and brandish'd in extent, is an action fit to brad and upbraide me with sloth, effeminacie, and notorious vices. This action is magistrall in Rhetorique'.[39] The middle finger is the lazy digit and

[38] Quintilian, *Institutio oratoria*, L.xi.c.3.

[39] With a splendidly lengthy title, the reference is: John Bulwer, *Chirologia: or the Natural Language of the Hand. Composed of the Speaking Motions, and Discoursing Gestures thereof. Whereunto is*

the longest, leading the 'chiro critics' to deem it helpful as a gesture relating to 'a more open way of expression, the notoriousness of their vices, who exceed others in wildness ... '.[40] For Antonio de Jorio, the analysis of the raised middle finger is similar although less magistral, detailing it as *infami digito*, but also as the finger of fate, of resolution, as in *digito destinare*.[41] To this complex and vivid lexicon of gestural meanings the Court proffers the simple conclusion that 'it is indisputable that Anderson approached Garcia at the counter and gave her the middle finger'.[42] Scrutiny of the image could proffer a range of interpretations, and the clip would be even better suited to analysis that takes account of colour, sound and movement, context, event and encounter, in which this magistral gesture, the digital member rather than the viscera or entrails, make the sign that the Court must determine. Even as immoblized in the CCTV still, there is a hint of movement in the blurring of the finger, and a sense of context in the closed eyes and smile. In its classical sense—*O digitum multum significantem*—the sign could well be that of sloth and inaction on the part of the defendants. In the modern vernacular the middle finger, flipping the bird, may be an insult and visual expletive, but how it is performed and the manner of raising and lowering, culture and context, tone and illocutionary force all play their role. The 'indisputable fact' of raising the middle finger is neither bare nor free of interpretation of viewing. If subsequently further fingers were raised it could be counting or enumeration rather than editorializing. Extispicy thus requires analysis not only of immediate context, but also of the past patterns and anachronic senses of the gesture and places of its use. The finger is attached to hand and body and as a corporeal sign merits analysis of the physical stance, grimace, and nature of the encounter with other bodies present, in this instance Maestre's aunt, who seems relatively passive or undisturbed so far in her response. The smile and the lowered eyelids suggest some element of humour, or at least a use of the indigitative expression that is closer to the anachronic sense of lassitude and indolence that the 'magistrall' rhetoric of the finger disposes. The pointer, the visualized digit, a vertical—arrect—middle tactile member is an enigmatic ministration and polysemic signal.

The Court makes its decision based upon discursive testimony rather than upon the one putatively indisputable, because visually captured, element of evidence presented in the judgement. The case is a relatively simple one which seeks to

added Chironomia: Or, the Art of Manuall Rhetoricke. Consisting of the Naturall Expressions, digested by Art in the Hand, as the chiefest instrument of Eloquence, by Historicall Manifesto's, Exemplified Out of the Authentique Registers of Common Life, and Civill Conversation. With Types, or Chyrograms: A long wished for illustration of this Argument. Manus membrum hominis loquacissimum (London: Tho. Harper, 1644) at 80.

[40] Ibid., at 81.

[41] Antonio de Jorio, *Gesture in Naples and Gesture in Classical Antiquity* [1832] (Bloomington: Indiana University Press, 2000)

[42] *La Michoacana*, at para. 8. For a contemporary US reading of the impudent finger, see Ira Robbins, '*Digitus Impudicus*: The Middle Finger and the Law', 1403 *U.C. Davis Law Review* (2008) giving free reign to the fingers as protected by freedom of expression.

remove Anderson from the case for unprofessional conduct. As he is an attorney from outside the jurisdiction, he is appearing *pro hac vice*, and his contumacious, unprofessional, expletive-ridden, dishonest behaviour and multiple misrepresentations to the Court make revocation of his admission appropriate: '[a]t bottom, Anderson repeatedly misled the Court'.[43] Far from being silenced in the service of vision, discourse is here used to write over the image. There is little to dispute in the outcome of the case. The finding is that the plaintiff lied to the Court and acted contemptuously. It is the retinal justice of the decision, the significance of the image which is reproduced as worth well more than a thousand words, as irrefragable proof, indisputable visual testimony to the veracity of the defendants' discourse, that is more open to criticism. It is overlooked, too familiar to bear examination, introduced and then talked over. Extispicy as a method would require rather that a picture that is the subject of judgement receive extended viewing and, as here alluded, insertion into the aesthetic and depictive history and circumstance of its usages and circulations. Indigitations, chironomic gestures, the signals of the finger grapes are fairly constant, as Antonio de Jorio, in particular, famously argued and as the Irish divine Gilbert Austin had also taken up in prosaic and erudite detail.[44] The finger, one might opine, is always more than it seems, a gesture that is an event, an encounter, a relationship to the recipient viewer, for sure, but also to the system and history of chironomic signs. What is seen is material, sensible, a matter of visual detail, the force of encounter, the quality of the gaze, the smack of colour, textures, hues, and tones.

The latter suggests a final frontier in juridical transmission of visual extispicy. Law reports are printed in black and white, gothic texts, times roman font, purporting to be free of colour and of affect, as if the whack of white and the portent of black were somehow outside the spectrum of pigmentation, tint, and taint. Monochrome, however, is a selection, a choice, and brings with it an affective and significant tinge and hue. An example, because that is how common law works, and in this instance colour was precisely the extispicious issue in contention. In *Melbourne's Cheapest Cars* the question before the Court was that of passing off under s. 52 of the Trade Practices Act 1974.[45] Had the respondent misled or deceived by using advertisements—hoardings—whose colours and lettering were so similar to the applicant's as to confuse the public? Had the respondent taken advantage of the applicant's profile and reputation? The question again, in variant form, is directly visual. Do these advertisements look sufficiently the same as to constitute passing off? Although the Court—McInnis FM—shows several photographs

[43] *La Michoacana*, para. 8.

[44] Gilbert Austin, *Chironomia, or a Treatise on Rhetorical Delivery: Comprehending many Precepts, both Ancient and Modern, for the Proper Regulation of the Voice, the Countenance, and Gesture* (London: Cadell and Davies, 1806).

[45] *Melbourne's Cheapest Cars v Melbourne Street Cars* [2004] FMCA 606.

of the signs, two are ultimately used as determinative comparata, photograph 1 and photograph 4. As below (Figures 6.9 A & B):

(a)

(b)

Figures 6.9 A & B Insertion by Federal Magistrate McInnis in *Melbourne's Cheapest Cars v Melbourne Street Cars* [2004].

The photographs are inserted in the judgement, but there is an appropriate notification of the law reporting context in that '[it] is important to appreciate that the Court had the benefit of a number of enlarged colour photographs which are clearer than some of those reproduced in this judgement. Viewers of this judgement by electronic means should be presented with the colour version'.[46] McInnis FM acknowledges, without irony, that the precedential images are not in fact precedents, but rather lower quality digital representations of colour photographs that had been viewed by the Court in enlarged, higher definition, forms. The overlooking or casual disregard for the visual detail, colour and definition, light, traces, and tinges of scopic capture is ameliorated somewhat by the Federal Magistrate's acknowledgement of the specific basis of decision in the comparison of colour schemes and wording, with allowance being made for the time of photographing the signage, stipulating that readers should 'note that some photographs appear to be taken when the signs have been in shade while others are in full sunlight'. That said, we are then told or rather instructed to view the two photographs in light of '[t]he irrefutable fact ... that both parties use a bright yellow background'. It is then further asserted by the judge that the shades of red used in the two signs, 'with the applicant's red being rather darker than the respondent's red colouring', does not preclude determination. 'I am able to draw [a] conclusion from the photographs'.[47]

The respondent argued that their signage was in palette and wording different to or only accidentally and innocently similar to the applicant's. Their advertising work had been outsourced to a sign-writer who had recommended the colours and had chosen a red that was distinct from the burgundy colour that had been used by the applicant. The judge, ignores the sign-writer and the colour and signage differences claimed, to find in favour of a substantial similarity of colour scheme. The dominant yellow is held to be the determinative conflation, and leads to the conclusion that 'the words, taken together with the colour scheme, which is similar to the colour scheme of the applicant, is likely to mislead or deceive the public'. To this, intriguingly, the judge adds the retinal observation that the words alone would not necessarily provide a basis for a holding of misrepresentation.[48] The colour is crucial. It is 'similar', a concept used twenty-five times in the judgement but nowhere defined or circumscribed visually in any express or direct manner. It outweighs the 'differences', not least in that 'difference' occurs only twice in the decision and so lexically comes off as twenty-three instances less, a verbal weighting clearly in favour of the applicant. That, however, is not an analysis, nor is it a visual apprehension or a defined mode of viewing, which is what is at issue as the object of the discourse. *Video et iudicio* is a version of the dismissive *video rideo*, connoting less vision than preordained and here at least instant punishment.

The judgement in *Melbourne's Cheapest Cars* reduces to the repetition of the perception of the similarity of the two photographs, a concordance of colours that misappropriates a profile and misrepresents a visual identity, the fair aspect and

[46] Ibid., para. 50.
[47] Ibid., para. 25.
[48] Ibid., para. 52.

visage of Melbourne's Cheapest Cars. Viewing the two determinative photographs, the applicant's signage is distinctive. Photograph 1 shows white lettering on a red background, encompassed by a white border line and then a yellow backdrop. There is the signature of the owner—Eddie Albernica—to the left of the main capitalized lettering. Above the signage is a globe with yellow and red colouring, a white centre, and lettering to the left that is indiscernible in the image. Below the sign are cars with brightly coloured price labels, while behind the Lot are two trees with what appears to be a luxuriance of green foliage, and a bright blue sky with nimb and nebula. The advertisement is emphatically for Melbourne's Cheapest Cars. To this, we are asked to compare the two advertisements in photograph 4, for the Cheapest Cars in Melbourne. This is a photograph of low quality, taken from a distance, of signage on a Lot. To the left, partially obscured by trees, out of focus, we see, although it is not entirely decipherable, in capitals, what might be 'APEST CARS IN MELBOURNP', or equally visually plausible, 'AREST CAPS 4 4ELEGSAWP' in red letters on a yellow background.[49] There are no borders, no white lines or background, no signature, and the wording lacks any apostrophe or claim that Melbourne owns the cheapest cars. The size and font of the lettering, the colours of the letters, the yellow background, the absence of signature all distinguish this visual statement. Then, to the right, in marginally better focus, a slightly larger signage, 'CHEAPEST CARS IN MELBOURI', the end of the city name being lost and out of frame. There is further writing to the left side of the red lettering, here in black, in different font, ending with *VEHICLES* but otherwise indecipherable. There is also considerable further lettering above and below the main statement, but this too is illegible in the Court report. The photograph is taken from outside the Lot and through the fence with a pale blue, late afternoon cloudless sky behind, throwing shadows on the ground in front of the signage. There is no globe, but there are telegraph wires and a lamp-post above the signage. There are trees in front and one behind. Such are the viscera, the visual elements of the photographs, which also differ in perspective, focus, definition, aspect ratio, framing, pixels, exposure, and depth of field.

The comparison seems less than extispicious. The decision, the judicial viewing, fails to observe the elements, the details, or indeed the striking differences in colour, arrangement, and order of wording. It might be that these are not the pivotal scopic features of the advertisements, but it is not even apparent from the discursive judgement that they have been seen and taken into optical, let alone optimal account. To hold, as a matter of law, as a retinal judgement, that signage with white letters on a red background with a slim yellow border is similar to a yellow sign with black and red letters, in different light, in a distinct context, with different wording requires analysis, explanation, visual justification. For this to

[49] The four in question is visually an open 4, the reverse of the typeface used here 4.

be possible and persuasive necessitates returning to the concept of extispicy and an ambulation of the eye through the process of viewing. To see is to open to the image, to wander scopically over the photograph, to gaze silently and, over time, to come to know, to feel what is seen. As Barthes has it, alluded to before in Chapter 2, to see requires 'an intimate cessation of all intellectual operations', an opening of the mind, a laying bare of the viewer before the viewed and, in cautionary mode, 'if not, *discourse* maintains itself in its little complacency'.[50] The jurist's reduction of the pictorial to the discursive has to be reversed because it is the primary symptom of the blindness of law and the acme of retinal injustice.

[50] Roland Bathes, *Inner Experience* (New York: SUNY, 2008) at 13.

7
Retinal Justice

Images matter and images are matter, external apparitions in the text that impact judgement. If judges deign to raise their eyes, to lift their penthouse lids of vision, the pictorial resources of easily relayed virtual visual environments and events can guide and enhance the reasoning and the retinal justice of their determinations. The imaginal context and character of politics and law can no longer be denied or evaded, the visual capture of persons and occasions propels an increasingly scopic power of judgement, the eye of law, into an optical domain of decision. As Bellido, for example, remarks of British copyright law, 'the majority of landmark cases ... shared that particular feature. They all had "support" structures (charts and diagrams); they all had visual objects to think "with" that served to expose the substantial infringement in copyright'.[1] It is the thinking with the visual, the lateral implications, ocular intimations and optical apprehensions and openings of the imaginal in judgement that are to be pursued now so as to develop rubrics for viewing, to give a point to the critique, as well as a lex*icon* of imaginal representations that have become precedents in law. To the archivists and librarians of the documentation of juristic decisions we need in short to add a custodian of image captures, a gallery attendant, a curator and keeper of the diversity of depictions that are inserted into judgements. The rubric of precedential pictures requires an awareness of their cathartic impact and knowledge of the aesthetic qualities of imaginal elaborations and expressions. Whether judge, jurist, or advocate, the lawyer too, in Augustinian terms, walks and dreams in images—*in imagine ambulat homo*. To appreciate such an hauntological legal condition, the *perpetuum mobile* of images, the dynamogrammatic modes of visual relay impel the not yet of albums of advocacy, the exhibitions of equity, and in sum and ticket the spectacle of norms.

That pictures are precedential is a logical corollary if not necessarily a conscious implication of their insertion into judgements. Their role, however, as extispicious interventions is to tear a rend in linear discursive abstractions, the still life of legal reasoning, to diffract into sight lines and atlases of affective visibilities. The case of *Gonzalez-Servin*, discussed in the Introduction, made this point vividly apparent if not judicially acknowledged, in the insertion of an ostrich with its head buried in the sand. The image, amongst its many implications, is comedically critical of

[1] Jose Bellido, 'Looking Right: The Art of Visual Literacy in British Copyright Litigation', 10 *Law, Culture and the Humanities* (2014) at 80.

Judicial Uses of Images. Peter Goodrich, Oxford University Press.
 DOI: 10.1093/oso/9780192848772.003.0007

those who refuse to see what accosts or threatens them. Later cases have slowly edged towards some form of reasoning by means of a largely untutored visual analogy or appearance of similarity. Thus in *Randolph v Forever 21*, the plaintiff had tripped and fallen over the wheels of a two-tiered display table.[2] She had gone with four friends to the Circle Center Mall in Indianapolis, never having shopped in a Forever 21 clothing store before. The Court continues, in the words of Mark J Dinsmore USMJ, to observe of '[t]he table, depicted in the photograph below' that '[t]he lower tier clearly sticks out from the upper tier, which is much smaller. The table was stationary at the time of Randolph's fall, and the wheels at the bottom were locked into place. The floor was light brown in color' (Figure 7.1).[3] After the colour photograph of the display table, its wares and pricing flag, the protruding wheels are inventoried as: 'The wheels at the bottom of the table were approximately five to six inches in diameter. The stem of the caster is offset from the center of the wheel, so the wheel, when rotated toward the front of the cart, stuck out more

Figure 7.1 Insertion by U.S. Magistrate Judge Mark Dinsmore in *Randolph v Forever 21 Inc* (2017).

[2] *Diana Randolph v Forever 21 Inc* (2017) WL 2901330.
[3] Ibid., at 1, column 2 (citations to Docket removed).

than three inches from the edge of the table'. The scene is set, an image is provided, we can see, in the judgement, amidst the monochrome prose, in full colour and reasonably high definition, that there are casters and wheels that might trip and injure.

In its defence, Forever 21 makes the argument that the wheels were open and obvious and that a reasonably observant shopper should have been aware enough to avoid them. In support of their argument for summary judgement, they wheel out precedent, though not a binding one, in which a shopper had tripped on caster wheels on a display rack in a Kohl's Department Store in Yonkers, New York (Figure 7.2). The precedent case involved a dispute as to the degree of protrusion of the caster wheels which the plaintiff had claimed to be 6 to 12 inches, but which a photograph of the item disproved in the eyes of the Court which followed the lead of the Supreme Court in *Scott v Harris* and held that '[w]hile the Court cannot make credibility determinations in deciding a motion for summary judgement, it need not credit assertions that are wholly contradicted by photographic evidence in the record'.[4] The Court, 'employing the reasonable use of their senses' to observe, upon looking, came to the conclusion that the wheels did not protrude more than two or three inches. There being no rubric or criterion for vision, the measurement is with the naked eye and according to the familiar, which is to say precedential, judicial criterion of obviousness of viewing. No actual calibration of the image or analysis of perspective and location is offered. It is simply taken to be what it seems. This is the visual authority, and the Court in *Randolph* cites to the case and reproduces a black and white, low-quality image of the offending rack.

Just as the grainy quality of the picture of the rack suggests a relative insignificance to the image, there is no analysis offered but rather a distinction which in essence could as likely be that between monochrome and colour as the extent or extrusion of the caster wheels. The later Court takes the view that there is a determinative distinguishing feature to the two cases, and one which renders the wheels on the rack impertinent to the instant decision. This is that Forever 21 had distracted the shoppers by enticing them to look at their colourful, alluring, and low-cost clothes. Indeed 'Forever 21 employs visual merchandisers to keep shoppers' eyes on the merchandise (and not elsewhere, such as the ground) and that Randolph was actually focused on the merchandise'.[5] The store had used visual expertise—versions of Bellido's visual literacy experts—to lure the shopper to her fall and this despite the unremarked fact that the wheels were red, signalling blood and danger. Desire upended her and the Court is sympathetic, dismissing the motion for summary judgement and allowing the case to go to trial on the basis that the display rack as inserted visually into the judgement is too different in context and visual purpose to serve as a pictorial precedent.

[4] *Zora Matteo v Kohl's Department Store Inc* 2012 WL 760317.

[5] *Randolph*, 4, column 2.

Figure 7.2 Insertion by U.S. Magistrate Judge Mark Dinsmore in *Randolph v Forever 21 Inc* (2017).

It bears noting that the two sets of wheels differ markedly in aesthetic and presentation. The colour photograph of display clothes on a gleaming stainless steel stand, on polished wooden floors is diametrically different to the lackluster, grainy, grey display rack of Jockey underwear in unalluring plastic packets. The Court takes no note of the visual differences, the distinct frame, colour and composition, context and content of the two pictures. It is simply obvious to the Court, though the apprehension is neither analysed nor commented, that they are strikingly or at least obviously divergent in scopic valence and optical value. What is not examined is the character of the representation as the cause of the sense of difference. The analogy is not between valid comparata, or at least some weighting needs to be given to the fact that the latter photograph is so tonally particular and separate from the colour photograph of clothes that are meant to be seen as opposed to underwear whose very name suggests covert operations or intimate seclusion. The display rack of Jockey personal wear indeed invites a deflection of the eyes, a turning away out of modesty or monochrome lack of interest.

Whatever the retinal failings of the Court in *Forever 21*, and however differently the images might be viewed, we are witness to a first step in retinal justice, namely a willingness to follow visual precedent, to look at and, even if in the most superficial and unwitting of manners, to compare pictures inserted in prior judgements as having optical relevance to and potential authority over later decisions. The birth pains of a theory of precedent *ad apparentiam*, a normative authority lodged in prior images, can be glimpsed in the juxtaposition of pictures. Just as with discursive authorities, the precedent will always be different in terms of time and place, circumstance and persons, and by similar visual token the pictures compared will necessarily differ in provenance and context, genealogy and associations. It is the role of the courts and the art of retinal justice to look, view, observe, and proffer the same or a greater degree of visual scrutiny as would be accorded to documentary and discursive authority. The insertion of pictures, the increasingly specular character of decision, the appearance of images across the page and often in colour on screen or by hyperlink, opens judgement to a novel medium and legal reason expressly, if slowly, cautiously, somewhat oneirically, enters the dominion of the imaginal and that of law as spectacle. The relevant rubrics will be elaborated in what follows and must begin with recognition and scrutiny of the novelty of this development of images as normative manifestations of judicial expression.

Much as the supposed visual turn has been announced, and however often jurisprudence or more exactly legal theory, the discipline of seeing law as theatre, as something strange, has made and makes use of images, this opening of the eyes has not extended any great distance towards viewing the images in judgements or accounting for the epistemic and ontographic significance of the visual in the juridical. The reason is in part that the speed cycle of contemporary academic fashions precludes depth of attention and in part that the creative impulse in the scholarly accounts of law tends to propel the inter- and sub-disciplinary focus away from law to other disciplines and aesthetic pursuits in a search for expansion of the remit and meaning of legal studies, of the pursuits of the jurist as scholar and humanist. There is also the question of the inadequacy of academic and intellectual training in the reproduction of the law school. The rush to specialism and the anxiety of employment generate status anxieties and exit velocity concerns, rather than scholarly focus. The push and pull between profession and podium, corporation and classroom, academic and clinic, distracts from and at times actively impedes the longer term of research methodology and durable treatises. The professoriate scribble on topics of short-term concern and law firm interest, eschewing questions of theory and the complexities of legal remediation, while on the bench the fear of the image reflects a judicial apprehension of the faltering of reason when confronted by visual precedents. The normative status of the depiction is evaded out of lack of qualification, absence of training and concern for error rendering research esoteric and anodyne. It is as if the picture were unconsciously deemed a fact, a brute presence, the wall of the real to which only superficialities can be directed. There is an anxiety, in sum, that intuitively recognizes that the image cannot be dissected or read, that its *implexity*, as Didi-Huberman coins it, precludes breaking the visual entity apart, a recognition that disentangling renders the picture unintelligible.[6]

The starting point for training in retinal justice is thus not simply recognition of novelty, of aesthetic, ontographic, and normative distinctiveness, but also acknowledgement that the visual has always been present, that the word is a visible sign, the text an aesthetic and haptic material form, the atmosphere and environment of law a luxuriance of spectacular installations and inventions in the city, town, and peripatetic paths of country and lawscape. It is for this reason that our study started with the use of maps and diagrams, tables and trees in early lawbooks and judgements. There is only a small and generally overlooked perceived novelty in the early use of the diagrams, charts, plans, schemata, and maps. These are still felt to be linear, graphic and lectoral, rather than the matter of aesthetic viewing. The diagrammatology of law has yet to emerge fully, but a trajectory can be discerned leading to evermore figurative visual forms. The map thus expands into the identity photograph, the cartograph of the face introduced into judgement to identify and demarcate its optical form. The visualization of the visage as an ID photo extends the diagram to the calibration of the face and inaugurates a future shift from line to figure, from linear to lateral, and from the left to right of reading to the ambulation of the eye over picture, painting, or photograph, animé or screen. A pause then to recognize the first instance of novelty, the eruption of the image in judgement as a new medium and a potential reversal of the order of precedence, in which the imaginal turns on, and potentially changes the scriptural into a more explicit and vivid visual form. The image is the beginning, the first conscious sighting of law, of text, of the spectacular and specular presence of judgement bringing with it a different and distinct cognition—conusance[7]—of

[6] Georges Didi-Huberman, 'Image, Language: *The Other Dialectic*' (2018) 23 *Angelaki* 19, at 22, and for more detail, Didi-Huberman, *La Peinture incarneé* (Paris: Editions de Minuit, 1985).

[7] I am guilty of using the antique but most apposite term conusance several times. It references knowledge of and through other jurisdictions and by extension other epistemes. A matter, to coin a phrase, of antiquity triumphing over novelty.

judicial decision as something visible, to be viewed, a material vision and haptic presence of an imaginal relay that is in and of law, an implexity to judgement. The sensible life of law resides in the relay of images, the apparitions that manifest externally and now also increasingly within the text.

Recognition of the materiality of the image, the extant and ontographic quality of the relay of depictions, whether virtual or plastic, that will appear at some point upon a screen, suggests beginning again with the matter of imagery and the multiple and mobile manifestations of the imaginal so as to better understand the haptic and sensory dimensions of looking and being looked at. The root of the material sense of image is the biological *imago*. It constitutes the last moment in a process of metamorphosis from *pupa* to what is termed the imaginal stage or maturity. The *imago* is the result of a process of metamorphosis, of matterphorical development which involves both motion and growth from the sessile stage to chrysalis to the appearance of imaginal discs and then the winged being, the insect, takes flight to a state of *perpetuum mobile*, of constant uprising. The image is in ceaseless transition, from metamorphosis to mobility and to flight. The imaginal, literally and matterphorically, takes the form of legs and wings, and thus has its proper definition as the means of motion, of walking and winging, both in physical and intellective senses. If the image is an entity, a being in motion and emotion, a mobile aura and atmosphere, then it defies reduction to text and reading because it is sensible, corporeal, and presupposes the entire panoply of affects, gestures, bodily movements that implicate also the unconscious and its altered temporalities and spaces. Even the diagram, even the map confronts the eye with the implexities, the layers and multiple media—fabric, lines, colours, key and code—that make it an entity that traverses time and occupies different spaces. The map more than any other diagram surely opens to prospect, suggests movement, travel, the expansiveness of opportunity for change that any journey brings.

The image cannot be rendered reasonable. It is not language. It is not there to be solved, proved, or definitively settled, but rather exists to open up to possibilities. This leads to a second feature and rubric which is that the novelty of medium requires a method and style of viewing that allows time and detail of optical examination. The image is a composition, and in the language just adumbrated engages an implexity of elements, one in another, like a living palimpsest in which excision of any element will alter the whole. In elaborating the category of surplusage it is precisely the cognitive dissonance as between image and text, depiction and discourse, the irreducibility of one to the other that triggers the need for a new dialectic, a specular dialogue of different media. What is at issue is the emergence in the legal text and particularly in its virtual relay, in colour, with sound and motion always possible, of a different mode of apprehension and of thought. Where law falters in the face of novelty, it stammers, stops, and eventually, from the reverberations of stasis, enfolds a new form. Surplusage is excess of meaning and so opens judgement to a novel twist, a fold of meaning and alternate matter as elaborated in the variable modalities of implexity, of colour, sound, movement, perspective, and apprehensive force. Surplusage introduces another scene of judgement, the something more that is the unconscious, the conception of decision, the pictorial remediation being the most direct available expression of the imaginal sources of legal invention, the vision in decision.

The surplusage of images moves the analysis of law from diagrammatology to the imaginal, adding to the sensorium and sensibility of schema and atlas, the affective and oneiric quality of seemingly random, dislocated, originary images. The beginning of the image is the image of beginning. For Freud, in *The Interpretation of Dreams*, 'We find the child and the child's impulses, still living on in dream'.[8] The figure of the *infans* links childhood indissolubly to visuality as the mode in which the baby attempts wishful hallucination and binds the unconscious mind to pleasure and the depictive: 'at the very origins of the human mind [is] a pronounced preference for ideas and feelings that can be represented in visual form'.[9] The infantile dimension of images, their inaugural and binding character, sketches the other scene of the juristic decision upon the fabric of kinship and early sociality. The *corpus iuris* too is a body in time and space, an ambulant image with its own implexities, an autobiography of affect and experience coded into the unconscious, the body that rises up and decides. It is a key point from Aristotle to Bottici's theory of the imaginal that pictures, *phantasmata*, precede and enable all intellectual work.[10] Every process of thought is an image and an imagining, a multiple progression of intellection and expression in diverse media across the irreducible surface of subjective ontography. As Didi-Huberman notably presents it: 'to think, you have first to imagine', and the gallery of imagery, the corporeal storehouse of affect and experience, the phantasms of the flesh, bodies enfolded in images, necessarily tie the unconscious to the visual reasoning of law.[11] Depictions, the insertion of pictures in judgements, gain their appeal and their insight, their value to retinal analysis, in being both singular and several, individual and social, personal and plural. The optical diversity that such inserted images provide is also what most directly bridges that divide, the cut of the text, in connecting the judicial subject to their childhood, their social origins, networks, and other imaginal modalities that move them in the world and in their professions.

Building upon Bottici's theory of the imaginal, the pictorial introduces a social unconscious into the analysis of legal reasoning by which she means that the visual opens judgement to viewing, and this brings with it cultural and communicative constraints of which the judge is only partially aware. The unconscious in this sense is a mobile and metamorphosing, active agency of thought in which

[8] Sigmund Freud, *The Interpretation of Dreams* [1900], Vol. iv, *Standard Edition* (London: Karnac, 1995), 191.

[9] Vicky Lebeau, *Childhood and Cinema* (London: Reaktion, 2008) at 102–103.

[10] Bottici, *Imaginal Politics: Images Beyond Imagination and the Imaginary* (New York: Columbia University Press, 2014) particularly Ch. 3, 'Toward a Theory of the Imaginal'.

[11] Georges Didi-Huberman, *Images in Spite of All: Four Photographs from Auschwitz* (Chicago: Chicago University Press, 2011) at 1.

thinking is simultaneously conscious and oblivious, ocular and occluding. What we are unaware of has a more powerful influence over us by virtue of being hidden, acting from a distance, fissured in the figures that appeal and, in their appeal, affect and effect judgement. Imaginal law is thus a field of possibilities, the images used in representing decision expand not only the dimensions of juridical authority but also the latitude of precedent and the distraint of the rule. What were historically the downcast eyes of the judge are now raised, the penthouse lids uplifted to provide a law, a verdict of vision, retinal justice as a mode of looking at pictures, as *in vivo* apprehension of the materials of depiction. As a question of viewing, of the juridical gaze or judicial speculum, the best avenue to defining both the practice and the precedential desiderata comes from cases where the detail of the depiction, the colours and forms of the visual, are the subject of judgement. Patent and copyright cases are the prime movers in this regard, and so the analysis of surplusage, in Deleuze's terms of the minor that becomes major, is to follow the reasoning of the eye where the ocular subject matter is inserted into judgement.

A leading UK case is *Designers Guild* and involved the claim of copyright infringement of a fabric design created by the plaintiffs.[12] As is not uncommon in such cases, the Chancery Judge and the Court of Appeal both insert pictures of the fabrics in issue into the decision. The House of Lords inserts a colour prosthetic of the fabrics as a comparison of the two designs into the archives, although not into the judgement. Three pairs of images make their appearances at the three different levels of the juridical hierarchy and the images differ significantly in colour, tone, and composition. The plaintiffs succeed at first instance and in the last instance, before the House of Lords. The defendants prevailed in the Court of Appeal. Three different sets of robed eyes, a trinity of distinct viewings and conclusions, can help make the judgement and justice of the retina, and the relevant rubrics of optical assessment more evident.

The starting point is aesthetic history and the genealogy, the influences and shadow gallery that the specific design derives from and to which it belongs and contributes. In this instance the painter of the Design Guild picture was given the brief, by the eponymous Tricia Guild, to produce a design that looked 'loose and hand painted' and to this end she suggested the 'handwriting' or the 'style and colour' as also the 'influence and feel' of Matisse. Guild provided two books with reproductions, and the designer also went to the library to consult further volumes on Matisse. A style was thus designated and an aesthetic paradigm, an impressionist style, was proposed and eventually implemented in the Ixia fabric. Although the trial judge wanders into the generalities that pervade the visual methodologies of copyright law, stating for instance that '[a]lthough there were differences between

[12] At first instance in the Chancery Division, before Deputy Judge Lawrence Collins QC, *Designers Guild Ltd v Russell Williams (Textiles)* [1998] F.S.R. 803. It went thence to the Court of Appeal, [2000] F.S.R. 212, and then to the House of Lords, as it then was, [2001] FSR 113.

Ixia and Marguerite, the overall impression was very similar', he follows this with the specification that something more than such an apprehension of proximity is necessary.[13] A comparable style and 'handwriting' is not enough, the 'fingerprints' of copying are needed and a chirological description of the manner of making the print design ensues in detail, in both its *specifica* and *differentia*. Inspired by Matisse's fabric designs but also by the desire to effectuate an impressionist feel, the translation of the borrowing to the fabric print is elaborated at technical length. Painting with acrylic, the design artist Helen Burke revised her initial drafts to soften the picture. A yellow flower was changed to a white flower to create 'a translucent and delicate feel' so that the flora stands out but does not do so too boldly. She adopted a hand brush stroke to create an almost transparent flower over the stripes and so as to avoid a hard look. After further detailed exposition of technique, of colours and colourways in particular, the judgement proceeds to comparison of the original artwork of the Ixia pattern and the similarities that were to prove a causal connection between the copyright work and the infringing Marguerite design.

The third rubric of optical apprehension is that of assessment of the visual axes and inventions of the picture. Here the reproduction of the two images in the judgement provides some general assistance, but the poor quality of the pictures and their reproduction in monochrome when much of the reasoning is based upon colourways and 'resistance' effects is rather counterintuitive. As for the vectors of visual comparison, there are seven ocular pathways examined. There is first the distribution of elements, the stripes, the spaces between the stripes, and the pattern of scattered flowers. There is the neo-Impressionistic style, the brush strokes and texture achieved. The vertical strokes and rough edges of the brush marks that merge into the background; the form taken by the petals; the fact that the colour of the stripes in the fabric shows through some of the petals; the representation of the centre of the flowers as a blob; and finally, the similarity in style, brush stroke, and colour of the leaves is noted. It is a high level of visual detail that is provided, and in addressing the technique of making the images with such specific focus a degree of method is introduced into the visual comparison. It is surprising in this regard that the images inserted are not probative of resist effects (a visible undercolour) or of the colourways, and it hardly aids in the comparison that it is curiously designated in terms of handwriting and fingerprints of style. The Court is concerned to assert the confirmation of the 'naked eye', but the image does not provide much for the eye to review, dissent or confirm.

It is very much to the detriment of retinal justice that after the commendably extensive analysis that Judge Collins provides of the optical details, material composition, and implexity of the designs, the Court of Appeal overrules the decision while using two different representations of the fabrics. The House of Lords, as it

[13] *Designers Guild* at 804. https://larc.cardozo.yu.edu/faculty-online-pubs/61/, eFigures 13 and 14.

then was, subsequently references a third pair of images, the visual prosthetic that is lodged, in high definition and full colour, in the Parliamentary archive. The judgement in the Court of Appeal, handed down by Morrit LJ makes short shrift of the technologies of reproduction and the specifics and differences of the two sets of visual comparata: 'The design is reproduced in black and white at the end of the judge's judgement as reported in [1998] F.S.R. 803, 830. The references to the trial judgement which follow are references to that report of it. The design in the pink colourway but reduced to 26.75 per cent of its original size is annexed to this judgement as Annex A.'[14] There is one further reference to the 'black and white' reproduction in the report of the Chancery Court decision, and then a reference to the Marguerite design and its pink pathway, reproduced at 26.75 per cent of its size, in Annex B.[15] These are the images that represent the sum and substance of determination, the vision in decision.

Morritt LJ offers some analysis of method, referencing the importance of the assistance of the eyes of experts in framing and explaining the composition of the picture and design, but it is the eye of the judge, the juridical speculum, that will decide. The first person singular eventually takes over as the optics of decision: 'I have examined both the painting of Ixia and the fabrics produced from it in each of the three colourways subsequently adopted. I have compared them with the fabrics made to the Marguerite design in each of the four colourways used to produce that fabric'. There are further incidental observations and then a preliminary yet determinative conclusion: 'I am bound to say that when I first saw Ixia and Marguerite I did not consider that the latter involved the copying of a substantial part of the former and the cogent arguments of counsel for DGL have not caused me to change my mind. On the broadest level they just do not look sufficiently similar'.[16] Judicial honesty generates a paradox, although it is a fairly common one in copyright cases where the judge is forced to look and decide upon the visuals. Tasked with deciding a complex aesthetic and medial dispute, the judge admits to falling back upon what their eyes saw, the initial impression, their intuitive perceptual sense of what these exhibits and annexes looked like to them. Being seen as 'just' not sufficiently similar, however, is far from just and is certainly not retinal justice. More is needed, and Morritt LJ endeavours dutifully to provide an analysis of the identities and differences which determine whether or not there has been substantial copying.

The low-quality monochrome reproductions of the pink colourways in Ixia and Marguerite are not particularly helpful precedential pictures, nor do they necessarily justify the appellate Court's analysis. As far as colourways are concerned the reproductions are without value, and hues, tones, paint stains and the like are

[14] *Designers Guild v Russell Williams* [2000] F.S.R. 121 at 123.
[15] Ibid., at 124.
[16] Ibid., at 133.

indiscernible. There is thus a limit to the analysis that follows, but the judge does make available the analytic visual framework that is marshalled to reinforce his initial impression. This follows the trial Court Judge's deconstruction of the images closely, but to opposite effect and reversal. The idea had been copied—the combination of flowers and stripes—but not the expression. What follows is a rebuttal of the three features of the painting that Judge Collins had found most similar. The Marguerite used bigger stripes and larger flowers and leaves. 'Different flowers, differently disposed' precluded a finding of substantial similarity. The overall effect was also distinct. As to the resist effect or undercolour brushstroke technique, this also differed: 'It is clear, as the judge recorded, that in both fabrics the colour of the stripes shows through some of the petals. But, so it appears to me, that verbal description conceals a significantly different visual effect. In Ixia the petals appear to be translucent. In Marguerite they appear to be multicoloured or perforated'.[17] This leads to the conclusion, express and direct, that 'my visual comparison does not ... coincide with the Judge's conclusion'. In a final apparently incidental flourish, or minor gesture, Morritt LJ remarks on policy grounds that it would 'obviously be dangerous' to cast the net of copyright protection too widely for fear of creating 'monopolies in ideas'.[18]

Entry for content and exit for style. The decision is grounded in a first impression, an untutored view of the fabrics, and is justified by a policy consideration that lacks even the pretence of visual justification. The derivative intermediate analysis of the trial judge's dissection of the image simply contradicts his perception while paradoxically affirming the structure of his analysis. It becomes a question of degree of impression or effect because the starting point is aesthetically wrong and, I think, also juristically questionable. The contemporary legal tradition should neither privilege the text nor impose the dominance of discourse over all other forms of intellection. Where it is a question of vision, the discursive has to be suspended and the doors of perception opened, the mind silenced so the eye can view, wander, track, and return to sense the image, stay with the picture and its variable associations, rhizomes, shadows, axes, and layers. That is the opposite of initial impression or immediate effect, feel or impact. As the legal humanist Barthèlemy Aneau puts it, and I am fond of the expression, in *Picta poesis*, it is necessary to struggle to fit the words to the image rather than subjecting the image to the words.[19] Rude though it may be, my suggestion is that too little time, too slight a viewing, too peremptory a scopic scrutiny has been accorded to the image by what is designated by judges as the 'naked eye'. Paradoxically, the oculus has resisted stripping down, and so never got naked, never bared itself to the picture. To address the picture with an uncluttered vision requires divestment,

[17] Ibid., at 134.
[18] Ibid., at 135.
[19] Barthélemy Aneau, *Picta poesis ut pictura poesis erit* (Lyon: Bonhomme, 1552) at 6.

stepping back, clearing the eye for the judicial opificers of the optical. The multiplicity of the image and the visual axes of sense that precede discourse and impact thought directly, which is to say unconsciously, require time and sensibility as well as a perceptual detail that is most visibly lacking in the monochrome reproductions in Annex A and Annex B of the Court of Appeal judgement. It is only then that analysis of direct viewing and the making of comparisons can properly begin and introduce in turn the history of the image, the sources of inspiration, the mode of composition, the context of fabrication, prototypes, personnel and then colourways, axes, inversions, patterns, and frames.

It is the juristic status of the pictures that needs to be changed, their remediation accounted for, and their precedents presented. Prior to engaging with the gallery of the sensible, however, a third decision, reversing the Court of Appeal's claim to find the images obviously and evidently different, is provided by the House of Lords. Here, as Bellido brilliantly extrapolates, the work of visual detection of the 'fingerprints of copying' requires a sophisticated technique of viewing and the disassembly of the imagistic configurations through technical scrutiny of its mode of fabrication as expounded by an expert in the techniques and media of design. Retinal expertise, technical knowledge of modes of fabrication, the instruments necessary for determining the markers of copying, such as high-quality images, samples of fabric for dissection of their composition, magnification equipment, acetates and prints in reverse negatives, light boxes, and on occasion infrared reflectography, x-rays, and sonar scans are necessary accessories for any serious investigation of the image. As the House of Lords stresses, copying is a question of quality and not of quantity. As comparison requires juxtaposition of material and means that have to be available for the composition of properly probative montages which may well be of features that are otherwise invisible. Just as one has to be taught to read the law, so too it will increasingly be necessary to be trained to look at precedent in pictures.

In *Designers Guild* the House of Lords was unanimously persuaded of the infringement of copyright by a photomontage constructed by the design guru, consultant, and self-confessed 'visual literacy expert', Victor Herbert. In his evidence to the trial Court, Herbert had created a montage comparing the two fabrics in the mode of mirroring so as to demonstrate that Marguerite was composed as an inverted image of Ixtia. (Figure 7.3) The two depictions are placed side by side, in the vertical mode of the fabrics, as opposed to the horizontal reproductions that the two lower courts had utilized. Focused exclusively on the design, the 'prosthetic image' creates a juxtaposition that indicates, in magnified form, the technical means by which the latter image reproduces the plaintiff's design.[20] As adverted earlier, the House of Lords does not include this dispositive image in the judgement, but it does place and retain it in the records of proceedings and thereby

[20] *Bellido*, at 81.

Figure 7.3 Insertion by the House of Lords in *Designers Guild Ltd v Russell Williams (Textiles)* [2001].

By permission of Parliamentary Archives, Houses of Parliament, Westminster.

incorporates it into the judgement and as part of the precedent. There are differences and there are also similarities in the juxtaposition and both are important. The technical expertise of the design witness and the care and attention paid to the image and the construction of the montage suggest that a considerable skill, medial proficiency, and well tutored vision are prerequisites for an aesthetic and ethical judgement of visual evidence. It is also no accident that the prosthetic image that decides is the best constructed, presented in colour and high definition. The substantial is a question, as said, of quality and not of quantity and thus is a technical question of whether the design—the painting—has been copied, as much as it is of the transfer of elements of the image. Much was not copied, the images are evidently quite different, but the esoteric legal question is that of the qualitative visual significance of the portion that is borrowed in relation to the whole. It may be a small portion and yet key to the design or pivotal to the picture. In *Designers Guild*, the infringement was one of 'altered copying'. The parts may all be different, but the whole may nonetheless be a copy: 'The Marguerite design is not an exact copy of Ixia, nor is any specific part of the Marguerite design an exact copy of any corresponding part of the Ixia design. It is an altered copy'.[21] Similarity and substantiality are both questions of visual degree, questions of the independence and originality in the source work, the technique and form of composition and then whether the altered copy takes the work of the artist, the creative expression, as its own.

The decision in *Designers Guild* had to trace an image from the school of impressionist painting to the fabric designs of Matisse, to a juxtaposition of a floral fabric design and an altered version of an original impressionistic hue. A complex array of artistic techniques and details of fabric fabrication were necessary to arrive at the final vision and last instance decision. The comparison actually made depended upon much that was not immediately visible to the naked eye of the law and thus tracing of visual sources, aesthetic history, and deep structures of composition and effect needed elucidation by eyes learned in aesthetic sensibility and artistic fabrication. Just as the text requires careful parsing, from lexical examination to syntactic scrutiny and semantic extension, implication, and connotation, the image requires its own material apprehension from the haptic matter of its appearance to the scrutiny of its context, construction, layers, elements, hues, tones, parts, and totality. This is not a matter of words, of reduction to the complacency of discourse, but rather a quite different attention to the affective force and mobile dynamics of vision. It is not a question of visual literacy, however comforting an intermediate term it may be, but rather and distinctly it must start from sensible apprehension, the optical scanning and visual appreciation and apperception of the imaginal exterior presence of a visible entity in its apparent and shadow parts,

[21] *Designers Guild* [2001] at 130.

in its context, aligned to its genealogy, and cognizant of its history, open to its mobility and morphosis over time.

The degree of detail, the apprehension of layering, the dissection of techniques and scrutiny of the force of colours, the vortex of sightlines, the diversity of perspectives, and the other symbolic proliferations of the imaginal return us to the retinal rubrics of the extispicious. The divination through the juxtaposition of visual elements requires contemplation of the multiple elements of visual matter that make up the image. This requires quieting of the mind, silencing of discourse, and contemplating the picture. As Didi-Huberman extrapolates, 'to contemplate means first of all to observe a natural reality by delimiting it like a *templum*', a reference which has particular force for jurists who have historically invoked the temple of justice as the site and the prospect of their work—*proprium et sanctissimum templum iustitiæ consecratum* as Francis Bacon rather hyperbolically defines a court.[22] The extispicious viewing is necessarily an act of interpretative transference, of translation from the elements inspected, dissected, and rearranged, to the end of drawing inferences, diagnoses, prognostications, alignments, intensities, and intimacies with the symbolic system, the imaginary of legal thought. Judges stumble, legal thought falters in front of what was never written, the spectral phantasm, the mattering of the visual, the a-lexical system of scopic signage and circulations. The code of the visible is the sensorium of imaginal relations, the associations, networks, and linkages that bind a populace and enlace the subject in the spectacular presence of legal sovereignty and now, and increasingly, in the desire of the imaginal norm. This is the atlas of particularities that for our interpretative purposes is constituted by the ever-growing corpus of images that the case law relays. Reason and image, *logos* and *eidôla*, day and night, come face to face in the spectral relationships between the particularities of things, the visual presence of the pictorial in the interstices of precedent. Where for Lord Coke each syllable was known and significant in law, we may soon have to add that each photogram, every pixel, is seen and sensible to the normative order, whether it recognizes such affectivity or resists the grip of all critical apparatuses of viewing.

The image, its colours, size and shape, matter and form, figures and connections, all present and potentially, through insertion, expose a distinct and unsettling epistemic and ontographic sensibility in the heart of the juridical. Images are the medium of memory, the sites of surviving knowledge that now significantly complicate legal reason with associations, inferences, intuitions, and desires of which it has long been unaware or at the least most reluctant to expose, let alone exhibit and insert as aspects of precedent. The stability of the textual, the order of linear juristic precedent decisions is broken up by the apparent disorder or unconscious

[22] Didi-Huberman, *Atlas, or the Anxious Gay Science* (Chicago: The University of Chicago Press, 2018) at 22. The definition of justice is from Francis Bacon, *A Collection of Some Principall Rules and Maximes of the Common Lawes of England* (London: More, 1630), preface—the most holy and consecrated temple of justice.

associations of imaginal transmission, by colours, sounds, and motion thrust into the text of judgements. For this reason, retinal justice dictates a protocol and rubric of legal viewing, as well as a complementary gallery of precedential pictures, a columbine of imagery with a curator as custodian, guard, and interpreter of how the law views, and of the pictures viewed. The sensible life of images belongs outside of linear textual analysis and the rubrics of scriptural exegesis and interpretation. Visual precedent merits and needs its own custody and curation, its art and artisans because retinal justice is not textual justice, nor is the equity of the visual reducible to the linear and monochrome expressions of the printed page. Retinal justice requires a revisioning of method in addition to the interpretative protocols already and critically reviewed in this work. These are envisioned as aids to curation of legal images and as a guide to articulating the critical perceptual criteria that allow for the imaginal in the legal in a scope that in principle of course impacts all judgement.

Protocols of Perception

1. *Colours of Law.* First, and still somewhat counter-intuitively, despite the prevalence of visual relays online, law has to enter a world of colour because precedent that relays pictures, paintings, photographs, and film will have to exceed the monochrome dominion of printed lines, the exegetical methodology of book bound legal bibliophilia, and the linear tools of textual decryption and decipherment for visual scanning, learning to look in a domain of multiple hues, tinctures, tones, and now often also sounds and motions. There are, of course, some precedents for colour. The illuminated manuscript, the emblems in sixteenth-century printings of the *Corpus Iuris*, and the genealogies, trees, and other schemata in other early printed legal treatises. The black gothic typeface of lawbooks would incorporate maxims in red typeface, to indicate their importance as the lifeblood, the sanguine sense of doctrine. Remaining with the primary distinguishing feature for our purposes of retinal justice, it is colour, bare pigment, the stains, hues, blushes, tinctures, and intensities of polychromasia that most strikingly mark the advenience of the album and gallery of visual precedents. The pivotal role of colours is simply the point of fissure and diffraction that delineates the transition from text to depiction, from the regimentations of the page to the ambulations of viewing and the implexities of the imaginal. Colour, brute colour in the sense of the pigment and stain that structures painting and acts as the condensation of the visual prior to figuration is the medium of vision. Resistance or accession to colour marks the tension between print and pictures. In many of the cases reviewed, colour images were reproduced in black and white as if that were a legally permissible mode of reproduction, Gutenberg's law, rather than infidelity to what was purportedly pictured. Colour is primary, it means and matters and has to be

accounted, which is to say viewed, experienced, opened up, and responded to, as the initial invocation of art, artisan, and visual expression.

As the point is central to retinal justice, a further example of the retinal detachment of law can be illustrative of this first protocol of visial equity, as a conscious yielding to colour. In *Hayuk v Starbucks*, the plaintiff, an internationally renowned artist, brought an action against the defendant coffee retailer chain claiming copyright infringement. The plaintiff, based in Brooklyn, New York, is a painter and muralist who has exhibited her work throughout the US and in the Ukraine, as well as publishing two books and numerous videos of her work. She has also, from time to time, allowed her work to be used commercially. The defendant, 72 and Sunny, is an advertising agency that approached Hayuk to see if she would create artwork for a proposed Starbucks advertising campaign. After discussions, Hayuk declined their offer. The defendants then went ahead with their advertising plan and created the Frappuccino campaign using artwork that was substantially similar to Hayuk's work and the action for copyright infringement ensued with the complaint and thirty-eight images, thirty-six in vivid colour, were incorporated into the judgement by reference.

The artist's work in question is of vividly coloured geometric designs, two of which, for reasons of space, and for the obscurities of the Press lawyers' view of the use of images published in judicial decisions, will have to be linked here, Kites 1 and Sexy Gazebo. The pair provide a reasonable sense of the colours and intensities, as well as the visual axes and lines of force within the compositions. These can then be compared to the imagery and colours used in the Starbucks campaign, from which two screenshots are linked here. The relevant law on infringement requires proof of 'substantial similarity' between the artwork and the defendant's copy. Exact copying, also indicatively enough termed 'literal copying', the analogy being regressively to the literary rather than the visual, is not required: 'misappropriating the "total concept and feel" of ... a particular work' can also constitute aesthetic conversion of the artist's work.[23] Adding that ideas cannot be protected for fear of a monopoly on the idea, the judge continues to cite to the 'ordinary observer test', which asks if this particular version of the reasonable person both fond and familiar to common law would regard the two works as having the same 'aesthetic appeal'. Proceeding to declaim that the test is not a carte blanche to 'vague or amorphous determinations', the judicial conclusion, *inter alia*, is that 'the total concept and feel of ... the Hayuk works and the expression of those ideas in the

[23] *Hayuk v Starbucks* (2016) 157 F.Supp.3d 285 at 290. See eFigures 15 & 16, https://larc.cardozo.yu.edu/faculty-online-pubs/61/ for the relevant comparison. For a different approach, though one that still ignores colour in favour of shape and design, see *Judy Stabile v Paul Smith Ltd* 137 F.Supp.3d 1173 (2015) where the official printed report reproduces the two designs contested in monochrome, in a case where the identity of the patterns can only be fully perceived in the colour image comparison.

Frappuccino Works are not substantially similar'.[24] The court then adds that the differences between the works 'overwhelm any superficial similarity'.

For those familiar with the Starbucks Frappuccino campaign and its myriad uses of the triangulated vortex of colours and stripes, and as visible in the patterns linked here, it is precisely the concept and feel, the visial lines and concordant colours, that appear similar and infringing of Hayuk's concept and performance. What is it that evades the legal retina and impales the judicial concept of the ordinary observer test upon the stake of dissimilarity or failed analogy of appearances? The answer is that for the District Judge, Laura Taylor Swain, concept and feel, or even better colour and sensibility, do not meet. The juxtaposition of vivid pigments escapes analysis. Here, in its most vital form, reason and emotion, the logic of law and the force of affect, fail to coincide, the twain do not meet in Swain. To open to colour and to inversions, rotations, vertex, and vortex of design requires a viewing that is in legal methodological terms non-standard and distinctive. Colour, vibrancy, shape, angle, and affective impact are not susceptible to analogy as if they were literary figures of narrative development, but must rather rest in the eye and the optical aesthetic of viewing. The affect of appearance and impact is pre-conceptual, and so the blast of intense colour, shape, and design, generates the event of the image and design that invents, implores, desires, allures, and astonishes. The coloured streams are immensely suggestive, while the colours themselves, in combination and strips, are a condensation of feelings, symptoms of motive causes, displacements of earlier patterns and hues that attach laterally and initially likely unconsciously to the perception of the work. To borrow from the humanist lawyer and artist Werner Gephart, what he terms the colours of law, once inserted into judgements, are real.[25]

The imaginal work of law is thus first to recognize that colour is primary and distinctive. It invokes, reminds, invents, and generates the experience of looking. It is the material of the image and transmits a prefigurative sense that will shape the viewing that follows. In the example of *Hayuk v Starbucks*, the prefigurative sense of the materials compared is of striking similarity in use of colour and design, the vertex and vortex of the triangulated pathways constitute vivid reasons—*vividæ rationes*—for the perception of a similitude, a sense of similarity in the passage of and to the eye, in the *ambulatio* or lateral and wandering of vision that justifies a determination that the affect and effect are significantly the same. The work of imaginal law is that of tracking not only the feel of the visual, but also the lateral avenues and shadow archive of imagery that colour, shape, pattern, and form

[24] *Hayuk*, at 293.

[25] Werner Gephart, *Some Colours of the Law* (Frankfurt: Klosterman, 2019). For further and important discussion of colour, see Georges Didi-Huberman, *Fra Angelico: Dissemblance and Figuration* (Chicago: Chicago University Press, 1995) and also Georges Didi-Huberman, *Confronting Images: Questioning the Ends of a Certain Art History* (State College: Pennsylvania State University Press, 2005) Ch. 4.

promote. Retinal justice has to be able to see and feel the colours of law and this means a slowing down of the linear, a cessation of the babble of the text, in favour of viewing, of sensing and in an aesthetically discriminating manner appreciating figures, forms, and their pigmented materiality. This involves a suspension of judgement, of prior or precedential discursive determinations of what is seen. To compare like with like requires working through the gallery of subjective imaginations as well as prior juridical albums of colours and depictions to the presupposed image, the lacerated part objects of scotomized legal viewing. Returning to Hayuk, the judge sees only parts, and restricts analogy to the lines and to the form, to an inarticulate concept that may struggle but inevitably fails to feel the conjunction of colours in their specific geometric patterns, the array of tints, as a work, as a conception instantiated visually in the art works from which Starbucks borrowed. Abstract art would appear to have no place in law, because the abstract colour pictures are the antithesis of legal abstraction.

The hues used may vary but the feel is the same, and retinal justice will require accession to that sensibility, to the look and its affective impact. It will also stipulate, in addition to time and attention to the medium of the materiality of the image, an inquiry into the lineage of the idea and the sources of its emotional impact. The defendant advertiser approached the artist and offered her a contract. They discussed the project. They were drawn by and desirous of her work, her colours and patterns, her prefigurative, abstract, artistic vision.[26] They then produced a strikingly similar advertising campaign that was gauged precisely to their desire to simulate the affective impact of Hayuk's work. After seeking to engage the artist, after viewing her work, the advertisers, for commercial gain, sought to imitate her work, to obtain the affective result that employing her would have achieved. Copyright law is clear that ideas cannot be duplicated, the concept being irreplicable, but in aesthetic and artisanal terms it is not the idea but the performance, the form and feeling, the affect and impact that is taken and manipulated to commercial ends and financial profit. These are intrinsically tied to the colours and deserved at the very least some viewing and reviewing, as also representation, description, and depiction.

It bears noting that the decision in *Hayuk* does not reproduce the colour images but incorporates them by reference, as if the subject matter of determination, the vivid hue of the designs, were somehow unviewable, illegible, or simply irrelevant to the reception and interpretation of the report as a precedent. In the same vein, and despite occasional and incidental judicial recognition of the importance of red as a sign of significance, of danger, of the mandatory, or of blue as indicative of a hyperlink, of non-descript grey as lacking impact, the use of colour tends

[26] If one shifted ground to the law of contract, there was a strong argument that the circumstances were significant of a contract implied in fact or, because Hayuk had declined a contract, an unjust enrichment. See *Wrench LLC v Taco Bell Corp.* 51 F. Supp.2d 840.

nonetheless to pass unremarked and unnoticed.[27] Moving to English common law, consider the rather extraordinary libel case of *Spicer v Commissioner for Police of the Metropolis.*[28] In an effort to show that the complainant had been racing and showing off, late at night and in proximity to a car that crashed and killed a student pedestrian outside Kingston University in South London, Mr Justice Julian Knowles reproduces numerous stills from CCTV footage. Ignoring the irony of using stills to demonstrate that a car was racing, the pertinent point for present purposes is that the Court, to use the proper synecdoche, manipulates the still images to such an extent that viewing is overdetermined by visual pre-judgement, manipulation of the images that purport to show in neutral guise what happened. There are numerous incidents of the manipulation of the CCTV stills through the judicial use of colour, particularly graphs that show the trajectory of the putative showing off. In one such depiction there is a so-called 'high G trigger point' in a bloody red, and then braking marked on a graph by a bracket in the orange of prison uniforms or high-level threat. Such insertions of colour cannot be ignored and any adequate comprehension of the legal history of colours as governed by sumptuary law would necessarily observe and comment upon the impact of such tints and hues. I will limit analysis, however, to a single egregious insertion.[29]

Utilizing the CCTV footage, Mr Justice Knowles reproduces a still of the scene of the accident (Figure 7.4). This image is inserted to prove that the Metropolitan Police Press release that had linked Spicer to the event in which another car had crashed and killed a pedestrian was not libellous because true.[30] Note however that neither the photographic stills nor the map of the street can be viewed without taking account of the directional and affective scopic character of the colours, nominate arrows, and the collision of pixels creating a blur effect in the stills. The visual images steal the show, attracting the eye and luring the mind to the material presence of the scenes that are captured and the affects invoked by their various representations of accelerated death, of speed, persons, vehicles, and the community of the urban night where these encounters and viewings took place, and the tragedy unfolded. The case is purportedly about the accuracy of the verbal description of Spicer's guilt, but the images invoke a different medium and optical composition in which words are simply accessories to the arrows and colours that draw and direct the eye in its scanning of the image. Although presented as

[27] On the importance of red asterisks, see *Berkson v GOGO LLC* 97 F.Supp.3d 359; on recognition of blue as indicating hyperlinking, see *Hubbert v Dell* 835 N.E. 2d 113 (2005), or *Anand v Heath* 2019 WL 2716213; and on non-descript grey, see *In re Zappos* 893 F.Supp.2d 1058 (2012), or *Nguyen v Barnes & Noble* 2014 WL 4056549.

[28] *Spicer v Commissioner for Police of the Metropolis* [2019] EWHC 1099 (QB).

[29] The graph is diagram 4C as reproduced in the judgement para 180.

[30] For those interested, the Police published a report on their website that stated: 'Two guilty of killing a woman while racing their cars. [Picture Hina Shamin] [1] Two men who raced their high performance cars along a street in Kingston, leading to the death of a young woman, have been found guilty by a jury'. The jury, however, had not found Spicer guilty, although under a substituted charge he did receive a fine and penalty points for careless driving. See *Spicer* para. 11.

Figure 7.4 From *Spicer v Commissioner for Police of the Metropolis* [2019].

a simple and logical diagramming of the locations, proximities, and speed of the vehicles 'racing and showing off', the visual or more properly diegetic ark of the judgement has a very different affective impact to the verbal narrative or purported calculus and proof of the disapprobated vehicular activities. The subjective state of the driver William Spicer as reported in the release by the Metropolitan Police Press office is prejudicially coloured and marked in both the CCTV stills and the coloured graphs of the path of his vehicle.

For the art historian Didi-Huberman the significance of colour is that of creating a distinct field of representation in which it is not the absent bodies that are depicted—figures or indeed faces could easily have been reproduced—but rather geometric shapes and patches of colour with arrows of direction painted on them.[31] The colour and figures tell a story that the words cannot relay. In the view of Mr Justice Knowles, the pictures and illustrative schemata demonstrate a race and showing off, although this is for him a question only of speed, of acceleration and braking with the addition of Spicer's illegal right turn and parking some way from the scene of the accident before returning. What is important is that while the words and the descriptions purport to represent and designate the absent actors in the narrative, at night, on Penhryn Road, what is present in the judgement is

[31] Didi-Huberman, *Fra Angelico*, 19.

a set of colour images and their coda. What is manifest in the judgement is thus the pixelated blur of the second frame of Figure 7.4 and the coloured rectangular figurations. The purple pen of the time stamp marks the equivalent of royal decree, or here the delegated temporal letter of the law, and then the rectangles with arrows in yellow, green, and red. The yellow, always yellow for Spicer, must also be accounted. The colour of cowardice, of chicken and of straw, as in a straw claim, are not far from this peculiar visual choice. In tandem and confluence these are the vivid reasons—*vividae rationes*—of the decision, and merit close further scrutiny in their optical presence.

Colour takes the image out of time and carries anachronic implications, visceral affects and effects. The blotches of red have a theological import, the blood of Christ, of a body pierced and bleeding, wounded, dying. The visual intimation of blood is linked in early modern law to printed law books in which red letters, cardinal flaming type, would indicate universal norms, most usually in the modality of Latin maxims or other dogmas.[32] The significance of law's red letters bequeaths to the colour the representation of the divine wound, the generative force of the Christian religion, as well as the promise that opens onto another life. There is nothing innocent in the use of the sanguine hue in a common law, Anglican context, and thus to mark the victim in red is to liken her innocence to that of Christ, while also making a visual connection to the blood red lipstick that Hina Shamin, the student who died, is wearing in the photo portrait that the Metropolitan Police Press release uses in the article complained of by Spicer. Compared to that, Spicer marked in yellow is a sorry contrast, significant of playing chicken in fleeing the scene of the crash, as also of cowardice in racing, seeing who could go faster, take greater reckless risks from the impunity of a luxury car. Then finally, at the bottom, the exhibit is coloured in police blue, the stain of authority and legitimate exposition. All of which is to say that some explanation, commentary, viewing, and critical accounting of this loaded use of colour in stills that purport to simply evidence the event in judicially neutral frame, are necessary for any semblance of retinal justice being done.

By the same token, in a very different context, there is a remarkable irony to the recent decision in *Andy Warhol Foundation v Goldsmith* in which the transformative use of colour was the sole issue to be decided. The judgement is reproduced in monochrome in the official printed reports and only three of sixteen highly distinct images from the relevant series are reproduced at all.[33] The case raised the question of whether the photographer's copyright had been infringed when the 'art-world colossus' created diversely and vividly coloured silkscreens of a part of

[32] On the common law status of maxims, see Edward Whitehouse, Fortescutus illustratus, *or a Commentary on That Nervous Treatise 'De laudibus legum angliæ'* (London: Roycroft, 1663), at 126 et seq.

[33] *Andy Warhol Foundation for the Visual Arts v Lynn Goldsmith* 11 F.4th 26 (2021). https://larc.cardozo.yu.edu/faculty-online-pubs/61/, eFigure 17.

the photo-portrait. In deciding against the Foundation, the Second Circuit determined that Warhol's remediation of the photograph was not legally transformative, and so was not protected by the fair use doctrine. The fact of remediation, that a half tone silkscreen was created from the top portion of the photograph, and not the photo-portrait as a whole, was ignored, and the variety of colours and changes to the impact and affect of the depiction of the iconic rock figure were glossed over with an atonal and monochrome eye (Figure 7.5). For the purposes of the protocols of retinal justice it is the absence of any discussion of colour and the affective viewing it promotes that is most significant. Circuit Judge Gerard Lynch engages in a literalist reading, as opposed to any more open viewing of the silkscreen images.[34] Acknowledging that depth and contrast were altered in the transfer of the image, colour is treated as an aside and as an observation that is irrelevant to monochrome literalism, the regimentations of the page, and a 'reading' of the subject of the picture.

The remediation shifts the form of the image from a photograph with its attendant presumption of realism, of an undoctored and direct view of the face, to that of an artwork, a creative invention that uses part of a photograph to generate a self-reflective viewing reaction to the underlying figure that is surrounded and, in some versions, covered by colour. The introduction, of blush and hue, tone and tint, patterns and intersections, is alone sufficient to warrant judicial notice and juristic significance. The alteration of foreground and background, the removal of details from the photograph, the flattening of the depiction, as also the cropping of the image to create a sense of a floating and somewhat spectral presence of aura and body is significant of the effect and affect that the artistic creation generates in the viewer. A new subject is formed, but in the case of the judicial viewer it is not a subject aware of their own novel disposition. The decision does not look at colour, but rather reads in literalist form, from memory as much as perception, from presupposition as much as viewing, the largely invisible but comfortingly monochrome outline of the photo-portrait, the recognizable if adeptly formulated mugshot, lurking beneath the vivid intensities and altered form of the silkscreens and drawings of the artist's remediations. Here is a golden opportunity to recognize and advance an instance of aesthetic jurisdiction, an exemplum of a retinal justice to come. Colour here should pre-empt text, and aesthetics should have epistemic priority over law. It is an ideal moment to advance the development of *ars iuris* as opposed to the prosaic lumberings and cognitive tumbrils of legal positivism.

[34] The trial court reproduces all sixteen, in colour online at least, and arrives at an opposite conclusion to the appellate court, in *Andy Warhol Foundation for the Visual Arts v Lynn* In the Supreme Court, *Andy Warhol Foundation for the Visual Arts v Lynn Goldsmith* 143 S.Ct 1258 (2023), the majority affirms the appellate decision. Justice Kagan, dissenting, remarks rather appositely that 'The majority doesn't see it. And I mean that literally. There is precious little evidence that the majority has actually looked at these images ...'

Figures 7.5 Inserted by Judge Gerard Lynch in *Warhol Foundation v Goldsmith* (2021).

By permission of Lynn Goldsmith.

Renaissance jurists referenced the goal of interpretation as apprehension *sub-auditio* and by extension *sub-intellectio*. What is referenced is an attention to an interposition of meaning, the mediation between interpreter and interpreted in which each feature of the hermeneutic and here visual transference is changed by the exchange. The argument is not that the monochrome photo-portrait was or was not infringed, but rather the prior assertion of method which requires that the legal actor recognize their changing role as the viewer and the viewed of the depictions. The legal concept of *interpositae personae* is of judges and jurists as actors and creators of meaning, as normative responders who now need to develop an awareness of the cognitive and affective impact of the imaginal, its triggers and symbols.[35] In the heraldic tradition, law coded colours and for that reason and background history alone, one would expect a minimal sumptuary attention to monochrome and colour, the implexities of remediation, the alteration of both matter and visible subject, the pigments, stains, tints, and tinctures by which the eye is guided, and discourse diffracted. Colour blindness, with all that it implies, does not behove the judiciary, nor does it further the legitimacy of law which is predicated precisely upon the jurist being able to address both conflict and the apprehensive diffractions of discourse that both generate divisiveness and call for the knowledge and equity, humour, and wit of jurisliterary, aesthetic, and colourist intervention.

2. *Diffractions of Apprehension.* The concept of points of diffraction of discourse was elaborated first by Michel Foucault who used the optical metaphor to denote points of incompatibility: 'two objects, or two types of enunciation, or two concepts may appear, in the same discursive formation, without being able to enter—under pain of manifest contradiction or inconsequence—the same series of statements'.[36] What is at issue for Foucault is the availability of distinct strategies or alternatives within a discursive formation, with diffraction allowing for the development of sub-discourses and different positions of desire. Tied to discourse and to questions of authority defined as the role that the statements must play in non-discursive practices, the insertion of images in legal utterances allows for an expansion of the points of incompatibility to embrace a diffractive fringe which takes the novel form of a visual splitting or breaking apart of the discursive chain of precedent in a videological form.

The key issue, as specified above in the matterphorical terms of colour, is that of authority. The concept of images as a diffractive fringe is in part a way of taking account of the dominance of discourse in the relay of law, but also a protocol of hinting in a proleptic manner to the incompatibility of visual insertions into precedent texts. In time, sensible life, the imaginal relay, the micro-ontology of

[35] On the Renaissance jurist's concept of interposition, see Ian Maclean, *Interpretation and Meaning in the Renaissance: The Case of Law* (Cambridge: Cambridge University Press, 1992) at 63–64 tracing the priority of the lawyer's sense of intention and meaning over that of the words alone.

[36] Michel Foucault, *The Archaeology of Knowledge* (London: Continuum, 2014) at 76.

images, will take precedence over precedent as text. The diffusion of rule in the distinct form of imaginal relay constitutes a fissure in the discursive formation, and it is one that has yet to be addressed properly because even where the image is introduced by the judge to make a point about precedent or on occasion as a precedent, we have seen that the imaginal form of the insertion is ignored and the interpretative apparatus activated in relation to the visual modality of judgement is unreflectively and variously that of the obvious, of believing one's eyes, of pictures speaking for themselves, of showing the real and so seeing in some strangely undirected form what took place or what is in issue. Professor and Judge, Richard Posner even argues for the greater use of pictures in judgements for two seemingly related reasons. The first is that judicial, as well as law review and law reporting resistance to pictures generates an unnecessary formalism: 'The aversion to the visual is of limited significance in judicial writing but it is an excellent example of the flight from concreteness to abstractness that is such a pronounced feature of the legal professional's style of thinking and writing'.[37] The second reason is to combat boredom: 'Wherever possible, use pictures, props (for example, trademarked items in a trademark case), maps, diagrams, and other visual aids, in your brief or at argument. Seeing a case makes it come alive to judges'.[38] This latter desideratum relates of course to advocacy and only by association to judgement and precedent, but it is predicated upon the internet availability of myriad visual resources and is part of a more expansive encouragement of judges to using the web to come alive, to engage with the contemporary, and also and less plausibly so that the judge can do what 'real people do', which is to look at the screen and surf the dominions of the virtual.

Posner wishes to bring the virtual world, sensible life as imaginal relay, into the courtroom and into judgement. He wants to see 'it', to view the real, to feel that his judgement is actual and concrete by virtue of introducing the *certum*—which is to say the particularity—of visibility. It should by now be evident that law lags behind social media, and that the shift to viserbality in decisions requires a dramatic reorientation of legal epistemology, one which specifically takes account of the diffraction of thought that occurs with the advent and advenience of imaginal relays of legal norms. The image is the point of fissure and of epistemic incompatibility within the discourse of law, if only because it is not discourse. The heuristic distinctiveness, and tralatitious independence of the picture from the text, requires protocols, community, and thought that diverges qualitatively from the *dis-currere*, the running away or flight to abstraction in the angelological frame of normative discourse. It is a point that is made well by jurists who work to provide visual essays as distinct though intentionally complementary features of viewing

[37] Richard Posner, 'Judicial Opinions and Appellate Advocacy in Federal Courts: One Judge's Views', 51 *Duq. L. Rev.* 3 (2013) at 23.
[38] Ibid., at 38.

the relation between law and image, the normative and the imaginal. The emergent argument of the visual turn in jurisprudence is one that commences with the visual, with the distinct imaginal relays of pictorial forms, because it is recognized that the preconceptual quality of the visual, the affective force and initially anarchic sway of the depicted will frame the perception of cause and its equities: 'Engagement with the visual involves a consideration of the ways in which images prepare people for a particular type of encounter with law and how art becomes an aspect of legal culture ... '.[39] The optical insertions constitute the frame through which the legal process is encountered and the pictures that judges import in judgements likewise will increasingly come to frame the event, the impact and interface of legal decisions. The diffractive fringe, like the minor language, increasingly comes to centre stage.

The image as fissure and point of diversion, as a site of incompatibility in the discourse of law, thus requires a grasp on looking, an attention to the gaze emanating from and looking into the record. The abstraction of the printed text—which in one medieval notion brings the sounds of one absent to the ears without voice—succumbs to the materiality of the image as diffractive presence, as colour, shape, pattern, sound, and motion on screen, and so as instigating another path of intellection, a distinctive avenue of perception and sight lines of decision. The cathartic impact of seeing has to be taken into account, and a rudimentary aesthetic of a sensory legality is necessary to the apprehension and working through of the novelty of the viserbal in decision. The image is matterphor remediating metaphor, a theme pursued in relation to laws of theory, by Gandorfer, and adumbrated by the artist and law professor Phillipopoulous-Mihalopoulos in terms of the flesh of law, meaning the regimen of haptic and material signs that emerge from or respond to the imaginal in the juridical.[40]

As adverted earlier, in discussing the morphology of the imaginal, the legal approach to viewing tends to analogize appearance to the familiar. Judge Posner thus reflects upon the use of images as illustrative of what real people look at, and thus assumes the quotidian and ordinary character of the signs that support, as opposed to subtending and framing, the encounter with words and worlds. The general and vague Posnerian jurisprudence of vision, which sees the image as conjunctive rather than diffractive, can be counterposed to some extent with practice and in particular, as pursued here, the use of photographic records and other visual matter in criminal law, copyright law, patents, and torts. In addition to the plethora of expressions of feeling and impression, of obviousness and belief

[39] Linda Mulcahy, 'Eyes of the Law: A Visual Turn in Socio-Legal Studies?', 44 *Journal of Law and Society* 111 (2017) at 122.

[40] Gandorfer, *Matterphor*, op cit. Ch. 1, as well as her edited collection, Zulaika Ayub and Daniela Gandorfer, 'Matterphorical', 24 *Theory and Event* (2021) 2–13. Andreas Phillipopoulos-Mihalopoulos, 'Flesh of the Law: Material Legal Metaphors', 43 *Journal of Law and Society* 45 (2016) and further in Andreas Phillipopoulos-Mihalopoulos, 'Performing Metaphors', 24 *Theory and Event* 268 (2021).

in what the eyes see, there is a deeper drive to take proprietorship of the image, to rule the visual and control the sign. The epistemic trajectory of legal vision is one of dominance, of 'control signs', icons which in their juridical mode 'function to make reality and representation indistinguishable'.[41] The result, as lengthily traversed, is that the image becomes a 'fact', inevitable, inescapable, subject to the regime of visiocratic governance. As new realities are viewed, they are reduced to and incorporated into the extant regimen of vision, but in an unconscious form for maximal effect, as in a dream defining the desire of the judge.

Diffraction marks sites of incompatibility because the image qua image, as diffracted, cannot be so simply assumed or controlled. An uncomplicated example from criminal law can provide an imaginal exemplum. The photo identification or mugshot, from an arrest, is a photo-portrait but legally it is a bare representation of a subject, a face named, profiled, and calibrated. A *propositus* controlled and inscribed in the records. In *State v Walter* the defendant was charged with manufacturing methamphetamine. In closing arguments at trial, the state prosecutor 'used a visual presentation with various photographs, diagrams, and lists. The final photograph used in the slideshow was an enlarged color photograph of Walter. In the photograph, Walter is wearing a bright orange prison jumpsuit and the word "GUILTY" is superimposed in large, block, red letters, running diagonally across Walter's face and filling the frame of the photograph' (Figure 7.6).[42] Walter was convicted and appealed on the ground that the altered visual evidence prevented a fair trial.

The most remarkable feature of the case is that neither the defence counsel nor the presiding judge saw the relevant image. The familiar is overlooked, and the coincidence of reality and representation in the identikit is seemingly too obvious to require scrutiny. The image slips past the conscious viewing and lodges in affect as the frame and scopic focus of determination. Once discovered and objection raised, the issue for the appellate court was prejudicial error. Here it transpires that the photograph is admissible, but the addition of the blood-red, all-caps guilty was improper. No detailed viewing or discussion of the visual specifics, composition, angle, calibrations, or colours ensues. The orange jumpsuit and the calibrated mugshot require no deliberation. Other photo-portraits used in judgements gain no precedential standing, even though the gallery of such photographic identifications or here aspersions is extensive.

In *Federal Election Commission v Christian Action Network*, for example, an opposite conclusion was reached, where the defendant lobbying group produced print and television advertisements assailing what the group believed to be the militantly homosexual agenda of candidate William Jefferson Clinton during the 1992

[41] Nathan Moore, 'Icons of Control: Deleuze, Signs, Law', 20 *Int. J. Semiotics of Law* 33 (2007) at 52.
[42] *State v Walter* 479 S.W. 3d 118 (2016) at 122.

Figure 7.6 Insertion by Judge George Draper III in *State v Walter* 479 S.W. 3d 118 (2016).

elections.[43] These included a photo-portait of Clinton in a circular frame with a bold black line through it, and a further monochrome profile picture of Clinton set against an American flag, the subject shown with a black moustache very similar to images of Hitler. In this case, the photo-portraits are determined admissible under relevant election law as freedom of speech, rather than express advocacy in relation to an election: 'The advertisements at issue do not contain explicit words *or imagery* advocating electoral action'.[44] In context, it would be hard to imagine what else the images did advocate, but what Suneel Mehmi depicts incisively as photographic literalism seems here to attach to the Court's viewing, and in the representation of the real, it is the real, which means here the judge's imaginal presupposition, that controls the interpretation of the representation while being framed unconsciously by the very image that is the purported object of

[43] *Federal Election Commission v Christian Action Network* 894 F.Supp. 946 (1995) appendices at 962, 968. Posted at https://larc.cardozo.yu.edu/faculty-online-pubs/61/, eFigure 18.

[44] Ibid., at 948.

deliberation and interpretation.[45] In all of this, to return to the arresting arrest image, its defiance, its orange and numbers, its gray and black tone accentuating the quizzical gaze of Chadwick Leland Walter is passed over, its prejudicial connotations being subordinate to the words emblazoned in vexillological manner, blood red, across the picture of the head, *caput lupinum* itself.

Borrowing in stochastic fashion from copyright law, the particular diffraction of discourse in the rebuked image in *Walter* is a form of unfair use, a prejudicial transformative use, a deforming infringement of the real. Leave to one side the fact that the use of the photograph of arrest is of itself prejudicial rather than probative, and that the prosecution manipulation of the jury through imaginal relays is more bludgeon than proof. It is a classic example of shark aesthetic which slips the image past conscious viewing to create an affective response prior to reflection and so generating the 'seeming' to be, the impression upon which the naked eye so feeds. It is highly significant that the particular optical representation of the defendant was never consciously perceived by either the defence attorney or the trial judge at the time of initial relay to the jurors. This of itself suggests that the mere use of imagery qualitatively changes the nature of the dialogue, or more properly legal agon. Recognition of such disjunction or splitting, the diffraction of discourse occasioned by visual arguments, perceptual rhetoric, requires a comparable diffraction of jurisprudential inquiry and relay to apprehend the new form. Retinal justice suggests a novel model and dispositive purpose that starts with a compilation of an atlas of judicial images and a curation of their circulation in such a manner as attends carefully to questions of provenance, composition, context, comparata, connotation, colour, sound, and form as well as the now recognized if dilettante inquiries into editing, focus, quality, angles, lenses, and platforms of reproduction and relay.

The question posed, indirectly in *Walter* but more presciently in fair use copyright cases, is precisely that of diffraction of the ruling, the incompatibility of the different instances and hence the lines of thought, ratiocination, and opination, that the distinct forms generate. There is an inverted form of the question of infringement that has to be asked of the judicial images. Namely that if the use is transformative, if it is in the language of copyright a fair use, then it is prejudicial and impermissible, whereas a use that infringes the copyright is retinally just. French copyright law treats the real as property and requires aesthetic transformation of the image of real property for it to escape copyright censure. Infringement of the real is precisely what the law must require of judicial imagery, of precedential pictures. There is no sense in which it can be argued that the image lacks sensibility and aesthetic affect. Every representation is a transformation, an aesthetic choice,

[45] Suneel Mehmi, *Law, Literature and the Power of Reading: Literalism and Photography in the Nineteenth Century* (Abingdon: Routledge, 2022) arguing that literalist viewing is associated 'with the seemingly naïve belief that everything in a body of writing is somehow manifest, given, transparent and easily read rather than having to be laboriously and creatively deciphered'.

an image in a fluid and different time and space. Such is the case at the most structural level of the visual depiction as a false truth, because however directly and factually it seems to reproduce the real, it is not what is represented, but a distinct and floating material form of another exterior being or thing, then extant but now a deviation, a different presence and form of the encounter or event relayed. To this it can be added that to infringe is to break, to injure, void, or foil, which here also means to plough, to change, to make something grow. That the judicial image should infringe makes neatly conscious the sense in which any depiction necessarily not only diffracts but specifically renders to view in a novel and remediated form, a changed, broken, excised version of the real.

Legal interpretation reduces to discourse, while the image diffracts into the visual. If every use of a picture is to some degree transformative, the question becomes one of a spectrum of visual features and narrative contexts of the putatively infringing use. A photographer skilfully frames a picture of a film star—Robert Pattinson—slumped over the seat of a car, and sells it to a licensing company which posts the image on its website. A for profit gossip website screen grabs the image and posts it on its website and displays it alongside a discussion of its significance on a 'rumor to real' scale that is featured beside the image.[46] The question of whether this is fair use turns upon the issue of whether the new work is transformative: 'does it merely supersede the objects of the original creation' or does it add something new, 'with a further purpose and different character, altering the first with new expression, meaning, or message'.[47] Without rehearsing the intricacies and vagaries of the fair use doctrine, the legal issue is predominantly treated as one of discursive context and critical description of the image, and in some jurisdictions the aligned consideration of whether there is acknowledgement of its source. If the discursive use is distinctive then a finding of transformative use is more likely. The question deliberated in relation to the Pattinson image is whether the gossip site discussion criticized the licensing site's use of the celebrity image for rumour and gossip. The question of the image, of viewing the picture, does not arise, nor is it reproduced in the decision but rather haunts as an absence, an invisibility that is referenced but not seen because it seems—though evidently this is not apparent—that it is the discursive parameters of use that matter, even though it is the image that is copied. The incompatibility of discourse and image again comes to the fore.

The priority and precedential value of discourse also dictates that visual features of the imagery tend to be glossed in textual terms. The sensible quality and colours of photographs are reduced to the geometric and diagrammatic so as to be viewed predominantly through the linear lens of the written and as if they are graphs or maps. The diffraction of the visual remains unexamined and probably unconscious in that the viewing of the image is of its denotative, which is to say

[46] *BWP Media USA V Gossip Cop Media* 196 F.Supp.3d 396 (2016) at 399.
[47] Ibid., at 404.

linguistic, features. It references the real, it shows and on occasion demonstrates an object, persons, things, or events, but it is not viewed as a sensible materiality nor apprehended as an optical essay that draws judgement into the domain of visual persuasion and the optical scope of the drives. In *Ferdman v CBS Interactive*, the point of diffraction is concealed by the monochrome of the image, the grey on grey of the actor Tom Holland photographed in Spiderman's motion capture suit (Figure 7.7). The image, which again has been screen captured from the photographer's website, is used as part of a story about the filming of the movie moving from

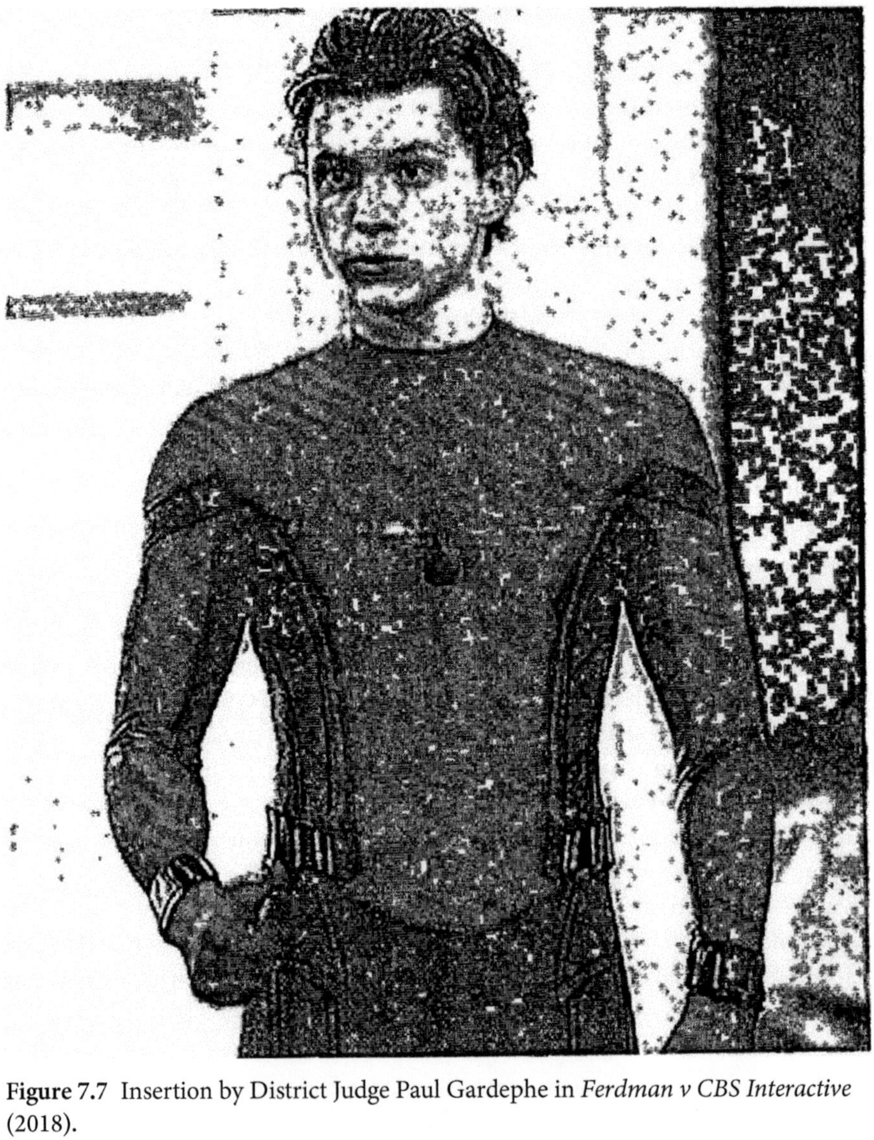

Figure 7.7 Insertion by District Judge Paul Gardephe in *Ferdman v CBS Interactive* (2018).

Atlanta to Queens, Spiderman's home neighbourhood. There is nothing said about the image other than that it has not been altered in shape or size and that it shows what it shows. It is replicated: 'the Photo was presented as an historic artifact—its significance was as the item' which it depicted and not any incidental feature or unnoticed aspect of the still, which in fact captured Holland breakdancing punk style.[48] There is something monochromatically graphic in the pixelated depiction of a motion capture suit which is to film what the typesetter's print workshop is to texts. The monochrome of the outfit comes as close as a figurative image can to the black and white of the printed page. It slips in. The diffraction is unnoticed and so a finding of infringing use follows seamlessly. The image copies the text. It mimics discourse. It is an unwarranted image, an intrusion purloined from another site where its use had been the same.

The absence of colour and the abstract patterning of the image incorporate it easily into the path of discourse and so, in looking at the picture as a mode of reference to the actor depicted, the photograph becomes the equivalent of a stolen word which infringes copyright by transposing the manifestation of an idea into the secondary or copying discourse. What is viewed can be treated as if it were being read. By way of contrast, the diffraction of viewing, the sight lines of looking are marginally more in evidence when the reproduction is in colour and the image is juxtaposed to different visual content. In another case, the plaintiff photographer Rebecca Fay Walsh photographed and copyrighted a picture of rapper and celebrity Cardi B (Figure 7.8). The defendant online magazine reproduced the copyrighted image in an article on Cardi B's collaboration with Tom Ford Beauty brand and reproduced the photograph as part of a screen capture of an Instagram in which the rapper herself had posted the picture alongside the bold blue lipstick shade that she was promoting (Figure 7.9).[49] As part of a story about the rapper getting into a fight with another rapper at a New York Fashion week event, the reposting of the Instagram image from a screen grab accompanies discussion of fans responses to the naming of the lipstick after her. The diffraction of the image and the remediation of discourse are much more evident in this judgement because the images are reproduced in colour, and the specific visual form of the asserted infringement gains some consideration. The image grabbed and copied has been resized and cropped. The colour and tone are muted in contrast to the larger than life depiction of the lipstick. The article reproduces a copy of an Instagram post that is in turn a cropped copy of the photograph. Remediation is here instantly evident, and the diffractive role played by the introduction of imagery, particularly in colour and visual juxtaposition with a product line and Instagram message, inclusive of roughly 2.5 million likes, renders the visual axis of the decision sufficiently distinct to be classified as fair use. The use made of

[48] *Steven Ferdman v CBS Interactive* 342 F.Supp.3d 515 (2018) at 531.
[49] *Walsh v Townsquare Media* 464 F.Supp.3d 570 (2020).

Figure 7.8 Insertion by District Judge Vernon Broderick from *Walsh v Townsquare Media* (2020).
Image courtesy of Rebecca Fay Walsh // FAYMOUS.

the image by the defendant website is transformative, but as concerns retinal justice the differentiating features are also, at least in potential, transformative of the judgement which now carries two colour photographs and takes on a discernibly optical, videological character.

The diffraction of discourse manifested in the use of colour pictures, figural optics, is a symptom of multiple levels of incompatability between the abstract linearity of legal discourse and the ambulatory and affective fluidity of the image. Building upon the first protocol, that of recognition and analysis of colour, the protocol of diffraction expands the viewing of judgement to include the associative chains that all aspects of the image introduce into the invention of judgement, the vision in decision. This protocol follows the eye in its lateral, ambulatory, wandering *perpetuum mobile*, its digressive criss-crossing of the visual subject of viewing,

Figure 7.9 Insertion by District Judge Vernon Broderick from *Walsh v Townsquare Media* (2020).

as well as in its reverie of other images, its regression to childhood play, its reconstruction of what was imagined and viewed in the final analysis of the optical in the verbal discourse of judgement. Apprehension and diffraction are also questions of impact, of seismography of the visible, and thus also of the dynamogrammatic force of the aesthetic relay. The dynamogram, being a question of force and not of meaning, seeks to track the tensions and the energies, the symbolic gradations and intensifications that the image introduces into judgement and relays the vision in the decision.

3. *Affective Norms.* In a medieval Augustinian maxim, *ubi oculus ibi amor*, the interior connection between sight and passion, the excitations and loves of the visible gain direct expression and led Protestant theologians to denounce the image as a strumpet, a term that lacks a recognized etymology but is most likely, which is to say in my opinion, a corrupt trumpet or abuse of the biblical power of Gideon's trumpet, the *effectus* of sound and motion. It is, in other and lesser words, a strange bedfellow for common law, a tradition and discipline that emerged in the modern era from the Protestant sermons of Richard Hooker and the technical strictures of Sir Edward Coke, who was a devout congregant of Hooker's church services and sermons. In more modern argot, in the current degree xerox, the saturation point of image streaming, we might expand the concept to lights, camera, emotion. The trinity reflects the predicate of visual representation in painting and now photography, the inscription of light as a variant mode of photosynthesis whereby the viewer engages and grows. What then of the legality and normative status of the depicted? Judicial illocution in images, the showing of judgement, the issuing forth in visual prospect of decisions that were historically scriptural is also a diffraction of the norm, and a visual essay on the rule. For Manderson, in his careful study of artistic representations of law's temporality, the image is not just another concept of law, but rather a novel mode of legal presence, a fabric and fashioning of governance that materializes law in a distinctive manner replete with both subliminal force and meaning: 'Affective and enigmatic, visual elements are crucial to the constitution, not to mention the seduction, of the law. Images are prime sites of law's theory, and ... *praxis*. They are also, on occasion, prime sites for the critique of law too'.[50] For Manderson this primacy of depiction generates a confrontation with time and specifically the anachronic character of both law and art. The image, in the sense defined in this work as the matterphorization of the visual sense of an event, is an imaginal presence, a mode of thought that bears the suspended status of being both present and absent, a medium that provides access to collective intellection, which for Hobbes was the angel of thought, the flash of the spirit. In the specific terms of this study of judicial insertions, the impact of the image upon the relay of judgement and rule posits directly the jurisprudential question of the normative status of the image and the role of affect in the seductions, and

[50] Manderson, *Danse Macabre* at 16.

anachronic and anterograde relays of law: 'Images give a figure, not only to things and to spaces, but to times themselves: Images simultaneously configure the times of memory and of desire'.[51]

The imaginal both implexifies thought as the sensory apprehension of visual relays and their extensive streams of depiction, but also intensifies the encounter with the subject matter of the rule. The unconscious may be structured like a language, but it is destructured like an album, subtended and rearranged through the stupefaction and passion attaching to images.[52] The sensible image impacts sensible life, and it is this tensor and connection that judicial usages most directly implicate and unwittingly utilize. An element of retinal reticence is necessary to engage the process of imaginal relay and to gauge the normative effects and affects of the emergent gallery of judicial pictures. The tensor, the funambulist path of vision propels the judge into the intimate relation of images and throws open the sensibilities of analogy, the affects of likenesses, the lures of similitude as a look, comparison as an aspect, as the visage of things. The norm is carried away by an image, by the *veritas falsa* of the picture which simulates the subject represented while dissimulating the medium of relaying it. The painting is the simulation, in French law the *semblable*, the effect of the cause, not itself the thing nor the creator of the image. The jurist has to step back from the visual relay to apprehend its difference, the force of diffraction and the alternate temporality of imagery, the heterochrony and heterogeneity of the visual insertion.

The image interrupts discourse, interposing the visual in contrast and disruption of the chain of reasoning, the logic of precedential judgement. The interruption literally breaks the syntactic and semantic verbal connections by introducing a different constellation, a configuration of affect and reason that is neither rule nor law but to the contrary an enigmatic and anterior witness to the imaginal work of judging. What interrupts the normative expression is the vision of decision in the letter of the law. If the rule is a generality applicable *in abstracto* to similar or future encounters and circumstances, the picture is a material singularity that matterphorizes a specific and past occasion. Its significance is not a directive but a configuration that belongs within an alternative gallery of images. Its meaning is generated not so much by the singularity of what is shown, but by the lateral connections and intimations it generates which in aesthetic and filmic theory are distributed by means of montage.[53] The emancipated lawyer, if I can so optimistically nominate the visually sensible jurist, the aesthete of the *ars iuris*, is one conversant with and skillful in viewing and reassembling legal methods of montage.

[51] Didi-Huberman, *The Anxious Gay Science*, at 27 (translation modified).

[52] Régis Debray, *Le stupéfiante image* (Paris: Gallimard, 2013) at 17.

[53] Didi-Huberman, *The Eye of History: When Images take Positions* (Cambridge, MA: MIT Press, 2018) at 122–127.

The lateral and meandering path of the eye engaged in imaginal relays and the suspended materiality of the depicted follows a different track of affect and apprehension. Images are gestures in judgement, expressions of movement that configure some intensive feature of the event pictured and of the norm that responds to it. The image opens law to viewing, to the lines of sight and paths of imagination and fantasy that the visual necessarily also imports. Vision provides a window—*ut pictura fenestra*—in the sense of a subject who views and reassembles the tableau through the intimate dialectic and inaugural act of looking, of opening to and opening up what is viewed.[54] The opening up disrupts the chain of deduction or flow of induction and in an involuntary and unwitting fashion injects affect, sensation, and sensibility into the reason of law. The visual figures inserted into precedent texts jolt the viewer precisely through the exposing and juxtaposing of encounters that are normally separated, moments frozen in time that will provide the material of future legal invention. The montage opens and uncovers constellations of events, fragments of action that have been torn from their context and relations to now circulate, anachronically and heterochronically, displaced and refigured to the precedential progress of common law.

If the image, to borrow from Deleuze, introduces 'a bloc of sensations ... a compound of percepts and affects', it reveals a background and sensibility to the event judged, as well as forcing the intimate relation of looking and perceiving, reconfiguring and sensing, feeling the norm. The montage is the visual array of images and senses that accompany the bare being of the depicted in the sensorium of the viewer. Images are matter and they matter to judgement because blush, tone, colour, the diffraction of the optical, scopic desire, embarrass and inform the creation of law. Spiderman appearing in visible form in a legal text is necessarily significant and especially so if there is complete absence of any normative sense of what this insertion means. It throws the web of the visual across the striations of the text and in doing so disassembles the verbal exposition and interrupts the logic of the text with the appearance of a star, Tom Holland, in facial close up. A superhero visibly on the page or more likely on screen with the letter of the law is a disruption, a rend in the fabric of precedent, a break in the supposedly unbroken chain of proceedings *ad similia*. It is not incidental that it is Spiderman, the subject of a series of movies, a cult figure and multimodal presence, in comics, in movies, in scholarly literature, and now also glimpsed in law.[55] The fantastical figures of justice, Spiderman, Superman, the Watchmen, Daredevil, and an expanding list have launched an academic flotilla, a small armada of essays in *lex comica*, graphic legal studies, superheroes and law. The danse macabre of this distinct window into the juridical expresses and brings with it a plethora of associations, condensations, and

[54] On intimacy and viewing, the painting as window, see the magnificent Gérard Wacjman, *Fenêtre: Chroniques du regard et de l'intime* (Paris: Verdier, 2004).

[55] For another instance of spiderman appearance in costume in a law report, see, look, view the image reproduced in *Courthouse News Service v Brenda Forman* 606 F. Supp.3d 1200 (2022).

displacements that attach to the image of the film star, to the superhero Spiderman, to the comic genre and film sequences that the photograph triggers.

The decision in *Ferdman v CBS* was that the reproduction of the photograph on the defendant's website infringed the plaintiff's copyright. It was a mere copy without transformative purpose or product. The story carried on the website was that the filming of *Spiderman: Homecoming* had now brought the hero home. As this was obviously enough the theme of the movie, and also the context and description of the images posted by the photographer, nothing of news or any other value had been added to the simple repetition of the picture. What is visually most dispositive is that the image of the hero in a motion capture suit, slipped into the judicial text unremarked, unanalysed, free floating, fails to capture either movement—the breakdance—or the location. The picture is of the actor, prior to filming, prior to law, in a state of prescience and process of becoming. There is no colour, no background, no Queens. All of which strongly suggests that the picture carries a considerable weight of judgement, that the strangely pixelated, monochrome frontal view is a screengrab of the celebrity, an infringing filching of the actor's image and not a depiction of the hero in their novel location, without any sense of the *nostos* of homecoming or of Spiderman being and becoming somewhere new.

The image may ornament the judgement, but its role is far more than ornamental. Retinal justice begins with the proposition that the image matters and thus that protocols of viewing, strict scrutiny, an analysis of the affect and anachronism of the image in legal discourse, and an account of what it conveys as well as how it relays is a precondition for judicial insertion. A curator of images could provide the relevant montages, the juxtapositions and associations that the image is likely to trigger, but in juristic contexts of use the primary methodological desiderata are first an extended viewing, a tracking of the eye as it wanders over the depiction, and secondly a disassembling of the image, an accounting of its history and composition, its elements as well as its juxtapositions to other images. The viewing has to silence discourse and open the mind of the spectator to the sensible apprehension of what is seen, the imaginal montage that it instigates, and so its role as installation in the judicial determination. Affect and response, repressed or unnoticed, will be acted out in judgement, accurately or erroneously, but without accountability it becomes the other scene of decision, the shadow law that disturbs and confuses rather than promoting and promulgating an aesthetics and ethics of judgement.

Cardi B has 45.2 million followers. Her photo-portrait, reproduced twice in the judgement, can hardly be deemed insignificant at any level, juridical or social, mediological or empirico-critical. The interface of affect and rule, sensibility and normativity, here take on a more colourful and substantial visual role. The court found the reposting of the photo-portrait met the criteria of fair use of the work reproduced. The transformative alteration lay in embedding the depiction, along with the header, subscript, and image of Tom Ford lipstick, from

Cardi B's Instagram message, into a story about the star endorsing the brand. 'In other words', the court reasons, the use is new, although of course it is the words, the discourse surrounding the image, that are held to meet the criterion of different purpose, while the differences between the two images juxtaposed in the judgement are only glancingly apprehended and never fully addressed. The mini-montage of the star, and then of star and lipstick, deserves some normative credit even if rather casually inserted in the printed report, in black and white, and on different pages. It is the rapper who has transformed the image. This is in part by virtue of cropping the sides and more significantly in juxtaposition and endorsement of the image of lipstick and insignia of the Tom Ford brand.

The altered image is reproduced in the online article about Cardi B's endorsement, and the spat with Nicki Minaj at Fashion Week. At this juncture it is no longer the photographer's photo-portrait of the celebrity picture, but the celebrity's own montage or mash up of the photo that is in issue and copied. Visually, the Instagram posting is a radical shift from a picture of the rapper celebrity surrounded by others to an advertisement for a product. In the manner of advertising, the juxtaposition is also strikingly sexualized. The open hand, palm facing out and pointing upwards, is an icon of attestation, the chirological manifestation of swearing before the divinity as your witness: 'to lift up the right hand to heaven, is the natural form and ceremony of an oath'.[56] She lifted up her hand and swore, seems a not inappropriate descriptor of the Instagram staging of the image, while in the original, in the context of a crowd, the right hand is raised in flirtation and greeting. The same image in a distinct context signifies differently. The left hand, open palm, pointing away and downward, is the chironomic sign of secrets to be revealed, described as 'an artificial conceit ... ', that makes it seem as if some hidden matter will be brought forward to confirm an argument or make reason apparent.[57] As the gesture of this hand has been partially cropped out of the image, its purport must be assumed to be less pressing.

The most significant change, however, is not in the photograph but in its juxtaposition. The open-mouthed expression, of surprise, delight, desire to consume, to bite, to lick, tongue extended is evidently enough now posed beside and directed towards the product. The erect stick of lip gloss, its shadow aligned with Cardi B's look is posed so as to be, in appearance, ready to be grasped, to paint the open mouth, to colour—to fellate—the lips, and to enter labia and mouth. While this might seem extreme, the sexualized character of the montage can be resisted but it cannot but be apprehended at some level, conscious or preconscious, hypnopompic or oneiric. It is a drastic visual change and a complete alteration of the depiction by virtue of the company it keeps. Another time, another place, and

[56] John Bulwer, *Chirologia or the Natural Language of the Hand* (London: Henry Twyford, 1648) at 50.

[57] Ibid., at 35

the picture lives again as something new, installed for different viewers and here to commercial ends. The juridical significance of the Instagram for the purposes of the copyright infringement claim is formulated discursively as being the inclusion of the image in a different narrative of celebrity and merchandizing. The words change the character of the posting and so it serves a transformative narrative goal, but that misses the visual point which is that the rapper's remediation and cut and paste juxtaposition with the image of lipstick and brand insignia, with followers and likes enumerated, sold out in all capital letters above the post, creates a wholly new scopic experience and visual apprehension. While it may diminish the aesthetic value of the original and distract from art in favour of commerce, sex, and sale, it could not be accused of being any longer, in this time frame, colour, and context, the same image. The reality has been infringed visually, and if such is the case then the office of the judge and the obligation of the court is to look carefully, with raised eyes at the implications—the implexities—of the images juxtaposed.

It remains to conclude these preliminary protocols with both a cautionary observation and an expression of opportunity. Attention to colour, to mark and stain, pigment and tincture as manifest in judicial perceptions inserted as images is never neutral. Sumptuary law which regulated early modern codes of dress, the colours, cloths, and codes of consumption provided ranks and hierarchies of clothes and colours that served to delimit and define gender and status for social, political, and legal purposes.[58] That appearances are a profound feature of law's presence and legitimacy is a doctrinal conundrum insofar as legal dress was supposed to hide the actors and promote the textual reason of law and decision. Now that recent studies have pointed importantly to the theatrical props, roles, and performances ever present in the manifestation of judges and jurists, the elements of race and affect, colour in its multiple senses will confront the law-making process in ever more direct forms. The materiality of the immediate sensorium of legislation, trial, and enforcement, takes centre stage. Legal procedure has to adapt to the diffraction of the traditional discourse of law in the face of visual materials, platforms, and fragmentations. The fissures of discourse are also opportunities, however, and constitute potentially egalitarian prompts suggesting something of a birth to the image and the imaginal, an opening of law, by virtue of the visual media it uses and the accessibility of a justice that can be seen. The image viewed creates the viewing subject, and in doing so introduces and opens legal reason to judicial affect. Judgement has to face up to the senses, decision can no longer hide the complex sensorium of taste, discrimination, atmosphere, smell, and the whole diversity of feelings that have to date played such an unacknowledged and often repressed role in precedent. Putting the two points together, the caution relates to

[58] Alan Hunt, *Governance of the Cosuming Passions: A History of Sumptuary Law* (Basingstoke: Macmillan, 1998).

the danger of unacknowledged affect, the desires, moods, untutored reflections of childhood fantasies that imagery will always also introduce into the legal forum.

The shades of populism and the pressures of public opinion press against the walls of the court. This also provides an opportunity. The remediation of law, an embrace of the diffractive pace of fissure as generative of an unsettling of legal procedure and an opening of judgement. Images diffract because they precede and resist words. Pictures demand new methods of curation, critical analysis, and careful viewing of the specific depiction introduced and of the rhizomes that any given image will also invoke, consciously or otherwise, into the logic of apprehension and reason of rule. Image and affect, which have always been present, finally gain a systematic recognition and place as vital alternative media of apprehension and contestation of the viscera, the persons, senses, colours that appear before and now also in the law.

At its boldest the remediation of legality, the advent of images in judgements, brings colour to law at a time when issues of colour, of minority, of racial discrimination, of xenophobia and unthinking discrimination are peculiarly present. Law, bereft of protocols of viewing, submerged in the monochrome fog of the text will be unsettled, and judgement will be changed by new modes of scrutiny and the novelty of image and colour in the face of decision. The regimentations of the page, the linearity and binary quality of print has generated over time a monochromacity of thought and vision. The judge is trained in the binary antinomy of black and white, the opposition of two poles of the spectrum, without any space in between. The antinomy of all or nothing, no colour, all of the colours plunged anarchically together works to distract from difference and to deflect viewing from detail, from the *certum* of particularity. Awareness of colour, of the full depth and range of tints, hues and stains opens up a sensorium of wild difference, of unique particularities, and of singularity as irreducible difference across an inordinate spectrum of persons, things and actions.

8
Conclusion
Remediations

The court is at a distance from the event, removed from the persons, things, and actions that are being tried. The judge who inserts pictures in their reasoned and now also depictive decision is again separated from the encounters, textual, visual, virtual, and interpersonal of the agon of the litigation. The reader and viewer of the law report, which arrives later, or not at all, since many decisions are unreported, is again further removed from the dialogues, exchanges, images, and other instruments of live judgement. This book has laboured to show that each stage of this transmission across time and distance is also visually mediated and imaginally relayed. The depictions matter, and when inserted in precedential judgements they merit close and attentive scrutiny, deliberative method and a critical apparatus of selection and viewing that has to date been lacking but is now supplemented by the protocols of retinal justice set out here. The judicial insertion of visual materials necessitates a juristic methodology of looking with attention to the normative and precedential import and effect of the image, the seismic reverberations and dynamographic effects of this aesthetic force suddenly present as precedent. For the jurists who view and use the visual, for the interested public, and the media that report, viewing will necessarily also or indeed primarily, which is to say initially, interpret judgements in optical fashion. What is now and inescapably the spectacle of decision is the novelty of affective relay of occurrence and event. What becomes law in the popular, socially mediated imagination is increasingly likely to be triggered as a question less of reading than of viewing. It is the latter platforms of transmission, the pixelated passions and imaginal spectres of virtual notice that will be the conduit of norms and as such will hold public and cursive, rather than discursive, sway.

Historically law fears the image and counsels downcast eyes, a blindfolded justice, and the monochrome linearity of *ius scriptum,* a variant of *ratio scripta*, symbolized in heavy Gothic typeface on the printed page or in the UK the vellum instruments of legislation. The heavy signifiers of legality, the weighty tomes, hushed halls, quiet chambers, the elevated gravitas of enunciative sites all bear the umbrageous fog of history, the theatrical colours, obscure habiliments and enigmatic argots of the past, the *traditio* of time immemorial, beyond memory and all too often out of mind. Law is supposed to project a sense of gravamen, to be safe, unchanging, old, recognized and comforting as esoteric tradition

Judicial Uses of Images. Peter Goodrich, Oxford University Press.
 DOI: 10.1093/oso/9780192848772.003.0008

and familiarity of the sovereign regime. Judicial vision, while necessarily taking the form of spectacle, like rhetoric, is to be restrained, juristically cautious and encrypted symbolically. *Obscurum per obscurius*, the tenebrous explained by riddles, is one facet of the appearance of juridism as the comfort of the mystery of government, the *arcana imperii* or enigma of rule. This tendency is enforced by the default method of precedent which is not to look but to read an antique argot in a specialized socio-linguistic register. The vision in decision is now elsewhere, and so long as the displacement of the visual remains the case, retinal justice fails to be done. Law looks away in supposedly objective insensibility.

The narrative of the visible in the juridical starts with diagrams, schemata, and maps, which are treated as the equivalent of text, as linear encodings that represent persons and places which should be read rather than viewed as sensible aesthetic matter intruding on and diffracting the sense and sensibility of the textual. They proffer a reality effect, an excess of meaning whose function is to convey only that the *certum* or particularity visualized is real. Surplusage is thus the initial category of the viewings that precede and then flower with the advent of the photograph, where the image becomes an increasingly frequent ornament or superfluity in the narrative of judgement, an incident of the incidental but one which is also there in the *dasein* or being of judicial exposition and reasoning, part of the matter of decision. It is in being present, in its character as legal surplusage, that the optical figure shifts the meaning of the deliberation because law's historical and interpretative trajectory has always been to incorporate surplusage as a feature of *mens legis*, and so as nuance and specification, refinement of ambit and intention.

The sense of excess out of abundance, as doctrine frames it, is followed by more self-consciously superficial and light uses of imagery as comedic and interruptive in the sense of theatrical presentations of judicial affect and as relief from the tedium of trial. The other face of surplusage is thus the flotsam or accidents of images, the real emergent in decision as humour, as eros, as libidinal tensors condensing affects of judgement. Again, however, and there is no need to invoke Freud to allude to the interpretative importance of the humorous, of laugh and critique, the significance of visual jokes, caricatures, and cartoons has its roots in renaissance legal humanism and the *serio-ludere* of the emblem tradition. Tracking judicial visual materials into the contemporary leads then to photograph and film, bytes and gifs, Instagram and Tweets, Tik Tok and online games that now join the digital relay of legal texts as they fragment onto the multiple platforms and mobile optimized media of virtuality. Evidential and extispicious images play a heightened and increasingly self-conscious role as an augmented form of reality effect in which the subject matter of the event judged can be viewed in and on camera, screened, decrypted, and held to visual account. It is here that images most often make their way into judgements and so come to play the significantly overlooked role, tracked in this work, of apprehending and communicating legal rules, while also facilitating a greater accessibility, popular appeal, and diversity of visual forms of law's social presence. It is this remediation of the juridical that has most directly generated the topic addressed by retinal justice, that of the image as a normative relay of judicial precedent and visual record of legal governance.[1]

The final questions raised by a law that becomes visibly imaginal, and viserbally transmitted, are those of aesthetics and politics, a version of beauty and the beast by which I mean that the image enlivens and matterphorizes legality in an ambivalent form. The visual relay creates an indelible and affective record of a legal past and precedential rule that can be viewed and sensed differently, as pictured, as captured on celluloid, digitally, in colour, with sound and motion. That means that lawyers have to learn to look as opposed to looking away or looking down in the myopic pursuit of exclusively textual details. Lifting the penthouse lids, becoming sensible to images that matterphorize the figures of judgement means diversifying, discriminating aesthetically and ethically, aesethically, mixing levity and gravity as part of attending to the material and political character of the world law shapes and is fashioned by. It is appropriate to recall in such a context the early modern maxim, frequented often enough by common lawyers, *dum vivo video, dum video rideo*, meaning while I live I look, while I look I laugh, which implies I break out, I respond, I change both physically and in affect and thought. But more than that, one particular version of the epigram continues to specify, while I live, I look at human error and textual terror.[2] The transition from epistemology to ontology, from abstraction to sense, leads into the feelings of laughter and terror of the *comédie humaine* that judges witness and perform. Law is taught through humour and examples, often enough through comedic cases because laughter not only binds in memory but moves and embraces both physical and intellective novelty. When we laugh we change, not only through the dissipation of the stasis of melancholy but also because it is the surprise or the strangeness of the juxtaposition that triggers invention of both form and idea.

It is in the introduction of affect, the law of the passions, that the insertion of images has its greatest presence and effect.[3] To look is to be drawn into, to gaze further, to enter and engage in the affective dialogue of imaginal work, which, like dream work, triggers subjective desire, wish fulfilment, and the pleasure principle.

[1] Remediation is used here in the sense of the representation of one medium in another, in which process of translation the new medium is usually a supplement and remedy for the failings and limitations of the prior media. The term was coined by Paul Levinson in *The Soft Edge: A Natural History and Future of the Information Revolution* (London: Routledge, 1997). For elaboration of the concept, see David Bolter and Richard Grusin, *Remediatiion: Understanding New Media* (Cambridge, Mass.: MIT, 2000).

[2] In full: *dum vivo video, et dum video rideo / dum vivo, video / errorem in humanis / terrorem in libris*. Epigraph from Francis Lenton, *Characterismi or Lentons leasures Expressed in Essays and Characters Never Before Written On* (London: Mitchell, 1631). The briefer *video et rideo* can be found in use in woodcuts and legal emblems of the early modern era.

[3] This argument is well made in outline, with reference to Jerome Frank's concept of saying it with music, and so of multilevel judgements, in Mateusz Stępień, 'Say it with Images: Drawing on Jerome Frank's Ideas on Judicial Decision Making', 32 *Int. J. Semiotics of Law* 321 (2019).

The legal fear of the image is the jurist's anxiety in the face of emotion, and specifically when dealing with the haptic and all too vivid presence of the materiality of judgement. Law does not wish to look up from the text at the bigger scenario and greater context of bodies embedded in the social and political, the other and visible scene of networks and domains that appear as the subject matter of decision. Take as an example a body that seeks to appear directly, as an image of the corporeal real, without clothes, unmediated, maskless, simply and barely as it is, in court, to make a case for freedom of visual expression. The saga of the naked rambler is well known and occupied the UK and European Courts for over a decade because Stephen Peter Gough's determination to appear naked in public, in town and country, on planes and trains, in court and in prison, at the dentist and at the doctor, was variously deemed contempt of court, breach of the peace, 'threatening, abusive, or insulting behaviour' under the 1986 Public Order Act, infraction of an Anti-Social Behaviour Order, and under Article 9 of the European Convention on Human Rights, a threat 'to the interests of public safety, [and] the protection of public order, health or morals'.[4] In consequence of such a battery of diverse offences paradoxically occasioned by Biblical innocence, Gough spent roughly a decade in prison *au naturel*. As Gary Watt puts it, Michelangelo's David stands proud and naked in full public view, the site of innumerable touristic visits and viewings, immobilized flagrant public nudity, while Gough, ambulant in his birthday suit, spent over ten years incarcerated. The nude and the naked, stone and flesh are apparently to be strictly distinguished.[5] One is deemed socially and juridically to be art, the other is bestiality, nature viewed as unnatural which is in diverse senses a wild judgement.

The crucial point, without needing to rehearse the legal and political arguments as to visual propriety and panic, is that of the prohibitions upon viewing, the censorious blind eye of law. What is it that judge and jury, in the seclusion of the law court, in camera if need be, in well protected portals, refuse to countenance and will not look upon? Addressing the later stages of the case, in 2014, Gough was tried at Winchester Crown Court without being allowed to appear before the jury, because he was undressed. Fronted by proudly phallic statues outside the courthouse, the judge asked the defence barrister's pupil to enter the dock to see if when Gough rose for the Court he would be covered or visible from the jury benches. It was determined that the standing Stephen would be hidden by the front of the dock and only the very top of his pubic hair would be public, or vice versa. Nonetheless, he was banned from the Court and appealed the decision. This landed him in prison and later in the Court of Appeal, where he was allowed to appear naked, but

[4] *Gough v United Kingdom* (2015) 61 E.H.R.R. 8 para. 187.

[5] Gary Watt, 'Dress, Law and Naked Truth: Some Further Coverage', 7 *Cultural Studies in Fashion and Beauty* (2016) at 118. For Watt's extended views, on nudity and dress, see Gary Watt, *Law, Dress and Naked Truth: A Cultural Study of Fashion and Form* (London: Bloomsbury, 2013). Summarizing the implicit legal view that nakedness is uncivilized, but the nude is art.

only via video-link, and his sentence to thirty months incarceration was upheld. Here, in the appellate division, the unapparelled appellant did appear in Court, but only in the remediated form of on-screen, pixelated presence. The visible image of the nude subject was obscured because, as remarked by Lady Justice Rafferty, his nether self or 'person' was covered by a table.[6] *Oh tempora, oh mores, oh mensa.*

Isobel Williams, an artist of considerable *imaginosum*—she is a translator of Catullus—took a break from her live drawing of Japanese rope bondage clubs, to address the undressed and sketch the proceedings in court.[7] She had followed the case and in image and blog had raised the visual question of what it is that so terrifies the judicial eye. Her sketches ask why an Edenic rustic figure in the highly confined and regulated space of a courtroom cannot momentarily appear naked so as to make their argument *in personam,* which is also and necessarily *in corpore.* Video, photographs, and drawings of Gough walking dressed only in socks, boots, hat and rucksack, are freely available online, and Isobel Williams has produced many colourful and monochrome sketches of our man in the buff in Court, yet she is still not allowed to sketch the pictures *in vivo* in the trial chambers. Her depiction of the naked rambler seated, from memory, from one of the many earlier trials, recreates the stark contrast between the costumed barrister in formal attire and the starkers defendant seated but not in visible nakedness (Figure 8.1). The artist has drawn away the curtain, the architectural clothing of the front of the dock, to reveal what the eye will have seen only in the substituted form of imagination. The colour and contrast, the hair and beard, watch and boots of the defendant, the thin wire upon which the barrister's extended finger suggestively rests, combine to proffer a reality, a visceral, incarnadine presence in court which is what Gough has been, amongst other things, campaigning for and espousing as his cause for more than a decade. His argument, and I have seen him make it nakedly online, is that it is only when he gets undressed, when he normalizes being without clothes, that he discovers who he is. *Dasein* in the altogether.

What is most intriguing is that his argument is his body. His writing is his naked passage in the world. It is that argument which the court would not allow, that image which it could not tolerate or see, that body which had to be censored. A common law predicated upon exemplars was unwilling to view the exemplum. Lord Justice Clerk (Gill), after the extraordinary projection of labelling Gough 'an incorrigible exhibitionist', proceeds to extrapolate that 'If he seeks to express the view that an individual has the right to be naked at all times and in all places, there is nothing to prevent his doing so orally or in writing while remaining properly dressed'.[8] The *petitio principi* or logical error of assuming what he has to prove seems to have escaped the noble and learned judge. In Clerk's clerical view, being

[6] *Regina v Stephen Gough* [2015] EWCA Crim 1079.

[7] Isobel Williams, *Catallus: Shibari Carmina* (Manchester: Carcanet, 2021). Her blog on Gough can be found at http://isobelwilliams.blogspot.com/2015/12/the-naked-rambler-and-sitting.html.

[8] *Gough v H.M. Advocate* [2007] HCJAC 63, para. 76

Figure 8.1 Naked Rambler seated, by Isobel Williams http://isobelwilliams.org.uk/.

undressed is contemptuous behaviour, even if he seems also to have missed the point that Gough did get dressed—he put on socks and shoes and stopped there, omitted to go further in sartorial habiliment. Making the argument while fully dressed is what Gough contests and exhaustively demonstrates that he will not and cannot do. His sensible argument is the authenticity of nakedness, the innocence of truth without rhetorical or sartorial embellishment. He is engaged in an authentic representation of the corporeographic and chorographic argument that he claims as his legal right. This is his *theatrum corporis et iustitiæ*, performance art, post-dramatic theatre, and exemplification of a specific cause in a specific location in the only form that is true to the argument being made. I am not advocating that Gough should necessarily be allowed, or not allowed, to roam unannounced and naked, but rather the more restricted point that his genital liberality or lack of loin cloth *is* his expression, his cause and his argument. Whatever view the instant Court might take of the behaviour out of court, it is the refusal to look, the censorship of the immediate visual argument that is most striking. He can say, the judge seems to imply, anything he wishes, but he cannot show it, cannot be it, not even here, in a court, before a blindfolded justice and judges *en banc*. Where Phryne won her case by throwing off her cloak and appearing naked before the judges, Gough loses his appeal for not getting dressed. A difference of gender.

There can be no question that dress is an addition—a covering, tegument, carapace, and painted cloth of clothing. Images are added to the epidermal facia and a cloak or curtain is hung to hide the frons and most immediate façade of being. Isobel Williams captures this well by removing the veil and contrasting form to sartorial costume, the similarity of extended fleshy outstretched fingers and hirsute head, to the literal *sedentariam vitam* of the appellant. She reveals the image, the nude, that imagination otherwise is forced to project. Lady Justice Rafferty admits as much in the appellate judgement when she remarks of Gough's videolink appearance:

> There was on the nursery slopes of the trial[,] dialogue about whether if he were in court he would sit or stand. We are grateful to Mr Scott (who did not appear below) for explaining to us that any point arising from it falls away. By videolink from prison today he sat unclothed from the torso upwards, his lower body obscured by a table. For all we know he was clothed other than above the waist.[9]

Gough does not get to appear, save in remediated form, and the judge makes a point of dismissing that appearance, choosing to remark that she has noticed that he cannot be seen in full and perhaps puns upon the sitting or standing person. Any point arising falls away, deflated by video, flaccid *in absentia*, and obscured by a table. The nursery slopes of dialogue and implicit infantilization of the naked *in cathedra* appellant are legally irrelevant and yet incorporated into the judgement by reference and by video-linked live performance. The Court is concerned with pronouncing a verdict, speaking the truth, but it does not wish to look at the truth

[9] *Regina v Gough* para. 7.

or confront the reality of the body. To say that 'for all we know he was clothed' is to mark a looking away, a stalling of vision and rejection of the image that is condemned—imprisoned—without being seen in full or glory.

The courtroom artist Williams makes the point quite brilliantly in a second sketch (Figure 8.2). The drawing itself, recollect, is from memory, already censored because she dare not sketch in court for fear of imprisonment.[10] She has to remember, she has to use the interior image, the memorized imprint, and it loses its colour and force. Now it is lines, the linearity of law's self-image and reports. Only Gough's face, the Christian *haec imago*, appears over the bar of the dock that he was not allowed to enter. He is smaller, somehow more frail, less real, and the barrister, *amicus curiae*, is in the pit, lower, distanced, and has faded into indistinction, features fallen away, an actor going through the motions in the process of seeming to shrink and disappear. Considering the contrast, witnessing the two images and their difference—viewing colour, skin, and flesh, as mattering—we realize that vision was stopped on the nursery slopes of viewing. What could be seen was left to the indeterminacy of 'for all we know', the scopic drive halted as Rafferty LJ looks away from the screen in exact replication of the trial Court's looking away from the defendant who is not allowed to appear. It is, to coin an expression, a form of scotomization, a species of *damnatio praesentiae et corporis*. It would seem that in addition to the classical maxim and foundational principle *audite et alterem partem*, the case of Stephen Peter Gough suggests that we now need to add, in the modern tongue, the more expansive visual principle that one must see the other side as it wishes to appear, and in the red letter of Latin maxims, *vide alterem partem*. In the French so fond to early modern lawyers, *gardez un œil pour l'accusé. Habeas corpus* might be supplemented by *video corpus*. In court, in camera if need be, but before the law, even if only temporarily—a screen can be provided, as one Scottish sheriff put up in court, and the defendant can be ordered to sit after making their stand—the image has a right to appear.

The case was about nakedness, the bare fact of being undressed constituting an offence—and as the Court also noted, numerous distinct offences in different jurisdictions and courts—through appearing clotheless in Halifax, as also, to name but a few sites of underdress, in Winchester, Basingstoke, Edinburgh, and Perth. The body as an image, bare appearance in the skin, 'genitalia and buttocks', had led to the appellant being tried without being allowed to be present. The legal issue was in significant part nakedness and yet even in coming before the law, with the liberty of the subject at stake, Gough was denied the right to appear. The trial court refused to look, to view the naked subject, and on appeal, precisely on the question of whether blind trial was unfair, he was consigned to a video-link of

[10] On the rules of contempt of court and specifically the 1925 Criminal Evidence Act, see Peter Goodrich, 'Remediation', 1 *Art, Law, Politics* 21 (2021).

Figure 8.2 Naked Rambler in the dock http://isobelwilliams.org.uk/.

which the judge makes a point of stating that she could not see him and did not care to inquire or look at the subject of her judgement. His right to appear was denied and denied again, and his appearance, his argument *in vivo*, *in nudo*, was prohibited by a table, by a video-link, by a judge who intriguingly does not require that he rise in the presence, virtual though it might be, of the Court. Justice was not seen to be done because the view of the body was shuttered out.

It seems extraordinary from the perspective of retinal justice that the law, in its search for truth, in pronouncing verdict and verity, dare not look at the unclothed, at the naked truth, and so refuses to even countenance the one claim, argument, and statement that Stephen Peter Gough had relentlessly sought to make for over a decade, namely the silent expatiation of his being and being bare. Why refuse the justice of seeing the event? Why close the doors of the Court in this bizarre reversal of the writ of *habeas corpus* in which the one body charged with seeing that imprisonment is justified cannot itself look at the imprisoned in their universal ontological state, as naked *dasein* that paradoxically cannot be there where his presence is cause and consequence of the trial. The Court chooses what it will see, and so selects, both repressing and unveiling the object of judicial cognition, or in the older and more replete language, conusance, upon which it will deign to deliberate. A different image, the reverie which mixes an oneiric or unconscious spectre of the naked Gough, substitutes for any actual appearance or visual statement of his case. The secondary and distanced images, projected mental depictions, remove the subject to the judicial interior, and in appearance at least an abstract, objective textual case, the shellac of positivism, takes the place of Gough's essentially optical claim.

The peculiarity of the continuing conflict over the naked rambler, and this seems in its way very contemporary, is that when the legal issue is a question of visibility in its barest form, a matter of depicting the limits of the image—call it *imago*, skin, covering, carapace, integument, protection—the decision is taken without looking or, on appeal, with viewing obscured, distanced and deflected. The courtroom artist Isobel Williams has to depict a trial that did not take place, the fantasm of an encounter, the interior and concealed imagery of the objective unconscious. Is it impossible to look at the sketch of the defendant being cross-examined? If not, and I have reproduced it here for that very reason, then what does it indicate of retinal justice that the scene depicted could not be looked at directly in those several cases where Gough was not allowed to appear? The occasions when he was placed behind a screen, hidden or exiled from the presence of the law, are lent an air of the comedic, of unnecessary blindness. The pivot of retinal justice and the all too frequent bar to vision that the law imposes has been lengthily pursued in the present work and has encountered variously impediments, blockages, and deflections by means of which judges glance, peruse, scan, and scotomize rather than allowing any extensive scrutiny or attentive and extended viewing, even where those images are reproduced in judgements. The image is deemed superficial and gains in the main only cursory examination. The practiced ambulation of the eye, the focus upon visual detail, aesthetic methodologies, historical artistic sensibilities are all side-lined. *R v Gough* is an extreme and so exemplary instance in which the judges refuse the image the right to appear in court and most decidedly do not include it in the judgement handed down. The image is too real, too haptic and visceral of the defendant's countenance to be countenanced. It is projected out of court and out of record and such exclusion marks a significant absence of retinal justice. Whatever the sentiment or sense of the anti-social behaviour at issue might be in substantive forms and formulas, exclusion of the image is a symptom of an unfortunate blindness of law, a missing of the point, replacement of examined depiction by interior phantasm.

The sketch by court artist, poet, and translator Isobel Williams is evocative of the tradition of *serio-ludere*, or playful instruction that this particular courtroom scene, replayed over some fifteen years of prosecuting and imprisoning Gough, can provide. The contrast between costumed barrister and nude defendant humorously borders on role reversal. The naked truth, the unconcealed evidence, the bare faced, although with beard and boots, crinose and crepidarian, is juxtaposed with the overdressed advocate who is supposed, purple at his back, to be seeking the truth. The colour, the tones and stains equally indicate a comedy of sensibilities in which the lawyer is garbed in black and white, as if a printed page, while the room and the accused are aesthetically a more vivid sensorium and fuller flesh tone. It is a remarkable record of an image that is absent from the trial. It has the curious status of a quasi-juridical record, a scene from the memory of prosecution, although it is much more likely to be seen than the law report—justice unseen—of the decision. The aesthetics of the image, the humour of these unconventional contrasts is peculiarly significant of an aesthetic in which it is precisely the image, in the text or here exterior to the judgement, that opens the trial to the world and evidences the sensibilities and insensibilities of jurists in their theatrical home, their world of play or juridical and emblematic *serio-ludere*. The aesthetic and ludic, sketches, cartoons, television, film, streaming are now ever more present and instructive. Indeed, insofar as law is aimed to teach, to instruct behaviour, to appeal to the young, the visual record, the diffraction of imagery becomes ever more central, as traced in this work, to the practice of precedent and transmission of rules.

It would be wrong to end by suggesting that something as serious as being imprisoned is simply comic, save in the sense that it belongs to the comedy, the theatre and records of law as seen in coloured sketch or photograph—*theatrum sexualis et iustitiæ*. The point of the naked example is a different one, that the Court would not look and would not allow the bare presence of the plaintiff. The trial is always itself but a sketch, an essay that attempts to re-enact encounters and events that occurred elsewhere and at other times. It is, however, also an *in vivo* process and so explicitly a matter of sensibilities, of aesthetic and dramatic character, of bodies, clothes, costumes, roles, and dialogic parts and performances. The history of law and particularly the records upon which its narrative is based have tended towards the monochrome and linear. The dead letters of the reports are a rather covert, distanced and, by linguistic argot, occluded manner of recording. If the image, to borrow from St Augustine, gives life, it is the coming to life, the *lex animata* of legal action that provides the fodder of theatrical and filmic courtroom drama, but also manifests most often the initial encounter of citizen—subject, lawyer, judge—with the nomosphere, the dominion, both exterior and interior, of the governance of behaviour, the *oikonomia* of administration. The narrative and depictions, the invocations of what was seen and heard, are the didactic record, the public face of the legal institution that subsists and that holds a citizen, a subject, kin, and compatriot, to a common path and law. The importance of such imagery in judgements, as instances of diffraction, is difficult to comprehend and equally hard to overstress in imaginal times when the juridical is likely to lose its force if it fails to stream its presence and legitimacy, trials and decisions, in accessible forms. The image becomes the deed that the public sees and that instrumentality is now incorporated into the text that relays precedent.

It is for the latter and compelling reason that the visible exscription of judgement, the imaginal transmission of legal decision necessitates the development of a methodology of viewing, and in scholarly and propaedeutic manners it is necessary *ridendo et pigendo docere*, to institute dramatic instruction in and through the affect and impact of images and the instruction of the body in the apprehension of appearances. This requires attention to what appears, scrutiny of the vivid reasons for deciding and so an aesthetics of law in the mode of retinal justice. We are impelled thus to a visual jurisprudence, an optical epistemic that looks at the colours and forms, contexts and composition of what we see at trial, recorded as decision and passed on as the imagery of precedent. Lived law is the memory of judgement, the incorporation of record and tradition, past practice brought to life in current encounters, as also in the imagination of future events. It is tempting not to look, or not to look too closely because the law is often the record of trauma and death, pathology and conflict. Failure to look is not only blindness rather than insight, it is abdication of responsibility, a shirking of the historical and political task of judgement, which is to recollect and direct, to act ethically in light, which is to say in the optics of the law's own prior practices, its symbolic atlas and now also augmenting gallery of events. Bare life, *zoē*, should not be excluded from that record, quite the contrary, as current philosophy stresses, the distinction between naked life (*zoē*) and political life (*bios*) has been the trigger of genocide and exterminism. Bare life is never simply bare, it cannot be merely expendable, it must not be wasted.

The argument in support of retinal justice, of looking and critically discerning the available images of persons, contexts, encounters, and events as manifest parts of judgement is simply an extension of the argument in favour of *in vivo* trial as opposed to paper determinations wholly *in abstracto*. Returning to the Court of Appeal decision and Lady Justice Rafferty's disdain for looking upon a naked body, further observations are pertinent. Stephen Peter Gough had been excluded from court for refusing to agree to wear clothes, when the right to be naked, in his birthday suit, was the essence of his plea. Lady Justice Rafferty excluded him from court again but allowed a video-link appearance from prison. When she now looks, she determines that his words may be false because for all she can see he might be dressed from the waist down. The table obscures his lower portion and parts, but in looking she does not know and cannot see. A whole new meaning to what troubled Winston Churchill about Latin, the vocative of *mensa*—oh table—but more importantly she does not want to see, does not have Gough rise upon the entrance of the judges, does not have him stand for the affirmation of verdict.[11] She positively resists looking at bare life and so long as judges, legislators, sovereign figures, and governments refuse to look, observe, attend, and acknowledge *zoē* in its primacy, it will remain excluded and expendable. She says 'for all we know' he was clothed below the table, but the point is that she does not know, and will not look, refuses to care, denies feeling, turns away. It is a short historical and theoretical step to bare life being unrecognizable, unseen, dispensable, and disposed. Closed eyes do not make for open justice. All that remains, ironically, is the image, as the exterior materialisation of the absent form, the matterphor of spectres, of the dead. This is the subject of the final case of judicial insertion of images with which this study will end.

The insistent question posed by judicial looking away, by the refusal to view, denial of optical scrutiny, is that of retinal injustice or scopicide. Looking would allow the eye to come alive to the image, the skin that is there to be seen and which often constitutes the ocular scope of *in vivo* discovery. To see, to quiet the chatter of discourse and open to look at the living matter of body, skin, painting, photogram, or clip is to encounter a haptic world of sense, sound, smell, breath, movement, and colour, both external, as viewed, and internal, as seen. It is in the spirit, record, and point of view of looking at the excluded, at bare life, in visual pursuit of the commonality of forms of life, the *zoē* that is shared and passed on, that I will look a last time in this exercise at judicially inserted images that were placed in a dissenting judgement as a record of lynching, exclusion, and liquidation of voting rights activists. The image of the dead, the spectre or ghost of lives excluded and ended, precisely because of their nude colour, their naked life, is the subject matter, the matterphor and image of a final instance, the last call of retinal justice to look and see again. In a voting rights case that was before the Ohio courts for a decade and finally decided in 2016, a section 1983 action was filed challenging the constitutionality of state laws requiring county boards of elections to reject the ballots of absentee and provisional voters whose identification envelopes or affirmation forms contained an address or birth date that did

[11] According to Françoise Wacquet, *Latin or the Empire of a Sign: From the sixteenth to the twentieth centuries* (London: Verso, 2001) at 140–141: when Churchill's Latin master explained that *mensa* could mean a table or o table, he continued to elaborate 'O table – you would use that addressing a table, in invoking a table ... you would use it in speaking to a table'. 'But I never do' Winston exclaims and thereafter gave up on Latin.

not perfectly match voting records, reducing the number of post-election days for absentee voters to cure identification-envelope errors, and for provisional voters to present valid identification, and limiting the ways in which poll workers could assist in-person voters.

In the dissenting judgement, holding the restrictions on voting to be unconstitutional, Circuit Judge Damon Keith, the grandchild of slaves, proffered the history of martyrdom suffered by those struggling in the cause of voting rights: 'The Majority's actions must be viewed in full light of their historical context ... the utter brutality of white supremacy in its efforts to disenfranchise persons of color is the foundation for the tragedy that is the Majority's effort to roll back the progress of history. I will not forget, I cannot forget ... '[12] Then there follows a photo essay aimed at contextualizing the facts of the case and their legal analysis. Thirty-six photo-portraits are reproduced, of subjects killed by lynch mobs, by the Klu Klux Klan, by white terrorists. The figures include Emmet Till and Martin Luther King. Two of the thirty-six montages will have to suffice here to resonate and demonstrate the case. The faces of those murdered while acting in the cause of enfranchisement, the collectivity, small though the example may be, places the visual history in the record and includes the narrative of discrimination in a remediated form as the policy concern underpinning the correct interpretation of the Equal Protection Clause of the Fourteenth Amendment and the later Voting Rights Act. To see is to witness, to evidence in the etymological sense of making visible and encountering the *certum* of what can be viewed. The judge follows the model of the Nuremberg trial in using images to engage with atrocity and represent the dead, who cannot be present except as images, as revenants, as spectres (Figure 8.3). It also remediates the judgement in a manner that indicates the affect, the sense of outrage, loss, and inequality that necessarily impinges upon decision and shifts medium and attention from the abstraction of linear rules to the haptic and affective materiality of images, of faces which constitute the viewer as a subject, someone who looks, and so triggers responses, feeling and thought.

To laugh, to cry, to learn in the blushes, tingles, insufflations and exhalations, grunts, groans and groinings of the body, is to encounter and engage. The *perpetuum mobile* of being joins legal subjects to vision as opening and response, as making what is visible matter to viewer and viewed. It is the task of visual jurisprudence to do retinal justice, to express in multiple media, modalities and forms, to enter the scene, join the event as it is now at issue and, even when inanimate, as brought to life, to image, as the living subject of judgement. The critical use of images can give law an aesthetic accessibility and credibility that allows it to open the specialism and argot of jurists to public view and so matterphorize the subjects of juridical abstraction and make law more sensible to the being that is judged. The goal of retinal justice is in this transhumanistic sense directed more at the

[12] *Northeast Coalition for the Homeless v Husted* 837 F.3d 612 (2016) at 639.

	In 1955, **Emmett Louis Till**, a 14-year-old boy on vacation, reportedly flirted with a white woman in a store.[6] Three nights later, two men took Till from his bed, beat him, shot him and dumped his body in the Tallahatchie River. One of Till's murderers reflected, "I just decided it was time a few people got put on notice. As long as I live and can do anything about it, niggers are gonna stay in their place. Niggers ain't gonna vote where I live."[7] An all-white jury declared the men innocent of murder.[8]
	In 1957, **Willie Edwards Jr**. was assaulted by several Klansmen who threatened to castrate him, took him to a bridge, and forced him to jump,[9] all for allegedly making advances toward a white woman.[10]

Figure 8.3 Insertion by Circuit Judge Damon Keith in *Northeast Coalition for the Homeless v Husted* (2016).

profession and via that guild, to the judiciary, the legal delegates of the sovereign, as an encouragement and protocol for daring to look, for lingering in vision and insight, and for deciding in full view of the living images, the visual records that history has thrust their way as the visceral moment and vivid form of precedent, born often enough from the trauma of trial. To see is to extend into the sensible, to acknowledge affect as integral to judgement and as an infringement of the real as seen in the record. What the dissent in *Husted* seeks to show is the image of bare life claiming political status, *bios*, when the mode of Emmett Louis Till and Willie Edwards Jr's inclusion was that of exclusion and death. They represent visually the impolitical exception, the foundation of imperialist politics in bare life. Sovereign power is predicated upon the double structure of law and anomie, lawful and outlawed, to which correspond, as Agamben details, the historical categories of authority (*auctoritas*) and bare power (*potestas*): 'The originary structure of Western politics consists in an *ex-ceptio*, in an inclusive exclusion of human life in the form of bare life.'[13] The imaginal presence of those who were sacrificed outside of law, martyred in their effort to engage and enter the political, represent, in

[13] Giorgio Agamben, *The Use of Bodies: Homo Sacer IV, Vol. 2* (Palo Alto: Stanford University Press, 2015) 264.

monochrome, the particular form and colour that *caput lupinum*, the perceived outlaw, took and to a degree still takes.

It is the phantasm of skin colour, the symptomatically incarnadine facial hue, that triggers unconscious affects which take in this history, our history, in the form of rage and homicidal intent towards the excluded, the figure of the outlaw and of life rendered bare. The image in the judgement introduces in stark form the subjects and matter of the particular decision. The imaginal medium of the record becomes the vehicle, the affective and material form of the murdered living on, the hauntological as ontological, entering the trial and looking back at the law.[14] The images necessitate response and constitute a viewing subject, who opens to or in the case of the majority shuts out even though the haunting and responsibility are necessarily there. The photo-portraits materialize and even where they provoke resistance to the occurrences and events that the depictions relay, they roam, looking at those not ready to see, which Derrida terms the *visor effect:* 'we do not see who looks at us'.[15] To borrow a cautionary note from Ertür, '[l]ike every ghost, the ghost of this trial that we encounter today is an impoverished and distorted version of the life, the live event it once was, inflected through various chauvinisms, or various modalities of resentment, enmity, frustration, grief, longing, and desire'.[16] The inclusion of photo-portraits and biographical thumbnails act as a passport to the present and to a sensibility that exceeds prose. They activate what can be hazarded as an unconscious of law, the disruption of the spectacle of trial, exposing its structures and activating ghosts – *revenants* – in counter-forensic engagement, in the generation of possibilities.[17] The visual portrayals institute a juridico-political aesthetic that challenges the viewer and dissents from the majority decision in medium as well as argument. Those killed become spectres haunting the judgement, making and continuing to make the claim to a right to be seen, to be heard, to matter, as the precondition to political existence and inclusion. Epidermal imperialism should be contested in colour, now that technology so allows. It is to that more proximate visual infringement of the real that retinal justice responds.

Custom is costumed, the face is the image and likeness, in Western aesthetic theology it is that of the Father in the Son, but however much sensible life and notions of civility require dress or death, the skin remains the primary image and colour. It becomes a fetish, an *objet petit a*, in the obscure orientation of desire, in the primal scenes of Pornhub, as well as the leisured ambience of fine art in the white cube of the gallery or statuary in Florence. The biblical body and its carnal

[14] On the pun, see Jacques Derrida, *Specters of Marx* (New York: Routledge, 1994) at 10.

[15] Ibid., at 7: 'This spectral other looks at us ... Here anachrony makes the law. To feel ourselves seen by a look which it will be impossible to cross, that is the *visor effect* on the basis of which we inherit the law'.

[16] Başak Ertür, *Spectacles and Specters: A Performative Theory of Political Trials* (New York: Fordham University Press, 2022) at 141.

[17] Ibid., at 184–185.

knowledge are originary images, and it is symptomatic that it is the gaze of the excluded, the look of Emmett Till, historically, ignominiously the other colour of what was purportedly white culture, that unleashes the inarticulate and aphasic, epidermal rage of the mob that kills him. When words run out it is often only images that remain, untamed, unconscious, and unthought. The image thinks the body that acts. In such cases, we do not see so much as we are seen through. Visuality is in significant degree the trigger of discourse, the exterior inside that propels dialogue that will both mark and mask the event. What then is to be done and where to end? The epistemic of the epidermis has to be undressed, addressed and redressed. The face is the body. It is the image. Haunted, ambulant, mobile, visible being. The superficiality of juridical vision, the lack of ocular focus, the blindfold that supposedly replaces opinion with impartiality, in fact operates here as projection of prejudice. Not to look closely is simply to impose a prior view, to presuppose the character, quality and color of the subject, to overlook by overlaying assumption upon fact. The process of abstraction whereby facts become norms and the 'is' transforms into the 'ought', *sein* into *sollen*, seems to entail a looking away, a blurring of detail and of focus which results in displacing the viewed by legal precognition which is also miscognition. Most importantly the absence of attention to colour, the insistence upon monochrome, generates an unthinking polarization, quite literally black and white, antinomy, with the space in-between erased, and the infinite degrees of difference also eradicated. All is difference, in colour, tone, hue, aspect and movement. Not to look is not to see but rather to abstract and generalize as if two colours were the same, as if difference was to be grouped as opposed to individuated, always dividuated.

As hinted throughout this work and now expressed with direct simplicity, judges as social examplars, need to open up to the vision in their decisions, and this means that they should be trained 'aesethically' in the use of images because at root the spectral mode of apprehension is a critical dimension of how they see and judge. As argued here, this means apprehending colour, diffraction, and affect as relayed through the imaginal presences in judgements. The gallery of judicially contrived precedential pictures should be catalogued and curated for all to see the juridical *in imagine*, in colour, as part of political life, as events of significance and visibility in the determinations of the law. What judges refuse to see, what Lady Justice Rafferty exiles, infantilizes to the nursery slopes of her case, is what she does not see but nonetheless imagines. Another haunting. What is not present is visible imaginally, in signs and words, pictures, portraits, statues that float in the reverie of perception and pre-judgement. The imperative of retinal justice is to look, to open up so as to open to the life that is viewed, the images that are seen, and either directly or indirectly judged or in their turn and wake trigger decision.

The zetetic passions of jurists deserve and demand a vision that is alive to the beings in motion, ambulant images, the insight and premonition that viewing engenders. Borrowing from T.S. Eliot, we end where we began, and so come to know the place where we started for the first time.[18] Technology has made law imaginal, more mobile, fragmentary, virtual and image-laden. This remediation, the increasingly visual relay of legality, inaugurates an ocular hermeneutics, a further layer and augmentation, but also a shift of focus and of the interpretative scrutiny that legal judgement requires. The protocols and rubrics of retinal justice are aimed at the future, at a visible and visualized spectacle of law's public presence and corporeal acts. The past, the pickle jar of precedent, the rear view mirror of case law, has of late seemed an increasingly inutilious and flawed methodology of decision. In one of the early depictions reviewed in the introduction the judge juxtaposed an ostrich and a besuited lawyer with their heads alike in the sand. The caricature was intended as an acerbic reprimand to derelict advocates for failing to cite precedents. The more significant optical import of the images, however, and an emblematic signification of the ostrich, is of the injustice of not looking, the civil wrong of blindfold and blindness. The remediation of the legal archive, the unloosing of text and image, the pictorial in the judicial, can catapult law into the lateral and ambulant dominion of retinal justice, the desideratum of slowing down discourse so as to attend to appearances and take the time to open up to and view subject and skin, the infinite particulars of persons, the individuation of individuals, as manifest in their colour, movement, signs and sounds. The scholastic tradition knew well enough that to think you have first to imagine. To judge you have first to look. In the old language one could say *ex visione lex*, which in our common law idiom means decision comes in vision.

[18] T.S. Eliot, 'Burnt Norton', in *Collected Works* (London: Faber and Faber, 1954): 'In my beginning is my end' (East Coker).

Table of Cases

All images are available in the cases cited but for ease of access, where the Press has had cold feet with respect to reproducing the image, they can be found as tabulated in the text at https://larc.cardozo.yu.edu/faculty-online-pubs/61/.

Australia

Aaron James Ring v Commissioner for Police (2019) QDC 32.	143
Ausbal Pty Ltd v Grandsea Holdings Pty Ltd [2014] VSC 625.	146
Australian Competition and Consumer Commission v Viagogo AG [2019] FCA 544.	147
Ben Pelech v Royle [2019] WASC 297.	147
Clare and Ors v Eva Bedelis [2016] VSC 381.	1, 60–64
Downie v Lockwood [1965] VR 257.	60
Emprja Pty Ltd v Red Engine Group Pty Ltd [2017] QSC 33.	146
Helen Sanders and Others v City of Perth [2019] WASC 226.	145–146
Kathryn Gill and Others v Ethicon Sàrl (No 5) [2019] FCA 1905.	147–150
Kelly Lange v Timothy O'Corrigan [2015] NSWDC 173.	168–174
Leichhardt Municipal Council v Daniel Callaghan Pty Ltd (1981) 46 LGRA 29.	60
Melbourne's Cheapest Cars PTY Ltd v Melbourne Street Cars [2004] FMCA 606.	146, 191–194
Metro Business Centre v Centrefold Entertainment Pty Ltd [2017] FCA 1249.	102–107
New South Wales Aboriginal Land Council v The Minister Administering the Crown Lands Act (Moira Park Road No 1 and Moira Park Road No 2 claims) [2015] NSWLEC 179.	49–56, 147
Ring v Commissioner for Police (2019) QDC 32.	143

Canada

R. v NS [2012] 3 SCR 726.	124
R v Nikolovski [1996] 3 RSC 1197.	150
R v Shaun Burgher [2016] O.J. No. 2738.	151–152

European Court of Human Rights

Gough v United Kingdom (2015) 61 E.H.R.R. 8.	242

Hong Kong

Chan Chuen v Forestside Limited High Court of Hong Kong HCA 2055/2011 (2016).	57–59

India

M. Siddiq v Mahant Suresh Das & Ors (2019) Civil Appeal Nos 10866-10867 of 2010. 33–39
Pramatha Nath Mullick vs Pradyumna Kumar Mullick & Another (1925) LR IA 245. 33
Ram Jankijee Deities v State of Bihar [1999] 5 SCC 50. 33

Ireland

Health Service Executive v Brookshore Ltd [2010] IEHC 165. 60

Israel

Dahan v. Shacharoff, 30823-08-16 (Herzliya Small Claims Ct. Feb. 24, 2017). 15–17

Seychelles

Popular Democratic Movement v Electoral Commission [2012] 5 LRC 109. 73

South Africa

State v Redhouse and Another (CC14/2017) [2018] ZAECPEHC 43 (26 July 2018). 174–177

United Kingdom

AAN (Veil) [2014] UKUT 00102 (IAC). 124
Croft and Howel (1578) 20 Eliz. Plow. Com. 537. 72
Designers Guild Ltd v Russell Williams (Textiles) [1998] F.S.R. 803. 204–209
Designers Guild Ltd v Russell Williams (Textiles) [2000] F.S.R. 121. 206
Designers Guild Ltd v Russell Williams (Textiles) [2001] FSR 113. 204, 209
Eaton College Case (1557) 73 Eng. Rep. 327. 73
Ener-G Holdings plc v Hormwell [2012] EWCA civ 1059. 73
European Central Bank v Document Security Systems Inc [2008] EWCA Civ 192. 108–111
Genner against Lucking (1614) Hill. 11 Jac. B. R. Roll. 499. 72
Gough v H.M. Advocate [2007] HCJAC 63. 243
Hearst Holdings v A.V.E.L.A. [2014] EWHC 439 (Ch). 112–117
In re Pascoe (1944) 170 Law Times 171 [Ch. Div.]. 73
Lancashire County Council v Mr A and Mr B The Children (By their Children's Guardian) (2016). 15
Marriot and Pascalls Case 1 Leonard 159. 3, 7–12

Continued

Continued

Mutual Energy Ltd v Starr Underwriting Agency Ltd. (2016) 165 Con. L.R. 220	73
Nigel Peter Moore v Brent Waterways Board [2009] EWHC B12 (Ch).	40–41
PMS International Group Plc v Magmatic Limited [2016] UKSC.	5, 178–180
R v D (R) [2014] 1 LRC 629.	124
R v MacFarlane [1994] Q.B.419.	72
R v Morris-Lowe [1985] 1 W.L.R. 29	72
R (on the Application of Ghai) v Newcastle City Council [2009] EWHC 978 (Admin).	61
Regina v Stephen Gough [2015] EWCA Crim 1079.	243, 245
Samsung Electronics (UK) Ltd v Apple Inc [2012] EWHC 1882 (Pat).	177–180
Samsung Electronics (UK) Ltd v Apple Retail Inc [2012] All ER (D) 176 (Oct).	177
Spicer v Commissioner for Police of the Metropolis [2019] EWHC 1099 (QB).	216–218
Sydenham and Worlington's Case (1585) Godbolt 32, 78 Eng. Rep. 20.	71
Temple Island Collections v New English Teas Limited [2012] EWPCC 1.	182
United States of America	
35 Bar & Grille, LLC et al. v City of San Antonio 943 F. Supp. 2d 706 (W.D. Tex. 2013).	87–89, 103
A.D. LLC v 2004 Partners LLC 860 N.W.2d 341 (2014).	129, 146
Aileen Brooks v IT Works Marketing 2022 WL 2079747. 2022 WL 2079747.	4
Anand v Heath 2019 WL 2716213.	216
Andy Warhol Found. for the Visual Arts v Lynn Goldsmith 382 F.Supp. 3d 312 (2019).	219
Andy Warhol Foundation for the Visual Arts v Lynn Goldsmith 11 F.4th 26 (2021).	218–220
Andy Warhol Foundation for the Visual Arts v Lynn Goldsmith 143 S.Ct 1258 (2023).	
Animal Welfare Institute v Beech Ridge Energy 675 F.Supp.2d 540 (2009).	52
Aquifer Guardians in Urban Areas v. FH.A 779 F. Supp. 2d 542 (2011).	55
Austin Gates v Hassan Khokhar 884 F.3d 1290 (2018).	121
Berkson v Gogo LLC 97 F. Supp. 3d 359 (E.D.N.Y. 2015).	142, 216
BWP Media USA V Gossip Cop Media 196 F.Supp.3d 396 (2016)	227
Capitol Square Advisory Board v Pinette 515 U.S. 811, 115 S.Ct. 2440 (1995).	8–10, 13
Carmen John Perri v Public Storage et al. 2019 WL 7881617.	146
Clark v Wodehouse 669 P.2d 101 (1983).	61
Conrad v AM Community Credit Union 750 F.3d 634 (2014).	178–179

Construction & General Laborers' Local Union No. 330 v Town of Grand Chute 834 F.3d 745 (2016).	1–2
Courthouse News Service v Brenda Forman 606 F.Supp.3d 1200 (2022).	19, 102, 234
Courtland Company v Union Carbide 2022 WL 2392871.	70
CX Digital Media Inc. v Smoking Everywhere 2011 WL 1102782.	14
David Jeans v John Varga 2019 U.S. Dist. LEXIS 171401, 2019 WL 4857720.	146, 152–153
Dariana Mizrahi v Yamaha Motor Corp. 2019 WL 3890311.	146
Diana Randolph v Forever 21 Inc 2017 WL 2901330.	197–200
Federal Election Commission v Christian Action Network 894 F.Supp. 946 (1995).	234–255
Fleischer Studios, Inc. v Freundlich, Inc 5 F.Supp. 808 (1934).	115
Gilles v Blanchard 477F.3d 466. (7th Cir. 2007).	44
Gonzalez-Servin v. Ford Motor Company 662 F.3d 931 (2011).	18–19, 21, 97, 196
Hayuk v Starbucks (2016) 157 F.Supp.3d 285.	213–215
HouseCanary, Inc. v Quicken Loans, Inc Civil Action No. SA-18-CV-0519-FB (2018).	53–57, 82–83
Hubbert v Dell 835 N.E. 2d 113 (2005).	216
In re Zappos 893 F.Supp.2d 1058 (2012).	216
Insite Vision Inc. v Sandoz Inc 2013 U.S. Dist. LEXIS 1602.	17
Jackson v Beasley 712 So.2d 162 (1998).	76–77, 80
James and Cynthia Kochanski v Speedway SuperAmerica LLC 850 N.W.2d 160 (2014).	129, 141–142
Jeannie Netherly v Martin Vincent Turco 2017 Tex. App. LEXIS 6053, 2017 WL 2774448.	19
Judy Stabile v Paul Smith Ltd 137 F.Supp.3d 1173 (2015).	213
Kochanski v Speedway SuperAmerica LLC 356 Wisc.2d 1 (2014).	129
Kruge v Workers' Compensation Appeal Board 2014 WL 273809.	42–43
Kuhn Constr., Inc v Diamond State Port Corp., 990 A.2d 393, 396–97 (Del. 2010).	72
La Michoacana Natural, LLC v. Maestre 611 F.Supp.3d 87 (2020).	188–191
La Sonya Robertson v Clarksville-Montgomery County School System 2018 WL 3199219.	92–95
Luis Rincon v Home Depot USA 2019 WL 6118406 (2019).	135–136
Michael Dick v Pilot Travel Centers, LLC 2018 WL 2761407.	85–86

Continued

Continued

Michelle Hunt v Sunny Delight Beverages Co 2018 WL 6786265.	152
Milatz v. City of Cincinnati 145 N.E.3d 1117 (2019).	129, 133–134
Nguyen v Barnes & Noble 763 F.3d 1171 (9th Cir. 2014).	216
Nikki Shivone Long v State of Maryland WL 4898877 (2019).	45–49
Northeast Coalition for the Homeless v Husted 837 F.3d 612 (2016).	252
Omar Grayson v Harold Schuler 666 F.3d 450 (2012).	90–91
Ray Evers Welding Co. v Occupational Health and Safety Review Commission 625 F.2d 726 16 (1980).	155
Richard Culotta v Doubletree Hotels LLC 2019 Tex. App. LEXIS 5272.	137–138
Roy Ruffino v City of Puyallup 377 F. Supp. 3d 1205 (W.D. Wash. 2019).	146
Sandifer v United States Steel Corporation 678 F.3d 590 (2012).	156–158, 161, 165
Sandifer v United States Steel Corporation 134 S.Ct. 870 (2014).	157
Schwartzwald v Oath Inc 2020 WL 5441291.	121
Scott v Harris 550 US 372 (2007).	76, 129–131, 143, 198
Sheryl Lynn Schaefer v United States 2017 WL 2506174.	139–140
Sikhs for Justice v Badal 736 F.3d 743 (2013).	184–186
State v Miller 260 Ga. 669, 398 S.E.2d 547 (1990).	122
State v Walter 479 S.W. 3d 118 (2016).	224–226
Steven Ferdman v CBS Interactive 342 F.Supp.3d 515 (2018).	228–229, 235
Trident Center v Connecticut General Life Insurance 847 F.2d 564 (9th Cir. 1988).	135
US v Lizarrago-Tirado 789 F.3d 1107 (2015).	43–45, 56, 75–76
Vintage Rodeo Parent LLC v Rent-A-Center, Inc (2019) WL 1223026.	72
Walsh v Townsquare Media 464 F.Supp.3d 570 (2020).	229–231
Wrench LLC v Taco Bell Corp. 51 F. Supp. 2d 840 (1999).	215
Zora Matteo v Kohl's Department Store Inc 2012 WL 760317.	198

Bibliography

Agamben, Giorgio. Opus Dei*: An Archaeology of Duty*. Palo Alto: Stanford University Press, 2013.

Agamben, Giorgio. *The Use of Bodies:* Homo Sacer *IV, Vol. 2*. Palo Alto: Stanford University Press, 2015.

Alciatus, Andreas. *Notitia utraque … Disputatio Adriani aug. et Epicteti philosophi*. Basle: n.p., 1552.

Alexopoulou, Sofia, and Antonia Pavli. '"Beneath This Mask There is More Than Flesh, Beneath This Mask There is an Idea": Anonymous as the (Super)heroes of the Internet?', *Int. J. Semiotics of Law* 34 (2021), 237–264.

Aneau, Barthélemy. *Picta poesis ut pictura poesis erit*. Lyon: Bonhomme, 1552.

Aneau, Barthélemy. *Jurisprudentia*. Paris: Ad Sagittarii, 1554.

Aoki, Keith, and Garrett Epps. 'Dead Lines, Break Downs & Troubling the Legal Subject: Or "Anything You Can Do, I Can Do Meta"', *Oregon L. Rev*. 73 (1994), 551–560.

Austin, Gilbert. *Chironomia, or a Treatise on Rhetorical Delivery: Comprehending many Precepts, both Ancient and Modern, for the Proper Regulation of the Voice, the Countenance, and Gesture*. London: Cadell and Davies, 1806.

Bachelard, Gaston. *Earth and Reveries of Will: An Essay on the Imagination of Matter*, translated by Kenneth Haltman. Dallas: Dallas Institute, 2002.

Bacon, Francis. *A Collection of Some Principall Rules and Maximes of the Common Lawes of England*. London: More, 1630.

Barthes, Roland. *The Rustle of Language*. New York: FSG, 1986.

Bataille, Georges. *Inner Experience*, translated by Stuart Kendall. New York: SUNY, 2014.

Beckett, Gilbert A. *The Comic Blackstone*. Sydney: Wentworth Press, 2019 edn.

Bellido, Jose. 'Looking Right: The Art of Visual Literacy in British Copyright Litigation', *Law, Culture and the Humanities* 10 (2014), 66–87.

Benjamin, Walter. 'The Work of Art in the Age of Mechanical Reproduction'. In *Illuminations: Essays and Reflections*, edited by Hannah Arendt, 217–253. New York: Schocken, 1968.

Berardi, Franco. *After the Future*. Chico, CA: AK Books, 2011.

Berliner, Moshe. 'When a Picture is not Worth a Thousand Words: Why Emojis Should Not Satisfy the Statute of Frauds' Writing Requirement', *Cardozo L. Rev*. 41 (2020), 2161–2201.

Bertetto, Paolo. *Le Miroir et le simulacre*. Rennes: PUR, 2015.

Biber, Katherine, Trish Luker, and Priya Devii Vaughan, eds. *Law's Documents: Authority, Materiality, and Aesthetics*. Abingdon: Routledge, 2021.

Bigg, Charlotte. 'Diagrams'. In *A Companion to the History of Science*, edited by Bernard Lightman, 557–571. Oxford: Wiley Blackwell, 2016.

Bittar, E.C.B. *Semiotics, Law, and Art: Between Theory of Justice and Theory of Law*. Geneva: Springer, 2021.

Bleecher, Donald et al. (eds), *Taking Exception to the Law: Materializing Injustice in Early Modern English Literature*, Toronto: Toronto University Press, 2015.

Blount, Thomas. *Glossograhia* [1656]. Menston: Scolar Press, 1969.
Blount, Thomas. *Fragmenta antiquitatis.* London: Atkins, 1674.
Boehme-Neßler, Volker. *Pictorial Law: Modern Law and the Power of Pictures.* Heidelberg: Springer, 2011.
Bolter, Jay David, and Richard Grusin. *Remediation: Understanding New Media.* Cambridge, MA: MIT Press, 2000.
Bond, Henry. *Lacan at the Scene.* Cambridge, MA: MIT Press, 2009.
Bottici, Chiara. *Imaginal Politics: Images Beyond Imagination and the Imaginary.* New York: Columbia University Press, 2014.
Brooks, Peter. '*Scott v Harris*: The Supreme Court's Reality Effect', *Law and Literature* 29 (2017), 143–149.
Brunschwig, Colette. *On Visual Law: Visual Legal Communication Practices and their Scholarly Exploration.* Bern: Weblaw, 2014.
Brunschwig, Colette. *Visual Law and Legal Design: Questions and Tentative Answers.* Bern: Weblaw Editions, 2021.
Bulwer, John. *Chirologia: or the Natural Language of the Hand. Composed of the Speaking Motions, and Discoursing Gestures thereof. Whereunto is added Chironomia: Or, the Art of Manuall Rhetoricke. Consisting of the Naturall Expressions, Digested by Art in the Hand, as the Chiefest Instrument of Eloquence, by Historicall Manifesto's, Exemplified Out of the Authentique Registers of Common Life, and Civill Conversation. With Types, or Chyrograms: A Long Wished for Illustration of this Argument. Manus membrum hominis loquacissimum.* London: Tho. Harper, 1644.
Burton, Robert. *Anatomie of Melancholy.* Oxford: Cripps, 1628.
Call, Lewis. 'A is for Anarchy, V is for Vendetta: Images of Guy Fawkes and the Creation of Postmodern Anarchism', *Anarchist Studies* 16 (2008), 154–172.
Camden, William. *Britannia: sive Florentissimorum regnorum Angliæ, Scotiæ, Hiberniæ et insularum adiacentium ex intima antiquitate chorographica descriptio.* London: Bishop & Norton, 1600.
Carnevali, Barbara. *Social Appearances: A Philosophy of Display.* New York: Columbia University Press, 2020.
Castañeda, Michelle. *Disappearing Rooms: The Hidden Theaters of Immigration Law.* Durham, N.C.: Duke University Press, 2023.
Castañeda, Michelle. 'Virtual Judges in Immigrant Detention: The Mise-en-Scène of No-show Justice'. In *Law and New Media: West of Everything*, edited by Christian Delage, Peter Goodrich, and Marco Wan, 169–196. Edinburgh: Edinburgh University Press, 2019.
Cavallar Osvaldo, Susanne Degenring, and Julius Kirshner, eds and trans. *A Grammar of Signs: Bartolo da Sassoferrato's Tract on Insignia and Coats of Arms.* Berkeley: University of California Press, 1994.
Coccia, Emanuele. *Sensible Life: A Micro-ontology of the Image.* New York: Fordham University Press, 2016.
Cole, Luke, and Keith Aoki. *Casual Legal Studies: Art during Law School.* Cambridge, MA: HLS Inc. Press, 1989.
Coras, Jean de. *Altercacion en forme de dialogue, entre l'Empereur Adrian et philosophe Epictéte.* Toulose: Porterie, 1558.
Cormack, Bradin. *A Power to Do Justice: Jurisdiction, English Literature, and the Rise of Common Law, 1509–1625.* Chicago: The University of Chicago Press, 2007.
Cormack, Bradin. 'Paper Justice, Parchment Justice: Shakespeare, *Hamlet*, and the Life of Legal Documents'. In *Taking Exception to the Law: Materializing Injustice in Early

Modern English Literature, edited by Donald Beecher, Travis DeCook, Andrew Wallace, and Grant Williams, 44–70. Toronto: Toronto University Press, 2015.

Critchley, Simon. *On Humour*. London: Routledge, 2011.

Daniell, Samuel. *The Worthy Tract of Paulus Iovius, Contayning a Discourse of Rare Inventions, both Militarie and Amorous called Imprese*. London: Waterson, 1585.

Davies, Christie. 'Judges and Humour in Britain: From Anecdotes to Jokes'. In *Judges, Judging and Humour*, edited by Jessica Davis and Sharyn Anleu, 41–74. Cham, Switzerland: Palgrave Macmillan/ Springer, 2018.

Debord, Guy. 'A User's Guide to Détournement'. In *Situationist International Anthology*, edited and translated by Ken Knabb, 14–20. Berkeley, CA: Bureau of Public Secrets, 2006.

Debray, Régis. *Cours de médiologie générale*. Paris: Gallimard, 1991.

Debray, Régis. *Vie et mort de l'image: une histoire du regard en Occident*. Paris: Gallimard, 1992.

Debray, Régis. 'The Three Ages of Looking', *Critical Inquiry* 21 (1995), 529–555.

Debray, Régis. *Le stupéfiante image*. Paris: Gallimard, 2013.

Delage, Christian. *Caught on Camera: Film in the Courtroom from the Nuremberg Trials to the Trials of the Khmer Rouge*. Philadelphia: Pennsylvania University Press, 2014.

Delage, Christian. 'Confronting the Nazis with Images of their Crimes'. In *Images of Conviction: The Construction of Visual Evidence*, edited by Diane Dufour et al. Paris: Editions Xavier Barral, 2015, 133–135.

Deleuze, Gilles, and Félix Guattari. *A Thousand Plateaus*, translated by Brian Massumi. Minneapolis: University of Minnesota Press, 1987.

Deleuze, Gilles. *The Logic of Sense*. London: Athlone Press, 1990.

Dellinger, Hamton. 'Words are Enough: The Troublesome Use of Photographs, Maps and Other Images in Supreme Court Opinions', *Harvard L. Rev.* 110 (1997), 1704–1753.

Derrida, Jacques. *Specters of Marx: The State of the Debt, the Work of Mourning, and the New International*, translated by Peggy Kamuf. New York and London: Routledge, 1994.

Derrida, Jacques. *Negotiations: Interventions and Interviews 1971–2001*. Palo Alto: Stanford University Press, 2002.

Desjarlais, Robert. *The Blind Man: A Phantasmography*. New York: Fordham University Press, 2019.

DiCioccio, Rachel, and Laura Little. 'Comedy Collides with the Courtroom', *Temple L. Rev. Online* 92 (2020), 1–24.

Didi-Huberman, Georges. *La Peinture incarneé*. Paris: Editions de Minuit, 1985.

Didi-Huberman, Georges. *Fra Angelico: Dissemblance and Figuration*. Chicago: Chicago University Press, 1995.

Didi-Huberman, Georges. *Confronting Images: Questioning the Ends of a Certain History of Art*. State College: Penn State University Press, 2005.

Didi-Huberman, Georges. *L'Image ouverte: motifs de l'incarnation dans les arts visuels*. Paris: Gallimard, 2007.

Didi-Huberman, Georges. *Images in Spite of All: Four Photographs from Auschwitz*. Chicago: Chicago University Press, 2011.

Didi-Huberman, Georges, *The Surviving Image: Phantoms of Time and Time of Phantoms: Aby Warburg's History of Art*. University Park: Pennsylvania State University Press, 2017.

Didi-Huberman, Georges. *Atlas, or the Anxious Gay Science*. Chicago: The University of Chicago Press, 2018a.

Didi-Huberman, Georges. *The Eye of History: When Images take Positions*. Cambridge, MA: MIT Press, 2018b.

Didi-Huberman, Georges. 'Image, Language: the other dialectic', *Angelaki* 23 (2018c), 19–24.
Douglas-Scott, Sionaidh. *Law After Modernity*. London: Routledge, 2014.
Douzinas, Costas, and Lynda Nead, eds. *Law and the Image: The Authority of Art and the Aesthetics of Law*. Chicago: Chicago University Press, 1999.
Dupont, Florence. 'La scène juridique', *Communications* 26 (1977), 62–77.
Eagleton, Terry. *Humour*. New Haven: Yale University Press, 2019.
Eliot, T.S. *Collected Works*. London: Faber and Faber, 1954.
Ertür, Başak. *Spectacles and Specters: A Performative Theory of Political Trials*. Palo Alto: Stanford University Press, 2022.
Favour, John, *Antiquitie Triumphing over Noveltie: Whereby it is Proved that Antiquitie is a True and Certaine Note of the Christian Catholicke Church and Verity, against all new and upstart heresies*. London: Field, 1618.
Feigenson, Neal, and Christina Spiesel, *Law on Display: The Digital Transformation of Legal Persuasion and Judgment*. New York: NYU Press, 2015.
Fish, Stanley. 'The Law Wishes to have a Formal Existence'. In *The Fate of Law*, edited by Austin Sarat and Tom Kearns, 159–208. Ann Arbor: Michigan University Press, 1991.
Fisher, Mark. *Ghosts of my Life: Writings on Depression, Hauntology and Lost Futures*. Winchester: Zero Books, 2013.
Forcadel, Etienne. *La sphère du Droit: Sphaera legalis* [1553], edited and translated by Anne Teissier-Ensminger. Paris: Garnier, 2011.
Foucault, Michel. *The Archaeology of Knowledge*. London: Continuum, 2014.
Freedberg, David. *The Power of Images: Studies in the History and Theory of Response*. Chicago: Chicago University Press, 1989.
Friedman, Lawrence M. 'Lexitainment: Legal Process as Theater', *DePaul L. Rev.* 50 (2000), 539–558.
Freud, Sigmund. 'The Interpretation of Dreams'. In *The Standard Edition of the Complete Psychological Works of Sigmund Freud, Volume IV (1900): The Interpretation of Dreams (First Part)*, edited by James Strachey, ix–627. London: Hogarth Press, 1953.
Freud, Sigmund. 'Humour'. In *The Standard Edition of the Complete Psychological Works of Sigmund Freud, Volume XXI (1927–1931): The Future of an Illusion, Civilization and its Discontents, and Other Works*, edited and translated by James Strachey, 159–166. London: The Hogarth Press, 1961.
Freud, Sigmund. *The Joke and Its Relation to the Unconscious*. London: Penguin Books, 2002.
Gandorfer, Daniela, and Zulaikha Ayub, eds. *Matterphorical: Special Issue of Theory and Event*. Baltimore: Johns Hopkins University Press, 2021.
Gandorfer, Daniela. *Matterphorics: On the Laws of Theory*. Durham, N.C.: Duke University Press, 2024.
Gennaro, Giuseppe Aurelio di. *La République des jurisconsultes*. Paris: Nyon, 1758.
Gephart, Werner. *Some Colours of the Law: Images and Interpretations*. Frankfurt: Klosterman, 2019.
Ghermani, Naïmi et Annonville, Caroline Michel de., eds. *Image et Droit. Du* ius imaginis *au droit à l'image*. Rome: École Française de Rome, 2022.
Giancaspro, Mark Anthony. 'Picture-Perfect or Potentially Perilous? Assessing the Validity of "Comic Contracts"', *The Comics Grid: Journal of Comics Scholarship* 10(1) (2020), 1–27.
Giddens, Thomas. 'Comics, Law, and Aesthetics: Towards the Use of Graphic Fiction in Legal Studies', *Law and Humanities* 6 (2012), 85–109.

Giddens, Thomas. *Fonts of Justice: Typography and the Common Law*. Edinburgh: Edinburgh University Press, forthcoming 2024.

Giddens, Thomas. *On Comics and Legal Aesthetics: Multi-modality and the Haunted Mask of Knowing*. Abingdon: Routledge, 2018.

Ginsburg, Jane. "Does 'transformative' fair use eviscerate the author's exclusive right to 'transform' her work', 17:9 *Journal of Intellectual Property Law & Practice* 687–689 (2022).

Goodrich, Peter. Oedipus lex: *Psychoanalysis, History, Law*. Berkeley: University of California Press, 1995.

Goodrich, Peter. 'Law'. In *Encyclopedia of Rhetoric*, edited by Tom Sloane, 417–426. New York: Oxford University Press, 2001.

Goodrich, Peter. 'Satirical Legal Studies: From the Legist to the *Lizard*', *Michigan L. Rev.* 103 (2004), 397–517.

Goodrich, Peter. '*Imago Decidendi*: On the Common Law of Images', Art and Law 1 (2017).

Goodrich, Peter. 'Faces and Frames of Government'. In *Law and the Visual: Representations, Technologies, and Critique*, edited by Desmond Manderson, 51–74. Toronto: University of Toronto Press, 2018.

Goodrich, Peter. 'Viserbal Laws: On an Arbitral Modality Recently Adopted in Judgments', *African Yearbook of Rhetoric* 9 (2019), 50–60.

Goodrich, Peter. 'The Mask as Anti-Apparatus: On the Counter-*Dispositif* of *V for Vendetta*'. In *Critical Directions in Comic Studies*, edited by Thomas Giddens, 238–262. Jackson: University of Mississippi Press, 2020.

Goodrich, Peter. *Advanced Introduction to Law and Literature*. Cheltenham: Elgar, 2021.

Goodrich, Peter. 'Remediation', *Cambridge J. of Law, Politics, and Art* 1 (2021b), 310–314.

Goodrich, Peter. 'Weird Judgement: Agon, Omniscience and the Absence of an "e"', *Ordine internazionale e diritti umani* (2021a), 130–139.

Goodrich, Peter. '"*Perpetuum Mobile*: Colour, Sound and Motion" 128 *Actes Sémiotiques* 87–102 (2023).

Gopaleen, Myles Na (Flann O'Brien). *The Best of Myles*, edited by Kevin Nolan. London: MacGibbon and Kee, 1968.

Hayaert, Valérie. *Lady Justice. An Anatomy of Allegory*. Edinburgh: Edinburgh University Press, 2023.

Hayaert, Valérie. 'Emblems'. In *The Oxford Handbook of Law and Humanities*, edited by Simon Stern, Maksymillian Del Mar, and Bernadette Meyler, 757–777. Oxford: Oxford University Press, 2019.

Hayaert, Valérie. Mens emblematica *et humanisme juridique*. Geneva: Droz, 2008.

Herbert, A.P. *Uncommon Law*. London: Methuen, 1935.

Heron, Nicholas. *Liturgical Power: Between Economic and Political Theology*. New York: Fordham University Press, 2018.

Hori, Lucas. '*Bons Mots*, Buffoonery, and the Bench: The Role of Humor in Judicial Opinions', *UCLA L. Rev. Disc.* 60 (2012), 16–37.

Hunt, Alan. *Governance of the Consuming Passions: A History of Sumptuary Law*. London: Macmillan, 1996.

Isidore of Seville, *Etymologies*. Trans. S. Barney et al. Cambridge: Cambridge University Press, 2008.

Jewel, Lucy. 'Does the Reasonable Man have Obsessive Compulsive Disorder?', *Wake Forest L. Rev.* 54 (2019), 1049–1088.

Jorio, Andrea de. *Gesture in Naples and Gesture in Classical Antiquity* [1832]. Trans. Adam Kendon, Bloomington: Indiana University Press, 2000.

Joubert, Laurent. *Treatise on Laughter*. Tuscaloosa: Alabama University Press, 1980.

Kahan, Dan, David Hoffman, and Donald Braman. 'Whose Eyes Are You Going To Believe? *Scott v. Harris* and the Perils of Cognitive Illiberalism', *Harvard L. Rev.* 122 (2009), 837–906.

Kelsen, Hans. *Pure Theory of Law*. Berkeley: University of California Press, 1960.

Krämer, Sybille. '"Epistemology of the Line": Reflections on the Diagrammatical Mind'. In *Studies in Diagrammatology and Diagram Praxis*, edited by Olga Pombo and Alexander Gerner, 279–293. London: College Publications, 2010a.

Krämer, Sybille. '"The Mind's Eye": Visualizing the Non-visual and the "Epistemology of the Line"'. In *Image and Imaging in Philosophy, Science, and the Arts: Preproceedings of the 33rd International Wittgenstein Symposium 2*, edited by Elisabeth Nemeth, Richard Heinrich, and Wolfram Pichler, 275–293. Frankfurt: Ontos Verlag, 2010b.

Lamb, Charles. *The Essays of Elia*. New York: Putnam, 1845.

Lebeau, Vicky. *Childhood and Cinema*. London: Reaktion, 2008.

Legendre, Pierre. *L'Empire de la verité: Introduction aux espaces dogmatique industriels*. Paris: Fayard, 2001.

Legendre, Pierre. *L'Autre Bible de l'Occident: le monument romano-canonique*. Paris: Fayard, 2009.

Legendre, Pierre. *God in the Mirror: A Study of the Institution of Images*. London: Routledge, 2019.

Legrand, Pierre. *Negative Comparative Law: A Strong Programme for Weak Thought*. Cambridge: Cambridge University Press, 2022.

Leiboff, Marrett. *Towards a Theatrical Jurisprudence*. London: Routledge, 2020.

Lenton, Francis. *Characters: Or, Wit and the World in Their Proper Colours*. London: Samuel Speed, 1563.

Lenton, Francis. *Characterismi or Lentons leasures Expressed in Essays and Characters Never Before Written On*. London: Mitchell, 1631.

Levinson, Paul. *The Soft Edge: A Natural History and Future of the Information Revolution*. London: Routledge, 1997.

Lippit, Akira. *Atomic Light (Shadow Optics)*. Minneapolis: University of Minnesota Press, 2005.

Little, Laura. *Guilty Pleasures: Comedy and Law in America*. New York: Oxford University Press, 2018.

Liu, Jairui. 'An Empirical Study of Transformative Use in Copyright Law', *Stan. Tech. L. Rev.* 22 (2019), 163–241.

Lyotard, Jean-François. *Libidinal Economy*. Bloomington: Indiana University Press, 1993.

Lyotard, Jean-François. *Discourse, Figure*. Minneapolis: University of Minnesota Press, 2011.

Lysyk, Stephanie. 'Love of the Censor: Legendre, Censorship and the Theatre of the Basoche', *Cardozo Studies in Law and Literature* 11 (1999), 113–133.

Maclean, Ian. *Interpretation and Meaning in the Renaissance: The Case of Law*. Cambridge: Cambridge University Press, 1992.

Maksimov, Vladislav. 'Politicization of Life and Auto-Thanatopolitics in *V for Vendetta*'. In *Critical Directions in Comic Studies*, edited by Thomas Giddens, 195–214. Jackson: University of Mississippi Press, 2020.

Manderson, Desmond, ed. *Law and the Visual: Representations, Technologies, and Critique*. Toronto: Toronto University Press, 2018.

Manderson, Desmond. *Danse Macabre: Temporalities of Law in the Visual Arts*. Cambridge: Cambridge University Press, 2019.

McNamara, Charles Joseph. *Quintilian's Theory of Certainty and its Afterlife in Early Modern Italy*. Columbia: Columbia University, PhD, 2016.

Mehmi, Suneel. *Law, Literature and the Power of Reading: Literalism and Photography in the Nineteenth Century*. Abingdon: Routledge, 2022.

Mnookin, Jennifer. 'Photographic Evidence and the Power of Analogy'. In *Images of Conviction: The Construction of Visual* Evidence, edited by Diane Dufour. Paris: Editions Xavier Barral, 2015, 9–15.

Mnookin, Jennifer. 'Semi-legibility and Visual Evidence: An Initial Exploration', *Law, Culture and the Humanities* 10 (2014), 43–65.

Moinereau, Laurence. *Le générique de film: De la lettre à la figure*. Rennes: Presses Universitaires de Rennes, 1995.

Moore, Nathan. 'Icons of Control: Deleuze, Signs, Law', *Int. J. Semiotics of Law* 20 (2007), 33–54.

Moran, Leslie J. 'What's a Box of "Bakewell Tarts" Got to Do With it? Performing Gender as a Judicial Virtue in the Theatre of Justice'. In *Judges, Judging and Humour*, edited by Jessica Davis and Sharyn Anleu, 211–239. Cham, Switzerland: Palgrave Macmillan/ Springer, 2018.

Moran, Leslie J. *Law, Judges and Visual Culture*. Abingdon: Routledge, 2022.

Moyne, Père le. *De l'art des devises*. Paris: Cramoisy, 1666.

Mulcahy, Linda. 'Eyes of the Law: A Visual Turn in Socio-legal Studies', *J. Law & Soc* 44 (2017), 111–128.

Murray, David. *Lawyers' Merriments*. Glasgow: MacLehose, 1912.

Murray, Michael. 'Toward a Universal Visual Language of Law', *Law & Psychology Rev.* 46:1 (2021–2022), 86–103.

Na Gopaleen, Myles (Flann O'Brien), *The Best of Myles*. New York: Walker, 1968.

Nagel, Alexander, and Christopher Wood. *Anachronic Renaissance*. New York: Zone Books, 2010.

Nietzsche, Friedrich. *The Dawn of Day*. London: Allen and Unwin, 1903.

Olson, Greta. *From Law and Literature to Legality and Affect*. Oxford: Oxford University Press, 2022.

Ovid. *Ovid's Metamorphoses*. Dallas: Spring Publications, 1989.

Pancirolus, Guido. *Notitia utraque dignitatum, cum Orientis, tum Occidentis ultra arcadia honorique tempora*. Lyon: Gabiano, 1608.

Parvulescu, Anna. *Laughter: Notes on a Passion*. Cambridge, MA: MIT Press, 2010.

Pedullà, Gabriele. *In Broad Daylight: Movies and Spectators after the Cinema*. London: Verso, 2012.

Perrière, Guillaume. *Le Thëatre des bons engins*. Toulouse: Janot, 1540.

Peters, Julie Stone. 'Theatrocracy Unwired: Legal Performance in the Modern Mediasphere', *Law and Literature* 26 (2014), 31–64.

Peters, Julie Stone. *Law as Performance: Legal Theatricality, Spectatorship, and the Making of Law in Ancient, Medieval, and Early Modern Europe*. Oxford: Oxford University Press, 2022.

Philippopoulos-Mihalopoulos, Andreas. *Spatial Justice: Bodies, Lawscape, Atmosphere*. London: Routledge, 2015.

Philippopoulos-Mihalopoulos, Andreas. 'Flesh of the Law: Material Legal Metaphors', *Journal of Law and Society* 43 (2016), 45–65.

Philippopoulos-Mihalopoulos, Andreas. 'Performing Metaphors', *Theory & Event* 24 (2021), 268–293.

Porter, Elizabeth. 'Taking Images Seriously', *Columbia L. Rev.* 114 (2014), 1687–1782.

Porter, Elizabeth, and Kathryn Watts. 'Visual Rulemaking', *N.Y.U. L. Rev.* 91 (2016), 1183–1278.

Posner, Richard. *Law and Literature: A Misunderstood Relation.* Cambridge, MA: Harvard University Press, 1988.

Posner, Richard. *Public Intellectuals: A Study of Decline.* Cambridge, MA: Harvard University Press, 2003.

Posner, Richard. 'Judicial Opinions and Appellate Advocacy in Federal Courts—One Judge's Views', *Duquesne L. Rev.* 51 (2013), 3–39.

Pugliese, Joseph. *State Violence and the Execution of Law: Biopolitical Caesurae of Torture, Black Sites, Drones.* Abingdon: Routledge, 2013.

Quintilian. *Institutio oratoria.* London: Loeb Classical Library, 1998.

Quintilian. *Institutio oratoria.* Cambridge, MA: Harvard University Press, 2001.

Retort. *Afflicted Powers: Capital and Spectacle in a New Age of War.* London: Verso, 2005.

Robbins, Ira. 'Digitus Impudicus: The Middle Finger and the Law', *U.C. Davis Law Review* 41 (2008), 1403–1486.

Rodgers, Alan Ferguson. 'Humour and Law', *Scots Law Times* (2009), 202.

Rouille, Guillaume. *Alenconiensis causidici in legibus licêtiati. Justicie et iniusticie descriptionû compeniû.* Paris: Chevallus, 1570.

Sarat, Austin et al., eds. *Law and the Visible.* Amherst: University of Massachusetts Press, 2021.

Selden, John. *Titles of Honor.* London: Stansby, 1631.

Shaw, Julia. *Law and the Passions: Why Emotion Matters for Justice.* Abingdon: Routledge, 2020.

Sheppard, Steve, ed. *The Selected Writings and Speeches of Sir Edward Coke Vol 1.* Indianapolis: Liberty Fund, 2003.

Sherwin, Richard. *When Law Goes Pop: The Vanishing Line between Law and Popular Culture.* Chicago: Chicago University Press, 2002.

Sherwin, Richard. *Visualizing Law in the Age of the Digital Baroque: Arabesques and Entanglements.* London: Routledge, 2012.

Sherwin, Richard, and Anne Wagner, eds. *Law, Culture and Visual Studies.* Dordrecht: Springer, 2014.

Siegert, Bernhard. 'The Map *is* the Territory', *Radical Philosophy* 169 (2011), 13–16.

Silbey, Jessica. 'Cross-Examining Film', *University of Maryland Law Journal of Race, Religion, Gender and Class* 8 (2008), 17–46.

Silbey, Jessica. 'Evidence Verité and the Law of Film', *Cardozo L. Rev.* 31 (2010), 1257–1299.

Silbey, Jessica. 'Persuasive Visions: Film and Memory', *Law, Culture and the Humanities* 10 (2014), 24 42.

Speed, John. *Theatrum Imperii Magnæ Britannicæ.* London: Sudbury and Humble, 1611.

Speed, John. *The Theatre of the Empire of Great Britaine.* London: William Hall, 1612.

Spiesel, Christina. 'More than a Thousand Words in Response to Rebecca Tushnet', *Harvard L.Rev. F.* 125 (2012), 40–46.

Stępień, Mateusz. 'Say it with Images: Drawing on Jerome Frank's Ideas on Judicial Decision Making', *Int. J. Semiotics of Law* 32 (2019), 321–334.

Steimatsky, Noa. *The Face on Film.* Oxford: Oxford University Press, 2017.

Stern, Simon. et al. (eds). *Oxford Handbook of Law and Humanities.* Oxford: Oxford University Press, 2019.

Sterne, Laurence. *The Life and Opinions of Tristram Shandy, Gentleman.* Harmondsworth: Penguin, 1978.

Suresh, Sabarish. 'Cartographies'. In *Research Handbook on Law and Literature*, edited by Peter Goodrich, Daniela Gandorfer, and Cecilia Gebruers, 174–199. Cheltenham: Elgar, 2022.

Suresh, Sabarish. *The Traumatic History of Constitutions: The Partition of India and the Laws of Repetition*. Forthcoming 2024.

Sutherland, Keston. *Stupefaction: A Radical Anatomy of Phantoms*. London: Seagull Books, 2011.

Trahair, Lisa. *The Comedy of Philosophy: Sense and Nonsense in Early Cinematic Slapstick*. Albany: SUNY, 2007.

Teissier-Ensminger, Anne. *Fabuleuse juridicité: sur la littérarisation des genres juridiques*. Paris: Classiques Garnier, 2015.

Tushnet, Rebecca. 'Worth a Thousand Words: The Images of Copyright', *Harvard L. Rev.* 125 (2012), 684–759.

Varma, Supriya and Jaya Menon. 'Was There a Temple under the Babri Majid? Reading the Archaeological "Evidence"', *EPW* 45(50) (2010), 61–72.

Vico, Giambattista. *The New Science of Giambattista Vico*, translated by Thomas Goddard Bergin and Max Harold Fisch. Ithaca: Cornell University Press, 1984.

Virgil. *Eclogues*. London: Penguin, 1953.

Virilio, Paul. *War and Cinema: The Logistics of Perception*, translated by Patrick Camiller. London: Verso, 1989.

Vismann, Cornelia. *Files: Law and Media Technology*. Palo Alto: Stanford University Press, 2008.

Vismann, Cornelia. 'Tele-Tribunals: Anatomy of a Medium', *Grey Room* 10 (2003), 5–21.

Wacquet, Françoise. *Latin or the Empire of a Sign: From the sixteenth to the twentieth centuries*. London: Verso, 2001.

Wajcman, Gérard. *Fenêtre: Chroniques du regard et de l'intime*. Paris: Verdier, 2004.

Watt, Gary. 'Dress, Law and Naked Truth: Some Further Coverage', *Critical Studies in Fashion and Beauty* 7 (2016), 109–121.

Watt, Gary. *Law, Dress, and the Naked Truth: A Cultural Study of Fashion and Form*. London: Bloomsbury, 2013.

Weitzman, Erica. *Irony's Antics: Walser, Kafka, Roth, and the German Comic Tradition*. Evanston: Northwestern University Press, 2015.

Whitehouse, Edward. Fortescutus illustratus, *or a Commentary on That Nervous Treatise 'De laudibus legum Angliæ'*. London: Thomas Roycroft for Thomas Dicas, 1663.

Widener, Michael and Weiner, Mark S. *Law's Picture Books: The Yale Law Collection*. Clark, N.J.: Talbot, 2017.

Williams, Isobel. *Catallus: Shibari Carmina*. Manchester: Carcanet, 2021.

Williams, Isobel. 'Drawing from an Uncomfortable Position'. IsobelWilliams [website], 2015, http://isobelwilliams.blogspot.com/2015/12/the-naked-rambler-and-sitting.html (accessed 31 August 2022).

Willock, John, ed. *Legal Facetiæ: Satirical and Humorous*. London: Literary Society, 1887.

Index

35 Bar and Grille v San Antonio, 87–89, 103

Aboriginal Land Rights Act 1983, 49–50
actus legitimi, 173
adverse possession, 57
aesthetics, 29, 41–42, 52, 55, 60, 68, 117, 128, 148, 154, 164–166, 176, 196, **204**–210, 240, 249
  Imperial, 20, 31, 253
  Shark, 4, 23, 131–132, 226
affect, vii, 22, 66, 86, 92, 106, 126, 154, 156, 165–166, 176, 232–233, 237–238
Agamben, Giorgio, 173, 253
agelasts, 99
agnosia (judicial), 19
agonism, 22
Aileen Brooks v IT Works, 4
album, 166, 172, 176, 233
Alciatus, Andreas, vi, 14, 97
Alien Tort Statute, 184
altered copy, 210
ambulatio, 3, 16, 67
ambiguity, 71–73
anachrony, 79–80, 88, 190, 218
Anderson, Leslie, 183
Aneau, Barthèlemy vi, 207
angelology, 173, 223
Anglia, 27, 39, 71
anima, 79
Anti-Mask Act, 121, 122
antiqui iuris fabulas, 22
appendices, 56, 81–84, 118, 185
Aquinas, Thomas, 64
arcana iuris, 24, 240
archive, 6, 13, 142, 196, 204
  shadow, 143, 204, 214–215
Aristotle, 203
arrows, 45–46, 55
as if, 42, 176
atlas, 20, 26, 29, 32, 184, 250
ars iuris, 23, 219, 233
Augustine, Saint, 160, 187, 196, 232, 250
audite et alterem partem, 246
au jus, 21, 98
Austin, Gilbert, 191

Bachelard, Gaston, 67
Bacon, Francis, 3, 211
bare life, 102–107, 250–254
Barthes, Roland, 7, 195
Bartolus de Saxoferrato, 16
Basoche, 98
Bataille, Georges, 35
Bellido, Jose, 196, 198, 208
Benjamin, Walter, 167, 171
Bentham, Jeremy, 3
Bertetto, Paolo, 161
Bible, 38
Biery, Judge Fred, 53–56, 87–88, 102
Bigg, Charlotte, 32
bios, 250, 253
Birss, Mr Justice, 114, 118, 177–179, 181
blindspots, ix, 4, 23–24, 133, 242, 246
Blount, Thomas, 98, 100
Bonaventura, 64
Bond, Henry, 175–176
Boop, Betty, 112–116
boredom, 164, 222
Bottici, Chiara, **14**, 27, 44, 203–204
Bradley, Judge Ann, 140–142
Breyer, Justice, 129
Britannia, 29–31
Brunschwig, Collette, 5
Bulwer, John, 189–190, 236
Burton, Robert, 81

cacozelia, 17
Camden, William, 26
Capitoll Square Advisory Board case, 8–9
caput lupinum, 226, 254
Cardi B, 229–230, 235–236
cartography, 20, 25–28, 39–40, 47–53, 66
cartoons, 112–117, 240
Casteñeda, Michelle, 75
cats (and humour), 108–110
certum, 8, **11**, **20**, 22, 39, 68, 70,112, 117, 132, 166, **222**, 238, 240, **252**
casuistry, vii
Carnevali, Barbara, vi
catachresis, 79
CCTV, 12, 92, 95, 141, 150, 152, 190, 216
Centrefold, 102–104

censorship, 243, 245–246
charta, **26**–28
childhood, 203, 238
Chirologia, 189–190, 236
Chironomia, 188–190, **236**
chorography, **26**–27
chromatics, 47
Churchill, Winston, 251
Clerk (Gill), Lord Justice, 243
Clinton, William Jefferson, 224–225
clothes, 159–161, 242–250
Coccia, Emanuele, vii, 14, 96, 167
Coke, Sir Edward, 116, 117, 211, 232
collage, 59, 129, 130, 139
colour, 23, 45–46, 48–52, 57, 191–194, 205–211, **212**–221, **217**, **237**
  antinomies, 238
  blindness, 24, 221
  blue, 50–51, 215, 218
  colourways, 204–210
  grey, 215, 228
  orange, 216, 224
  pink, 52, 57–58, 206–210
  purple, 218, 244, 249
  red, 45–47, 57–58, 105, 107, 115, 182, 191–193, 198, 215, 216, **218**, 224
  yellow, 191–193, 205, **218**
comedy, 21, 53, 84, 86, 95, **97**–99, 100–107, 111–116, 121, 124–126
  comœdia, 100
comics, 116, 234
Conrad, Catherine, 118–120
Contempt of Court, 242
con- trahere, 71
contumely, 190–191
conusance, 16, 180, 201, 248
copying, 207–210
copyright, 177–179, 196, 204–210, 213–215, 226
Coras, Jean de, 14
Cormack, Bradin, 25, 31, 74
Corpus iuris, vii, 212
copying (literal), 214
craft, 72
Cruiskeen Court, 25–26
Critical Inquiry, 103
Croft v Howel, 72
cross, 9–11

Dadaism, 86
Dahan v Shacjaroff, 15
Daniell, Samuel, 180
Danse Macabre, 232
Darling, Charles, 101
dasein (naked), 240, 243, 247
Debord, Guy, 100
Debray, Régis, 74, 233
déchirure, **viii**
De Fraude v Snafflebit, 101
Deities
  Legal persons, 33–34
  Ram, 33–35
Delage, Christian, 11–12
Dellinger, Hamton, 9
Deleuze, Gilles, 14, 160, 204, 234
Derham, Associate Justice David, 61–63
Derrida, Jacques, 20–21, 87, 254
Designer's Guild v Williams, 204–209
Desjarlais, Robert, 148
détournement, 90, 99, 117
diagrammatics, 20, 25, 32, 39, 52, 67, 68
diagrammatology, 25, 32, 38–41, 203
dies nec fasti, 121
Didi-Huberman, Georges, viii, x, 8, 29, 79, 164, 166, 174, 201, 203, 211, 217
Digest of Justinian, 17, 25, 116
digitus impudicus, 16, 188–189
dimwit observer, 9, 11
Dinsmore, USMJ, 196–198
discourse, 37–38, 96, 222
  diffraction of, 221–227, 229–230, 236–237
  dis-currere, 35, 222
dispositif, xi, 63, 174, 178, 183
dissimulation, 159–161, 233
dogma, 65, 68, 131, 164, 218
downcast eyes, 7, 22
dreams, 22–23, 79, **203**
dress, 159–161
Duchamp, Marcel, 86
Dupont, Florence, 97
dynamogram, vi, 24, 117, 154, 164, 196, **232**

Eaton College case, 73–74
Easterbrook, Judge, 1
Edwards, Chief Judge, 156
Einstein, Albert, 109–111
elegantia iuris, 23–24, 111
Elias, Norbert, 99
Eliot, T.S., 255
emblems, 42, 76, 79, 84, 88, 98–99
emojis, 5, 15–17
epidermal facia, 245
Erasmus, Desiderius, 98
Eros, 101–102, 115, 117–119, 156
Ertür, Başak, viii, 20–21, 254
Eton. *see* Eaton
European Central Bank case, 108–110
European Convention on Human Rights, 242
ex abundantia, 70–72, 86, 96

ex abundantia cautela, 72–73
ex gratia, 71
extispicy, 23, 164, **166**, 172, 173–174, 176, 184, 190–191, **211**
exception, 253
eye
  accuracy, 137, 170–172
  ambulatio, 3, 16, 67, 163, 195, 196, 214–215
  downcast, 7, 22, 101, 204, 241–242
  judicial, 100–104, 131–133, 138, **178**, 184, **205**–206
  monochrome, 219
  naked, 205, **207**, 226
  record and, 3, 48, 196

fair use, 6, 219, 226–229, 235–236
fashion, 159–161
Favour, John, 172
Fawkes, Guy, 122–125
Ferdman v CBS, 228
finger (giving the), 16, 189–190
Fish, Stanley, 135
Fisher, Mark, 173
First Amendment, 87–88
Flaccus, Valerius, 98
Flèches. see arrows
flowers, 51–52, 205–207
Fog. *see* jurisprudence
Forcadel, Etienne, 116
Ford, Tom, 229–230, 236
Fortescue, Sir John, 31
forum non conveniens, 18–19
Foucault, Michel, 221
Franzosi, Professor Mario, 108–109
French Connection, 131
Freud, Sigmund, 13, 16, 70, 79, 87, 89, 97, 100, 105, 111–112, 118, 126–127, 203, 240
Friedman, Judge Daniel A., 48

gallery, 8, 23, 74, 76, 80, 143, 160, 208, 250
Gandorfer, Daniela, xi, **50**, 223
Gates v Khokhar, 121–124
Gephart, Werner, 214
ghosts, 38
Giddens, Thomas, v, 116, 123
Gill v Ethicon, 148–150
Ginsberg, Ruth Bader, 157, 159
Ginsburg, Carlo, 70
Gonzalez-Servin, 18, 21, 97, 196
Google Earth, 32–34, 42–43
Gough, Stephen Peter, 242, 244–248, 250–251
Gough v H.M. Advocate, 243–244
Grand Junction Canal Act 1793, 40
graphosphere, 74
guilders, 110, 112
Gutenberg, 212–213
Gynemesh, 147–149

habeas corpus, 246, 248
haec imago, 124–125, 246
Hamm, Jon, 121
haruspex, 173
Hastings, battle of, 55
Hayaert, Valérie, 98–99
Hays Code, 115
Hayuk v Starbucks, 213–215
hepatoscopics, 22–23, 143, 164–165
haunting, 20, 35, 173, 196, 227, 254–255
heraldry, 161
Herbert, A.P., 101
Herbert, Victor, 2008
hermeneutics, 11, 18, 22, 221
  ocular, 11, 22, 90, 256
histrions, 21, 98, 104, 106, 121, 126
Hobbes, Thomas, 14, 26, 45, 99, 124, 176, 232
homo fenestris, 79
Hooker, Richard, 232
HouseCanary Case, 53–55, 81–84
humour, 100–101, 108–109, 126–127, 190, 240–241
Hunt, Alan, 237

Iconicity, vii, 224
Idols, 34, 162, 211
If, 183
Image
  affect, 6–7, 11–13, 20–22, 47, 59, 66, 92, 155, 156, 162, 201–204, 232–233, 244–246
  ambulant, 203
  atlas, 6, 20, 32, 35, 59, 203, 202
  beginning (as), 201, 203–204
  body as, 246
  comic, 53, 81, 84, 102–105, 115, 196–197
  dasein, 240, 243, 248
  discourse (and), 22, 95–97, 108, 116, 118, 152, 207–210, **236**–238
  dogma (as), 64–65, 68, 187
  erotic, 97, 102–107, 113–116
  extispicious, 23, 164 et seq
  gallery, 142, 160, 166, 196, 203, 212, 215, 224, 233
  humourous, 21, 101–108
  idol, 33–34, 125, 161
  infringing, 226–227, 235
  micro-ontology, 222
  normative, 10–12, 18, 111–113, 118, 164–167, 324–236

Image (*Continued*)
objective unconscious, viii, 17–18, 95, 167, 248
opening, 79–81
resistance to, 14
sensory, 8, 18, 23, 67, 95, 143, 200–201
skin, 253–255
symptom, 70
temporality, 174, 189–193, 233
text, 6, 16, 18, 104, 112–118, 149, 163, 169, 180, 207–**211**
veritas falsa, 6, **14**, 103–104, 176, 227, 233
vivified, 33–34, 39, 47–48, 201
imaginal, viii, 4, 8, 14, 16–18, 20–21, 29, 75, 88, 106, 132, 154
biological, 202
evidence, 159–162
heterotopic, 17, 29, 105, 142, 202
impediments, 140, 147–148
implexity, 103, 176, **233**
literalism, 225–226
norm, 210, 221
relay, 166, 201–203, 222, **226**
simulation, 160–161, 173
window and, 76–78
imago, viii, 8, 84, 124, 185, 202, 248
imago decidendi, vii, 4, 5, 22–23, 68, 75, 133
implexity, **ix**, 24, 119, 201–202, 233
imperialism, 20, 31, 252–254
epidermal, 254
impresa. see impresses
impresses, **180**
impressions (judicial), 177–181, 204–210, 226
first, 181, 184, 198, 205–207
indiscipline, 27
informed user test, 177–779, 181
infringement, 177, 196, 204–208, 210, 213–214, 218, 229
of the real, 226, 237
injustice (depicted), 27–29, 252–254
in ludo veritas, 84, 111
Insite Vision, 17
interpositae personae, 221
Interpretation of Dreams, 203
inventio, 69–70, 75, 166
isolarion, 48, 105
iura imaginaria, 22
ius imaginum, 19, 22–23, 64, 76, 79
ius submovendi, 25, 45

Jackson, Mr Justice Peter, 15–16
Jackson v Beasley, 76–79
Jacob, Lord Justice, 108–109
Jorio, Antonio de, 190–191
Joubert, Laurent, 99
Jovius, Paulus, 180
jurisdiction (visual), 12–13–14, 20, 25–26, 41–42, 75, 121, 219
jurisliterature, 23, 98, 221
jurisprudence
colour and, 208–212, 214–216
diffracted, 221–222, 226
minor, 121–122, 204
positivist, 38, 219, 248
theatrical, 104–107, 121, 124–126, 200
visual, v, 12–14, **223**–224, 250
wild, 52, 242
justice
retinal, v, ix–x, 5–6, 12–13, 17, 23, 68, 131–134, 141–143, 165, 174, 191, 200, 204, 206, 211–**212**, **226**, 241, 248, 252–253, 256
temple of, 211
Justinian, 17
justissima tellus, vii

Keith, Judge Daimon, 252
Kelsen, Hans, 68, 75
Knowles, Mr Justice Julian, 216–218
Kozinski, Judge Alex, 44–46, 56, 75
Krämer, Sybille, 32, 52
Kwok, Deputy High Court Judge, 57

Lacan, Jacques, 100, 126
Lamb, Charles, 102
Lange v O'Corrigan, 167–171
laughter, 98–99, 117, 121, 241
risus paschalis, 121
risus sardonicus, 120–121
law
a comicis, 84, 99, 102, 103–105, 120–121, 127, 241
aesthetics, vi, 31–32, 164, 208–210
bananas, 119–121
Christian, 81, 89
comedy, 21, 52, 84, 86, 95
diagrammatolgy, 31
fictions, 174–**176**
frivolous, 119
in forma pauperis, 120–121
lex animata, 250
living law, 259
psychoanalysis, 173–174
scholarship, 200–201
scripture, 172
spectacle, 200
theatre, v, vi, 3–4, 22, 102–104, 121–126, 164, 200, 245
web, 164

lawyers
judicial affect, 131, 154, 214–215, 224, 237
emancipated, 233
insensibility, 240
OUP – censor function, v–vi, 103, 213
perception of, 132, 178–180
Lebeau, Vicky, 203
Legrand, Pierre, 71, 128
Legendre, Pierre, vi, 25, 64–65
Leiboff, Marett, 38, 101
Lenton, F., 99
Leviathan, 75, 164
lex icon, 196
libidinal force, 21–22, 97, 104, 117–118
liturgical effect, 164, 172, 232
literalism (photographic), 183, 219, 226
Little, Laura, 99
ludi liberales, 98
Lincoln, Abraham, 53, 81–84
locus fluitem, 40
Lyotard, Jean-Françoise, 166

Mannequins, 174–176
maps, 26, 31, 41, 42, 45–47, 52–53, 56–57
meiosis, 120–121
Makaula, Judge, 174
Manderson, Desmond, 79, 232
Mann, Judge, 40–42
Marley, Bob, 90–92
Marriot and Pascals Case, 3, 71–73
Marx, Chico, 131
mapping, 25–36, 38, 45–54, 68–69, 105
masks, 23, 121–123
masochism, 101
materialism (new), 63, 66–67, 142, 157, 201–202, 214, 241–242, 251, 254
Matisse, Henri, 204–205
matterphor, 50, 64, 86, 99, 166, 202, 221, 223
McInnis, Federal Magistrate, 191–193
Maclean, Ian, 221
McNamara, Charles J., **11**
Mehmi, Suneel, 225–226
Melbourne's Cheapest Cars, 191–193
mens emblematica, 19, 23, 98
mens legis, 240
Michelangelo, 242
Minaj, Nicki, 236
Mnemosyne, 17
Mnookin, Jennifer, 7
modelling, 159–161
Moinereau, Laurence, 166
moiré effect, 109–111, 112
monochromacy, v, 9, 19, 24, 45, 76, 149, 152, 183, 191, 200, 206, 238
monotheism, 124–125
montage, 29, 139, 208, 210, 233–235
Moore, Nathan, 224
Moran, Leslie, 107
Morellian method, 70
Morrit, Lord Justice, 206
Morton, Justice, 72
Moyne, Père le, 76
Mulcahy, Linda, 5–6, 223
Murder, 174–176
mute eloquence (*muta eloquentia*), 70, 111, 126, 119, 140

Na Gopaleen, Myles, 25
nakedness, 242–248
naked rambler, 242–248
narcissism, 100–101
Narcissus, 66, 187
Negligence. *see* Tort
Neuberger, Lord, 180
Nietzsche, Freidrich, 132
Non-Entia imaginaria, 42
normativity, 165–166, 200, 222–223, 233
affective, 232–238
nomos, vi, 250
novum omne cave, 7
nuper, 71–72
Nuremberg, 11, 252

oath, 236
O'Brien, Flann. *see* Na Gopaleen
obiter depicta, 8, 68
obscurum per obscurius, 240
obviousness, 67, 90, 109–111, 129, 133–134, 139–141, 152
oikonomia, 250
oneirics. *see* dreams
ontography, 74, 99, 120, 180–181, 202
optics
claim of, 248
heterotopic, 13, 14, 17, 108
pathways, **204**–210
ostrich, 19–20, 21, 97, 196, 256
Ovid, 66, 67, 100

Parvelescu, Anna, 99
Pascoe's Case, 72–73
passing off, 101–106, 191–194
Pattinson, Robert, 227
Pedullà, Gabriele, 131
patent, 108–111
perambulation, 66
performance, 8
Periam, Justice, 71

Perrière, Guillaume, 124
persona, 3, 23, 52, 124–125
Peters, Julie Stone, vi, 3, 74, 98, 100
pettifoggers, 81, 84
Pfizer, 17
phantasmata, 203
phantasmography, 11, 147, 160
Philippopoulos-Mihalopoulos, Andreas, 44, 223
photogram, 11, 211
photographs, 7, 9–11, 33, 56, 57–61, 73–74, 135–136, 147–148, 158–162, 181, **193**, 200
  selective chromatics, 11, 181–184, 252–254
Photoportrait, 109–111, 224, 235, 254–255
Phryne, 245
Picta poesis, vi, 207
pigendo et ridendo docere, 98, 117, 250
pigment, 191, 212, 214, 215, 221, 237
plan subjectif, 60, 132–133, 140
Planning, 60–62
Plato, 29
PMS International v *Magmatic*, 5, 180
polychromasia, 212
populism, 238
Porter, Elizabeth, 157
Positivism, 38
Posner, Judge, 1–3, 18–19, 102, 118–120, 157–160, **185**, **222**
Precedent (visual), 19–20, 21, 55, 66, 70–72, 122, 132, 135–138, 163, 171, 174, 196–201, 208, 211, **215**, 222, **234**, 253–256
Prendergast, Matthew, 102–107
Proboscis, 99
Procedere ad apparentiam, x, 7, 19, 95, 173, 200
Procedere ad similia, 7, 70, 74, 95, 181, 234
Promissory estoppel, 15, 17
psychosis, 175–176
Public Order Act 1986, 242
Pugliese, Joseph, 143
Punning, 87–88
Puttenham, George, 75

Quintilian, 98–100, 127, 189

R D (R), 124
R v Gough, 243, 245–246, 248
R v Morris-Lowe, 72
R v Nikolovsi, 151–152
R v NS, 124
Rafferty, Lady Justice, 243, 243–246, 250–251
Ram Lala Viragman, 34–35
rambo tactics, 53
Randolph v Forever 21, 197–198
Rares J., 103–107
rastafarianism, 90–92
ratio decidendi, 133
ratio scripta, 14, 23, 37
reality effect, 1, 6–7, 20, 41, 59, 86, 133, 160, 240
reasonable person, 181–182
remediation, 60, 67, 92, 208, **219**, 229, **241**, 256
resistance, 132
restrictive covenant, 60–63
retinal (justice). *see* justice
revels, 98, 120, 121
revenants. *see* ghosts
reverie, 67, 84, 108, 254, 257
rhetoric, 17–18, 38, 75, 87, 104, 240
  catachresis, 79
  chironomic, 188–190, 236
  effectus, 38, 104, 164, 173, 232
  figures, 75, 106, 109–111, 119–120, 157
  inventio, 3, 21, 66, 70, 108
  metastasis, 55
  meiosis, 120
  synecdoche, 109, 135, 160, 216
rhizomes (optical), 12, 14, 76, 89-90, 92, 163, 183, 188
Rhodes, Justice, 71
right of appearance, 246, 248
riparian rights, 40–41
Rodger, Lord, 109
Rouille, Guillaume, 27–28

Samsung v Apple, 177
Sandifer v US Steel, 157–161, 165
Savignac, Mark, 159–160
Scalia, Judge Antonin, 129–130
Schreber, Judge, 86
Schindler's List, 183
scilicet, 176, 183
Sciography, 67
Scopic drive, 12, 17, 68, 101, 129–133, 165, 174, 180
Scotomizing. *see* blindspots
Scott v Harris, 76, 129–131, 135, 198
screenshots, 4
seeming, 157–162, 226
seismography, 232
semiotics, 23, 26, 27, 121, 161, 173
sensibility, 29, 68, 96, 108, 132, 167, 174, 176, 181, 208, 210, 233, 235, 249
serio-ludere, 21, 25, 84, 98, 111, 121, 240, 249
seven, 115–116
Seville, Isidore, 26
Shamin, Hina, 216, 218
Shapiro, Timothy, 158–159
Shaw, Julia, 155
Siddique v Suresh, 32–35
Siegert, Bernard, 31

Sikhs for Justice, 184–185
Silbey, Jessica, 67
Sileni Alcibiades, 34, 35
similarity (presumption of), 193
simulation, 159, **160**–161, **233**
Smith, Sir Thomas, 73
SMS, 14
sola scriptura, vi
Souter, Justice, 9, 13
sovereignty, 44, 66, 164, 253
spectrality, viii, 14, 20, 38, 164, 173–174, 200, 251–252
speculum, 173, 184
Speed, John, 29–31, 53
Speilberg, Stephen, 188
Speisel, Christina, 5, 128
Spicer v Met. Police, 216–218
Spiderman, 229, 234–235
Stabile v Smith, 213
Star Wars, 55
State v Walter, 224–226
Sterne, Laurence, 99
Stevens, Justice, 9, 11
storeys, 60–61
stupefaction, 100, 233
sub-auditio, 221
sub-intellectio, 221
sumptuary law, 161, **162**, 216, 237, 216, 237
superfluity. *see* surplusage
Suresh, Sabarish, 39
surplusage, 20–21, 69–74, 95–96, 202–204, 240
Sutherland, Keston, 100
symbolæography, 16, 72
symbolic proliferation, 164–166, 176, 183, 211
Swain, Judge Laura, 214
synaesthesia, 5, 180, **181**
synecdoche, 109, 135, 160, 216

taking, 115–117
Taylor, Rev. John, 88–89
Teigen, Chrissy, 104
Temple Island Collections, 182
Tessier-Ensminger, Anne, 23, 116
tetratheca juncea, 51–52
Texas Lawyers' Creed, 81–83
Thanatos, 156
theatre, 27, 98, 104–106, 120–122, 124–126, 245
throne (empty), 35, 106
Till, Emmet, 252–254
toilets, 85–87, 175
tort, 94, 112–114, 133–135
  Negligence, 86, 94–95, 133–141, 169
  Passing off, 112–115
Torture Victim Protection Act, 184
trademarks, 102–107, 112–114
Trade Practices Act, 191–192
traditio, 239
tralatitious, **67**
transformative use, 218–219, 226
trial (*in vivo*), 22, 245, 249, 250, 253
Twinfeet, Justice, 25, 64
tympanum, 5, 104, 128
typography, v, 114, 128, 164

ubi oculus ibi amor, 232
unfair use, 226
unconscious, 13, 41, 76, 80–81, 92, 97, 112, 118, 126–127, 143, 151, 167, 180, 203, 211, 224
  as album, 233
  jokes, 97–99, 109, 119, 126–127
  objective, viii, 17–18, 96, 167, 248
  optical, 167–172
  skeletal, 167–172
  social, 203–204
US Supreme Court, 130–133
US v Tirado, 44–45, 56, 75–76, 94

V for Vendetta, 121–123
vagina dentata, 105
vanishing sign, 35
veils, 124–125
verballing, 38, 42, 134–135, 140, 164
veritas falsa, vi, 14, 160, 233
verum, **11**, 20, 68
vestigium, 64
vexillology, 41, 226
Vico, Giambatista, 9, 20, 22
vide alterem partem, 246
video corpus, 246
video et rideo, 99, 193, 241
videosphere, x, 74, 221, 230
viewing, vi, 38, 63, 104–106, 118, 152–153
  protocols, vi–vii, **212**–238
  reasonably informed, 101, 112, 1187
views, 60–62, 146–147
Virgil, 126
Virilio, Paul, 43–44
virtual, 147, 222
viserbality, **12**, 56, 59, 155, 221, 222, 241
visial lines, 117, 213, 214
visiocracy, viii, 17, 174, 184, 224
vision in decision, 20, 23, 54, 59, 64, 65, 96, 131, 163, 165, 173, 203, 206, 230, 240
Vismann, Cornelia, 6
visor effect, 254

visual
  advocacy, 19
  apprehension, 7, 12, 129–131, 179–181, 232–238
  atlas, 7, 17, 19
  comedy, 103–106, 111–112, 116, 121
  comparison, 204–210
  evidencing, 139, 164–165
  literacy, **vi**, 18, 129–132, 198, 208, 210
  mapping, 20,6466, 104–106
  merchandising, 198
  prosthetic, 204, 206–210
  watching, 132–133
vividæ rationes, 5, 29, 47–48, 104, 214, 218
voting rights, 252

Wacquet, Françoise, 251
Wajcman, Gérard, 78–79, 234
Walsh, Rebecca Fay, 229
Warburg, Aby, 8, 24, 117, 164
Warhol Foundation v Goldsmith, 218–220
Water, 40–41
Watt, Gary, 161, 242
Weizebbluth, Judge Amir, 14–15
Williams, Isobel, 243, 244, 246–248
Wiggles, Miss, 88–89, 97
Windows, 76–79, 234
Workers, 155, 161

x-ray, 167–173, 208

zetetics, 255
zoē, 143, 250, 251–254